THE DISTRICT MAGISTRATE IN LATE IMPERIAL CHINA

Studies of the East Asian Institute
Columbia University

D0208240

The district magistrate
in late imperial China

JOHN R. WATT

COLUMBIA UNIVERSITY PRESS

1972 New York and London

COPYRIGHT © 1972 COLUMBIA UNIVERSITY PRESS
ISBN: 0–231–03535–7
LIBRARY OF CONGRESS CATALOG CARD NUMBER: 79–187299
PRINTED IN THE UNITED STATES OF AMERICA

Erratum: Mei Liang-fu (Bibliography, p. 310: Glossary, p. 321) should read Chiang Liang-fu.

for Duncan

The East Asian Institute of Columbia University

The East Asian Institute of Columbia University was established in 1949 to prepare graduate students for careers dealing with East Asia, and to aid research and publication on East Asia during the modern period. The faculty of the Institute are grateful to the Ford Foundation and the Rockefeller Foundation for their financial assistance.

The Studies of the East Asian Institute were inaugurated in 1962 to bring to a wider public the results of significant new research on modern and contemporary East Asia.

Acknowledgments

This work is essentially the dissertation which I submitted to Columbia University, with a number of condensations and revisions. It was completed in January 1967 and revised between then and August 1969.

Like all thesis writers, I owe many obligations to relatives, colleagues, and advisers. In particular, I would like to thank A. Doak Barnett, Paul Ch'en, John K. Fairbank, Chao-ying Fang, Thomas Metzger, George Potter, Irene Rubin, Eugene Wang, and C. Martin Wilbur for their support at various stages of progress, and especially my wife Anne and our children for fostering and living with it throughout.

I am also indebted to recent studies on Ming and Ch'ing society by Chang Chung-li, Ch'ü T'ung-tsu, Ho Ping-ti, and Hsiao Kung-ch'üan, for opening up the administrative literature of these periods and bringing into focus their political and social conditions. Another recent author who deserves great thanks is Morohashi Tetsuji, for the outstanding contribution which his *Dai Kan-Wa Jiten* has made to the study of Chinese civilization.

The research for this study was made possible by grants from the Foreign Area Fellowship Program of the SSRC and the ACLS. None of the above are responsible for any opinions or errors in the present study.

CONTENTS

THE DISTRICT MAGISTRATE IN LATE IMPERIAL CHINA

INTRODUCTION

CH'ING ADMINISTRATION AS A SUBJECT OF WESTERN RESEARCH: SOME PERSONAL CONSIDERATIONS

Ch'ing administration is becoming a major field of inquiry within the Western study of Chinese civilization. As academic fields go, it is relatively well financed. Recently, it has produced several substantial social and institutional studies. It has its own journal, which is helping to attract new students to its cause, and in the process of development, it has moved well beyond the interests which initiated it to American higher education.

This situation, and the presentation of this study, tempts one to ask, why study the Ch'ing era and Ch'ing administration? What do Westerners stand to get out of this subject? What can they hope to contribute to it? More specifically, what considerations led to the making of this particular study? What are its intentions, and what can be expected of it?

Why study Ch'ing administration? Clearly, Westerners study Ch'ing administration for some of the same reasons that they study the Chinese body politic and civilization as a whole, and these reasons should require little explanation. The Ch'ing period itself has the particular character of being recent in time, yet still carrying much of the inherited civilization with it. It offers valuable opportunities for comparing old and new, and contrasting continuity and change. Its proximity to the modern East–West confrontation forces Westerners to ask what it was that they challenged, and face up to the antagonistic course which its successors have taken.

The Ch'ing period is also remarkably well documented and largely untouched by Western historians. Recent study of this documentation is bringing back to light the institutional significance of the Ch'ing period. For any who feel that Western writing on China is top-heavy in study of traditional philosophy and culture on the one hand or of contemporary revolution on the other, the Ch'ing period offers absorbing opportunities for study of institutions as cultural agencies, or as settings for interaction between what a society believes and what it does.

While this period is somewhat less prone than the present era to inspire political bias, it is nevertheless highly applicable to general subjects of political and sociological interest. It offers a remarkable example of empire, enforced by military power, but rooted in civil institutions. For all the studies of imperialism there are hardly any of Ch'ing imperialism, and few analyses of its basic military power and the relationship of that with its civil and social institutions. Its administrative sophistication is well known, but until recently Western knowledge of that administration was largely limited to the civil service examination system. We assumed, following Weber, that Ch'ing administration was bureaucratic, but we have had little grounds for making this assumption, and little basis for knowing whether that characterization is relevant to the analysis of Ch'ing administration.

The Ch'ing, or more strictly Ming–Ch'ing period, also provides complex evidence on the interaction of political centralization and social and economic expansion and diversification. Its documentation provides detailed evidence of the relationship of ideology to action and social change, or the relationship of political and social power to ideology. It allows us to study such concepts as social mobility or urbanization, whether at the center of power or scattered throughout the provinces and districts.

Another major interest of the Ch'ing period, and of Ch'ing administration as a catalyst of that period, is in the political questions which it raises. Because the Ch'ing period experienced so much conflict and change, this has stirred up much critical questioning, particularly for Chinese intelligentsia, both at the time and subsequently. The mid-seventeenth century, a time of internal social upheaval leading to the catastrophe of the Manchu conquest, raised fundamental issues regarding the organization of power and its relevance to social ends. The immediate pressure was taken out of these issues after the Manchus finally established control, but the issues themselves remained very much alive in subsequent administrative analysis.

The early and mid-nineteenth century represents another period of general crisis in Chinese political and social life. An accumulation of administrative corruption, social disease fed by Western opium imports, defeat by minimal Western forces, rebellion and civil war of unparalleled length and destruction, enforced further questioning of the existing system and inevitably fostered the twentieth-century drive to isolate and reject the past.

For Westerners, the absorbing issue of the Ch'ing period has been the weakness of the Chinese "response" to the West. This response, defined in terms of Westernizing capability, appeared to prefer weakness to Westernization, especially when compared with the Japanese reaction. Such a response challenged the reigning Western political conventions, and as such demanded explanation. Since 1949 China's acceptance of Western conventions but rejection of the West itself has intensified the problem of China's "response" and almost defied our ability to interpret her modern historical processes.

Lately Western historians have begun to move away from looking at modern China as a challenge to the Western self-image. Instead, there is more interest in relating China's experience with general experience. From this viewpoint, the Ch'ing period again has much to offer. Its administration provides a remarkable example of the application of limited resources to the organization and distribution of power. Study of its far-reaching use of legal and administrative regulations will indicate much about the general social function of laws and regulations. In the process, the investigation of this aspect of the Chinese body politic is certain to modify our characterization of the imperial Chinese political system, which at the present time is too much based on understanding of its formal social ideology.

The Ming–Ch'ing period is also crucial to an understanding of modernization and change as a general social process. Westerners are bound to think of modernization primarily in terms of industrialization, as its most tangible end product. Yet, as a process of transformation away from the organizing principles shaping the traditional order, it manifests itself throughout the Ming–Ch'ing era. The continuing growth of population, the monetization and diversification of the economy, the increase in social mobility, the spread of tenancy and economic competitiveness, coupled with centralization and systemization of the political order, point to changes in the body politic which, in combination, appear qualitatively different from previous eras. What one appears to see is a growing demarcation of the society itself, coupled with a loosening of social bonds, surely critical elements in any characterization of "modernity." If we regard technological intensification as a particular manifestation of a Western modality and reserve "modernization" for a broader and more basic drift away from equilibrium as a social goal, then it would seem that Ming–Ch'ing society, with its indifference to political attempts to restore equilibrium, is a modernizing society, although obviously not in precisely the terms found in the West. As such, it lends itself to examination of precisely the trends which have been obscured by the impact of technology in and on the West.

Such questions seem to hold out the possibility of developing a new relationship between Chinese and Western experience. Compared with the area studies approach, for which the study of the Western impact on China has been a central theme, or the sinological approach, which has grown out of a Chinese impact on the West, the emerging relationship should be interested in studying questions of mutual significance, in order to raise the general level of human social and cultural perception. Seen from this perspective, Chinese experience becomes essentially a mirror image of the West's, revealing man to man and society to society.

In this respect, the Ch'ing period is especially interesting because it presents characteristically modern issues: for example, population growth, political corruption and disunity, loss of values, institutional violence, conflict between public and private morality, emergence of new political movements, and also of complex techniques for the maintenance of political control and sociopolitical balance. In this connection, the recent upsurge of doubt in the West about the authority of Western institutions may have helped the development of a more relativistic relationship with Chinese experience.

It would have been helpful if such a perspective had guided the making of this study. Unfortunately, I can claim only to have been groping from the outset for some such formulation. Initially, I was interested in avoiding the issue of Westernization and in examining Chinese institutions for their own inner dynamics. This meant beginning before the nineteenth century; accordingly, I settled for the early Ch'ing period, in order to preserve a limited experience as a Ch'ing specialist and also to build on an interest in the relationship of history to modernity.

My reasons for choosing to study local administration in general, and the role of the district magistrate in particular, were more complicated. In part, the subject was suggested by the nature of the documentary holdings at the Harvard Yenching library. The library has excellent collections of Ch'ing institutional documents, as well as a vast mass of primary material on local administration. This material has recently been explored there and elsewhere in a number of studies on Ming–Ch'ing social institutions. These studies demonstrated the wealth of interest available in this material. They also drew new attention to social forces at work in Ch'ing society and to the significance of local administration in relation to those forces.

In choosing to study local administration and district magistrates, I was also guided by personal considerations. Ch'ü T'ung-tsu, in particular, had emphasized the importance of local administration in the maintenance of imperial authority, and described the pressures placed on the character and competence of district magistrates in upholding this political responsibility. It seemed, from Ch'ü's study, that the magistrate was the linchpin of the administrative system. Moreover, he appeared to enjoy extensive powers in relation to his subordinates, while at the same time being highly vulnerable to superior authority. This raised interesting notions about the relationship of authority to responsibility. I was especially struck by the stress which this office placed on the character of its incumbents, particularly in the context of physical and moral corruption, by which it was held to be surrounded. This challenge of authority to character appealed strongly as an analytic theme, and I intended to take it up through a biographical study.

An explanation for the form of the present study may help to state why this theme gave way to a more general institutional analysis. To provide such a theme with an institutional and social environment, it proved necessary to undertake a good deal of introductory groundwork. This groundwork began with a characterization of the role of the district magistrate, by noting the contrast between its powers and the checks to its powers which had stirred my initial interest. The authority of the role had been broadly characterized in Ch'ü's study; on the other hand, the control system, although much illustrated there, was not analyzed in terms of its objectives, form, or institutional impact. I attempted a preliminary analysis of the way in which imperial regulations limited the authority of the district magistrate, without feeling able to embark on a major investigation of this issue. Later, I discovered that the form and impact of the control system were far more extensive and systematic than I had realized, and could not be neglected in a study attempting to characterize district administration.

The next requirement was for a characterization of district magistrates themselves. Here I wished to find out what sort of men they were through use of personal material available in biographies, appointment lists, and genealogies. There is a mass of quantifiable evidence which could be brought to bear on this question. The findings which I offer here are, of course, initial and tentative. Ideally, they should be followed up by exhaustive, Namier-like studies if we are to achieve any sophisticated socioeconomic characterization of district officials.

Having seen this groundwork already grow beyond its expected proportions, I wished to go on to the controversial issue of whether or not magistrates came into office with any prior administrative experience. Since it was known that the office was directly open to examination graduates, there were *a priori* reasons for believing that magistrates came, or could come, into office without such experience. Yet, it seemed hard to believe that such a significant office could be held by inexperienced men who, in any case, seemed relatively well on in age by the time they took office. If they had not been obtaining relevant experience during the often long time between qualifying for this challenging office and actually receiving an appointment, what had they been doing?

The examination of this question led into an analysis of the unexpectedly elaborate and complicated appointment system. The findings, which I hope are relatively close to actuality, indicate that the question of prior administrative experience is far more complex than could be guessed by merely studying the examination system or the hierarchical organization of local and regional administration. In fact, when the experience of deputies and probationers is further explored and given temporal context, the picture is likely to become considerably more detailed than is already the case.

These findings pointed to the existence of a major system for channeling and controlling access to office. Compared with the examination system, this appointment system has attracted little attention from Western specialists. This is no doubt because the intellectual content of the former has given it a unique association with eligibility for office which has fully justified the attention it has received. Furthermore, the appointment system, in its Ch'ing form, is evidently of more recent vintage and exerted much less impact on the population as a whole. On the other hand, as a means for manipulating desire for power, while judiciously allocating control between central and regional authority, the Ch'ing appointment system must be regarded as an extremely subtle and effective instrument. As such, its implications deserve further investigation.

To round off the institutional environment, I wished to obtain some idea of the career prospects of district magistrates. This seemed significant to the mental health and behavior of the individual while serving as magistrate. If promotion was a reasonable expectation, as it is in most civil service structures, one would expect to find some relationship between qualifications for promotion and administrative behavior. If, on the other hand, promotion was difficult to obtain, this could imply that other objectives guided the magistrate's conduct while in office. An examination of the system of promotion indicated that it was extremely difficult for magistrates to rise more than one rung up the civil service ladder, and hard even to rise up that single rung. Preliminary studies of individual career patterns support this finding. This situation, if true, raises many implications about organizational relationships, use of office, loyalty to public values, etc., especially in view of the added problem of vulnerability to demotion or dismissal. I have noted some of these implications without being able to pursue them at length.

In my initial plan, I intended to complete the groundwork with an examination of the ideas and values which district magistrates brought into office with them. Rather than simply assume that they were Confucianists at heart, it seemed desirable to find out what relationships existed between Confucian philosophy and eighteenth-century local administration. Given the political setting in which that philosophy originated, those relationships could hardly have been self-evident. What, then, could Confucianism have to say about local administration, and how was this construed by Ch'ing writers on local administration? Woven into this question was the implication that Confucianism must also have affected the evolution and survival of the office itself, ringed as it was by institutional barriers, as well as by human inducements to highly un-Confucian behavior.

The main conclusion to be drawn from this inquiry was that Confucian classics differed sharply in their approach to local administrative conduct. Later classics dealing directly with local administrative duties seemed to conflict in values with the four basic Confucian books defining administrative leadership itself. Ch'ing officials, as students, had spent twenty or more years in preparation for office, absorbing the values of the four Confucian books. Yet, as administrators, they seemed to lean in crucial ways towards the later classics. This involved a conflict in roles, which could hardly have helped influencing administrative conduct. As such, it raised the question of what had happened to the institutional and social environment, to expose local administrators to such a conflict?

The rest of the study constitutes an exploration of this issue, in terms of historical changes directly affecting the conduct of the Ch'ing local administration. It concludes that behind the conflict in roles there existed a conflict between the values inculcated by Confucian theory as such, and those prevailing in Ch'ing administrative performance. Reduced to its essentials, theory required administrators to give priority to the welfare of the people. Central government policy, while not denying this emphasis, in practice demanded priority to the interests of the state and enforced its demands with stringent sanctions. A great many factors contributed to the growing conflict between theory and practice, among them political centralization itself, the evolution of private ownership, the imposition of alien regimes by military conquest, and the transformation of rural society in southern and eastern China into densely populated areas. These developments made it increasingly difficult for local administrators in the early Ch'ing to fulfill either the theoretical or practical obligations of their role.

This being the argument of this study, what content can be expected of it? Essentially, it offers an analysis of the institutional and historical setting in which Ch'ing district magistrates operated. In this respect, it attempts to explore questions suggested by Ch'ü's study and should be regarded as complementary to that work. It offers for Western readers an analysis of some of the problems facing Ch'ing local officials. As a background study, it does not attempt to conclude how the resolution of these problems affected individual judgment and character. There are also other major subjects—such as the relationship of provincial to local administration, the role of the district magistrates in the administration of criminal law, or the social setting of Ch'ing district administration—on which others have worked or are working, and which are impossible to go into deeply here. Lastly, I have not attempted to assess local administrative conditions after the early nineteenth century, in the belief that they were substantially affected and altered by extraneous social and political changes.

A final note about the analytical form adopted here. Some have suggested that the institutional analyses in the first part of this study be reincorporated in the historical treatment of the second and third parts. After some consideration, I have avoided this change, in the belief that it would obscure the exploratory character of the work and superimpose a synthetical character which the treatment as a whole does not warrant. I also believe that the counterpoint between the institutional present examined in Part I and the historical movement through past and present explored in Parts II and III enables one to look at the past in the light of the historical present, and thus come closer to the historical perspective of early Ch'ing district magistrates.

PART I

THE OFFICE AND ITS INCUMBENTS

1

POWERS OF THE DISTRICT MAGISTRATE

The district magistrate played a leading role in Ch'ing administration. His position made him both the highest official in close contact with the lives of the people and the only local official whose power was of any immediate concern to them.

The significance of this position was not lost on either the regime or its subjects. "The department and district magistrates," wrote the Yung-cheng emperor (reigned 1723–1735), "are the officials close to the people. The integrity of one man involves the peace or unhappiness of a myriad."[1] Writing over one hundred years later, during the Taiping rebellion, a president of the Board of Officials repeated this view. "No officials," he stated, "are as close to the people as district magistrates. If the district magistrates are all capable, then government will be simple, punishment clear, the people peaceful, and material things in plenty. How could there then be military upheaval?"[2] In the aftermath of the rebellion, another official reaffirmed that "the order or disorder of the people is tied up with the district magistrates."[3]

Despite its alleged importance, the position of district magistrate was one of the lowest in the administrative hierarchy and was certainly the lowest of any significance. Although barred to native residents, it was available as an opening appointment. Many *hsien* magistrates, as will be shown, had never previously held administrative office. On the face of it, novices would seem to have been quite unsuited for a role to which such weight was attached. What then underlies this administrative paradox?

Let us start by considering the authority of the office. The function of the district magistrate was to take charge over all matters affecting the maintenance of public order. An imperially sponsored source of the late eighteenth century listed his duties as "superintending the government of a district, regulating its taxes and labor services, hearing and administering its legal suits, promoting education and culture, and controlling its customs." It said that "all help for the aged, sacrifice to spirits, provision for scholars, and regulation of study he is personally responsible for and diligently manages."[4] These functions were not of equal importance. A similar compendium was nearer the truth in saying simply "the department and district magistrates are the officials close to the people. They personally manage all judicial and fiscal affairs."[5]

As judge of the court of first instance, the magistrate conducted investigations of criminal cases, issued warrants for arrest, examined suspects and witnesses, decided the case and gave sentence according to the detailed prescriptions laid down in the Penal Laws and Statutes, and supervised its execution. In cases for which the sentence was no more serious than a beating or the wearing of the cangue (a large wooden halter), the magistrate could decide the punishment and have it administered on his own authority. In cases calling for more severe punishment, the magistrate conducted the preliminary hearing and recommended the appropriate sentence. The case was then reviewed by superior courts, the level of review depending on the degree of offense.

Once a charge had been set in motion, the magistrate was bound by law to obtain a conviction. In return he was permitted when examining a suspect to use various forms of torture. The setting of the courtroom also favored the magistrate. He sat at the end of the hall in formal attire behind a high bench. The suspects and witnesses knelt on the stone floor, flanked by guards and lictors. When a magistrate wished to use torture, he tossed down bamboo chips from a container on his bench, each representing a given number of strokes, or otherwise indicated the device to be used. The lictors then hurried forward and carried out whatever had been indicated.

The atmosphere of the courtroom is vividly portrayed in contemporary works. In a case from *The Scholars*, a famous critique of eighteenth-century social conditions, the magistrate was confronted with a crime difficult to bring home on its perpetrators. A salt convoy passing through his district had been robbed, and the helmsman and salt clerk were advised by scholars traveling with the convoy to take the case to the local magistrate. When they did so, the magistrate rejected their story ("Such a thing couldn't happen in a quiet law-abiding district like this") and had the helmsman given twenty strokes with the bamboo "till his flesh was torn to shreds." The young clerk, "terrified" to see the magistrate pointing at him and reaching for another bamboo chip, immediately volunteered whatever the magistrate wanted to hear. "Kowtowing as quickly as a pestle pounding onions," he begged that his life be spared. One of the scholars now "politely" intervened, and the magistrate concluded by warning the boatmen to be more careful in the future, and driving them out of his court.[6]

Despite, or even because of, the summary nature of such proceedings, magistrates could be highly conscious of their judicial power and of the effect it could have on the life of an individual. To illustrate this point Wang Hui-tsu, a late eighteenth-century private secretary and magistrate, cited a proverb saying "if the hurt of the punishment exceeds the offence, it is a disgrace for one's entire life." He recalled an occasion in which he had heard a country person gratuitously insulted because his father had been punished, and asked "as father and mother of the people, how can a magistrate lightly view the administration of a flogging?"[7]

As the above implies, magistrates enjoyed considerable latitude in their administration of justice. In principle, the judicial authority of the magistrate was limited by the comprehensiveness of the laws and by the right of the defendant to appeal his sentence. In practice, it predominated because it combined all local security functions under one head and because the magistrate received all criminal and civil cases brought before administrative authority. Moreover, going to court was an expensive and time-consuming business, and appealing prolonged this economic attrition. Consequently the people derived their first and often only experience of administrative ethics from the magistrate or his subordinates.

In his fiscal role, it was the magistrate's task to raise annually a fixed quota for delivery to the higher authorities. In fixing assessments, the magistrate's initiative was limited. By the middle of the eighteenth century, taxes were assessed principally on property. Once the assessments had been recorded, force of custom made it difficult for magistrates to alter them, or even to gain full access to the taxation files in the district office.[8]

The magistrate's principal opportunity came through the method of collection. By manipulating exchange rates, keeping firm control over fees for administrative services, and enlisting the support of runners and local dignitaries in rounding up taxpayers, a magistrate could expect to take in a wide margin of profit. In doing so he was expected to conform to local precedents and expectations, or risk the opposition of powerful local families.[9] Success in tax collecting thus depended on a magistrate's ability to manipulate the local situation.[10] Nevertheless, society assumed that a magistrate would do well out of his office. One clan assessed magistrates holding substantive appointments at a higher sum than department heads in metropolitan boards, censors, assistant prefects, and independent department magistrates (administratively on a level with prefects). Another assessed magistrates less than the independent department magistrates but more than the higher ranking assistant prefects.[11]

As chief district administrative officer, the magistrate's influence easily surpassed that of all other local official personnel. The local educational officials held sinecures. The assistant district officials lacked authority. Their powers were extremely curtailed and their salaries and staff insignificant. Except for the unclassed jail wardens, there were few of them to be found. (See Tables 1 to 3) The district clerks and runners, some of whom enjoyed considerable local power, also lacked authority. For the slightest mistake they could be physically beaten and frequently were. The magistrate's senior personal secretaries, who were generally degree holders and also well versed in administrative procedure, enjoyed a good deal of informal authority. But they lacked office and were obliged to act in an advisory capacity. The magistrate was the only local official whose role combined both authority and power.

Toward the gentry (as defined by Ho), the magistrate held a symbiotic relationship. He required their help in obtaining information on local customs and current problems, and in financing welfare and public works. In many districts their cooperation was essential to the fulfillment on time of his tax quotas. In return he was important to them as the sole significant local representative of imperial authority. He could act as a conduit between the local gentry and higher provincial authority. He constituted an official arbitrator of their disputes with each other. His authority could underwrite their local economic activities. In conflict the magistrate and the gentry could cause a good deal of mutual trouble, the former by damaging their social prestige, the latter by obstructing local administration or by interfering at higher administrative levels. In concert they represented an almost unchallengeable local combination of political authority and social and economic power.

Table 1. Prefectural and district officials, showing number and distribution by office between 1758–1899

	LATEST DATE FOR INFORMATION				
	1758	1785	1785	1812	1899
ADMINISTRATIVE OFFICIALS					
Prefecture					
Prefect	186	182	184	182	185
1st-class asst. prefect	202	202	208	116	110
2d-class asst. prefect	180	152	177	108	82
Commissary of records	177	165	178	167	167
Independent Department					
Dept. magistrate	67	65	65	67	72
1st-class asst. magistrate	21	16	21	22	20
2d-class asst. magistrate	34	40	34	35	35
Jail warden	58	58	65	?	?
Department					
Dept. magistrate	154	146	150	147	145
1st-class asst. magistrate	47	37	48	32	32
2d-class asst. magistrate	61	51	50	44	35
Jail warden	164	142	158	?	?
All dept. jail wardens	222	200	223	219[a]	221[a]
District					
Dist. magistrate	1282	1297	1302	1293	1303
Asst. magistrste	406	417	358	350	345
Registrar	108	106	85	58	55
Jail warden	1282	1292	1298	1294	1296
Totals					
Head officials	1689	1690	1701	1689	1705
Asst. officials	2740	2678	2680	2445	2398
Subdist. magistrate	923	916	896	947[b]	935[b]
EDUCATIONAL OFFICIALS					
Pref. director of schools	190	184	191	189	190
Dept. director of schools	198[a]		198[a]	210	
Dist. director of schools	1109		1108	1111	
Asst. directors	1531[b]		1561[b]	1521[b]	

SOURCES. 1758: *TCHT:CL*, 4/11b–15b; 1785: *T'ung-tien*, pp. 2210–11; 1785: *T'ung-k'ao* pp. 5589–90; 1812: *TCHT:CC*, chs. 4 and 5; 1899: *TCHT:KH*, chs. 4 and 5.
NOTES. The *TCHT:CC* and *KH* give the following information on subprefectural administrative posts. *TCHT:CC*—independent subprefects, 18; commissaries, 18; subprefects, 47; asst. subprefects, 31. *TCHT:KH*—independent subprefects, 32; 1st-class asst. subprefect, 1; 2d-class, 11; commissaries, 18; subprefects, 48; asst. subprefects, 30. The table excludes both miscellaneous and unpaid cultural officials (who were few and insignificant).
[a] Includes independent depts.
[b] Includes prefectures, departments, and subprefectural posts.

Table 2. Examples of official salary and staff of magistrate and assistant officials

	SALARY			STAFF	
	BASIC	SUPPLEMENTARY	TOTAL	CLERKS	RUNNERS, GUARDS, ETC.
CHIN-SHAN MAGISTRATE	45	1,200	1,245	12	90
Asst. magistrate	40	60	100	1	6
Jail warden	31.5	60	91.5	1	6
Subdist. magistrate	31.5	60	91.5	1	47
Asst. director of schools	40	—	40	1	3
P'ING-LO MAGISTRATE	85	920	1,005	12	101
Asst. magistrate	40	120	160		6
Jail warden	31.5	80	111.5		6
Director of schools	40	—	40		11
Asst. director of schools	40	—	40		8
LI-YANG MAGISTRATE	45	1,000	1,045		
Asst. magistrate	40	60	100		
Jail warden	31.5	60	91.5		
Director of schools	40	—	40		
Asst. director of schools	40	0	40		

SOURCES. *Chin-shan hsien-chih*, 1st ed., 2/5a–7b; *P'ing-lo hsien-chih*, 4/14a–18b; *Li-yang hsien-chih*, 1st ed., 9/3b.
NOTE. District salaries varied considerably according to the importance of the post and its distance from Peking. Overall figures are given in *TCHTSL*, ch. 261, and in *HPTL*, ch. 75. See also Ch'ü, *Local Government*, Tables 6 and 7.

With the people at large the magistrate was significant as the dominant symbol of political power. In the actual exercise of power, his authority depended on whether he was dealing with individuals or groups. Individual commoners had little means of protection against his power. Those who were taxpayers could be summoned to hearings and beaten for any default. As litigants they could wait for months to be able to present a case. As suspects they had no means of defense other than appeal to higher authority after sentence had been passed.

On the other hand, groups such as clans or secret societies were at a much greater advantage. The magistrate was one man in the district city; they were a multitude dispersed throughout hundreds of villages and hamlets. In the south their power rendered the magistrate's influence negligible in outlying areas, and also came between the magistrate and the people in fiscal and judicial administration.[12] Because of the diffusion and atomization of rural society, the magistrate was heavily dependent on the gentry to assist in organizational control, and this was assured only in activities serving gentry interests, such as public works and civil defense.[13]

Nevertheless the people, as political unsophisticates, were always susceptible to the authority of the magistrate's role, because of its identification with transcendent human and supernatural powers. As representative of the local city god, or as counterpart of the judge of the underworld, magistrates were able to use these relationships to secure confessions or compliance resistant to purely terrestrial authority.[14] As imperial delegate, the magistrate represented the local symbol of the unitary power of the Son of Heaven, and as such the district's legitimate source of authority. On arrival at their districts, magistrates were accordingly treated to elaborate ceremonials of welcome and similarly revered at the end of a successful tenure. While in office they constituted the sole "father and mother official" and could expect great respect whenever making a formal appearance.

All this indicates that the office of district magistrate was heavily endowed with legal and moral authority. On this basis adept officials holding regular appointments were in a position to exert a good deal of power over the fortunes of the local inhabitants.

The extent of this power is borne out by the extent of the controls mounted to contain it. In principle, many ideological, political, and social factors existed to limit the magistrate's freedom of action. In the first place, Confucian teaching stressed his responsibility both as a servant of the ruler and a beneficiary of the people. To the ruler and to all superiors, he should be sincere, deferential, and loyal. Toward the people he should be just and sensitive, balancing strictness with magnanimity. He should "promote benefit, dispel adversity" and impart the nourishment of the Confucian way itself. Magistrate's handbooks stress these duties and give attention to illustrating what they imply in practice.[15]

Despite these moral sanctions, successive imperial administrations had also developed a stringent system of rewards and punishments. This approach to administrative control had met with considerable opposition from Confucianists. They had argued that, as educated persons, officials were alive to moral influence, and that to control them by rewards and punishments was demeaning and would reflect on imperial prestige. On this issue the Confucianists were defeated. The system of rewards and punishments remained a basic part of official management until the end of the imperial era.[16]

Under the Ch'ing dynasty the system of rewards and punishments played a leading part in controlling administration. It was embodied in a series of Disciplinary Regulations, which for civil affairs were under the management of the Board of Officials.[17] The Disciplinary Regulations were distinct from the Penal Laws and Statutes in function and content. Both dealt with offenses, but the former were limited to administrative performance, while the latter covered both administration and society. Moreover, the Disciplinary Regulations were designed to produce action rather than prohibit it. As dealing with administrative offenses, they were confined to administrative punishments such as fines, demotion and reduction in salary, demotion and transfer, and dismissal.[18] The Penal Laws and Statutes dealt in physical punishments, ranging from ten strokes of the bamboo to lingering execution. The Laws and Statutes were, however, more far-ranging in their treatment of administrative offenses than the Disciplinary Regulations. An offense which, under the Disciplinary Regulations, called for administrative punishment such as dismissal, might also call for physical punishment under the Laws and Statutes. In such a case, the physical punishment would also apply.[19] Similarly, if there was no article in the Disciplinary Regulations adequately applying to an apparent offense, the Laws and Statutes became the statutary authority. If they also failed, the matter was dealt with on the basis of precedent or deliberation.[20]

The Disciplinary Regulations laid down the duties of an official in any anticipated situation calling for administrative action, and the punishment for every degree of failure in the performance of those duties. For example, a magistrate who failed to collect from 10 to 40 percent of the annual tax quota within a stated period was punished by one to four demotions in grade. The punishment for collecting less than half the assigned quota was dismissal. For collecting the quota within the allotted period, merit recordings and advancements in grade were awarded, according to the size of the quota. In the capture and punishment of criminals, similar sanctions, rewards, and time limits operated.[21]

The Disciplinary Regulations varied greatly in severity. For delaying a civil suit, or exceeding the first deadline for the trial of criminal cases by less than one month, the punishment was loss of three months nominal salary, a very minor sum. On the other hand, a magistrate could be dismissed for such offenses as conniving at bribery by a clerk, failing to conclude a criminal trial within four months, or incorrectly recommending someone for death, as a result of which the sentence was approved and executed.[22] He could also be dismissed for a variety of fiscal offenses.

To be punished by dismissal was not necessarily as serious as the English term may suggest. In the Collected Institutes the punishment of dismissal ranked above that of demotion three grades and transfer. The punishment of "dismissal but retention in office" ranked above demotion three grades and retention in office.[23] A dismissed official could register for reappointment and be put on the quotas for reappointment of reinstated officials. On the other hand an official could face much more serious punishment than simple dismissal. He could be dismissed and permanently disbarred for such an offense as failing to report a natural calamity.[24] His actions might implicate him with the Penal Laws. If he made unlawful instruments of torture, his punishment under the Disciplinary Regulations was dismissal, but under the Penal Laws it was dismissal and one hundred strokes of the heavy bamboo.[25] For willfully recommending an unjust sentence, the penalty was the sentence itself. If the sentence was death and was subsequently carried out, the punishment was death for the magistrate.[26]

In return for all these sanctions, a magistrate could hope for rewards ranging from one recording in merit to immediate promotion before the completion of his current term of duty. For certain achievements, such as arresting over ten thieves within one year, he could be recommended for an imperial audience.[27]

There are several distinctive features to the system of administrative rewards and punishments. In many cases superiors were held responsible in the offense of an inferior; in such cases the punishment was made proportionate to the nature of the offense and the rank of the superior. The more immediate the superior, the greater the responsibility and the punishment.[28] Second, the Disciplinary Regulations distinguished between public and private offenses, i.e., whether or not the private interest of the official was involved in a given administrative offense. This concession, first introduced in the late sixth century A.D., could mean an appreciable difference in the fate of the offender.[29] Public offenses could be offset against any merit recordings or advancements in grade; private could not.[30] In addition, punishments for administrative offenses computed in the Penal Code in strokes of the bamboo could be commuted to fines and demotion according to specified sliding scales. The commutation was greater if the offense was public than if it was private.[31]

The system of rewards and punishments confronted an official with opposing decisions. For example, if he failed to effect an arrest or complete a trial, he was subject to punishment. But he was also liable for detaining, torturing, or sentencing an innocent person. He could be disciplined for selling too little salt and for forcing people to buy salt.[32] Moreover, these sanctions faced him every time he took an administrative decision. In short, all performance in administration was defined and evaluated by the system of rewards and punishments. As far as the dynastic regime was concerned, moral stimuli played an acceptable but subordinate role.

In provincial government, the administration of the Disciplinary Regulations was one of the major functions of the superior officials. They were expected to see that the magistrate was performing his duties as specified in the regulations, and to impeach him for any infractions.[33] A magistrate was to some extent guarded from victimization by a superior, since every accusation of misconduct came before the emperor and the Board of Officials. Nevertheless, the weight of this surveillance by prefects, intendants, traveling censors, provincial judges, treasurers, governors, and governors-general was certainly an influential factor in limiting a magistrate's exercise of his authority. The low rank of his position put the magistrate at a further disadvantage. The magistrate's rank of 7A (see Table 3) put him below assistant prefects who, administratively speaking, held comparatively unimportant positions, and put him well below prefects. Magistrates were required to report regularly to their immediate superiors on all important aspects of their duties. All this obliged magistrates to be extremely careful in their dealings with their superiors and take good care either to cover their tracks or to remain as far as possible above reproach.

To check officials from utilizing existing personal contacts in the districts allocated to them, imperial regimes established the principle of avoidance. Under the laws of avoidance, a magistrate was not allowed to serve in the province in which his native district was situated, nor to serve in a district within 165 (Western) miles of his native district. In his first district post he would ordinarily be unfamiliar with its local customs, dialect, and subordinate office personnel. If he held an "immediate" or

Table 3. Comparative ranks of selected offices and changes in rank during early Ch'ing

METROPOLITAN OFFICES		
Board Dept. director	3	changed to: 5 (1659); 4 (1661); 3 (1667); 5A (1670)
Board asst. dept. director	4	changed to: 5 (1659); 4 (1665); 5B (1670)
2d-class secy. of board	4	changed to: 6 (1659); 5 (1667); 6A (1670)
Han-lin bachelor	7	
PROVINCIAL OFFICES		
Prefecture		
Prefect	4A	changed to: 4B (1763)
1st-class asst. prefect	5A	
2d-class asst. prefect	6A	
Commissary of records	8A	
Independent Department		
Magistrate	5B	changed to: 5A (1767)
Department		
Magistrate	5B	
1st-class asst. manager	6B	
2d-class asst. manager	7B	
Jail warden	9B	
District		
Magistrate	7A	
Asst. magistrate	8A	
Registrar	9A	
Jail warden	Unranked	
Local Educational Officials		
Director of pref. schools	9A	changed to: 7A (1735)
Director of dept. schools	Unranked	changed to: 8A (1735)
Director of dist. schools	Unranked	changed to: 8A (1735)
Asst. directors of schools	Unranked	changed to: 8B (1735)

SOURCES. *TCHTSL*, 18/last five pages; *TCHT:CL* ed., chs. 3–4.

"acting" appointment* he could expect to require as much as a year (if he stayed in office that long) to establish effective personal control.[34]

In important posts such ignorance was avoided by limiting appointments to those who had already gained some experience in the administration of that province. Moreover, once appointed to a province a magistrate could expect to continue his career as a magistrate in that same province.[35] On the other hand, he would have to leave his post and province if, for example, his parents died, or if a close relative was appointed to a senior position in that province, or if he needed to recover from an illness, or if

* The meaning of this appointment terminology will be explained in chapter 3.

he was dismissed. If he subsequently resumed his career, it would very often be in another—and unfamiliar—province.[36]

Such a network of administrative control implies a striking imperial distrust of local administrative power, or of the power of local society in conjunction with local administration. Later, we shall examine the effect of this control, as well as that exerted by local society, on the conduct of local officials. For the present, let us consider the qualifications and personal authority of the men appointed as magistrates.

2

QUALIFICATIONS OF DISTRICT MAGISTRATES

Intellectual attainment

The district magistrates were virtually all men of considerable educational training and attainment. The majority held high degrees under the civil service examination system. Most of the rest had been educated for the examinations, but had failed because of the intense competition. They had made their way into officialdom by purchasing examination statuses which qualified their owners for administrative appointment. A very few had risen from the lower ranks of the bureaucracy and subbureaucracy or had been given status because of outstanding parental attainment.

Because of the prominence of the degree system in the administrative and social life of the country, it is necessary to summarize the different degrees and statuses.[1] There were three main degrees: licentiate (*sheng-yuan* or *hsiu-ts'ai*), provincial graduate (*chü-jen*), and metropolitan graduate (*chin-shih*). The degree of licentiate was the first step in the path to public service. It differed from higher degrees in function as well as status. The higher degrees qualified their recipients to hold public office. Licentiates were not normally so qualified.[2] The purpose of this degree, besides giving some prestige to scholastic effort, was to begin the narrowing down of those from whom the majority of the administrative officials would ultimately be chosen. Functionally, a licentiate was merely entitled to sit the qualifying examination for entrance to the examinations for the second degree. Moreover, the award of the degree was conditional. Triennial supervisory examinations were held, and licentiates who failed them three times lost their title. Only those of thirty years' standing or over seventy years old were permanently exempted from these examinations.

The second degree, that of provincial graduate, was the most critical of the examination system. This degree carried formal qualification for public office and the right to take the metropolitan examinations for the third degree. It also ensured access to the bureaucratic–intellectual elite of imperial China. During the early Ch'ing period, it stood between roughly half a million licentiates, plus a group of roughly 350,000 Imperial Academy students (*chien-sheng*) who had purchased the right to sit the provincial examinations, and the group of approximately 18,000 who had succeeded in these examinations.

To these few must be added a group of approximately 40,000 senior licentiates (*kung-sheng*), who were chosen mainly from licentiates on the basis of seniority, examination, or purchase. The senior licentiates also enjoyed a range of legal and social privileges, as well as access to office, which ensured their entry to elite status. For the aspirant administrator, however, the status of senior licentiate was little substitute for that of provincial graduate. Apart from some 3,500 first-class senior licentiates (*pa-kung*), who were graduates of a special Court examination, the initial appointment of the remainder of the senior licentiates was confined largely to the low-paid and ineffectual assistant administrative or local educational offices. And only provincial graduates could sit the examinations for the final degree.[3]

The provincial examinations were thus the crucial test for the student who aspired to public service. They were therefore keenly contested. In the eighteenth and early nineteenth centuries, there were up to a hundred or more competitors for each degree offered. No limits were set on the number of times a qualified candidate could sit the examinations, and there are cases of candidates continuing through as many as fourteen or sixteen failures, a span of effort involving thirty-five or forty years.[4]

The content of the provincial examinations presented an exacting challenge, especially to the novitiate. Its syllabus called for compositions on themes from the four core texts of the Neo-Confucian canon and a further five or more classics, extended dissertations on the classics, history, and contemporary subjects, verse composition, and at various times the ability to write formal administrative statements and dispatches. To be at all hopeful of success, the candidate should have read widely in the extensive historical literature, thoroughly digested the classics, developed a fluent calligraphy, and mastered several poetic styles. Above all he should have mastered the essay style, known as the "eight-legged" essay from its eight-section format, which was the peculiar product of the examination system. The technicalities of this literary form were the undoing of many candidates. Finally the candidate was obliged to observe a host of miscellaneous regulations. His first papers were carefully screened for any procedural faults which, if found, would disqualify him from sitting the remaining examinations for that session.

The candidate who triumphed in the provincial examinations could compete in the metropolitan examinations held the following year. This examination was divided into two main parts. In the first part the syllabus was not unlike that of the provincial examinations. Those few who passed this part were presented for the palace examinations, the principle function of which was to determine the category and order of selection for official appointments. In the majority of these examinations, all candidates passed and were then entitled to the degree of metropolitan graduate.

The metropolitan examinations were likewise closely contested. Beside the special academic honors awaiting the highest graduates, all successful candidates could hope for a reasonably prompt selection to some metropolitan or provincial post. Up to 8,000 candidates competed for these prizes. Because of the limited number of offices available, only 200 to 300 degrees were normally awarded.

Such was the examination system. What then was the distribution of the district magistrates in terms of examination rank and status?

In an analysis of the seasonal registers of officeholders for the years 1745 and 1850, Ch'ü found that 74 and 69 percent respectively of the *hsien* district magistrates and slightly under half of the department magistrates were examination graduates. Within those groups 71 and 64 percent respectively of the district magistrates held the prestigious metropolitan, provincial and first class licentiate degrees. In these years, therefore, the substantial majority of the magistrates held advanced examination degrees.[5]

Were these distributions representative of the period as a whole? To gain light on this question, a survey has been made of the lists of magistrates in six districts and one department. There are several differences between these jurisdictions. Wu-hsien and Ch'ang-chou *hsien* were rated as "most important" districts. All magistrates appointed to these two districts had to have held office elsewhere and earned the recommendation of the

Table 4. Rank or status held by magistrates when taking office

REIGN PERIODS	WU-HSIEN								
	SC	KH	YC	CL	CC	TK	TOTAL	SC	KH
EXAMINATION									
chin-shih	2	8	1	1	3	5	20	4	4
chü-jen	1	7	5	5	5	4	27	1	4
pa-kung	2	2	1	5		1	11	3	1
yu-kung									
fu-pang	1	1					2	1	1
en-kung	1	1					2		1
sui-kung	1	1					2		1
sheng-yuan			1				1	2	
TOTAL	8	20	8	11	8	10	65	11	12
PURCHASE									
lin-kung		1					1		
fu-kung									
kung-sheng	1	1		2			4	1	8
fu-chien									
chien-sheng		7	7	4		2	20		20
TOTAL	1	8	7	6		2	24	1	28
OTHER									
yin-sheng		3					3		2
clerk									
office elsewhere		2	2	2	1	1	8		3
Banner (no rank indicated)				1			1		3
no rank indicated				19	3	3	25		
TOTAL		5	2	22	4	4	37		8
GRAND TOTAL	9	34	17	39	12	16	127	12	48
Average term per reign, in years	2.0	1.8	0.8	1.5	2.1	1.9		1.5	1.3
TOTAL ACTING		10	11	21	4	5	51		20
TOTAL BANNER		6	2	3					16

CH'ANG-CHOU					CHIN-SHAN					LI-YANG			
YC	CL	CC	TK	TOTAL	YC	CL	CC	TK	TOTAL	YC	CL	CC	TOTAL
1	6	1	5	21	3	7	1	4	15	1	4		5
4	10	2	4	25	4	21	10	7	42	2	11	9	22
1	3	1	1	10		3	1		4	1	6	2	9
			1	1									
				2									
				1									
				1									
				2				1	1				
6	19	4	11	63	7	31	12	12	62	4	21	11	36
						1			1				
							1	2	3				
4				13	1				1				
							1		1				
3	3			26	3	10	4	7	24	2	4		6
7	3			39	4	11	6	9	30	2	4		6
		1		3		1			1				
						3	1		4		2		2
1	5			9	2				2		5	1	6
				3		1			1				
	9	8	2	19		4		1	5	1	7	1	9
1	14	9	2	34	2	9	1	1	13	1	14	2	17
14	36	13	13	136	13	51	19	22	105	7	39	13	59
0.9	1.7	1.9	2.3		1.0	1.2	1.3	1.4		1.9	1.5	1.2	
8	22	4	?		8	33	11	13	65	2	24	6	32
1	3				1	7					4		

(*continued*)

Table 4. (*continued*)

REIGN PERIODS	NING-YUAN						
	SC	KH	YC	CL	CC	TK	TOTAL
EXAMINATION							
chin-shih	3	2	1	4		7	17
chü-jen	1	5	2	8	6	3	25
pa-kung							
yu-kung		1		1			2
fu-pang				1		1	2
en-kung							
sui-kung		1		1		1	2
sheng-yuan	2	1					3
TOTAL	6	10	3	15	6	11	51
PURCHASE							
kung-sheng	1	1		1			3
fu-chien						1	1
chien-sheng		2		2		2	6
TOTAL	1	3		3		3	10
OTHER							
yin-sheng							
clerk							
office elsewhere							
Banner (no rank indicated)		1		2			3
no rank indicated				5	1	3	9
TOTAL		1		7	1	3	12
GRAND TOTAL	7	14	3	26	7	17	74
Average term per reign, in years	2.6	4.0	4.3	2.3	3.6	1.8	
TOTAL ACTING							
TOTAL BANNER		1		3		3	7

	HSIN-T'IEN							TAO-CHOU					
SC	KH	YC	CL	CC	TK	TOTAL	SC	KH	YC	CL	CC	TOTAL
	4	1	3	1	2	11	1			3		5
	1	13	5	3		22	1			15	3	19
		2		3		5				2	2	4
	1					1						
1	1					2						
3						3			1		1	2
4	6	4	16	6	8	44		2	1	20	7	30
1	1			1	4	7	2	1	1	7	1	12
			2	1	3	6		5	1	3	4	13
1	1		2	2	7	13	2	6	2	10	5	25
								2				2
										1		1
4	1					5						
	1		1			2				1	1	2
5	1					6	4	5		9	1	19
9	3		1			13	4	7		11	2	24
14	10	4	19	8	15	70	6	15	3	41	14	79
4.3	6.1	3.2	3.2	3.1	2.0		3.0	4.0	4.3	1.5	1.8	
7	1		4	5		17						
	2	1	1			4		5	1	1	2	9

sources. Wu-hsien and Ch'ang-chou: *Wu-hsien chih*, 3/1a–17b; Chin-shan: *Chin-shan hsien -chih*, 3/1a–2b, 2d ed., 2/9–28; Li-yang: *Li-yang hsien-chih*, 9/39a–42; Ning-yuan: *Ning-yuan hsien-chih*, 7/8a–14b; Hsin-t'ien, *Hsin-t'ien hsien-chih*: 7/1b–4b; Tao-chou: *Tao-chou chih*, 4/22b–30b.

governor or governor-general.[6] The remaining jurisdictions were rated "medium" or "easy." Candidates for office could be appointed to all such districts without having held office previously. Lastly, the first four districts were in Kiangsu, one of the most politically and economically advanced of the eighteen provinces. The other three were relatively obscure districts in Hunan.

The rank and status of these magistrates is shown in Table 4. This table shows certain differences from the distribution in the two seasonal registers. A smaller proportion of the total were examination graduates, and in every instance more were *chü-jen* than were *chin-shih*. There is a greater proportion of Imperial Academy students (*chien-sheng*) in the sequential lists, especially in the K'ang-hsi period. This is partly because many of the "students" appointed under the K'ang-hsi emperor were bannermen, i.e., from the Manchu, Mongol, or Chinese families which supplied the permanent standing army of the Manchu regime. In Ch'ang-chou, nine out of the twenty *chien-sheng* appointed in the K'ang-hsi period were bannermen. In Tao-chou, five *chien-sheng* bannermen were appointed consecutively between the forty-eighth and sixth-first years of the K'ang-hsi period (serving from 1709 to 1724). In the K'ang-hsi reign, the Manchu dominion was still widely challenged. To find the funds to suppress a serious rebellion, the emperor was forced to sell ranks and titles in large numbers. Opportunities were provided to officials in many different categories to purchase qualification for appointment or "immediate" appointment as magistrates. Apparently the generous proportion of *chien-sheng* in these years reflected a need to give priority to military and financial security.

Magistrates holding examination status by purchase were also relatively favored in the Yung-cheng reign. The Yung-cheng emperor preferred to maintain an alternative channel of appointment to the examination route to prevent the domination of administration by cliques. For the first half of the Ch'ien-lung reign, the opportunities to gain office by purchase were cut back. When financial need caused the authorities to expand this route to office once more, the provision of substantive appointments remained limited, and many applicants had to be content with the purchase of "probationary" appointments.[7]

The findings also show that a substantial proportion of the magistrates held "acting" posts. This raises the question whether the acting magistrates reflected a degree or status distribution similar to the substantively

Table 5. Rank held by acting magistrates

	WU-HSIEN	CH'ANG-CHOU	CHIN-SHAN	LI-YANG
EXAMINATION				
chin-shih	4	3	10	1
chü-jen	7	9	18	7
pa-kung	5	3	4	8
other *kung-sheng*	1	1		
TOTAL	17	16	32	16
PURCHASE				
kung-sheng	3	5	2	
chien-sheng	13	12	21	5
TOTAL	16	17	23	5
OTHER				
yin-sheng		2	1	
clerk			3	
other office (no rank indicated)	7	11	1	6
no rank indicated	11	8	5	
TOTAL	18	21	10	11
GRAND TOTAL	51	54	65	32
Total other office	22	32		

SOURCES: See Table 4.

appointed magistrates? If not, what proportion of the total years of service did they occupy? Table 5 has been compiled to give an indication on the first of these questions.* It shows that in Chin-shan and Li-yang the distribution between examination graduates and those not indicated as examination graduates is approximately even. In Wu-hsien and Ch'ang-chou it is approximately one-third for the former to two-thirds for the latter.

This indicates that the findings in the previous table are influenced by the inclusion of those holding acting appointments. Moreover, most of those holding acting appointments served much shorter terms than those holding substantive appointments. In the two "most important" districts many of the acting magistrates were simultaneously holding other appointments and were only briefly filling in until a substantive appointment could be confirmed. It may be concluded, therefore, that in terms of years of service the higher examination graduates constituted a greater proportion than that reflected in Table 4. Whether or not they provided the

* The gazetteers of Ning-yuan and Tao-chou do not indicate whether the magistrates in office in those districts held acting or substantive appointments. The recorded length of the appointments indicates that most were substantive.

same distribution for the period as a whole as that indicated in the two
seasonal registers, they should be regarded as forming the substantial
body of the magistrates in service.

On this basis it is possible to make some deductions about their intellectual qualifications. First, they possessed a high degree of political
consciousness. They knew the prevailing ideology and could express it
unusually well. Second, they had proved an ability to analyze questions
and form conclusions under intense pressure. These are not scholastic
attributes, and this was a source of grievance to the many scholars who
competed unsuccessfully for the only accredited tests of intellectual
prowess. But the examination system was specifically designed to produce
political administrators; it was perhaps more successful in doing so than
is sometimes realized.[8]

Finally, as high degree holders, magistrates enjoyed great social prestige
independent of their political appointment. Those who were provincial
graduates would, it is true, be at a social disadvantage with the few
local gentry holding the metropolitan degree, but for the vast majority
of people they possessed the authority of an exclusive and revered
attainment.

Age

The examination career was often a long and taxing process. What
would have been the advantage of demonstrating capability if the candidate
had been exhausted in the process? Did the examination system produce
old magistrates? There has been a recurrent impression that this was the
case. The Yung-cheng emperor commented on the old age of those appointed magistrates in edicts of 1723 and 1724.[9] The contemporary impression
was that, until 1724, metropolitan graduates had to wait ten years for
appointments, while provincial graduates had to wait up to thirty years
or more.[10] Between then and the middle of the eighteenth century, the
appointment system was in fact expanded and modified in an effort to
bring more examination graduates within reach of an official appointment.

To check the authenticity of these impressions, three tables have been
compiled on the age of degree-holding magistrates. Table 6, taken from
the class list for the graduates of the 1829 metropolitan examination,
shows the ages of those graduates who subsequently became magistrates.

Table 6. Appointment and age of metropolitan graduates of the 1829 examination

Age in 1829	UNDER 25	25–29	30–34	35–39	40–44	45–49	50 AND OVER
TOTAL IN AGE GROUP	10	45	65	65	28	8	3
RECEIVED METROPOLITAN APPOINTMENT	5	13	12	16	3	1	0
HAN-LIN BACHELORS	3	16	20	11	6	0	1
appointed prefect		1	1[a]	1			
appointed magistrate		1	5	4[b]	1		
await promotion from magistrate			1				
FOR IMMEDIATE APPOINTMENT AS MAGISTRATES	2	13	26	29	15	7	1
received substantive position	2	12	25	27	11	5	
obtained transfer		1	9	6	2	2	
obtained promotion				1[c]			
awaiting promotion		2	1	1	1		
not yet received substantive position		1	1	2	4		
transferred to director of schools							1
EXPECTANT MAGISTRATES	0	3	6	9	4	0	1
took position as director of schools			1	3			
APPOINTED DIRECTOR OF SCHOOLS	0	0	1	0	0	0	0

SOURCE. *Hui-shih t'ung-nien ch'ih-lu* for 1829 examination; revised and printed 1836.
[a] 1st-class asst. prefect.
[b] One was an expectant.
[c] To dept. magistrate.

The age groups are those of 1829; the information was drawn up in 1836. The appointments were made between those years.[11]

From the information in the table, it appears that the average age of all those appointed and all those awaiting appointment as magistrates was in both cases thirty-five in 1829. Thirty-three of the graduates, representing 15 percent of the total, had not yet received an appointment as magistrate by 1836. Their average age was then forty-four. The majority of the magistrates from this class list were therefore men in their early middle age. However, perhaps the most significant feature of the table is that only one had been promoted by 1836, and that promotion was only to the position of department magistrate. The rest were still magistrates or expectant magistrates seven years after they had graduated.

Table 7. Appointment of metropolitan graduates (chin-shih) as magistrates

CHIN-SHIH OF LI-YANG AND CHIN-SHAN DISTRICTS

NUMBER ON LIST	DATE OF DEGREE	DATE OF APPOINTMENT	YEARS BETWEEN	TYPE OF APPOINTMENT	YEARS IN OFFICE
Li-yang					
15	1742	1752	10	S	2y 5m
22	1751	1763	12	S	8m
30	1761	1771	10	S	2y 1m
44	1789	1789	0	S	5y 6m
Chin-shan					
9	1713	1732	19	A	$4\frac{1}{2}$m
11	1730	1735	5	A	1m
12	1730	1735	5	A	7m
19	1724	1740	16	A	1m
23	1730	1741	11	S	2y 9m

CHIN-SHIH OF T'AN AND SHEN CLANS

NUMBER ON LIST	(A) DATE OF *chü-jen*	(B) DATE OF *chin-shih*	(C) DATE OF APPOINTMENT	(D) YEARS BETWEEN (B) AND (C)	(E) LAST RECORDED YEAR IN SERVICE	(F) YEARS BETWEEN (C) AND (E)	(G) YEARS BETWEEN (A) AND (E)
T'an clan							
59	1654	1655?	1662	7	1687	25	33
50	1690	1700	1707	7	1711	4	21
15	1713	1715	1725	10	1735	10	22
5	1732	1733	1740	7			
9	1736	1737	1748	11	1751	3	15
54			1761		1769	8	
16	1759	1760	1769	9	1770	1	11
44	1768	1772	1784	12	1787	3	19
7	1774	1775	1786	11	1801	15	27
40	1800	1808	1810	2	1822?	12?	22?
Shen clan							
4	1678	1685	1692	7			
7	1723	1733	1741	8	1745	4	22

SOURCES: Li-yang and Chin-shan districts, see Appendix III; T'an and Shen clans, see Appendix II.
S = Substantive
A = Acting

The list also bears out the view that the younger (and generally higher classed) graduates received metropolitan appointments, while the older were the ones who were appointed district magistrates. This continues the distribution pattern noted by the Yung-cheng emperor a hundred years earlier.

On the other hand, there are various reasons why the list may be more representative of nineteenth- than eighteenth-century appointment procedures (see next chapter on appointment of metropolitan graduates). Unfortunately, no earlier class lists giving comparable information have been available for consultation. To obtain a broader impression of the age of magistrates holding metropolitan degrees, the information in Table 7 has been compiled. The district data is taken from two gazetteers recording the date of the degree held by their officeholders. The clan data was obtained by checking degree and officeholders in two clan lists against the gazetteers of the districts in which they were recorded as holding office.

There are several limitations to this table. The sample is disappointingly small. It is also always questionable whether the appointment recorded was the first appointment. Li-yang and Chin-shan were both districts to which graduates could be appointed directly by the Board of Officials as soon as their turn came for appointment. But in all cases there is no certainty that there might not have been an earlier appointment elsewhere. One would expect to see more appointments within five years or under, more especially from 1724 on. However, in two respects the table is of use. It confirms that metropolitan graduates waited far less long for office than did provincial graduates, as will be seen from a comparison with Table 8. Second, the last column under clans shows graduates still in office twenty years on the average after receiving their provincial degree. If Chang is right in calculating the average age of admission to the provincial degree as thirty or thirty-one, this would mean that they continued to be magistrates up to the age of fifty or over. This is a finding that will be given support by evidence on the duration in office and promotion of magistrates.[12]

Since this passage was written, an analysis of metropolitan graduates holding office in Chekiang, Shensi, and Kwangsi provinces, as recorded in the Blue book for the third quarter of 1840, provides the following information: forty-five men holding Board-appointed magistracies (i.e., appointments open to examination graduates: on this see below, chapter

3) waited an average of five-and-a-half years from the time of receiving the metropolitan degree for appointment to their current position and had been in office on average a further two-and-a-fourth years by the time the list was compiled. In the case of Chekiang province alone the figures are seven-and-a-half and three-and-a-half years respectively. Eleven men holding province-appointed magistracies (to which officials must be promoted or transferred: see also below, chapter 3) had been metropolitan graduates for an average of fourteen years by the time of receiving the appointment and had been in office on average a further two-and-a-half years. Such a record does not, of course, show for how long the post was held. Some men are still in their first or second year; others have been in one post for well over ten years, and degree holders for well over twenty.

An indication of the age of magistrates who only held provincial degrees is offered in Table 8. This table, although still minute in terms of the total statistical population, provides a larger and more consistent sample than the previous table on the metropolitan graduates. There is also better reason for supposing that each appointment recorded is the first appointment. The provincial graduates had less preferential treatment than the metropolitan graduates in selection for office. They had also to compete for office against a much larger group. The table shows in each part that the time spent in waiting for office averaged twenty years. This makes these graduates about fifty years old at the time they achieved office.[13]

In the case of the first-class senior licentiates (*pa-kung*), a few examples can be cited to give an idea of their age. The cases are taken from the T'an clan genealogy and Li-yang gazetteer (Appendices II and III).

Apart from Number 53 on the Li-yang list, the wait in these cases is of the order of twenty years. Taking Chang's calculation that the average age of becoming *pa-kung* was in the early thirties, this suggests that *pa-kung* became or were magistrates in their fifties. This accords with their relative order of priority on the appointment lists.

It is impossible to determine precisely the age of magistrates qualified for appointment by purchase. The date of purchase is never indicated in any of the degree or appointment rosters. This is because a purchased status was no cause for particular honor and no index of a class affiliation. The only group of any significance in this category is that of Imperial Academy students (*chien-sheng*). Chang put their average age at the time

Table 8. Appointment of provincial graduates (chü-jen) as magistrates

NUMBER ON LIST	DATE OF DEGREE	CHÜ-JEN OF T'AN CLAN		YEARS BETWEEN
		DATE OF RECORDED APPOINTMENT		
43	1648	1671		23
12	1654	1671		17
3	1678	1691		13
10	1693	1712		19
28	1699	1716		17
37	1713	1727		14
4	1726	1750		24
38	1732	1759		27
51	1744	1767		23
24	1760	1784		24
33	1768	1795		27
45	1777	after 1795		18+
8	1789	1809[a]		20
35	1794	—[b]		—
41	1807	—[c]		c.20–25
11	1821	1836		15
22	1834	1861		27

CHÜ-JEN APPOINTED TO LI-YANG DISTRICT

NUMBER ON LIST	DATE OF DEGREE	SELECTION PROCEDURE	DATE OF APPOINTMENT	YEARS BETWEEN	TYPE OF APPOINTMENT	YEARS IN OFFICE
9	1723		1744	21	A	11m
11	1732	t'iao	1745	13	S	3y 5m
13	1726		1749	23	S	2y 7m
17	1723		1754	31	S	4y 2m
21	1756	chien-hsuan	1763	7	A	4m
23	1724		1764	40	S	1m
25	1753	chien-hsuan	1764	11	S	6y
32	1756	i-hsu	1773	17	S	2y 10m
40	1771		1785	14	A	6m
41	1771	ta-t'iao	1787	16	S	2y
43	1780		1789	9	A	6m
47	1771	ta-t'iao	1796	24	S	8m
48	1777	ta-t'iao	1796	19	S	4y 10m
49	1779	ta-t'iao	1798	19	A	2m
50	1780	ta-t'iao	1800	20	S	2m
51	1788	ta-t'iao	1801	13	A	2m
54	1768	chien-hsuan	1803	35	S	4y
56	1779	ta-t'iao	1807	28	S	1y 8m
57	1783	ta-t'iao	1809	26	A	2m
58	1794	ta-t'iao	1809	15	S	1y 5m

SOURCES. Li-yang district, see Appendix III; T'an clan, see Appendix II.
S = Substantive
A = Acting
ª Second post.
ᵇ Not on list ending 1828.
ᶜ Listed well on in Tao-kuang period, but no year given.

Table 9. Appointment of first-class senior licentiates (pa-kung) as magistrates

NUMBER ON T'AN LIST	DATE OF DEGREE	DATE OF RECORDED APPOINTMENT	YEARS BETWEEN
18	1654	1673	19
29	1741	1763	22
56	1807	1838	31
NUMBER ON LI-YANG LIST			
20	1741	1762 (acting)	21
53	1801	1803 (acting)	2
59	1801	1811	10

SOURCES. See Table 8.

of purchasing their status at roughly twenty-seven. They had to wait three years before qualifying for any appointment. They then had to wait for the issuance of a contribution list. In the late eighteenth and early nineteenth centuries, this happened in 1774, 1798, 1801, 1803, 1814, 1819, 1826, 1833, 1841, and 1850. Having made the necessary contribution they could then be picked for substantive appointment as magistrates at the rate of four a month, according to their order of contribution. One list was seldom cleared before another was opened. Because of this it was the practice to choose one from an old list for every four or five from a new. Given this procedure, it is clear that in an issuing year it would be possible for young men to make a quick contribution, get high on the lists, and be picked early. But as no prestige was attached to purchase it is more likely that, in the eighteenth century, at least, the younger men would continue to try their luck through the examination system.[14]

The above evidence points to the conclusion that magistrates on the whole were not young men. Most were well into middle age when they took up the office of magistrate and near to retirement by the time they left it.

Economic means

If the magistrates as a whole gained their first administrative office relatively well on in life, it would be pertinent to know something of their economic means. Were they a relatively wealthy group? Or were they a group who expected to make a good living out of their office in the limited time it was available to them?

Unfortunately there is hardly any quantifiable information on this subject. Officially, the question of an administrator's wealth was immaterial. Confucianism placed its stress on mental and moral character and on material frugality. It catered to an economy of recurrent scarcity, and what it required in its administrators was the ability to economize and abstain. It did not need evidence of material success.

Nevertheless, there are good reasons for wishing to know about the economic means of magistrates. If the economic power of their office was substantial, so were its expenses.[15] The magistrate had to pay his secretaries and servants out of his own income, entertain his superior jurisdictions, and pay fees when doing business with the personnel of superior offices. He had to contribute to the costs of public works, famine relief, and other public charities. He might have to pay fines or redeem other unaudited losses incurred by his predecessor. Successful officials were also expected to help finance their relatives and support projects for their clans and home districts. In a society lacking hereditary aristocracy, it was their business to provide a sound financial inheritance for their descendants while the family line was provided with the means to do this.

Yet an official's salary was limited, and before the introduction by the Yung-cheng emperor of the extra salaries for "nourishing honesty," it was nominal. The magistrate provided for himself and his expenses by taking fees. Although irregular, this way of financing administration was universal and within limits openly accepted. The introduction of the extra salary was intended to legalize those fees which could be legalized and reduce the level of those which could not. Only the ranking administrators received supplementary salaries. The educational officials and all the members of the subbureaucracy did not. The level of the salaries was permanently fixed, but the cost of living was not; and during the eighteenth century it rose substantially. Consequently the fee-paying system continued. It was its misuse which was the basis of the corruption which already by the late eighteenth century had become a major administrative problem.

Moreover, officials might have accumulated debts before they arrived in office. Many had waited a long time for substantive employment. Those appointed as probationers to the provincial administrations received no formal income except from whatever temporary assignments they received. It was in the provincial capital that magistrates normally hired their personal aides; some magistrates were apparently obliged to borrow from these individuals to tide them over until they could begin making a surplus out of their appointment.

The problem of corruption was one of the dominant issues in Confucian administration. It was commonly believed to be one of the chief factors in causing dynastic decline. It was no accident that the extra salary introduced by the Yung-Chang emperor was entitled to "nourish honesty." In view of the Confucian anxiety over honest administration, it may, therefore, be asked why the salary system failed to be effective.

In fairness to Chinese imperial regimes, it should be pointed out that the failure to finance administrative appointments adequately is far from untypical in premodern regimes. Some regimes not only failed to finance administration, but instead expected to make an income out of their administrators.[16] The problem of financing administration assumes significance in imperial China because the administrative staff was not expected to be drawn from a well-funded aristocracy but from examination graduates of sharply contrasting wealth. It is true that the Ch'ing dynasty sold examination status, aristocratic titles, and qualification for office but such sales were vigorously resisted throughout the eighteenth century by officials who were examination graduates, and did not reach substantial proportions until after the outbreak of the Taiping rebellion.[17]

What evidence, then, is there on the independent means of magistrates? A fair indication can be gained from the rank of the official. In his study of social mobility, Ho has shown that Ch'ing dynasty metropolitan graduates came primarily from families whose three preceding generations had produced one or more holders of higher degrees or offices. Moreover, the provenance of metropolitan graduates from this group increased as the dynasty proceeded.[18] This means that the majority of the metropolitan graduates came from families who had already established themselves in society and had been able, among other things, to finance the laborious education of their children.

However, there is broad evidence that the acquisition of the provincial degree could be of basic economic as well as social significance. As a candidate for office, the provincial graduate could attract patronage and private employment, gain privileges under the law, put up flagpoles outside his door, and be on familiar terms with local officials. This is why those who became provincial graduates were described as having "established themselves."[19]

If the fortunes of provincial graduates rose in the aftermath of their examination success, there is the question of how well they survived during the wait for substantive office. Those who served as secretaries could expect adequate remuneration because of the high demand for literate and resourceful persons in this employment. In the middle of the eighteenth century, the senior secretaries of law and taxation could obtain over 200 taels a year. Thirty years later they were getting as much as 800 taels a year. In the nineteenth century, some were receiving up to 2,000 taels a year, much more than the official salaries of most of the magistrates.[20] Teachers in private academies were also adequately remunerated. Chang calculates their average annual remuneration at 350 taels.[21] On the other hand, junior secretaries, or those who took work as private tutors or village teachers, or those who accepted appointment as educational officials, were much less well paid. They could receive as little as 40 to 50 taels a year or less. In his analysis of the social background of provincial graduates, Ho found that approximately half of those graduating in the early nineteenth century came from families whose three preceding generations had produced no degree holders or none higher than licentiate or Imperial Academy student.[22] Provincial graduates were thus less well endowed by their families than metropolitan graduates. The incentives to do well out of the opportunities provided by their degree must have been correspondingly greater.

The officials by purchase were for the most part better endowed. For senior licentiates and Imperial Academy students, the cost of purchasing qualification for substantive appointment as district magistrate stood at 4,620 taels in 1774. In 1797 it was up to 5,090 taels, although four years later it had reverted to the previous level. In the later years of the Chia-ch'ing reign (1796–1820) the price dropped to 4,070 taels. From 1819–1850 it rested at 3,700 taels. The cost of qualification for department magistrate was 1,500 to 1,000 taels higher.[23] These are substantial sums, beyond the means of the great majority. But the eighteenth century was an era of economic expansion and prosperity, and when the Ch'ien-lung emperor broadened the scope of the purchase system there was a rush to purchase the qualifications for every provincial rank from prefect down. The cost of purchasing qualification for appointment as probationary magistrate was, however, only 1,200 taels in 1775.[24] A probationer could expect income solely from whatever acting positions he held, and these were generally for a few months at most. Thus while a probationer required less means than one buying straight into substantive office, the opportunities for remuneration were substantially less and the incentives to do well out of the office accordingly more.

The conclusion is that the magistrates as a whole were relatively wealthy before coming into office. But the pressures to make a living were many-sided, and the means to do so honestly limited and inflexible.

The foregoing offers a preliminary insight into the authority of the office and its incumbents. The role of district magistrate was important, because of its moral influence over the local population and because of the power which it combined under one authority. For that reason it was by no means left to the mercies of its occupants but was kept under close restriction and surveillance by central government authority.

On the other hand, despite their low administrative rank the magistrates themselves were far from being socially junior. The great majority enjoyed high intellectual and social prestige. Their age accorded them social seniority in a culture attaching respect to age. Most were from well-to-do backgrounds. This leaves open the question of their administrative experience, to which the next chapter will turn.

3

THE PATH TO OFFICE

Appointment

We shall now proceed to examine the system for appointment of magistrates. One might expect that in a civil service enjoying a highly articulated examination system, those who succeeded in the examinations would automatically be admitted to office. This was not the case under Ch'ing administration. The period between qualification and appointment was seldom less than a year or two and could stretch up to over thirty years. The main reason for this delay was that the examination system constituted a test not simply of qualification for office, but of membership in an entire social elite. In spite of this, the members of that elite had been conditioned through their long education to look forward to receiving office. They expected it both as a mark of social fitness and as a reward for hard and costly years of study.

The problem for the regime was how to correlate the limited number of official posts with the pressure of candidates for office. One solution would have been to expand the number of offices. Two factors seem to have inhibited the Manchu regime from taking this action. First, it chose to keep a disproportionate number of metropolitan positions available solely for Manchus or for Mongol and Chinese bannermen. Second, it was averse to permitting any expansion in the official structure of local administration. Instead, as Table 1 indicates, a steady attrition in local administrative assistantships continued throughout the dynasty. The substantial bureaucratic expansion which did take place during the early Ch'ing period was at the unestablished level, among the private secretaries, clerks, and runners (see below, chapter 10, on changes in the staffing of local administration).

Despite these restrictions, the regime could hardly reduce the examination quotas. Its stringent quota policy already made the examination system into one of the chief points of tension in the political fabric. By the beginning of the nineteenth century, feelings of disillusion were widespread among the hosts of repeatedly unsuccessful candidates. The Ch'ing regime was very conscious of this problem. It chose to resolve it by providing more degrees qualifying for office than available offices, and adjusting this difference by developing a highly coordinated appointment system.

The appointment of *hsien* or district magistrates constituted one of the most conspicuous features of the whole appointment system.[1] This office provided one of the largest number of individual posts available. It could also be obtained without prior administrative experience. This does not mean that such experience was discounted. Altogether, twenty-four subordinate metropolitan and provincial offices qualified their occupants for the position of district (*hsien*) magistrate. They included second-class assistant department magistrates, prefectural commissaries of records, assistant district magistrates, and directors of schools. As can be seen from the appendices, a number of such officeholders were appointed magistrates.[2] Despite these provisions, the lion's share of the appointments went to degree and status holders who had not hitherto held subordinate office.

For the purpose of making appointments, the districts were divided into several different categories. Appointment to 944 of the districts (three-quarters of the total) was directly under the control of the Board of Officials.[3] Of the remainder, roughly 100 were classified as "preferment" (*t'i*) posts. These posts went to officials nominated by the governor or governor-general from among the acting or probationary magistrates under his authority or from officials due for promotion. The appointments had to be ratified by the Board of Officials.[4] As of 1748, candidates for a preferment post had to have served five years to qualify for such an appointment.[5] The remaining 250 or so districts were classified as "transfer" (*tiao*) posts. These posts were limited to officials who had already served three years in other substantive positions of the same rank. Nominations to transfer posts were also made by the governor or governor-general and cleared by the Board.[6] The preferment and transfer posts were also distinguished from the rest by their relative importance. They formed the posts classified as "important" or "most important." That means they had three or all four of the characterizations of being "frequented" (centers of communications), "troublesome" (much official business), "wearisome" (many overdue taxes), and "difficult" (a violent populace).

The preferment and transfer posts were distributed wherever circumstances warranted these classifications. In the advanced and active province of Kiangsu, 33 out of 67 districts were classified as transfer posts. In Hunan, out of 70 departments and districts listed in 1745, nineteen were preferment and six transfer posts. In distant Yunnan, out of 73 district jurisdictions in 1745, only nine were preferment and thirteen transfer posts. In thirty-six of these posts belonging to four prefectures, only four were preferment or transfer posts.[7]

The restriction of these posts to officials nominated by the provincial chiefs limited them to experienced men who had earned the confidence of their superiors. This policy constituted an important concession to decentralization. That is why there were comparatively few such posts and why the nominations of the provincial chiefs had to be screened by the central government. Reclassification of the posts was very uncommon and, apparently, required an exchange between Board-controlled and province-controlled appointments.[8]

Certain other procedures existed which also somewhat increased the influence of the provincial authorities. Under a procedure known as "retain" (*liu*), a provincial chief could make an appointment to a Board-controlled post when there was no time to wait for a Board appointment.[9] A provincial chief could also make an "acting" (*shu*) appointment. He could do this while awaiting Board clearance of an official recommended for a preferment or transfer post or as a means of employing an official without having to make a substantive recommendation for him.[10] Such an appointment did not require prior clearance from the Board. From 1799 on, the provincial chiefs were also entitled to examine magistrates sent to districts controlled by Board appointments within half a year after their arrival at the post. If they did not seem up to the job, but were otherwise in good health and noted for literary talent, the provincial chiefs could request to have them transferred to educational posts. If they were infirm, they were to be retired.[11] The provincial authorities could also, under certain circumstances, prevent a Board-appointed official from taking up his position until he had first been tried out in a temporary commission.[12]

Finally, it should be pointed out that department (*chou*) posts were not available to candidates for a first appointment. This held true, whatever the appointment classification of the department might be. All department magistrates had held prior administrative office in either the capital or the provinces. The departments were roughly evenly divided between Board-controlled and province-controlled appointments. The majority of the appointments appear to have been from provincial officials.[13]

The appointments to the great majority of the district posts were under the sole management of the central authorities. We must now turn to the procedures by which candidates for office obtained these appointments.

First, let us take the procedures for making appointments to magistrates' posts. All candidates were divided into separate lists, according to rank and qualifications. Appointments were normally made once a month (none were made in the lunar intercalary months). Those for Chinese personnel, who constituted over 90 percent of the total number of district officials,[14] were made on the twenty-fifth of each month. In the even months, the quota consisted of five metropolitan graduates, two new metropolitan graduates, five provincial graduates, two local educational officials who had completed a six-year term of office, four qualified by financial contributions, three serving officials qualifying for promotion, and two sons of outstanding officials, making a total list of twenty-three persons. If there were not enough individuals to fill a given category, substitute categories were indicated, usually consisting of metropolitan or provincial graduates. After so many even months, certain extra categories of candidates were included. Thus after two even-months lists, there would be added two palace instructors, two senior licentiate instructors, two provincial graduates studying as government instructors, and one third-class senior licentiate (*yu-kung*). Certain other categories also qualified after one or two lists.[15]

In the odd months, the quota consisted of four officials who had completed mourning and reapplied for substantive appointment, two officials who had been impeached and lost their positions but who were qualified to be restored to substantive appointment, four qualified by contributions, four metropolitan graduates, two new metropolitan graduates, four provincial graduates, two local educational officials who had completed six years' service, and one salt-administration official who had completed five years' service and who was recommended for the office, making a total list of twenty-three. In 1802 there was added one metropolitan official qualified for promotion. In 1834 two more restored officials were added, making a total of twenty-six.[16]

Certain candidates for office were exempted from taking their turn on the monthly lists. They included officials returning to their original position after completing mourning, officials deprived of employment through the abolition of their post, officials receiving permission to serve in a province near to their elderly parents, or officials receiving an imperial order to proceed to a given Board or province. Officials quitting office in obedience to the avoidance laws or returning to office after recovering from illness were placed at the front of the odd-months list, whatever their degree or status.[17]

To get on the monthly lists, a candidate first registered at the Board of Officials as soon as he acquired the degree or status qualifying him to apply for office. His name was then added to the list for the degree or status applicable to him. Unless he qualified for immediate appointment, he had then to return to his native district and wait until his name reached the top of the list.[18] When that happened he would be notified by the Board to return to Peking.

On arrival he would have to notify the Board and present his credentials fifty-five days before the date for distributing appointments. A few days before the day of selection, all those listed for appointment appeared before senior ministers, who checked their place of origin, age, suitability, and administrative experience.[19]

Meanwhile bamboo tallies indicating the location of the appointment were prepared and sealed.[20] Early on the twenty-fifth day of the month, the candidates for selection gathered outside the Gate of Heavenly Peace.[21] They drew the lots according to the sequence of the categories on the monthly list and according to their order within each category.[22] After having received the appointments, they were again examined on the uprightness of their conduct, correctness of their entry into the service, and on their age and state of health. Those not cleared on these counts were removed from the group. The infirm were put down for educational posts. The rest, before proceeding to their posts, were presented to the emperor. They were then dispersed to the various provinces.[23]

This was the general procedure by which candidates for the Board-controlled appointments were processed for appointment. Let us now see how the candidates of each major category qualifying for appointment were specifically handled.

The senior group were of course the metropolitan graduates. As Table 6 indicates, not all metropolitan graduates were appointed magistrates. Those who passed highest in the Palace examinations went into the Hanlin academy. Of the rest, the younger were chosen for metropolitan positions. The rest went on the lists for appointment as district magistrates.[24] Before this happened, the emperor marked the names of those designated for immediate appointment as magistrates. These then went on the immediate appointment list. The order of placement on the lists depended on the order of placement in the Palace examinations. The Yung-cheng emperor ordered that an exception to this be made for those more than fifty years old. These were selected according to age. All who were not then notified as being high enough in their respective lists to justify waiting in Peking returned to their native districts until their turn came.[25]

The composition of the metropolitan graduates checked for immediate appointment appears to have changed between 1723 and 1850. The Yung-cheng emperor had selected elderly men for this category. In 1805, however, the Chia-ch'ing emperor stated that in marking off new metropolitan graduates for immediate appointment as magistrates the original purpose had been to get them quickly into service, so that provision could be made for giving them some training. Recently the number of those marked off had become quite large, and this had been an obstacle to their selection. He gave special orders for the graduates of that year to be sent to the Board to draw lots and be dispatched to the provinces for immediate employment. He also noted that many graduates of the previous two examinations who had been marked for immediate employment had not yet received appointments, and ordered that they all be summoned to draw lots and be sent out to the provinces.[26] These graduates were not, however, given immediate substantive office. Instead, they were sent out for employment as deputies before being appointed to a substantive district position.[27]

The most fortunate among the metropolitan graduates appointed as magistrates were the graduates of the Hanlin academy who were not retained for metropolitan appointments. They could be appointed without having to wait in turn on the monthly lists. Others were left to wait years for the summons for appointment. Any who wearied of this delay could apply to be appointed to the innocuous post of prefectural director of schools.[28]

The next major group were the provincial graduates. The procedure established by 1700 was that those from distant provinces could register for appointment after one attempt at the metropolitan examinations. The rest had to wait until after three attempts. Candidates went onto the appointment lists according to their placing in the provincial examinations. In case two or more candidates received the same place in the examinations of different provinces, they were placed by order of province.[29]

The candidates from near provinces thus began with a minimum normal delay of seven years between graduation and qualification to register for appointment. Between graduation and appointment it was clearly possible for an individual to grow too infirm to be of any practical administrative use. In view of this, it was decided in 1723 that the provincial chiefs should examine all those succeeding in the provincial examinations who wished to become magistrates. The young and vigorous were to have their records sent to the Board. The old and infirm, together with those who were not of outstanding intelligence, were permitted to request to be registered for educational positions.[30] Ten years later it was decided that the provincial authorities should carry out a second check at the time a graduate received a summons for selection. If he was old, they were to notify the Board to register him for an education appointment. In 1739 the first examination was discontinued. Those waiting for a magistrate's position who declared themselves no longer fit enough to hold the post but who still wished to receive the title could also forego the second examination.[31] Provincial graduates could also be employed in the less taxing position of first-class assistant department magistrates.[32]

The imperial authorities felt far from easy about the substantial aging experienced by large numbers of provincial graduates between graduation and appointment. Every three years some 7,500 or more would congregate in the capital for the metropolitan examinations, only to be disappointed. This situation prompted the genesis of the so-called "great selection" (*ta-t'iao*) system. The first effort to find wider employment opportunities for provincial graduates was taken in 1727. In that year the ever-observant Yung-cheng emperor, noticing that the local educational officers were all "old and effete," ordered the provincial chiefs to examine them in conjunction with the provincial commissioners of education. Those who were "senile" and "incapable of expressing themselves" were to be ordered to retire. Their places were to be reserved for those provincial graduates failing the metropolitan examinations, whose essays were stylistically "lucid and correct." Those who, after six years' service, proved effective in directing their scholars were to be recommended for selection as magistrates. Seven years later, the emperor directed his attention to the difficulties encountered by provincial graduates from distant provinces in competing for the metropolitan degree. He commissioned senior officials to examine those who failed and recommend the able for selection for office. Those from the distant provinces who were willing to be registered for any immediate employment were to be examined and selected by the commissioners.[33]

The "great selection" proper began in 1752. The Ch'ien-lung emperor, who was then on tour, ordered commissioners to choose unsuccessful provincial graduates for presentation before the emperor. Forty were to be selected from each of the large provinces, thirty from medium, and twenty from small. These were to be divided into probationary magistrates and substantive educational officers.[34]

Between then and 1813 several different selection systems were tried in an effort to make the procedure equitable. In 1781 the emperor found that some of those coming up for selection had waited thirty-five years since becoming provincial graduates. In the distant provinces the gap was not more than twenty years or so. He ordered there to be no further distinction in the great selection system between near and distant provinces. The selection was arranged for every six years. But this produced too many officials. In 1800 the Chia-ch'ing emperor disbarred those who had sat in only the last three metropolitan examinations. This still left too many officials being sent out to the provinces. In 1813 the selection was reduced to once every four metropolitan examinations. Provincial graduates who had sat in only the last three metropolitan examinations continued to be disqualified.[35]

The provincial graduates selected as magistrates under the great selection system registered at the Board and drew lots just as in the monthly selection system.[36] But they drew only for provinces, not for substantive positions. They went out as probationers, without regular salary and for training in acting positions. After they had served one year in this capacity, the governor-general and governor then formally reviewed their record and notified the Board. Those found still fit for use as magistrates were allotted to any available Board-appointed posts that happened to have been vacated through the promotion, transfer, sickness, death, or retirement of their incumbents. If none were available, they could be temporarily employed as department or district assistant magistrates or prefectural commissaries of records. Those who were found unequal to the task of magistrate, or deemed too old, were employed only as subordinate or educational officials.[37]

The great selection system thus helped to get more provincial graduates into some form of administrative employment. A few were lucky enough to attain substantive appointments (see, for example, Appendix III, numbers 41, 48, 56). Others held short, acting assignments. But since its function was only to create more potential officials and not more actual positions, the great selection system could not substantially alter the prospects of the majority for receiving substantive employment. Only an increase in the number of positions or a major reduction in the quotas of other categories of candidates for office would have achieved any real difference.

Among the remaining candidates for the office of district magistrate the most prominent were the first-class senior licentiates (*pa-kung*) and the senior licentiates and Imperial Academy students by purchase (*kung-sheng* and *chien-sheng*). The first-class senior licentiates were selected for appointment on the basis of the performance in a special Palace examination, held once every twelve years. Those passing highest could be appointed court educational officials or probationary magistrates.[38] Those who were selected as government educational officials also qualified under the intermittent quota for government instructors provided in the even months. Those who did not participate in the Palace examination were divided along with the rest of the senior licentiates by examination into first- and second-class assistant department magistrates and assistant district magistrates. A few of these might eventually be promoted to magistrate, or serve in an acting capacity.[39]

For those wishing to purchase the office of district magistrate, the procedure was as follows.[40] Every so often the central government would open a subscription list for a given period of months or years. The terms of each list would indicate which offices and ranks were available for purchase. There were eight such lists during the Ch'ien-lung reign, six during the Chia-ch'ing, and four during the Tao-kuang. Those wishing to purchase qualification for office would go to Peking during the period in which the list was open, pay the requisite sum to the Board of Revenue, and then return to their districts to await selection. The price paid depended on the rank and qualifications of the payer. In the list opened between 1774–1776, the price of qualification for appointment as district (*hsien*) magistrate was 4,620 taels for a senior licentiate or Imperial Academy student, 2,020 taels for a substantive director of schools, and 2,570 taels for an expectant director of schools. A second-class assistant prefect paid 2,870 taels; if expectant, he paid 3,410 taels. An assistant magistrate paid 3,160 taels; if expectant, he paid 3,640 taels.[41]

The payment of these sums qualified the purchaser to be entered for selection on the even-months lists. If he paid a further 660 taels he could also have his name entered on the odd-months lists, which would double his chances of selection.

A candidate for office was well advised to pay the extra sum. Usually it proved impossible to clear those qualifying for office under each issue before the opening of the next issue. For this reason a quota system operated in the selection procedure. During the Ch'ien-lung reign, the practice was to choose four new subscribers for every one belonging to a previous issue. The heavy subscription for the 1774–1776 issue led, however, to a serious backlog in the appointment of those qualifying for office. In the early Chia-ch'ing period, the ratio was reduced to three new to one old in an effort to clear the earlier lists. But in 1816 the ratio went back to four new to one old. In 1819 it went up to five new to one old and stayed at that point during the Tao-kuang reign.

In addition to purchasing qualification for substantive appointments, it was also possible after 1776 to purchase the right to appointment as a probationary magistrate. After the establishment of the great selection system for provincial graduates, it had been discovered that even under this system there were not enough appointments for the degree-holders. The extension of probationary appointments to purchasers was therefore unpopular, including with the emperor himself. Nevertheless, a temporary demand for extra officials in Kweichow and Yunnan provinces opened the way to the purchasers, and thereafter it stayed open. This opportunity was limited to candidates subscribing for both kinds of monthly lists.[42] Even so, a memorial of 1811 indicates that a good many officials by subscription were going out as probationers.[43] In the nineteenth century, probationers were obliged to serve one or two years before qualifying for substantive office. If their purchased rank was higher than, or level with, the office in which they were tested, the term was one year. If lower, it was two years.[44] Unlike the degree candidates, they could, however, choose the province to which they were to be sent as probationers.[45]

The system for the appointment of magistrates acted like a valve between the flood of applicants and the number of positions available. In this capacity it was highly discriminating, but also very hard-pressed. It made much of distinguishing between districts and between applicants. Districts were not all distributed on a random basis. The most important went to the most experienced officials. There was a finely adjusted balance between the various categories of candidates for office, with the main share going consistently to senior examination graduates. There were several checks on the record and physical capability of each candidate. The infirm were disbarred and transferred to innocuous positions. Emperors took a personal interest in the appointments. A study of the voluminous *Statutory Amendments to the Collected Institutes* shows how careful they were to deal with problems that arose. They were particularly sensitive to the delay between graduation and appointment. But this problem remained unresolved. The expansion in number of the deputy and probationary magistrates merely meant that some expectant officials never received substantive office to the end of their careers or lives. As the Japanese editors of the *Ch'ing-kuo hsing-cheng fa* commented, "that is the extraordinary feature of the Ch'ing official system."[46]

Prior administrative experience

An examination of the system for the appointment of magistrates confirms the judgment that those who held substantive office were not on the whole young men. They were certainly old enough to have had the opportunity to have been exposed to prior administrative experience. Were they exposed to such experience, and if so, of what sort?

We already know that the incumbents of the roughly 350 preferment and transfer district posts and of all the departments, that is, at least one-third of the total body of district magistrates, had had such experience. An examination of Appendices I and II also shows that a number of magistrates accumulated years of experience from prior service in other districts. We also know that seven of the officials appointed on the odd months (in the nineteenth century, ten) had had prior administrative experience. Of those appointed in the even months, three were officials qualifying for promotion. Several government instructors were added in the substitute appointments. Some appointments went to officials exempted from the monthly lists. Finally, each month, two appointments were given to educational officials who had served six years in a local government office. This means that, every two months, from fifteen to twenty or, roughly, one-third to two-fifths of all those appointed by the Board had had prior administrative experience or long exposure to administrative service.[47]

What of the metropolitan and provincial graduates being appointed by the Board to substantive office for the first time? Some, at least, would have served as private secretaries. On a rough calculation there were at least some 7,500 secretaries serving in the departments and districts alone in the late eighteenth century. In the nineteenth century, this number probably increased.[48] In addition there were private secretaries serving at the higher levels of provincial administration. Chang estimated the total number of secretaries in all provincial administration at 16,000.[49] This would be too high for the eighteenth century, but might be reasonably close to late nineteenth-century conditions. These men shouldered much of the routine administrative business. They helped to supervise the subadministrative staff. The senior secretaries of law and taxation also gave essential advice on administrative action.[50] Some of them later rose to office themselves. The number of these cannot be calculated since their qualifications came from their degree, not from their service as secretaries.[51] Various examples are to be found in the biographical sections of local gazetteers.[52] The number could probably be sizably increased but for the tendency of biographers to omit mention of unofficial service in those who attained office. Certainly some of the most noted Ch'ing magistrates had previously served as private secretaries.[53]

The other major activity in which many magistrates had previously engaged was tutoring. In imperial China this involved teaching texts dealing with politics and administration. Teaching did not provide administrative experience, but it could provide a sound basis for developing political consciousness. Thus, effective tutors could be expected to have developed some awareness of the ideological aspects of the role of district magistrate. Some of the most distinguished of the Ch'ing district magistrates had previously been tutors. Among them were Chang Ch'i, Lan Ting-yuan, Li Chao-lo, Ts'ui Shu, and Tuan Yu-ts'ai. The first four were noted for effective administrative management, as well as for success in such tasks as controlling litigation, spreading education, and giving a sense of political well-being to the people under their administration. Clearly, tutoring should not be discounted as a background in the Confucian state to political administration.[54]

These findings indicate that at least half of the magistrates holding substantive office had had prior administrative experience. An unknown number had also had experience in other relevant activities. Others had been tested as deputies or probationers before being cleared for substantive appointment. All these officials were also reviewed by their superiors every three years.[55] There were thus many ways in which magistrates were able or required to gain administrative background, and were then checked for their success in this task.

There remained, however, a substantial proportion of officials who arrived in office without prior administrative experience. These were the officials who were most dependent on secretarial aid and most vulnerable to disciplinary sanctions. But it should not be assumed that these officials were entirely dependent for their own practical guidance on what they had learned from the classics and histories. There existed a large body of literature on practical administration. This included general handbooks by magistrates, guides on the promotion of agriculture and famine control, and records of the cases of officials famous for forensic ability. There were also simple expositions of the laws and regulations, and specific guides on how to give sentences or conduct post mortems.[56] Some of these handbooks were imperially sponsored.[57] In addition, the provinces, prefectures, and districts had their local histories, giving information on local customs and problems and local administrative regulations and procedures. There were many such guides and local histories in circulation throughout the eighteenth and nineteenth centuries.

In the late eighteenth and early nineteenth centuries there also appeared large collections of essays on every aspect and for every level of public administration.[58] These books and essays were written by officials for officials. The best of them give firm and trenchant advice. Incoming magistrates especially were urged to read them.[59] Efforts were made to make them widely available.[60]

For officials who took their position seriously there was no lack of professional manuals in convenient shape and form, from which they could very quickly obtain guidance on almost any aspect of local administration, if they had not already done so before coming to office. All this does not necessarily contravene the widely held opinion that incoming magistrates were inexperienced and ignorant. But it does show that if they were ignorant, the problem was not due to lack of available guidance.

4

LENGTH OF SERVICE AND SUBSEQUENT CAREER

The Ch'ing official had spent considerable time and crossed a good many hurdles to get into the office of district magistrate. How long could he expect to stay in that office? And what were his chances of promotion?

Length of service

The normal term of office was three years in any given post. The official stipulations for an official's qualification for promotion and transfer were as follows: a magistrate serving in an interior post was qualified for promotion after five years of service, and in a border, coastal, or river post after three years of service. He was also qualified after three years of service for a transfer post. In insalubrious areas he could be promoted in under three years.[1]

Various institutional factors governed a magistrate's duration in office. Action under the Disciplinary Regulations could result in premature dismissal, demotion and transfer, or promotion. The death of a father or mother would, except in rare cases, cut short an official's career for over two years. He might also retire temporarily in order to provide terminal care for parents or to recover from an illness. The triennial service ratings could also cut short an appointment. Officials characterized as dilatory, badly behaved, weak, or blameworthy were dismissed. If judged cruel or venal, they were permanently disbarred.[2]

How do the terms in office appear to have worked out in practice? Chang, on the basis of the analysis of two districts, found that the terms of office of district magistrates were "quite short" throughout the Ch'ing dynasty, and shrank abruptly during the nineteenth century.[3] A similar analysis of the seven districts shown in Table 4 does not present so consistent a picture. Average terms per reign go consistently down in Li-yang and consistently up in Chin-shan. In Wu-hsien and Ch'ang-chou they go down to a low in the Yung-cheng period and then rise back to the same or a higher average thereafter. In the three districts in Hunan, there is no immediately distinguishable pattern. Clearly it is unsafe to generalize on the basis of a few districts.

But these averages did not in any case allow for fluctuation within reign periods; nor did they distinguish between substantive and acting appointments or between Board-controlled and province-controlled appointments. To gain a closer idea of terms of service in any one district position, Table 10 has been constructed. The table shows the average number of persons in office by six-year periods. Where the records allow,

Table 10. Appointments to office of district magistrate by six-year periods

REIGN PERIOD		YC 1–6	YC 7–12	YC13 CL1–5	CL 6–11	CL 12–17	CL 18–23	CL 24–29	CL 30–35	CL 36–41	C 42–
WESTERN CALENDAR		(1723–28)	(1729–34)	(1735–40)	(1741–46)	(1747–52)	(1753–58)	(1759–64)	(1765–70)	(1771–76)	(1777
DISTRICT											
Chin-shan	all	5	5	10	4	6	7	2	7	3	
	s	2	2	2	2	1	1	2	3	1	
Li-yang[a]	all	3	4	1	3	4	2	8	3	5	
	s	3	2	1	1	2	1	4	*	4	
Wu-hsien	all	9	6	6	4	2	6	3	4	6	
	s	4	1	*	2	2	4	1	1	4	
Ch'ang-chou	all	8	6	2	5	4	4	4	8	2	
	s	5	1	2	3	2	1	1	2	1	
Yuan-ho[b]	all	3	3	1	2	6	4	4	6	5	
	s	3	2	1	1	4	2	4	4	3	
Ning-yuan		2	1	1	2	2	2	3	4	4	
Hsin-t'ien		2	2	2	2	1	2	2	1	2	
Tao-chou		2	1	2	2	3	2	4	5	7	

SOURCES. See Table 4 and Appendix 3.
Reign periods: Yung-cheng: 1723–35; Ch'ien-lung: 1736–95; Chia-ch'ing: 1796–1820; Tao-kuang: 182
S = Substantive appointment.

it distinguishes between all those holding appointments and those only holding substantive appointments.

The table shows that there was a comparative regularity in substantive appointments. In Chin-shan and Li-yang, the average turnover in this category was just slightly under two persons every six years. In the three province-controlled districts, the average turnover was exactly two persons every six years for Wu-hsien and Ch'ang-chou. In Yuan-ho it was also two every six years until 1837. The sudden rise thereafter may merely be a result of faulty record-keeping. In Ning-yuan the overall turnover rate was slightly over two persons every six years until 1819. It then doubled. The record for Tao-chou shows a substantial increase in turnover in the late eighteenth century, but this almost certainly includes acting appointments.

The regularity in the substantive appointments is not surprising. As we have seen, the rate of Board appointments was largely restricted by the monthly quota system. It would have been inherently impossible to produce a dramatic increase in the turnover of substantive Board appointments.

CL 48–53	CL 54–59	CL 60 CC1–5	CC 6–11	CC 12–17	CC 18–23	CC24–25 TK1–4	TK 5–10	TK 11–16	TK 17–22	TK 23–28
(1783–88)	(1789–94)	(1795–1800)	(1801–6)	(1807–12)	(1813–18)	(1819–24)	(1825–30)	(1831–36)	(1837–42)	(1843–48)
3	5	10	1	4	4	4	2	4	7	4
*	3	4	*	1	2	2	*	2	3	2
3	3	5	4	5						
1	2	3	1	3						
2	1	4	4	2	2	4	2	3	3	4
1	1	2	2	2	1	3	2	3	2	3
3	2	1	3	4	4	2	3	2	3	3
3	*	1	3	3	2	2	3	2	3	3
3	1	1	5	3	4	1	4	7	7	5
1	1	1	1	*	1	*	3	4	7	5
3	2	1	2	1	1	4	4	5	3	4
2	3	1	2	1	3	2	4	3	3	5
6	7	2	5	4	4					

* No new substantive appointments.
ᵃ Series ends with appointment in 1811.
ᵇ Series begins at the end of 1725 (YC 3/11).

Other factors limited the turnover in the province-controlled substantive appointments. For the three transfer districts listed, each candidate for appointment had to have served three full years at a comparable rank. His appointment had to be cleared with the Board. Such appointments were effectively limited to officials already serving within the same province, since the recipients were expected to be already familiar with local conditions and to have earned the confidence and trust of the provincial chiefs. In a province such as Kiangsu, in which half of the districts were transfer districts, these requirements limited the number of qualified persons available.

When the acting appointments are added to the substantive appointments, the picture once again becomes less clear. The rate of turnover appears to be heaviest in the Yung-cheng, middle to late Ch'ien-lung, and Tao-kuang periods. But it is doubtful if an overall generalization can be made from so limited a sample. One possibly significant difference may be noted between the overall rates of appointment in the first two Board-controlled districts and the next three province-controlled districts. In Chin-shan and Li-yang there are over twice as many overall appointments as there are substantive. In Chin-shan the ratio is 105 to 38. In Wu-hsien, Ch'ang-chou, and Yuan-ho, there are less than twice as many overall appointments.[4] Since the three province-controlled districts were all "most important," whereas Chin-shan and Li-yang were only "medium" districts, one would expect the conditions of service to be more difficult in the former districts and therefore the chances of duration to be correspondingly shorter. But the actual appointment patterns do not bear out this inference. It is quite possible that these patterns instead reflect the greater confidence felt by provincial chiefs in their own appointees than in Board-appointed officials.

It is also possible to compare the duration in office of metropolitan and provincial graduates and officials who qualified only by contribution. Here the question is whether or not those qualified by examination and those most highly qualified by examination lasted longest in an administrative post.

Some light is thrown on this question by Table 11. In the column of substantive appointments, it transpires that the average terms of service of metropolitan and provincial graduates compare very closely. The only exception to this is in Chin-shan. But the number of metropolitan graduates

Table 11. *Duration in office of chin-shih, chü-jen, and chien-sheng, comparing length of single substantive and acting appointments*

DEGREE AND DISTRICT	NUMBER		TOTAL SERVICE		AVERAGE TERM	
	SUBSTANTIVE	ACTING	SUBSTANTIVE	ACTING	SUBSTANTIVE	ACTING
Chin-shih						
Chin-shan	5	10	17y 7m	2y 2m	3y 6m	2½m
Li-yang	5		11y 1m		2y 3m	
Wu-hsien	6	3	13y 11m?	1y 6m?	2y 4m	6m
Ch'ang-chou	9	2[a]	19y 1m?	1y 7m	2y 1m	9m
Yuan-ho	13	2[a]	35y 2m	9m	2y 8m	4½m
Ning-yuan[b]	12		33y		2.7y	
Tao-chou[b]	5		6y		1.2y	
Chü-jen						
Chin-shan	20	18	37y 11m	10y 6m	1y 11m	7m
Li-yang	14	8	35y 6m	2y 11m	2y 6m	4m
Wu-hsien	12	6[a]	29y 7m?	3y 6m	2y 5m	7m
Ch'ang-chou	14	7[a]	28y 10m	4y 3m	2y 1m	7m
Yuan-ho	12	8[a]	28y 2m	5y 8m	2y 4m	8m
Ning-yuan[b]	19		53y		2.7y	
Tao-chou[b]	18		26y		1.4y	
Chien-sheng						
Chin-shan	5	21	6y 9m	14y 9m	1y 4m	8m
Li-yang	2	5	6y	1y 4m	3y	3m
Wu-hsien	3	7[a]	4y 6m?	3y 7m	1y 6m	6m
Ch'ang-chou	3	2[a]	11y 7m	2y 9m	3y 10m	1y 4m
Yuan-ho	5	2	12y 8m	9m	2y 6m	4½m
Ning-yuan[b]	5		11y		2.2y	
Tao-chou[b]	7		15y		2.1y	

SOURCES. Table 4 and Appendix 3.
[a] Excludes magistrates known to be holding substantive office of magistrate or higher rank elsewhere.
[b] The numbers are inclusive; the periods of office are only recorded in years.

holding substantive office there is too small to allow for a reliable calculation. In the remaining four districts distinguishing between substantive and acting appointments, the examination graduates all served an average of two to two-and-a-half years. The low average for Tao-chou again implies the inclusion of acting appointments.

The table also suggests that the Imperial Academy students were not unduly handicapped by the lack of an examination degree. This is a rather surprising result. It is true that in their youth they were probably as thoroughly exposed to Confucian education as were the examination graduates. But the lack of a prestigious degree might be expected to have put them at a disadvantage, at least with their provincial superiors, who above the rank of intendant were virtually all degree-holders. The table does not, however, indicate that degree-holders were either more efficient or more protected from their mistakes than were non degree-holders. This would seem to imply that once an official became a magistrate, achievement depended more on performance in a post than on past effectiveness in the examinations. The same might also be said of the officials holding acting appointments.

Table 11 indicates only the average length of service in a single appointment. If we wish to gauge the relation of service to future prospects, it is also desirable that we know how long a particular official remained at the rank of magistrate. Table 12 has been drawn up as an index to this question.

In this table some distinctions must be made between the various sections. Sections 1 to 3 refer to magistrates serving in more than one district. Sections 4 and 5 each deal with only one district. Section 1 also differs from sections 4 and 5 in that each of the three districts included in it were transfer districts. Thus each official had actually served three years longer in a substantive office of comparable rank than is indicated in the table. In terms of service, every official in Appendix I qualifies under the three-year criterion chosen for this table; but it does not follow that the prior office or offices held were invariably that of magistrate. The size of the entry in sections 2 and 3 is also understated. If more dates could be put to the recorded appointments, the list would certainly increase in number of individuals recorded as well as in the number of years that they served.

It should be stressed that the number of years indicated as standing between the first and last recorded dates in office indicates the known

Table 12. Length of time spent at rank of district (hsien) magistrate (criterion: over three years in rank)

	NUMBER ON LIST	DEGREE	DIFFERENT DIST. APPTS. RECORDED	YEARS[a]
1. WU-HSIEN, CH'ANG-CHOU, AND YUAN-HO	2	*chien-sheng*	3	$9\frac{1}{2}$
	16	*chien-sheng*	4[b]	4
	18	*chien-sheng*	4	7+
	19	*chien-sheng*	3[b]	7
	23	*pa-kung*	3[b]	4+
	24	*pa-kung*	3[b]	$4\frac{1}{2}$
	35	*chin-shih*	3[b]	$4\frac{1}{2}$
	39	*chien-sheng*	3	6
	40	*chü-jen*	4[b]	$10\frac{1}{2}$+
	44	*chü-jen*	2[b]	4
	52	?	1	$5\frac{1}{2}$
	53	*pa-kung*	2	6
	55	*chü-jen*	2	10
	57	?	1	9
	58	*chien-sheng*	1	5
	60	*chih-shih*	2	11
	66	*yin-sheng*	1	9
	67	*chü-jen*	1	$7\frac{1}{2}$
	68	*chü-jen*	12	6?
	70	*chü-jen*	3[b]	7
	71	*chin-shih*	1	7
	75	*chü-jen*	2[b]	4?
	77	*pa-kung*	3	7?
	79	*chin-shih*	2	11?
	80	*yu-kung*	2	5+?
2. T'AN CLAN	5	*chin-shih*	2	10
	7	*chin-shih*	4	15
	11	*chü-jen*	4	3+
	12	*chü-jen*	1	4
	22	*chü-jen*	2	7+?
	15	*chin-shih*	2	10
	28	*chü-jen*	1	5
	34	*pa-kung*	3	5+
	38	*chü-jen*	1	4
	40	*chin-shih*	2	11
	46	*chü-jen*	4	16+
	47	*chü-jen*	5	14+
	50	*chin-shih*	1	4
	55	*chü-jen*	2	13+
	59	*chin-shih?*	4	25

Table 12. (*continued*)

	NUMBER ON LIST	DEGREE	DIFFERENT DIST. APPTS. RECORDED	YEARS[a]
3. SHEN CLAN	4	chin-shih	2	5+
	7	chin-shih	1	4
	14	pa-kung	5	?
	21	?[c]	7	?
	9	chü-jen	3	?

	NUMBER ON LIST	DEGREE	YEARS[a]	
4. LI-YANG	6	chien-sheng	5y	8m+ [d]
	17	chü-jen	3y	4m
	25	chü-jen	6y	6m
	32	chü-jen	3y	8m
	36	?	9y	2m+
	44	chü-jen	5y	7m
	48	chü-jen	5y	11m
	54	chü-jen	4y	

	DATES	DEGREE	YEARS[a]	
5. CHIN-SHAN	1741–52	chin-shih	10y	4m
	1752–57	chin-shih	5y?	
	1772–78	chü-jen	6y	7m
	1782–87	chü-jen	5y	3m
	1788–92	chü-jen	4y	2m[d]
	1800–08	pa-kung	22y	6m
	1801–14	chü-jen	13y? [d]	
	1816–22	chien-sheng	6y	5m[d]
	1823–33	chü-jen	10y	7m

SOURCES. Appendices I, II, III; *Chin-shan HC*, 3/1–2b, 2d ed., 2/9.
[a] Period between first and last recorded date in office.
[b] Includes concurrent appointment.
[c] Purchased brevet title.
[d] First appointment acting.

period of time spent at the rank of magistrate. It does not refer to the length of time in which an individual actually held substantive or acting appointments. Some of the indicated time was taken up by retirement for mourning, assignment as assistant provincial examiners, transfer to unspecified appointments elsewhere, or simply by unexplained absence from acting service. With such interruptions in tenure, it was possible for a magistrate to return to the same post two, three, or even four times, sometimes after intervals of several years.

The table shows that it was by no means uncommon for officials to spend well over three years at the rank of magistrate. One-quarter of the T'an clan magistrates are included in the table. The number in section 1 represents one-third of the total given in Appendix 1, all of whom served in more than one post as magistrate after qualifying for a transfer position. The number for Li-yang is slightly under a third of those holding substantive positions, and for Chin-shan one-quarter. Both seem unexpectedly high proportions, given the fact that no other district appointments are included.

Can any connection be discerned between the degree or status held and the length of time spent at the rank of district magistrate? The table allows the following breakdown by degree. In overall figures there are fourteen metropolitan graduates, twenty-seven provincial graduates, five first-class senior licentiates, nine Imperial Academy students, two from other sources, and four unknown. If the transfer officials are omitted, the proportions are ten, twenty, one, four, none, and two, respectively. For the transfer officials who put in nine years or over (six or over on the list), the proportions level down to three, four, two, three, one, and one unknown respectively.

There is an implication in this that the metropolitan graduates may not have served as long at the rank of magistrate as the rest. As we know, the appointment quotas favored them. In the seasonal registers analyzed by Ch'ü, they outnumber the provincial graduates. In Wu-hsien and Ch'ang-chou their numbers even out if the acting officials are subtracted (see Tables 4 and 5). Li-yang and Chin-shan appear on the face of it to show a disproportionate total number of provincial graduates (Table 4). But the overall sample available here is too small to permit a conclusive finding about this matter.

Subsequent career

A *hsien* magistrate who qualified for promotion could in theory rise to any one of sixteen different metropolitan and provincial offices. They included Board second-class secretaries, certain junior officials of the

censorate, courts of judicature and sacrificial worship, and other speciali-
zed metropolitan organs. The main provincial posts available were first-
and second-class assistant prefects and magistrates of departments and
independent departments. Table 13 indicates the number of metropolitan
posts available for Chinese officials in each of these offices.

Clearly there were not many metropolitan posts available to magistrates.
Moreover, the magistrates were not the only officials competing for these
posts. The position of Board second-class secretary, for example, was
available to twenty-five different categories of official, among them
Hanlin bachelors and secretaries of the imperial patent office. Nearly all
of the new metropolitan graduates indicated in Table 6 as going into
metropolitan posts were appointed second-class secretaries. Of the appointments made under the monthly appointment system, only two out of
twelve possible even-month appointments of Chinese officials to this
office were saved for provincial officials. As of 1751, no magistrates
could be appointed to this office in odd months. In short, few magistrates
could rise to this position.[5]

Therefore, magistrates had a better chance of promotion to provincial
offices than to metropolitan ones. Table 14 indicates the number of such
posts available.

Table 13. Promotion of district magistrates to metropolitan offices

TITLE OF OFFICE	NUMBER OF POSITIONS	SOURCE IN *TCHT:CL*	REFERENCE IN BRUNNERT AND HAGELSTROM
Board 2d-class secy.	55	3/3b–6	292
Officials of censorate chancery	1	3/8a	211
Registrar of censorate	1	3/8a	212
Senior and junior asst. secy. of court and judicature	2	3/9b	215/5 and 6
Doctor of the Court of Sacrificial Worship	1	3/11a	304B/933
Secy. of the imperial patent office	30	2/1b	137A
Commissary of records of transmissions office	1	3/9b	928
Archivist of transmission office	1	3/9b	928
Registrar of imperial equipage Dept.	1	3/13b	117
TOTAL	93		

SOURCES. *LPCHTL*, han-kuan, 3/4b–5; *TCHT:CL* as indicated.

Table 14. Promotion of district magistrates to provincial offices

TITLE OF OFFICE	NUMBER OF POSITIONS	SOURCE IN *TCHT:CL*	NUMBER OF POSITIONS	SOURCE IN *TCHT:CC*	REFERENCE IN BRUNNERT AND HAGELSTROM
2d-class asst. prefect of metropolitan prefecture	(2)		2	4/16a	794
Metropolitan dist. magistrate	(2)		2	4/8b	794A
1st-class asst. prefect	203	4/9a–b	116	4/16a	849
Magistrate of inde- pendent dept.	67	4/11a	67	4/5b	851
Dept. magistrate	154	4/11b	147	4/7a	855
Dept. asst. salt controller	1	4/8b	1	5/25a	855A
2d-class asst. prefect	182	4/9b	108	4/16a	849A
TOTAL	611		443		

SOURCES. *LPCHTL*, han-kuan, 3/4b–5; *TCHT:CL* and *CC* as indicated.

None of these posts were restricted ethnically. Each could, however, be competed for by officials other than magistrates. For example, appointment to department magistrate was from the offices and numbers of officials shown in Table 15.

Eighty-two of the one hundred and forty-seven department magistrate posts available in the early nineteenth century were Board-appointed posts. To these the Board made two appointments in the even months (one of them a promotion) and three in the odd months. The latter consisted of one official awaiting reappointment as department magistrate, one by contribution, and one metropolitan promotion.[6] The remainder of the appointments were initiated by the provincial chiefs. Thus, about one hundred department magistrate appointments were in principle accessible to the 1,300 district magistrates.

A department magistrate who qualified for promotion could, in turn, be appointed board assistant department director, metropolitan subprefect, assistant salt controller, first-class assistant prefect, or magistrate of an independent department. In each case, he would, of course, have been in competition with a variety of other metropolitan and provincial officials.[7] He would also have found that the monthly quotas of the Board

Table 15. Promotion of officials to department magistrate

TITLE OF OFFICE	NUMBER OF POSITIONS	SOURCE IN *TCHT:CL*	NUMBER OF POSITIONS	SOURCE IN *TCHT:CC*	REFERENCE IN BRUNNERT AND HAGELSTROM
2d-class asst. prefect	182	4/9b	108	4/16a	849A
Dist. magistrate	1282	4/12b–13a	1293	4/8b	
Commissary of provincial treasury	15	4/6b	15	4/28a	826
Law Secy. of provincial treasury	7	4/6b–7a	7	4/28a	826
Subasst. salt controller	6	4/8b	7	5/15a	835A
1st-class asst. magistrate of independent dept.	21	4/11a	22	4/16a	851A
1st-class asst. dept. magistrate	47	4/11b–12	32	4/16a	855A
TOTAL	1560		1484		

SOURCES. *LPCHTL*, han-kuan, 2/7b–8; *TCHT:CL* and *CC* as indicated.

appointments to metropolitan offices continued to discriminate against provincial officials. For example, the even months regular list for Chinese board assistant department directors called for five metropolitan promotions to every one provincial promotion. In the odd months, the list consisted of one official awaiting reappointment to the office, one by contribution, and one by promotion.[8]

Let us now look at the records of actual magistrates to see what sort of promotion they achieved. Table 16 presents the record of the magistrates in the T'an and Shen clans.

From the table it transpires that sixteen out of eighty-two individuals achieved promotion, the majority to the position of department magistrate. Two members of the Shen clan subsequently moved to other departmental magistrate posts. One held an appointment as acting prefect. Twelve promotions are also recorded in the Wu-hsien, Ch'ang-chou, and Yuan-ho lists, between 1723–1850. Of these, one was to subassistant salt-controller, two were to department magistrate, four to magistrate of an independent department, four to first-class assistant prefect, and one to acting prefect. This limited number of promotions contrasts strongly with the large number of transfers to other appointments as magistrate (see Appendix I, passim). But given the restrictions on promotion indicated above, it is hardly surprising.

The scarcity of promotions to prefect calls for brief comment. The promotion to prefect was from circuit censors, Board department directors, metropolitan subprefects, assistant salt-controllers, first-class assistant prefects, and magistrates of independent departments.[9] Of the fifty-nine Board appointments, one out of six went to a provincial official qualifying for promotion. Two were available for purchasers. All the "important" prefectural posts were, however, reserved for the emperor, who appointed to them by special edict. Thus although the prefect was the immediate administrative superior of the district magistrate, he was two removes from him by the appointment system. An examination of official biographies suggests that many of the prefects who later rose to high provincial office had, in fact, previously held metropolitan appointments.[10]

On the other hand, a district magistrate could rise directly to any one of the sixty-seven posts of magistrate of an independent department. This office was administratively on the same level as a prefecture. Fourteen of the posts were under Board control. The rest were at the disposition of the provincial chiefs.[11] Though few in overall number, they were thus more readily accessible to provincial officials. Finally, district and department magistrates could qualify for promotion, providing they were not

Table 16. Promotion of district magistrates in T'an and Shen clans

TITLE OF OFFICE	RANK	CHIN-SHIH	CHÜ-JEN	PA-KUNG	OTHER	TOTAL
1st-class asst. dept. magistrate	6B	1				1
2d-class asst. prefect	6A		1			1
Dept. magistrate	5B	2	1,[a]*1*	2,*1*	2	9
1st-class asst. prefect	5A		2,1[a]			3
Prefect	4A/4B			*1*[b]		(1)
Board 2d-class secy.	6A	1				1
Board dept. director	5A	*1*				1
TOTALS		5	6	3	2	16

SOURCE. Appendix II.
Figures in italics = member of Shen clan.
[a] acting position.
[b] acting, held by dept. magistrate.

in active service, if they made the necessary contribution at the right time. But, if they wished to qualify for an office higher than that to which they could normally expect to be promoted, the cost was, of course, substantial.[12]

Besides promotion and transfer, a magistrate could also be moved to a subordinate post, be dismissed or demoted under the Disciplinary Regulations, or retire for a variety of personal reasons. If a metropolitan or provincial graduate appointed magistrate proved unequal to the position, the provincial chiefs could memorialize to have him transferred to an educational post. He would then have to return to his native district, after which his province would notify the Board to register him for an educational appointment. Magistrates who had retired for personal reasons, or because of a disciplinary punishment, and subsequently registered for reappointment, could declare themselves unsuitable for administrative employment and request an educational position.[13] The T'an clan list provides three examples of magistrates who ended up in educational positions (Numbers 20, 36, 37). The one who is recorded as transferring voluntarily obtained the one educational appointment ranked equal to magistrate. The others, who were clearly old men, were effectively demoted, unless it be that their administrative appointments were not substantive.

A question at obvious issue is, how many magistrates were demoted or dismissed under the Disciplinary Regulations? The available local records are unfortunately far from frank on this point.* Most give no reason for departure. The Wu-hsien gazetteer throws interesting light on this problem. According to it the pattern of removal for administrative reasons was as shown in Table 17.

It can be seen that in Wu-hsien a substantial proportion of the officials appointed in the first two reigns lost their offices for disciplinary reasons. All but one held substantive appointments. The one who did not was a prefect acting as magistrate. In addition, two others not listed above left "because of an affair." The cases are evenly spaced throughout the reigns and cannot be attributed solely to temporary crises. The one case in the Yung-cheng reign is unusual because it concerned a simple licentiate who

* It has not been possible to consult Peking gazettes dating from the period under study here.

Table 17. *Demotion and promotion from Wu-hsien and Ch'ang-chou districts*

REIGN PERIOD	WU-HSIEN							CH'ANG-CHOU						
	SC	KH	YC	CL	CC	TK	TOTAL	SC	KH	YC	CL	CC	TK	TOTAL
Total number of appointments	8	34	17				59	12	48	14				74
Total substantive appointments	8	24	6				38	12	28	6				46
Impeached and left	4	6					10	6	14	4	2			26
Removed from office	1	1					2	1						1
Demoted and transferred		3	1				4		2	1				3
Demoted									1					1
TOTAL penalized	5	10	1				16	7	17	5	2			31
PROMOTED		3			2	1	6	1	2	1	4			8

was demoted and transferred but then two months later reappointed.*
No further disciplinary actions are recorded, though some almost certainly
must have taken place.

In Ch'ang-chou the proportion of disciplinary removals in the early
reigns is even higher: over half of all substantive appointments ended this
way. There is a heavy rate of failure in the earlier K'ang-hsi period; five of
the cases took place after 1700, by which time the Manchu dominion
was fully and finally imposed. The high level of impeachment of substantive officials continued in the Yung-cheng reign, with four out of six
leaving in this way. Two impeachments were recorded as occurring right
in the middle of the Ch'ien-lung period. Then again there is silence on all
reasons for departure, disciplinary or otherwise. The records may have
been lost; on the other hand, the lack of indication may well have been
deliberate.

One gazetteer which maintained a frank editorial policy throughout the
eighteenth century is that of Li-yang. From it one can gain an idea of the
range of causes which could take magistrates from their posts and of
distributions within that range. Table 18 indicates the experience of the
twenty-eight (Board-appointed) substantive magistrates holding office
between 1723 and 1811.

The series includes frequent cases of temporary assignment as provincial assistant examiners. A number of individuals served in this capacity
two or three times. One individual was twice seconded to an acting position
elsewhere, on each occasion for roughly six months. The causes for
permanent departure divide rather evenly between personal reasons,
administrative punishment, and regular career progression. The distribution of transfers is also even and undiscriminatory; one took place to
comply with avoidance laws. There are no direct promotions, but this is
not altogether surprising in a Board-appointed district.

The above evidence all points to the conclusion that few magistrates
were able to advance up the administrative ladder. The reasons for this
may be summed up as follows. The officials who became magistrates were
well into middle age by the time they took up office. The promotion ladder
narrowed very rapidly. Promotion to metropolitan offices was out of the
question for the great majority. Provincial promotion was a much better

* He subsequently served for seventeen months.

Table 18. *Departure of substantive magistrates from Li-yang*

	Chin-shih	Chü-jen	Chien-sheng	OTHER	NO RANK INDICATED	TOTAL
TEMPORARY DEPARTURE						
Audience			1			1
Provincial asst. examiner	2	4			1	7
Acting transfer					1	1
No reason				1		1
PERMANENT DEPARTURE						
Illness	2	2		1	1	6
Care of parents		1				1
Death		1				1
Impeached and left	2	4				6
Demoted and transferred		1			1	2
Transferred	2	3	2		1	8
Special assignment		1				1
Promoted		(1)				(1)
No reason		1		2		3
TOTAL PERMANENT	6	14	2	3	3	28

prospect, but even this was cut back by the substantial attrition of inter-mediate assistantships between the mid-eighteenth century and early nineteenth century. A number of officials holding substantive office ended by going down rather than up. Others were obliged to leave office for personal reasons. Many years had to be put in to qualify for promotion; yet large numbers of officials frittered away time waiting for brief acting appointments. If a magistrate finally did achieve promotion, it could not raise him directly to the position of prefect, his own immediate superior.

In view of these findings it may be appropriate to think of the imperial Chinese local administration in terms of career strata. The lowest stratum of all consisted of the clerks, personal servants, and runners, in other words, the members of the subbureaucracy. Virtually none of these rose into the ranking administrative service. The private secretaries, on the other hand, represent a transitional layer. As secretaries they were effectively outside the administrative service system, but as low-ranking examination graduates, they could hope, through one further examination success, to cross into it.

The subordinate district officials belonged to the administrative service, but few could expect promotion to the position of their immediate superior. The district magistrates were largely high examination graduates, yet few of them could expect promotion to the position of their immediate superior. Instead they were transferred, promoted in rank but not function to department magistrate, or filtered into the comparatively innocuous prefectural assistantships. A new career stratum begins with the prefects. For many of these, the post is the first, and by no means the last, provincial appointment.

A curious interrelationship emerges from this picture. Confucian morality urged unquestioning loyalty to seniors; it also urged respectful deference to elders. As older men, the magistrates holding substantive office could expect to be assisted by ethical bonds in their relationships with their subordinates. But this may not have been the case in regard to their superiors. If a new career stratum began with the prefects, more especially with those who were sent out from metropolitan appointments, there is likely to have been a tendency to have had older magistrates serving under younger prefects. It would be of great interest to know how this situation affected their administrative and disciplinary relationship. Regard for others in administrative conduct is a recurrent theme in magistrates' handbooks. It was possibly an attitude on which they themselves were highly dependent.

In summing up the balance between the authority of the district magistrates and its control, it was noted earlier that their authority was confined by the detailed system of disciplinary controls. It now appears that their considerable experience was blocked by the appointment and promotion systems. While their chances of demotion or dismissal are still unclear, they obviously were given little prospect of rising to higher office. Whether or not this represents a deliberate imperial device to keep local administrators local, it certainly had that effect.

Given these indications of discrimination against magistrates, it remains surprising that the considerable authority of their role was retained in one individual, and not more broadly distributed over the various sinecures at both the district and prefectural levels of administration. That this was not done must indicate that forces for the polarization of authority on the district magistrate outweighed those for its distribution. We must now turn to an examination of what those forces were, and how they influenced the conduct of local administrators.

5

INFLUENCE OF CLASSICAL THEORY ON THE
ROLE OF MAGISTRATE

It would be hard to exaggerate the influence of classical Confucian theory on Ch'ing administration. Its values permeated Ch'ing political and social structure. It provided society with its basic educational texts and gave its education a profoundly political cast. For administrators it represented an enduring and authoritative guide to the never-ending problem of maintaining order. Throughout the early and mid-Ch'ing, the tyranny of the examination system ensured that the minds of officials were steeped in classical views on administration.

How then did Confucian theory influence Ch'ing administrative consciousness?

The administrative role in classical theory

The core of Confucian theory, as constituted in the Ch'ing dynasty, is contained in the Four Books, reinforced by the Five Classics.* The themes of the Four Books are responsibility and reciprocity. They insist on society's need for moral leadership and stress both the beneficence of superiors and the right of subordinates.

* I.e., the *Analects* of Confucius, the *Great Learning*, the *Doctrine of the Mean*, and *Mencius*, and the Books of *Changes*, *Odes* and *Documents*, the *Spring and Autumn Annals* and the *Record of Rituals*. A table of the various compilations of classics is given in Fairbank and Reischauer, *East Asia: the Great Tradition*, p. 68.

The Confucian belief in moral leadership arises from its view of the political character of the people. Both Confucius and Mencius insisted that the people's support was essential to political order, but they also emphasized popular instability. In the *Analects* the people are seen as ignorant and powerless. Their moral power was as grass; "when the wind blew, the grass bent." Mencius even feared them capable of abandoning all restraint. But believing human nature basically good, he maintained that the people would turn to benevolent rule "as water flows downwards."[1]

This view of human nature was embodied in the theory of social origin found in *Mencius* and the *Book of Documents*. According to this theory, the world began in a state of chronic disorder. After intense labor the sage emperors Yao, Shun, and Yü brought cultivation out of chaos and taught the people how to subsist. But, as Mencius argued, if the people were well fed but not taught the Way, they were still near to being like birds and beasts. Leadership had to civilize human nature. The sage emperors could not perform this task single-handed. They had to have the help of assistant administrators.[2]

Such reasoning served as a backdrop to the role of the ideal public servant, or *chüntzu*. The role of the *chüntzu* was a primary concern of the authors of the Four Books. *Chüntzu* originally meant "son of a lord" and was still used in this sense in Confucius' time. But in the hands of Confucius and Mencius the term is principally used to mean one morally fitted to assume the responsibilities of administration.[3]

The chief characteristic of the role of *chüntzu* was its ethical commitment. This is expressed as *jen* or humanity to others. The *Analects* makes it clear that *jen* is the essence of public administration. *Jen* was necessary to secure power. It came before wealth, rank, poverty, or obscurity. It was the means to purify the people and win their confidence and service. The *chüntzu* was one who manifested *jen*. As Confucius put it, "never for a single moment does a *chüntzu* act contrary to *jen*. He is *jen*! He cultivates himself so as to give peace to the people." Because of the primacy of *jen*, Confucius insisted that the *chüntzu* should avoid serving a corrupt ruler and live in a state where *jen* prevailed.[4]

An essential attribute of the role of *chüntzu* was its totality. The *chüntzu* was a *chüntzu* whether or not in public service. In its expression of *jen*, the role of the *chüntzu* allowed for emotional fulfillment and was throughout life its own reward.

Another important feature of this role was its alleged naturalness. Its ethic was instilled from birth through the familial attributes of *ch'in* or parental affection, *ti* or deferential affection for elder siblings, and *hsiao* or affection and service for parents. The *Great Learning* showed how the cultivation of the personal life led step by step to political capability and was in fact necessary for political wellbeing. The *Doctrine of the Mean* held that the achievement of equilibrium in human nature enabled man to support the natural harmony of Heaven and earth. It argued that the cultivation of the self according to the Way of Heaven and earth would develop sincerity, and this would of itself liberate the transforming power of *jen*.

Mencius also affirmed the naturalness of government by humanity and justice, and in face of the political warfare of his day held such government essential to political survival. He insisted that *jen* was inherent in all men, and defined justice, *i*, as humanity in political action. But it was the special function of rulers and administrators to manifest *jen* and *i*. The *chüntzu*, said Mencius, "seeks to be *jen*" and "seeks to guide his prince in the ways of *jen*." A prince who employed *chüntzu* would achieve peace and honor, while the people would be roused to virtue. Conversely, rulers who neglected *jen* and *i* invited overthrow and would forfeit whatever they had.

From this Mencius concluded that only men of humanity ought to occupy high position. To hold authority without humanity was to plunder the people and spread evil among them. States led in such a manner could survive solely by good luck.[5]

In the hands of Mencius the *chüntzu* had become the guarantor of political stability. Once the imperial state took Confucianism, and in particular the Four Books, as its ideology, this became its theory of administrative morality. The *chüntzu* became the paradigm of those training for officialdom, and the image of those who had entered it.

The social group for whom this ideal was primarily created were the *shih*, a term translated as "knights" or "officers" depending on context. In the middle and late Chou period, the *shih* consisted of small landowners or minor assistant officials, distinguished by their traditional association with a feudal code. The term survived into the Ch'ing dynasty, when it referred to the Imperial Academy students and licentiates. These unestablished career-seekers identified with the Chou dynasty *shih*, partly because of their comparable social status and partly because many of the disciples of the philosophers were in fact *shih*.[6] But unlike the Ch'ing licentiates, the *shih* of the middle and the late Chou were more and more moving into positions of authority. With the decline of hereditary power, men whose ancestors had been "knights" were obtaining positions as territorial magistrates.[7]

The role of the *shih* is discussed at length by Confucius and Mencius. Both commit the *shih* to the lifelong support of *jen*. In the *Analects* the *shih* are still differentiated from the *chüntzu* by their military values. In *Mencius* their roles have become interlocking. Both exalt humanity and justice, merit office but do not claim it, and find their reward through following the Way. The *chüntzu* is the model for the *shih*, and the *shih* are the material for the *chüntzu*.[8]

While the Four Books go deeply into the general aims of public service, they have little to say about the specific functions of office holders. This matter is taken up in the ritual texts, particularly in the *Chou li* or Rites of Chou. In the process a much more authoritarian theory of administration is set forth. According to the *Chou li* only the king establishes the state. He appoints central officials to supervise its administration and local officials to manage the education and pacification of its peoples. These officials are responsible for upholding the ruler's authority, checking their subordinates, and controlling the affairs of the people. They regulate taxes, issue edicts and prohibitions, hear suits, examine faults, and punish criminals. Every year they account for their administration and are penalized for any mistakes.[9]

The content of the *Chou li* differs in several respects from the teaching of Confucius as developed by Mencius. There is little emphasis on humanity and justice. The stress is rather on conservation and control, on warning and punishment. The *Chou li* gives the same importance to education as Mencius. But because it views human nature as intractible, its concept of education is austere and coercive. In short, it looks at administration from the position of the superior. It talks about the prerogatives of power and the necessities of control.

The *Chou li* was admitted to canonical status almost a thousand years earlier than Mencius. In that time it came to exert a far-ranging influence on the structure of local administration. Its institutions provided the basis of many of the rural control systems of later dynasties.[10] In the Ch'ing it appealed especially to the Yung-cheng emperor, who cited it frequently in his administrative writing.

Its support for authoritarianism was also reinforced by other classics, in particular the elementary *Classic of Filial Piety*. This specious tract used filiality to provide the rationale for unconditional loyalty to political authority. It was able to back up the spirit of the *Chou li* through the influential medium of early childhood education.[11] It too was highly favored by emperors. The K'ang-hsi emperor had a hundred-volume exegesis published, and under the Ch'ing it figured prominently as a required examination text till the middle of the eighteenth century.[12]

In consequence, the Ch'ing administrator was reared to conflicting concepts of responsibility. In the Four Books it was seen as an internal quality, in others it was demanded of him. In his education the former approach predominated. But once he entered administration—particularly local administration—he came under a deliberate system of coercion and control. Would such an administrator maintain a Confucian orientation to such an administration? We can consider this by examining Ch'ing interpretations of the role of local administration.

Role of magistrates in Ch'ing administrative writing

THE PEOPLE: Ch'ing local administrators seem to have agreed well enough with the classical Confucian appraisal of the people. The people were seen as the foundation of the state. The security or endangerment of a district depended on them. "If the foundation is firm," wrote Yuan Shou-ting, "the state is peaceful. Ordering the whole world consists in this. Ordering a single district consists in this."[13]

The people were also viewed as essentially well-meaning. Human nature, although "hard and uninstructed," was basically good. It was natural for men to long to do good and to fear to do bad. The people would, therefore, be responsive to enlightened leadership. Their hearts were not made of "wood and stone." If led with sincerity, they could be converted; if loved, they would be happy and peaceful.[14] Moreover, the vast majority were considered amenable to the existing political order and "good" in the sense of compliant. A few troublemakers such as beggars, bandits, notaries, and random criminals who were not, could be "weeded out" and got rid of. Other undesirables identifiable by profession, such as actors, prostitutes, government runners, and certain isolated groups descended from former rebels, were branded "base" or "mean." These were legally barred from entering the privileged socio-administrative order.[15]

The major political problem was still felt to be the intellectual and social immaturity of the people. "Simpleminded," "small," "inferior," were attributes commonly applied to them. The people were ignorant and unenlightened, and unable to "regulate themselves." They were like "children," or even "new-born infants."

Such being the case, Ch'ing administrators emphasized provision for the people's physical and mental nourishment. "Government of the people," said Ting Jih-ch'ang, "has a myriad aspects, but only two obligations. These are education and physical nurture; and nurture is basic for education."[16] Physical nurture involved the promotion of agriculture and sericulture, and the maintenance of irrigation facilities and famine control supplies. It required that administration "economize on the people's wealth and be sparing of their energies;" or, as Wang Hui-tsu bluntly put it, "not fleecing the people is the source of life and nurture."[17]

Local administrators must know the strength and weakness of each family and settlement and exhort them to be economical. They must particularly encourage care of the old and succor of the orphaned and impoverished, the hungry and cold.[18] In the context of physical and moral nurturing, magistrates were reminded that they were the "pastors" of the people: the cultivation and betterment of the people was their concern.[19]

While nurture involved individual welfare, education dealt with social relations. Its purpose was to bring the people into a state of social harmony. Its content was filial and fraternal respect, conscientiousness and trustworthiness, and social and familial concord.[20] Its function was largely preventive. "Laws," wrote Governor Ch'en Hung-mou, "restrain what has already happened. Education provides for those who are not yet criminals."[21] In view of the association of education with security, the educational role of administration was seen as extremely important. It was not just a question of "issuing orders and regulations," but of "changing" the people, bringing them to see the error of their ways and the enlightened example of the official's. In practice, the magistrate's court became a forum for public education of the people, and educational method included exemplary correction of offenders, as a means of persuading onlookers to desist from stirring up trouble.[22]

But educationally minded officials stressed that education could not be equated with legal correction. "To wait until they affront the law and then discipline them according to the law is not education but punishment," wrote Ch'en Hung-mou.[23] Education required that administrators go out and actively exhort the people. "There is a way to do it, there is an attitude of mind to it," wrote Ch'eng Han-chang. "Have a clear heart and single desire to make them upright. Be diligent with litigation so as to spare their strength. Pay attention to agriculture and irrigation so as to make abundant their food. Promote the schools so as to open up their powers of growth. Respect the old and show love to the young so as to establish their rules of conduct. Point out the good and punish the bad so as to motivate their behavior. Every way of educating and nourishing the people you must press to the utmost. If you do this diligently, you will find in anyone the means to transform him."[24] But this task required considerable perseverence. "The people's infection of themselves is not a one-day affair," wrote one magistrate. "You cannot transform them in an instant." "When transforming the people with education," agreed Ch'en Hung-mou, "it is at first hard to see any result. But if you stay at it for a long time, there must be a change."[25]

The task of providing educational leadership fell squarely on the district magistrate. Ch'ing administrative writing was unanimous in assuming that this leadership could best be supplied by magistrates, and that magistrates should only concern themselves with providing it. "There are only two important offices in the empire," wrote one local educational official, "those of grand secretary and district magistrate . . . . When it comes to witnessing the troubles and burdens of the people and personally seeing what benefits and harms them, then the former office cannot be compared with the latter. . . . The actual government and administrative control of the empire is effectively in the hands of the district magistrates."[26] An official who rose from district magistrate to high provincial office confirmed this pointed omission of the senior provincial offices. "The senior provincial officials," he noted, "are close to the ruler, but district magistrates are close to the people. The former can talk about 'promoting benefit and dispelling adversity' but they cannot carry it out. Their words are empty words. Only in the case of district magistrates can one really see this carried out."[27]

By the same token, district magistrates were too distant from the "source of moral power" to think in terms of directly assisting that power. Their only function, in the words of Yuan Shou-ting, was to be for the people; their effort only to be exerted on behalf of the people. It was in that way that they fulfilled their duty to the ruler.[28]

The accomplishment of such objectives required that leadership be intimate and highly motivated. As Yuan Shou-ting put it, "the district magistrate must see himself as a father and mother and the people as children. He must not look on himself as an official and the people as people." Moreover, said Yuan, he should look on the people as if they were his own children, and administer them as if they were his own family. He should protect them "as if he were protecting his infants." [29]

What did being the people's father and mother mean in practice? It meant, said Wang Feng-sheng, "that as with your own children and grandchildren the pain and itch are closely connected. When they call, you must at once respond." It meant, said Ch'en Hung-mou, "promoting their good fortune, nourishing and transforming them, working with a real heart and real effort." [30] In effect, the "father and mother" role was a political rather than administrative role, in which the official must show that his concern was genuine. If he did, the benefit would accrue to both the people and himself. The magistrate who labored over strengthening his character and promoting good government would provide the people with "the blessing" of a father and mother. The people would see that his intentions were on their account, and none "would not treat him as a father and mother and respect him as a sage." [31] Magistrates who ruled the people with affection earned the popular accolade "clear sky," and were showered with thanks on their departure from office. [32]

Conversely, the magistrate who failed to serve the people as a parent was abandoning his duty. "The father and mother official," wrote Wang Hui-tsu, "who doesn't come to grips with the vicissitudes of the people, as parents do for children, will have failed as an official." This stricture included magistrates concerned for their own future, who did not want to take the time or trouble necessary to understand the conditions of the people under their authority. "This," said Wang, "is like when a wealthy family hires a wetnurse, and as soon as she has become familiar with the infant, she collects up the contributions of her employer and makes off. After the infant has had many changes of wetnurse, the employer has gained nothing but loss for his outlay, and the infant derived no lasting benefit from the suckling. What does it *mean* to be a father and mother official? Alas . . . can we afford to plan anything that is not on behalf of the people?" [33]

It was from this familial concept of administration that the idea of "closeness" derived. In its immediate sense, closeness referred to physical proximity. The magistrate was close to the people and distant from the ruler; the high officials were close to the ruler, but distant from the people.[34] But "closeness" (*ch'in*) also implied emotional proximity. It was the distinguishing characteristic of parents, particularly mothers, just as filiality was that of children and *ti* (fraternal respect), that of younger siblings.[35] Anyone assuming a "parental" role should assume the attitudes belonging to that role. These had their distinctions: as Yuan Shou-ting put it, "The idea of father evoked awe (*tsun*) and of mother affection (*ch'in*)."[36] But in any consideration of the parent as an administrative concept, it was *ch'in* which emerged as the overriding attribute. The district magistrate was to be mother as well as father of the people.

The point was well put by Wang Hui-tsu. "One in a position of authority over the people," he wrote, "doesn't worry about their not showing him awe but about their not being close to him. Awe arises from fear of the laws, closeness from gratitude for kindness. If you want the people to submit to education, there must be closeness, or this will be impossible. The way to be close to the people entirely consists in having sympathy for their hardships. If you are sparing of their strength and their resources, and meet them with sincerity and trustworthiness, they will feel the official is someone not to fear but instead to show gratitude to. Then there will be the image of the official and the people as one body undivided."[37]

What did it mean to be close? "It means," said Wang Feng-sheng, "mutually meeting with the small people from morning till evening and not letting there be any obstruction between you."[38] In hearing lawsuits, it meant an ability to see things from the people's point of view and understand their motivation and predicament. It meant getting out into the countryside to communicate with the people and finding out what they were doing, giving advice, commending good conduct, and admonishing bad conduct. All this could only be done with any effect by the magistrate, since his superiors were too removed from the rural masses and his subordinates too lacking in power and prestige to be of influence. The district magistrates were the political parents; closeness was their primary function. As one subordinate local official put it, "those in such a position have nothing else to wonder about: just closeness. If they can understand this and carry it out, then everything will flourish and nothing obstruct."[39]

Since the role of the district magistrate was couched in such intimate and exacting terms, its performance called for sensitivity and diligence.

The magistrate must be alert to the mood of the people, their feelings about their way of life, local customs, and personal relationships. These could often seem unfamiliar and irrational to a magistrate, coming as he did from a distant locality. But it was precisely their irrationality, their basis in emotional attachment, that it was his duty to understand. The magistrate could apply the law to behavior which seemed disturbing and unjustified on grounds of reason. But often what might seem an infraction of reason actually involved an infraction of feeling. As father and mother official, it was the special function of the magistrate to sense this distinction and treat the matter accordingly on the basis of feeling. To apply only methods of reason to its solution indicated an insensitivity which could merely court further trouble.

Ch'ing administrative writers left no doubt as to the importance of sensitivity. "There must," said Yuan Shou-ting, "be a communication of feelings between above and below (i.e., administrators and people). If there is, then there is order. If there is not, then there is lack of order."[40] "Among the troubles of district," agreed Ch'eng Han-chang, "there is nothing like above and below being divided and the sense of feeling not getting across. . . . I wish that all *chüntzu* would be diligent at government and be close to the people in order to communicate feeling between above and below."[41] In the same vein Wang Hui-tsu wrote, "Officials and secretaries are united in having the benefit of the people at heart. But secretaries can advise according to reason and law. . . . The official must also take account of feeling and circumstance. If your judgments are not in accord with popular feeling, they will stir up murmurings. And if you maintain your decisions afterwards, the employment of force will be comparatively difficult." The goal was to bring feeling and law into conjunction. Then the management of affairs would be as it should be and giving orders to those below would be like "running water."[42]

The fulfillment of such a role called for prolonged application. From the outset the magistrate must be a man of determination. As one writer put it, "maintaining order requires ability, developing ability requires knowledge, accumulating knowledge requires determination."[43] The magistrate was urged to study the penal code, the biographies of upright and harsh officials, the handbooks of other officials.[44] He must get to know his district, an injunction symbolized in his title of *chih-hsien*, "know the district."[45] He must personally examine tax-registers, compare them with the layout of the land, meet with the village people and hear their complaints, no matter what the time and trouble involved. He must not delegate his duties to others.[46]

He must always maintain an uncompromising sincerity. As Yuan Shou-ting said, "this is what will move others. . . . If an official is scheming by nature, the people will always know it, for nothing conceals it. How can those occupying a position of responsibility afford to be anything but sincere?"[47] To affirm this sincerity he must persevere at his job. According to Wang Hui-tsu, it took a full year to get to know the conditions, feelings, and customs of a district. It took another year to know how to act in harmony with them.[48] According to Chu Tse-yun, it would take a magistrate one year to gain the people's confidence, three years to establish the makings of good order, and five years to accomplish it in full.[49] In short, it took considerable time for a magistrate to use his authority effectively, and an official must stay at the job if he was to achieve any results.

Finally, an official must watch for signs of overconfidence in himself or his superiors. He should examine his affairs daily. If for all his diligence the people still appeared to hold back, this, said Ch'eng Han-cheng, meant that his approach was still lacking in some respect. He should look into himself and see what was wanting. Then he should press ahead with all the more sincerity and perseverance.[50] Wang Hui-tsu went so far as to say that to be given a position of authority over the people was a starting point for seeing one's errors, not one's merits. The magistrate's lot as an official, in his view, was simply to be able to fulfill the charge assigned to him.[51]

6

DISTINCTIVENESS OF CH'ING ADMINISTRATIVE THEORY

Relationship of Ch'ing conceptions
with classical Confucian theory

How do the foregoing views relate to positions taken in classical Confucian texts? In many cases they derived from direct extrapolation. The appraisal of the people as "newborn infants" stems from a passage in the *Book of Documents* in which a newly enfeoffed prince is enjoined to deal with the people "as if guarding his infants"; the people would then be tranquil and orderly.[1] The statement is utilized in the *Great Learning* to drive home the connection between familial and political government. So strong did this connection remain that the *Cheng-tzu t'ung*, a dictionary compiled during the Ming dynasty and published in the K'ang-hsi period, was able to define the term for infant as "a small child in the first period of life; when a ruler (*chün*) refers to the people he also calls them 'infants.'" Understandably the Yung-cheng emperor could not resist saying of his father that he looked on the people as his infants.[2]

The idea of the people as "children" also occurs several times in early classics. One passage in the *Tso chuan* said of a certain ruler that "he is showing affection (*ch'in*) to his people. He regards them as his children and shares in all their sufferings."[3]

The concept of the ruler as father and mother similarly finds expression in the earliest records. The *chüntzu* of the *Book of Odes* was father and mother of the people. The "Son of Heaven" of the *Book of Documents*, was father and mother of the people and thereby king (*wang*) over all under Heaven. This concept was not taken up by Confucius but was resumed in *Mencius*, where it still refers primarily to the supreme ruler.[4] Its application to the district magistrate dates at the latest from the Sung dynasty, and appears to have been customary from then on.[5] Such being the family orientation of Chinese politics, the practice allegedly developed, during the Ming dynasty, of referring to magistrates as "father and mother" and senior provincial officials as "distinguished forbears"; but this seems to have been carrying consanguinity too far.[6] By the Ch'ing, the title is still residually the emperor's, but principally the local magistrate's.

The stress on the ruler's affectionate closeness derived from the politicization of these patriarchal notions. It was said of the sage-ruler Yao that he was able to manifest his exceptional virtue and so make close the "nine branches" of the family. Shun then found that the "hundred families," i.e., the next major social group below the supreme ruler, were "not close." His appointment of Hsieh as Master of the Multitudes was specifically to rectify this situation.[7] The *Great Learning* was the first source to relate closeness to the common people in general. The way of learning to be great, it said, consisted in manifesting the bright character, becoming "close" to the people and remaining in the highest good. Mencius, in his effort to make *jen* a viable political guideline, preferred to limit affectionate closeness to a strictly familial relationship. The *chüntzu*, he said, treats the people with humanity, but not with familial affection. But he who feels close to his family will feel humanity for all men.[8] But the association between family and state was too strong to maintain this distinction. Already by A.D. 100, the *Shuo wen* was defining *jen* "humanity" as *ch'in*, affectionate closeness.

The identification of the magistrates as the source of political closeness was an early development. Already by A.D. 750, an Imperial order noted that "as to officials who are close to the people, none exceed the district magistrates."[9] In fact, once the Ch'in and Han dynasties had established the prefectural (*chün-hsien*) system as the prevailing system of local administration, the district magistrate automatically became the administrative chief closest to the people. Recognition that under Confucianism this proximity carried emotional obligations was merely a matter of time.

The emphasis on nurture and education is more specifically Confucian. A famous passage in the *Tso chuan* declares that a good ruler will reward the good and punish the bad. He will nourish the people as his children, overshadowing them as Heaven, supporting them as the Earth. Then the people will maintain him and love him as a father and mother.[10] Confucius himself stressed that the people must be first enriched and then taught. He praised Tzu Ch'an for his kindness in nourishing the people and defined kindness as "doing what truly benefits the people." He held that the people should be taught for seven years before they could be obligated to serve the state in war; to lead untaught men to war was to abandon them.[11]

Mencius in particular stressed nurture and education. He identified nurture as applying primarily to care of the aged and education to care of the young. To him, nurture and education were the means to win the submission of the people. One who tried to be good at making the people submit would fail. One who was good at nourishing them could get the whole world to submit. Similarly, it was he who held that good government was not like good education for winning the people. He maintained that to punish the people for falling foul of the law was to "set traps" for them; to make exactions without ensuring that they had adequate means of support was tantamount to "eating" them. The sage-ruler ensured that food was as plentiful as water and fire. Those who had achieved the mean nourished those who had not; those who were talented nourished those who were not.[12]

Classical Confucian writing also left no doubt as to the importance of consideration for others, diligence, and self-examination. The *Analects* regarded altruism (*shu*) as the nub on which to base personal conduct.[13] In the political realm, *The Book of Changes* urged understanding between above and below, holding it to be the index of the advance or decline of the way of the *chüntzu* and of political order.[14] Diligence in a ruler was equally important. The people's livelihood depended on it. When asked about government, Confucius replied, "lead them, encourage them, tirelessly!" The *chüntzu*, he added pointedly, was diligent in his work.[15] Above all, the *chüntzu* reflected on his role as an exemplar. He practiced what he preached. He made demands on himself before making demands on others. Where the small man thought of the material, he thought of moral power. Where the small man thought of benefit, he thought of punishment.[16] So, too, the *Book of Changes* stated that a *chüntzu* set his mind on danger. When secure, he did not forget the possibility of ruin. He knew what was weak and what strong. He composed himself before trying to move others. He was a model to the myriad people.[17]

These judgments left their mark on texts dealing with the functions of actual office-holders. The Master of the Multitudes of the *Record of Rituals* nourished the aged, showed pity to orphans, exalted the worthy, and banished the disobedient. Each level of officer concentrated on avoiding failure in their service. Men taught as a way of stimulating themselves to effort. They learned as a way of knowing their deficiencies.[18]

Much of this thought not only underlies Ch'ing thinking on administration, but is actually cited by Ch'ing writers as support for their viewpoint. A scholarly writer like Yuan Shou-ting used one or more classical statements, or citations from biographies in the dynastic histories, as the theme for virtually every essay he wrote. Most writers cited on a more occasional basis, but did so to good effect. Ch'eng Han-cheng pointed out that Yao, although a sage-ruler (and therefore one who could have maintained order without exertion), and Hsieh, although also sage-like, exerted themselves "to the utmost" in the education of the people. How could the ordinary administrator be content with any less an effort? If he was, who was to blame for any difficulties?[19] The statement in the *Analects* that the *chüntzu* gains the trust of the people before imposing burdens on them: "If he has not gained their trust, they will think that he is oppressing them," was also used to good effect by both Ch'eng and Wang Hui-tsu to urge local magistrates to be diligent and to stay at a given post.[20]

More significant is the extent to which classical Confucian ideas are embedded in Ch'ing writing. The common Ch'ing idioms for people and rulers, or such concepts as goodness, sincerity, seriousness, diligence, affection, communication, nourishment, were all of Confucian provenance. Moreover, each represented functional parts of a whole theory of administrative order. This does not mean that either the whole or the parts remained unchanged. The people may have stayed "immature," but their political parent underwent a radical metamorphosis. However, it does show that the Ch'ing administrator's twenty-year study of the Confucian classics made a deep impression. Clearly Confucian ideas were of considerable effect in shaping the Ch'ing administrator's conception of local administration.

Differences between Confucian and Ch'ing concepts

One radical difference between Confucian and Ch'ing administrative theory is in their treatment of *jen*. In Ch'ing administrative writing, *jen* is far from being treated as the central concept. It is for the most part mentioned sporadically. Yet *jen*, as the cornerstone of Confucian and Mencian political theory, had been specifically applied both to the ideal administrator and to the actual class of men supplying the most administrators. Since much of Confucian theory passed effectively into Ch'ing administrative writing, the comparative neglect of *jen* by Ch'ing writers calls for explanation.

At first sight this neglect is unexpected. The concept of *jen* was given new impetus by the T'ang and Sung dynasty Neo-Confucianists, and became, as Chan has pointed out, the basis of Neo-Confucian ethics. In their study of *jen*, the Neo-Confucian thinkers concentrated on its basic meaning as much as on its practical implications. In this study, as in most Western language works, *jen* has been represented as "humanity" or "love of others." Strictly speaking these are manifestations of *jen* and, in effect, values or desired states. *Jen* is what generates these values. This meaning is implicit in the *Analects*, but since Confucius' emphasis was on the practical application of *jen*, he refused, it seems, to be drawn into an examination of its innate content. No doubt he feared that the study of its content would deflect attention from the study of its application. In the Confucius of the *Analects*, metaphysics is never permitted to distract attention from practical politics. But the search for a metaphysical definition could not be denied; and Mencius supplied one with his statements that "*jen* is man" and "*jen* is man's mind."[21]

The Sung Neo-Confucianists developed these definitions. *Jen* was nature, said Ch'eng I. Its identifying characteristic was growth, its signal the beat of the pulse. It was, said his brother, Ch'eng Hao, the vital force in living things. As such, it was in all things without differentiation. The immediate source for these interpretations was the *Western Inscription* of Chang Tsai. In this powerful manifesto, Chang presented Heaven as father, Earth as mother, the substance of the universe as body and its directing force as nature. Therefore, he said, all people were his brothers and sisters and all things his companions. The emperor was the eldest son of his parents. True filiality was to rejoice in Heaven and have no anxiety. On the basis of this identification of man with life, Chang urged respect for the old, sympathy for the weak, and a service that would contribute to the fulfillment of life as represented in human society.[22]

The ethical connotations of *jen* arose from reflection on its identification of the self with all life. As Ch'eng Hao wrote, the man who had grasped *jen* viewed Heaven and Earth and all things as one body. To him there was nothing that was not himself. Since he had recognized all things as himself, could there be any limit to his *jen*? Similarly, Ch'eng I held that in a man who had grasped the principle of *jen* (identified as impartiality) there would be no distinction between himself and others. These interpretations gave new emphasis to the Confucian stress on *chung*, "self understanding," and *shu*, "understanding of others," or altruism, which Ch'eng Hao explained as the way to practice *chung*. From this view, love and altruism were seen as *jen* aroused: love as the function of *jen*, altruism as its application. Chang Tsai, who served as a magistrate, tried to apply these views to practical living by reviving the "Well Field" system, a system of land division espoused by Mencius, in which land was grouped into equal shares with one central share for the support of the public interest.[23]

The Neo-Confucian effort to elucidate the nature of *jen* ran the risk of diffusing its political emphasis. The enquiry had led to the conclusion that *jen* was universal in all things. This view may be implicit in Mencius, but it is doubtful if it was entertained by Confucius. Etymologically the graph for *jen* consists of two elements, one representing "man" (also pronounced *jen*), the other "two." Of these elements, "man" is the coordinate; it is the "man-ness" of two which is represented. In the *Analects*, the emphasis is on the "man-ness" of *jen*. There is no relating of *jen* to all life. It is the nature and performance of man, specifically man in politics, which is examined. The Neo-Confucian interpretation does not neglect the social and political function of *jen*. But its universalization of *jen* reduced the concentration on human political behavior.

The Neo-Confucian tendency toward broad speculation was unwelcome to Ch'ing thinkers and administrators. The collapse of the Ming dynasty, in the wake of ill-organized peasant rebellion and humiliating conquest, raised fundamental doubts about the validity of the existing political and social structure. As we shall see, other economic and political rifts were to add to this intellectual malaise. The Manchus repressed it by winning the imperial mandate, reimposing the Neo-Confucian classical exegesis as the syllabus for the examinations, and by harshly policing literary output. While these measures reinstated orthodoxy, they could not restore its philosophical validity. Ch'ing scholars remained distrustful and devoted their energies to problems of scholastic methodology and administrative practice.[24]

The Ch'ing reversion from the speculativeness of Neo-Confucianism cannot by itself account for the neglect of *jen*. Since Ch'ing writing accepted practical orientation of classical Confucian theory, why not also the practical orientation of its ethics? Why did it accept the practical political interest in goodness, sincerity, seriousness, and discuss these in good measure, without also discussing the concept binding them together?

Clearly some part was played by the differing institutional situation. It was argued that for the classical Confucianists ability to manifest *jen* was the essential qualification for holding office. The Ch'ing official needed no such behavioral qualification. His qualifications were already institutionalized through the examination and appointment systems. Moreover, twenty-five years of study for the examinations and up to a further twenty or more years of waiting to get through the laborious screening of the appointment system, constituted by any standards a formidable test of qualification. Those who were appointed local magistrates received a seal of office. On all reasonable institutional grounds, the official was well certified for holding office. In practice this system never laid to rest the idea that an official should qualify on ethical grounds. But it overshadowed this idea to such an extent that criticisms of the system on moral grounds could seldom carry much weight.

It is also likely that the Ch'ing political and social situation helped to inhibit the local administrator's commitment to *jen*. Even in the *Analects*, not to mention Neo-Confucianism, *jen* calls for human identification. Evidently the educated, status-minded, and nonindigenous Ch'ing local administrator found it far from easy to identify with the "simpleminded," "small," "inferior," multitudinous and, to him, strange and dissimilar people. The repeated emphasis on the need for closeness to the people is an indication of this.

There is also the question of the ability of the Chinese officials to identify with their Manchu political leadership. In the middle to late seventeenth century, many careers were abruptly terminated or indeed never actualized because the alien and militaristic leadership of the Manchus was unacceptable. Thereafter, opinions were generally muted; moreover, resumption of the search for a career was inevitable and made easier by the determined effort of the Manchus to win the support of the Chinese scholar-gentry class. But in many administrative, legal, social, and ethnic ways, the distinction between Manchu and Chinese remained, with the Manchus invariably set apart as the privileged group. Educated hostility to the

Manchus remained, accounting for the harsh and continuing Manchu surveillance of Chinese literary output. Secret societies made hostility to the Manchus a basic theme, which came out into the open in their rebellion manifestos. Even at its most stable, the political climate was never wholly conducive to the identification of subordinate Chinese officials to the dynastic leadership on innate human terms.

As it was, the radical change in the structure of the body politic undermined the original reasons for that identification. The rulers of the Confucian and Mencian era operated within a highly competitive situation. Their problem was how to retain the active support of their existing subjects and if possible attract solid support from subjects of competing rulers. In both the *Analects* and *Mencius*, and particularly in the latter, *jen* was affirmed as the magnetic force for attracting political allegiance. Ch'ing local administrators had no such need to attract allegiance. Their problem was to maintain the goodwill of superiors and creditors. Their policy was to ensure sufficient quiessence to exact revenues and punish subversives without causing unnecessary tremors. Rather than radiate magnetism, they were much more concerned to "soothe" and "tranquilize."

For a guide to the policy of tranquilization, the *Chou li* was the most persuasive source. It was the *Chou li* which provided the classic precedents for systems for equitable land allotment, registration systems, provision of famine relief, arbitration of minor litigation, or forensic techniques for solving criminal cases. Above all the *Chou li* was the classic source for the public security systems of later ages. Its method of combining close-knit communal organization with leadership warning the people of the laws, educating them against disobedience, and punishing offenders, was the method which reached down to the Ch'ing period. Moreover, although the *Chou li* provided for special legal and security officials to manage arrest of malefactors and arbitration, it is in it that the Master of the Multitudes and his subordinates acted jointly as educators and punishers. The Master of the Multitudes of the *Book of Documents* was first and foremost an educator. There was another official to deal with punishment. Once again it was the *Chou li* which forecast Ch'ing local administrative conditions; for while Ch'ing district educational officials were concerned with the "education" of licentiates, it was the district magistrate who had charge over both the education and punishment of the people.

A final difference between the classical Confucian and Ch'ing administrator is in the method of administrative control under which each operated.

The Ch'ing local administrator functioned under an ever-increasing complex of administrative regulations. His eye was necessarily on the minutiae of daily business. The Disciplinary Regulations limited his freedom of maneuver and required him to keep a constant eye on his own security. The mid to late Chou dynasty administrator lived in a time of frequent political danger, and was far less shackled by routinized regulations. His success could depend as much on being in accord with the people as the Ch'ing administrator's could on being in accord with the laws.

It is no doubt to the different structure of the body politic and the different emphasis in administration that the Ch'ing administrator's comparative neglect of *jen* can be attributed. But the lack of emphasis on *jen*, although to some extent replaced by the *Chou li's* emphasis on tranquility, could not be achieved without cost. Confucian administrative theory had made it clear that *jen* was the special concept which gave meaning to the processes of government. Take away *jen* and the administrator had taken away the concept which illuminated why and how to be sincere, in short how to govern. The attention of the Confucian administrator had to be first and foremost on *jen*. That was why the Neo-Confucians insisted that their disciples not confuse love, unity, and so on, with *jen* itself, but see them as functions or attributes and therefore always focus on *jen*.

Of course, after twenty years of study of the Four Books with their Neo-Confucian commentaries, the Ch'ing administrator could hardly be unaware of the importance attached to *jen*. Some effort was therefore made to reconcile *jen* with the actualities of Ch'ing political order. Yuan Shou-ting wrote that the Ch'ing *Penal Code* was based on the penal concepts of the *Chou li*; its target was to implement the humanity and justice (*jen* and *i*) of Mencius. Another writer, commenting on the first chapter of the *Classic of Filial Piety*, wrote that in virtue nothing came before *jen*, and in *jen* nothing came before filiality. Therefore, filiality was indeed the highest virtue, and the necessary Way (as the classic tried to argue).[25] Neither of these statements can be squared with the genuine Confucian antipathy to laws and regulations or with the Confucian insistence that manifesting humanity was particularly the responsibility of the political senior and superior.[26]

In effect the Ch'ing administrator was involved with a conflict of roles: between the role learned in study and the role required in practice. There was an effort to reconcile this conflict, but it was achieved only at the impairment of the essential Confucian emphasis, a loss for which none of the adherence to secondary Confucian attitudes could properly compensate. The reduction of this emphasis could not help but prejudice the conduct of administration by trained Confucianists. How, then, did the Ch'ing administrator come to be faced with such a conflict? For an answer to this question, we must turn to an examination of political changes in the area of local government.

PART II

EVOLUTION OF THE OFFICE

7

CENTRALIZATION AND DIVERSIFICATION IN CHINESE
POLITICAL DEVELOPMENT

The Chinese political system underwent considerable change
during the last nine hundred years of the imperial era. In the administrative
structure there was, up till the mid-nineteenth century, a deliberate and
far-ranging trend towards centralization of power. In social and economic
life there was an equally strong trend toward diversification of power.
The local administrative system stood between these divergent forces.
Its own evolution was heavily influenced by both. As a result, local
administrators came under considerable pressure to make adjustments to
these influences, if they were to continue to fulfill their political functions.
The next four chapters will examine the effect of these influences on the
evolution of local government and consider in what way they affected the
magistrate's conduct.

First, let us examine briefly the nature of the two trends noted above.
The pursuit of a unified power structure has been a recognized trend
through Chinese history. The early abandonment of political feudalism
had been precisely because its diffuse structure had tended to undermine
political control. Under feudalism power was dispersed and authority
passed through discrete hereditary channels. Similarly, responsibility
was divided, and in return for loyalty, control surrendered to subordinates.
In England such conditions had paved the way for the gradual control of
the superior by the inferior, which provided a vital premise for the development of a universal franchise. In China, political and geographical conditions combined to favor the coordination of power and responsibility.

The imperial prefectural system established this coordination, placing the burden and the initiative in one central source. Once imperialism had emerged around 200 B.C., no other administrative system received serious consideration. Future history, particularly in the eras of the universal dynasties (Han, T'ang, Sung, Yuan, Ming, Ch'ing) devoted itself to evolving the institutions best suited to express the unity conceived in imperialism.

Much of the support for centralization came from philosophical speculation as well as from the political power struggle. It is no secret that philosophy and politics are closely related in Chinese culture. Even the most abstruse speculation, such as that contained in the *Book of Changes*, is found to go hand in hand with practical political teaching. In Chinese thinking oneness and unity very early emerged as prevailing concepts. The *Book of Changes* itself opens by saying: "Great is Heaven the originator. All things obtain their beginning from it. It unites and commands all things under Heaven." The idea of oneness as the origin of things is actually Taoist and not Confucian. But it was taken over by the syncretist thinkers of the Han dynasty (which provided the first example of a solidly unified imperial system) and incorporated into subsequent Confucian thinking. In the early Han, the philosopher and statesman Tung Chung-shu wrote: "The origin means the beginning. It expresses the Kingly way. The King is the beginning of man." He added, "the origin is the source of all things, and the origin of man is found in it." The collapse of the Han empire did not involve the collapse of the concept of oneness. The post-Han philosopher Wang Pi wrote: "one is the beginning of number and the ultimate of things. All things are produced by one and this is why it is the master of all. All things achieve their completion because of one." [1]

One of the major achievements of Neo-Confucian thought was to obtain a synthesis between oneness and universality. Chou Tun-i, who laid the basis of Neo-Confucian metaphysics, confirmed the unity of origination. He held that this source, the "Great Ultimate," produced activity and differentiation, and generated the creation and transformation of all things. On this basis he inferred that the many were one and the one differentiated in the many. Later Neo-Confucian thought, while stressing the role of principle in the creation of form, confirmed its indivisibility. Principle was one, its manifestations many. When the many were united by the one, there could not be any contradiction. [2]

From the earliest times this thinking had its political counterpart. The emperor was "the one man." The domain of political activity was "[all within] the four seas" or "[all] under Heaven." The people were the "multitude people." "Origination" or names of primal constituents or phases in the generative process such as "Heaven" "beginning," "outset," became key elements in the titles of imperial reigns or sections of reigns. Once again Neo-Confucian thinking coordinated these concepts. "The foundation of the multitude," said Chou Tun-i, "lies in one person" (the sage-emperor). The sage had in him the power to "penetrate all things" and "transform all people." Through him the way of Heaven operated and all things were in harmony.[3]

This thinking without doubt helped to promote the centralization of imperial institutions. Already the function of the bureaucratic and prefectural systems was to administer the imperial will and break up independent power. Similarly the function of the examination and appointment systems was to get rid of independent access to power. The trend in metaphysical thinking helped to give conceptual emphasis to these functions and reduce the rationality of any power not clearly emanating from the center.

Finally, historical experience seemed to confirm the advantages of centralization and the hazards of decentralization. The T'ang dynasty had achieved an inspiring degree of unification only to lose it all in its declining years. In its place, regional military governors took over control. They had their own armies and made their own civil appointments. Local government officials looked to them for leadership and protection. Central civil service recruitment and employment standards broke down. A loss of political confidence set in. Major rebellions hastened the collapse of the empire. A period of active maneuvering for power then ensued until unity was reestablished in 960.[4]

The lesson learned was that regionalization of power heralded disintegration. This was not the first time that such a lesson had been learned. It was the first time that a unified bureaucratic state had proved vulnerable to this disorder. Subsequent dynasties, therefore, assiduously promoted systems for centralizing regional power. Under the Ming dynasty, the central government took too much power for itself and allowed it to fall into irresponsible hands. In its downfall regional groups of rebels and powerful officials reestablished local power. Whatever their individual merits or demerits, their rise to power involved the breakdown of institutional order and led to prolonged bloodshed. In the midst of this, the

Manchus invaded and started taking control of Eastern China. Despite their efficient military organization, it took them forty years of often ruthless fighting to reestablish unified control.

In the end, at the cost of frightful destruction, history had repeated the lesson that the breakdown of central power spelled disaster. The memory of Ming despotism and the subjection of unity to barbarian control were to produce a temporary crisis of confidence in the institutions of centralization. But the Manchus succeeded in surmounting this threat. Thereafter, centralization regained control as an administrative objective, and localization resumed the aspect of a disintegrating force.

Because centralization took a political form, its political influence tended to be readily apparent. This was not so of the forces of diversification. These functioned for the most part in the society and economy, below the rather thin administrative surface. Thus, they often escaped notice until they had assumed significant proportions. Prominent among them have been population expansion and migration, various forms of productive diversification, and the development in society of local power structures such as clans or lineages and secret societies, which were largely independent of the state.

Population expansion has been a major factor in Chinese history. The form which it has taken is still far from clear, especially in periods before the Ch'ing dynasty. Present estimates indicate a series of repeated expansions and contractions from the Han dynasty on. From the T'ang to the end of the Ming, new expansions appear to have gradually pushed up the mean size of the population. After 1700 the rate of expansion increased and although declining somewhat in the nineteenth century, produced a population of some 430 million by 1850.[5]

This spiraling effect is also hinted at by changes in the demographic definition of different categories of district, as indicated in Table 19. These definitions are essentially fiscal and as such operate at somewhat lower levels of density than those actually obtained. That also is why the early Sung definitions are unusually low. However, by the time the Chin took over north China in the 1120s, the administrative definitions were moving up beneath the natural increase. The contrast between the figures for the Chin and the north under the early Yuan reflect the damage caused to both the population and its administration during the Mongol conquest. The south had now drawn well ahead in overall population density. By the time of the Ming survey at the end of the fourteenth century, some

Table 19. Variations in number of recorded households per district

DYNASTY AND DATE	SPECIAL CATEGORIES	UPPER	MIDDLE	MIDDLE LOWER	LOWER
T'ang					
618–626	not determined by size	5,000+	2,000	1,000+	
730		6,000+	3,000+	under 3,000	
	frontier	5,000	2,000	1,000	
Sung					
963	3,000/2,000	1,000	500	under 500	
changed to	4,000/3,000	2,000	1,000	under 1,000	
Chin	25,000 and 20,000	10,000	3,000	under 3,000	
Yuan					
1266 north		6,000	2,000		under 2,000
1283 south		30,000	10,000		under 10,000

SOURCES. A variety of sources contain these figures. See *Ch'in hui-yao ting-pu*, 214; *Hsi Han hui-yao*, 33/345; *T'ang hui-yao*, 70/1a–b; *Sung shih*, 4886–7; *Hsu t'ung-tien*, 1348.3; *T'u-shu chi-ch'eng*, ming-lun, kuan-ch'ang, 645 hui-k'ao/11a–b. These sources also give breakdowns for other local government jurisdictions. Local gazetteers usually indicate under which category their jurisdiction was placed.
NOTES. "Special categories" referred primarily to districts at or near the capital. "North" indicates north of the Yangtze; "south," south of the Yangtze and Huai rivers. The Ming began by distinguishing districts by productivity. Upper were those producing under 100,000 bushels; others were middle if under 60,000 and lower if under 30,000 bushels. Subsequently all categorization was abolished. Much earlier, the Ch'in and Western Han dynasties had distinguished districts by whether they were above or below 10,000 households in size.

southeastern districts were recording actual densities of over 60,000 or 70,000 households.

Migration has also been an important feature in China's demographic history. Prior to the Ming dynasty, the general thrust of migration was from the north and west toward the south and east. After the occupation of the more accessible arable areas, migration patterns became more complex as migrants pushed up into hill country or down toward marshes and estuaries. Demographic research indicates that migration could assume substantial proportions, shifting streams of people across provincial frontiers and away from their registered and ancestral home areas. Thus population movement tended to create a ground swell of expansion, contraction, reexpansion, migration, which became particularly unstable during the Ch'ing dynasty. The central government could do little about this force. Despite legislation to make people stick to their registered localities or professions, the movement continued.

The operation of the market has been another destabilizing force. As the illuminating articles by Skinner have shown, the marketing structure of an agricultural economy is capable of expanding, maturing and propagating, even though the economy itself remains generally at a near-subsistence level. (Near-subsistence indicates that the units of production in the economy are in large part self-sufficient, not necessarily that they are near to minimum standards of subsistence.) This motility is an outcome of the activity of the population itself and is primarily caused by increase in household density, and secondarily by increase in household participation in marketing.[6] Under these influences, standard rural markets expand in size and eventually throw off new offshoots. These in turn begin the process of maturation, while the parent market rises to higher levels of distribution. The importance of the standard rural marketing area is, as Skinner has shown, that it provided a central focus in both the economic and social life of the peasant household. As a distributive mechanism it could, on every market day, attract the attention of at least "one out of every five" adults living in its dependant villages. It also may very well have provided the chief framework for the social life of the peasant household and for the transmission of local customs and beliefs.[7] In any case, the tendency of the rural marketing system to generate new markets, rather than absorb old ones, helped to localize rural social life and keep it in a state of flux.

Another basic change, which can only be hinted at here, is in the system of land tenure. From the mid-Ming period on, there occurred an increasing struggle for the control of land. In the fertile southeast region, this trend was characterized by a gradual stratification of society along landholding lines. The struggle for land contributed in some cases to forced migration, in others to fragmentation of holdings, or to partial or complete relinquishment of title. More often this process has been described in terms of concentration of landownership. The essential point here is that it contributed to a general cultural differentiation, based on control of property and education. This helped social mobility; it also enforced instability and impermanence in social and familial status.[8]

The economic diversification which developed during the Ming and Ch'ing also was important in promoting social flux. Large areas in the south and east began to specialize in cash crops. Interregional commerce was extended, and with it the monetization of the economy. Mobility was injected into the labor force by the demand for porters and the opportunities for trading. Already before the end of the Ming dynasty, observers were noting the "almost incredible number of boats passing hither and thither," and the groups of several thousand porters moving produce across watersheds.[9] In sum, there was a surge of movement going on in the Ming and Ch'ing population, whether permanent, as in migration, or temporary, as in marketing and distributive services. This movement expanded or altered settlement patterns, shifted labor, spread commerce, altered land utilization, and prevented the maintenance of any status quo in the organization of social and economic life.

Finally, a word should be said about the role of social institutions in counteracting centralization. In a feudal or aristocratic society, the domain or estate stands against centralization by focusing local loyalties and combining them permanently behind the temporal owner. The Chinese state and society had succeeded in eliminating the basis for a powerful aristocracy. Property was divided on death so that family estates failed to remain intact for more than a few generations at most; while by the end of the Ming the examination system barred most landowners from administrative power. But in the absence of an effective hereditary aristocracy, society provided new means for permanent group identification and interaction through the development of the clans and secret societies. These provided organization, discipline, and a variety of social services, and were capable of raising armed bands for mutual defense or offense. In areas on the peripheries of administrative jurisdictions, these institutions came close to monopolizing popular loyalties.[10]

The ways in which these countervailing trends influenced local government were, in brief, as follows. Through administrative centralization, the number and scope of assistant local officials was reduced. Central control over the appointment and surveillance of the remainder was increased. Regulations were enacted to extend central influence over administrative conduct and reduce local initiative and flexibility. Second, rural control institutions were developed in an effort to increase the influence of the central government over the lives and behavior of the rural population. Their management became an added responsibility of local administrators.

In return, the diversifying trends acted to reduce the effectiveness of these controls. Population expansion and migration continually weakened the rural control systems and created new settlement areas outside the existing control structure. The expanding marketing systems challenged the static and exclusive territorial structure of the administrative system.

Monetization of the agrarian order forced local administrators to abandon the household and substitute land as the primary unit of taxation. This was of crucial significance in replacing social with economic criteria in the relationship of administration to the social order. Another feature of this change (which took place in the late Ming and early Ch'ing) was the replacement of much of the corvee labor serving local government with an expanding professional and locally based subureaucracy, able to compete with the official establishment for control of local power. Furthermore, social organizations, such as lineages and secret societies, developed alternative authority for dealing with the social problems of their members and acted to reduce their dependence on established governmental authority.

Caught between opposing forces, local administrators were pulled one way by the forces of political centralization and another by the challenges of social diversification. This dilemma, already apparent by the end of the Ming era, was intensified in the early and mid Ch'ing. We must now examine more specifically how it affected local magistrates, and how they attempted to deal with it.[11]

8

CENTRALIZATION OF DISTRICT ADMINISTRATION UNDER
THE SUNG AND MING DYNASTIES

By all accounts civil administration of district government reached a low ebb in the period preceding the Sung dynasty. With the breakdown of central appointment procedures, local administrative authority had become hereditary. Assistant officials were being appointed and paid by their immediate superiors. Subordinate provincial officials were putting their loyalty in local governors. In addition, military garrison administration had developed at the expense of civil district administration. The district magistrates, in the words of Ku Yen-wu, had become no better than "incompetent rustics, narrow-minded and good for nothing."[1]

The Sung administration took several important steps to alter this situation. It put court or metropolitan civil officials in charge of the more important districts and kept their titular incumbents at the capital. In the least-populated districts, it temporarily abolished the office of district magistrate, leaving its duties to be performed by the registrar. It also changed the title held by its own appointees. Previously this title had been *hsien-ling* or "district commander." The new court-appointed officials were given the attenuating title "knows the affairs of the district." This was later reduced simply to "knows the district" (*chih-hsien*). The same form of title was given to court-appointed civil officials set in charge of intermediate local jurisdictions. The change in title made clear that the new official was the delegate of the central government, not a local boss. It implied that henceforth "knowing" was to take precedence in local administration over "commanding." As such it proved an effective move in the central government's campaign to "pare down" local authority.[2] Under the Mongol dynasty's abnormal dualistic system of regional administration, this form of title was dropped. But it became and remained the standard form from the beginning of the Ming dynasty.

The Sung emperors also moved to bring the assistant local administrators under central control. Districts were reclassified according to population and importance. In those having between 1,000 to 2,000 known households (an intermediate category), no assistant magistrate was designated. In those having between 400 to 1,000, no assistant or registrar was designated. Until well into the eleventh century, no appointments at all were made to the post of assistant magistrate. Thereafter appointment of assistant magistrates was limited to important districts. Candidates had to be metropolitan examination graduates and have already served in assistant civil prefectural posts.[3] From the start, local administrators were also ordered not to appoint any subordinates without reference to the capital. In districts lacking senior assistants, the more junior were ordered to assume the duties of the senior posts. In 996, registrars were ordered for all districts; subsequently, in districts lacking the post of assistant magistrate, the registrar assumed its duties.

This policy of cutting back the higher rather than the lower assistant offices had the effect of putting assistant administration into the hands of lower-ranking individuals and diminishing its prestige. In addition most of the minor assistantships seem simply to have been left vacant. The Han and T'ang district magistrate possessed a large administrative staff under the management of senior assistants such as the registrar, who were his own nominees. The subordinate bureaucracies had provided an important basis for the independence of local officials during the interregnum between the late T'ang and early Sung periods. In the Sung, the only positions recognized by the central government were those of assistant magistrate, registrar, and sheriff or security officer. The rest seem to have vanished.[4]

Two other aspects of the Sung contribution to centralization should be mentioned. The Sung did not establish the examination system as the prevailing channel to appointment as district magistrate. It relied on sponsorship by senior officials. It did, however, establish conditions for sponsorship as magistrate. Candidates must have served three or more years in an administrative position and have been tested and approved as to character and competence. Thus, the sponsorship system served to increase central interest in the evaluation and rating of local officials.

Furthermore in 962 it was ordered that, for the purposes of promotion or demotion, district magistrates were to be evaluated according to the increase or decrease of households and cultivated fields. Later edicts required their success in deciding criminal cases to be taken into account. Evaluation of character was to be according to criteria first established during the T'ang dynasty. Later still, rewards and fines were established as a means of stimulating the magistrate's control of clerical staff, exhortation of the people, and increase in planting of trees and shrubs required in sericulture. The task of appraisal was under the control of prefects and assistant prefects and fiscal and judicial intendants; it was performed yearly.

This annual appraisal system, although built up in conjunction with the sponsorship system of appointment, survived the Ming replacement of sponsorship by examination. It remained an important aspect of the duties of intermediate provincial officials during the Ch'ing period.[5]

While Sung central policy is important for its long-range influence on the structure of Ch'ing local administration, the institutional developments of the Ming dynasty were of still greater influence. In this respect a decisive role was played by Emperor T'ai-tsu (or Hung-wu), the founder of the Ming dynasty. This brilliant but vindictive ruler was the first of any importance since the founder of the Han dynasty to have been born into humble circumstances. The son of a poor peasant who was early left an orphan, he had in his youth a familiarity with local conditions unequaled by any subsequent ruler prior to the present day. After he had successfully seized power, he used this knowledge to carry out a comprehensive reorganization of local administration.

The concepts by which Emperor T'ai-tsu was guided and much of the institutional structure designed to put them into practice remained intrinsic features of the Ch'ing local administrative system. Their durability also contributed in the end to many of its problems. Consequently, an understanding of their strengths and weaknesses is necessary to an awareness of the problems inherited by Ch'ing administrators.

Emperor T'ai-tsu's policies were deeply influenced by his familiarity with rural conditions. At the time that he took power, rural society was in a state of breakdown resulting from maladministration and civil disorder. In this situation, the emperor's sympathies lay predominantly with the poorer and less powerful majority. He felt that the life of the peasantry was at its best full of hazard and uncertainty. Now he saw them exhausted by unequal taxation, ruined by civil disorder, and disillusioned by civil administration.[6]

At the same time he believed that their vulnerability to oppression was in part due to their own ignorance and foolishness. They failed to requite forces of nourishment and preservation. They promoted corruption by bribing officials, and strife by feuding and litigating against each other. They were lazy about doing a day's work. Their condition called for greater fiscal equity and also for closer moral supervision.

Toward the officials and wealthy landowners the emperor's attitude was quite different. Evidently, he held them responsible for civil order and felt they had betrayed their trust. To the officials, in particular, he showed an implacable distrust. At this time local officialdom appears to have been suffering from the effects of prolonged lack of morale and responsibility. The Mongol dynasty had been ineffective in attracting Chinese recruitment into the civil service. It had also extended central surveillance of local administration and inserted a parallel hierarchy of non-Chinese administrators down to the level of district magistrate. These officials received more favorable terms of examination and appointment and were paid more than their Chinese counterparts.[7]

Whatever the grounds for official discontent, Emperor T'ai-tsu refused to excuse it. The function of officials, he charged, was to create happiness for the people and correct the ruler's failings. Instead, they had indulged in cruelty, squeezing others to fatten themselves. This contravened the constitution of the state. More pointedly, it "obscured the ruler's brightness and lengthened his bad points."[8] The emperor warned that such conduct was suicidal. But he did not stop at warnings. Officials were harrassed and humiliated, and offenders were rounded up in large numbers and dragged to the capital, where they were variously flogged, flayed, and executed. All newly appointed local officials were warned to substantiate the emperor's intentions, soothe the people, and avoid misconduct, at their peril. Signs were hung beside administrators' chairs reading, "flay the skin and reduce to grass," to reiterate the drastic punishments for misconduct.[9]

Toward the wealthy landowners the emperor expressed his indignation by deporting many from their native districts, in some cases to distant provinces. But he appears to have seen in them potential allies in his campaign against officialdom, and this hindered him from maintaining a consistent policy. In the end the wealthy were retained for influential roles in rural administration, despite reservations as to their integrity.[10]

Armed with this approach to rural society and administration, Emperor

T'ai-tsu proceeded to set in motion his remarkable system of rural administration known as the *li-chia* system. Under this system, all households throughout the empire were organized into groups of 110, representing a *li* or "administrative neighborhood." The ten wealthiest families were appointed to serve annually and in turn as "neighborhood leaders." The remaining hundred families were divided into ten *chia* or units of ten families. Each of these families also served annually and in turn as unit head.

The immediate aims of the *li-chia* system were to equalize the tax burden and to have the people collect it themselves. The tax burden consisted of the land tax and labor services, including the management of the *li-chia* and the provision of money or manpower for local administration. Fair allocation of the land and labor taxes was to be based on careful surveys and decennial revisions of the number of persons and property of each household, to which was added the original tax rating of the land presently in its possession. This information was reported by individual households and recorded in registers, copies of which were deposited in the *li*, the district, prefectural, and provincial offices, and the Board of Revenue.

The collection of taxes was equalized by apportioning duties according to economic means. Collectors at the *chia* level were responsible for only 10 households; the wealthier collectors at the *li* level were responsible for 110 households. Above them were *liang-chiang* or principal tax collectors. These were selected from the largest landowners in each district and were in charge of areas assessed for 10,000 bushels of grain. In practice their areas appear to have been generally smaller and involved the management of anything from five to twenty *li* or more.[11]

The remaining labor services were equalized by being assessed on the basis of property as well as manpower. If two households had the same number of adult males, the one with more property was assessed for more labor. Moreover, these services were divided into those requiring physical labor and administrative expenses requiring a monetary payment. Given the current scarcity of labor, the former were considered to involve a greater loss than the latter and were, therefore, to be allotted to the wealthier households.[12]

The principle of universal popular collection was an essential element in the emperor's drive toward fiscal equity. Before the establishment of the *li-chia* system, tax collection had been in the hands of local officials, clerks, and rural tax middlemen, all of whom were felt to have abused their monopoly. Under the new system there were no specialists. Everyone participated in turn. The people assessed themselves and collected from themselves. Moreover, the land-tax collections were handed up from the lower units to the tax collectors, who delivered them direct to their receiving points, thus bypassing local officialdom. Finally, the decimal structure and ten-year rotation of service limited the number of unit households in relation to the economic and social means of each collector, while at the same time providing for relatively infrequent tours of duty.[13]

The emperor's organization of rural society was designed to assume much broader functions than the provision of taxes and the management of tax collection. In his later years he initiated side by side with the *li-chia* system a structure of rural jurisdictions. This is referred to under the term *li-lao* or "neighborhood elders." Each *li* was to nominate elders for selection by local officials who were more than fifty years old, just, upright, and still robust enough to undertake the position. These elders were to assume legal and social functions. As judges their jurisdiction extended over matrimonial and property suits and cases of physical assault. It was expanded to include certain types of robbery, homicide, and sexual offenses. The elders were also empowered to punish "unregistered rascals and mischief-makers" and send them to the civil authorities if they failed to reform themselves.

As might be expected, an important feature of the system was the curtailment of the judicial powers of local officials. No plaintiff was to bypass the elders in any case over which they were given jurisdiction. If this happened, both the plaintiff and the officials who accepted the case were to be punished. The emperor claimed that the system worked to the convenience of the local officials, but he revealed his underlying motives in adding that it was intended to prevent officials and their subordinates from taking advantage of litigation to extort wealth from the people.[14]

To give further substance to these intentions, the elders were given various immunities and powers vis-à-vis officials. They were not to be subject to arbitrary arrest and prosecution by the local civil authorities. They were authorized to send in reports either supporting good officials against unfair charges or implicating oppressive officials. If local officials thwarted their judicial powers or rights, they were permitted to memorialize or bring their complaint in person to the capital. In addition, the elders had certain powers in relation to tax collection. If local officials or *li-chia* personnel were found to have tampered with the registers, the elders were to point it out by arresting the offender, proceeding to the capital with the records, and requesting the execution of the culprit. All officials conniving at malpractices were to be sentenced to death.

In their social functions the elders were to act in collaboration with the *li-chia*. These functions included the maintenance of security, moral exhortation, and agricultural promotion. The elders and the *li-chia* were responsible for assembling groups to arrest bandits, fugitives, and other law-breakers wanted by the civil authorities. The elders were also required to warn households against sheltering such persons. As senior citizens selected for their integrity, they were to take a lead in upholding the prevailing values. For example, they were to conduct ceremonies prescribed by the *Chou li* for honoring good behavior. They were expected to memorialize the names of the filial and chaste. Similarly they were to exhort the people against ruining themselves in litigation and to rebuke bad behavior wherever they found it. Finally, they were to see that cultivators attended to their work in the fields and help promote water-conservation projects.[15]

The most significant feature in this rural organization is the reliance which the emperor placed in grass-roots leadership. It will be remembered that the society and economy were in a state of breakdown following long repression and civil disorder. Clearly the emperor did not trust the general body of local officialdom with having either the conviction or the familiarity with local conditions required to restore prosperity to rural society. On the other hand, as emperor he felt himself too far away to be able to take a direct hand. So the leadership must come from the society itself.

At the same time, the emperor believed that the rural society was capable of producing the necessary leadership. The elders and *li-chia* personnel, he argued, lived side by side with the people of their community and their fields adjoined. They knew about everything that went on, whether good or bad.[16] They enjoyed the proximity to rural conditions which the administrative leadership lacked. The emperor seems to have felt confident that rural society was capable of producing men of experience and integrity, and that the village people, if given the opportunity, would bring these people to the front. In this matter the emperor displayed a confidence in village society unequaled before the present day. No doubt this confidence was warranted. What rural society lacked, however, was an organizational structure capable of giving scope to that leadership, while also serving the legitimate needs of both state and society. The *li-chia* system was designed to provide that structure.

But the emperor was not content merely with system-building. He saw that organizations were dependent for survival on acceptance by their members of the values which they incorporated. So he devoted attention to identifying the requisite values and having them promulgated amongst the people. These were eventually framed into six clear-cut maxims. The first, "honor and obey your parents," signified respect and service for the forces of creation and preservation. Thus in another context the emperor argued that the people paid taxes in return for the nourishment and tranquillity provided by the ruler, without which there was no firm support for life. The rest of the maxims urged respect for seniors, promotion of community harmony, instruction of the young, pursuit of a peaceful livelihood, and avoidance of bad conduct. The emperor specifically urged the young to respect the old, arguing that this would bring mutual respect and social concord. In fact there is in his writings a preoccupation with the value of peace and order and the advantages which it would spread through "field and village." [17]

Finally, there is little doubt that the *li-chia* system was designed to diminish the power of officialdom over rural society. This is worth stressing, as it has often been argued that the principal function of the *li-chia* system was to extend imperial control over rural society, i.e., to serve the imperial rather than rural interest. Emperor T'ai-tsu's interest in control is undeniable. However, it is clear that the emperor, with his long formative experience of rural poverty and disorientation, saw himself as a champion of the rural underdog. The enemies of this cause were not only the hazards of agriculture and the human weaknesses of rural society. They included the exploitation by organized officialdom and its hangers-on. The restoration of rural peace and order must, therefore, involve the establishment of a balance of power in the countryside between organized bureaucracy, on the one hand, and village society on the other.

The *li-chia* system was to provide this balance. By having much, if not most, of the collection procedure bypass the local administration, it would neutralize various forms of fiscal oppression. Giving neighborhood elders the right to report on officials, arrest and bring them to trial, and notably to address the capital directly, would balance the punitive powers of officialdom. Above all, the villages were to manage most of their public affairs themselves, with the minimum of official interference consistent with the maintenance of the system. In this way the system was to be the means of giving village leaders a framework in which to exert their influence, and of putting leadership as much as possible into the hands of villagers.

These policies were intended to provide a remarkable rearrangement of power. If they had succeeded, they would have substantially affected the development of rural society.

With this structure in the making, the emperor was able to develop policies for the control of officialdom. Here our concern is with those policies for controlling local officials. An early step was to begin reducing the local bureaucracy in size. Apart from executions and dismissals, this was also accomplished, as in the Sung, by limitation of appointments. For departments including subordinate districts, it was decreed that if the registered households did not amount to thirty "neighborhoods" (approximately 3,300 households), the office of first-class assistant magistrate was to be abolished. For departments under that size which lacked subordinate districts, the offices of both the first-class and second-class assistant magistrates were abolished. Similarly the offices of assistant magistrate and registrar were abolished in districts with a registered population of less than twenty neighborhoods.

Thus the less populous departments and districts were to be left with only two administrative offices, those of magistrate and recorder (later jail warden). The latter, which was unranked, did not properly belong to the category "principal official" as did the magistrate and registrar, but to the subordinate category of "chief officer." Its duties were restricted to having charge over the transmission of documents and letters.

This official staff compared in size with the complement in the smallest Yuan district of Mongol administrator, magistrate, registrar, security officer, and recorder. The largest Yuan districts had had, in addition, an assistant magistrate and an extra recorder. Ming districts never had regularly more than four administrative offices, although the emperor allowed for the provision of more educational offices.

The Ming also abolished the former threefold division of districts and fixed the rank of all magistrates (except those serving in capital districts) at 7A, which meant a demotion of half a rank for magistrates of large districts and an increase of the same amount for those in small ones. This reform was more significant for reducing the rank and prestige of magistrates in populous and wealthy districts than it was for increasing the rank and prestige of those in small and uninfluential districts.[18]

Emperor T'ai-tsu also issued various directives indicating his view of the function of local officials. His early edicts, aimed at officials newly receiving appointments, stressed the exhaustion of the people and the need to bring them peace and nourishment. He urged officials to reduce administrative exactions, encourage the virtues of filiality and loyalty, and familiarize themselves with the problems of rural life.[19] After the establishment of the *li-chia* system, he issued new regulations on what officials should know on arrival at their offices. Finding that officials were still not observing the spirit of his policies, he issued specific injunctions for each major provincial office. The magistrate's job was defined solely as follows: to oversee the *li-chia* and promulgate official regulations; to get rid of the bad, pacify the good, and not to promote the wicked or injure the well-intentioned. Seldom had the duties of a district administrator been more circumscribed.[20]

At the same time the emperor went to considerable lengths to seek out officials for local administration capable of carrying out his policies.[21] In 1370 he ordered a special examination of all assistant magistrates. Those "without fault" were to be promoted to district magistrate.[22] If he found the right man, he thought nothing of brushing aside regular terms of promotion. On one occasion he raised an assistant magistrate to prefect of Ningpo. Characteristically, he demoted the prefect to the post of assistant magistrate. An assistant magistrate who obtained the highest ranking for probity and industry was promoted to secretary in the Board of Civil Office. However, when an inhabitant of his district came to Court with the message that "since Chou Ch'uan (the assistant magistrate) left, the people have been disturbed and unsettled," the emperor without hesitation ordered Chou to return to the post of assistant magistrate. He also instructed the Board of Rites to give him a feast and bestow gifts on him before his departure.[23]

Besides locating able officials, the emperor was equally concerned to investigate and weed out the incompetent or undesirable. Under his system of investigation, officials were examined both on their professional competence and their personal qualities. But there was a difference in emphasis between these two inquiries. The former was in terms of three balanced categories: capable, normal, and incapable. Its purpose was to grade an official's record during, and at the end of, his tour of duty to determine whether to promote or demote him. The latter was designed to seek out failure. Its categories were covetousness, cruelty, intolerance, inadequacy, senility, sickness, inertia, and disrespect. Whereas officials marked as incapable would merely suffer demotion, those picked out for lack of probity were sent for punishment. The negligent were reduced to commoner status.

The difference between this system of surveillance and that of the Sung was that as well as determining future office, it also threatened the security of official status itself. All officials were henceforth suspect. Failure was the norm, and it was up to them to prove themselves or suffer the consequences. Moreover, the emperor made it clear that in either inquiry his first concern was with the official's political loyalty. When a district magistrate and registrar were given the top grade, for excellence respectively in the supervision of grain transportation and management of commercial taxes, a note came down stating "the duties of magistrates and assistant officials consist in bringing peace and comfort to the people. How can you take managerial performance as relevant? Examination of officials does not consist in this." [24]

Emperor T'ai-tsu made a point of letting his distrust of officialdom be known to the people at large. The *Notice for Instructing the People*, which enumerated the duties of neighborhood elders and *li-chia* personnel, contained such remarks as "when officials are appointed there is no knowing whether they are virtuous or not....," "some officials and their subordinates have been incompetent to teach the people to be good ...," as well as other statements threatening officials or limiting their powers. What were such passages doing in a document for instructing the people in the management of their public life, if not to give them the idea that officials were not invulnerable? Evidently the emperor intended local officials to be hemmed in between pressures and controls issuing from all levels.

This major experiment in rural planning brought about several lasting changes in the relationship between administration and rural society. Most important, probably, were the effects resulting from the shift in initiative away from administration and toward rural society itself. As we have seen, the goals of the emperor's internal policies were rural concord and harmony. There is a distinction between these and the more typically Confucian goal of attaining popular allegiance and support.

The emperor's goals, while not at variance with the maintenance of central power, were also society-centered. They dealt with the question, "What goals would rural society wish for itself?" Allegiance, however, is primarily state-centered. The bureaucratic administration, as an instrument of the state, was well suited to press the cause of allegiance, and "humanity" and "justice," as defined in Confucian writing, were well suited as its values. Bureaucracy was less well suited to attaining the goals of rural society. It was too closely identified with the state; and it was becoming too distant, in location and in the provenance of its leaders, to be able to root itself in rural life and in the special conditions of each locality.

Therefore, the emperor chose to involve rural society itself in the attainment of its goals. This decision came from a different view of the capability of rural inhabitants than that typically expressed in Confucian theory, and called forth emphasis on values intended to give substance to that capability. That is why the emperor's maxims urged society to work for a situation of harmony and productive effort, in which its *natural* leaders, i.e., heads of households and elders, could be given a lead. In this undertaking, therefore, officialdom was given a supporting rather than a primary role. This does not mean that the emperor turned his back on the administrative values appropriate to bureaucracy, but that his approach to the goals of administration called for emphasis on others.

The values thus enunciated were to remain a permanent feature of imperial administration of rural society. The idea that the people had a responsibility for cooperating in achieving the goals of the state was to appeal strongly, albeit for different reasons, to the foreign Manchu leaders. Exhortation of the people in these values became a notable and unpopular duty of Ch'ing local officialdom.

Another feature which survived was the use of rural organization for the maintenance of state security. Although this was not a primary function of the *li-chia* system, it became a primary function of ensuing systems. The increased central pressure on local administration and the reduction in the complements of administrative offices were maintained and extended. While the initiative of local administrators remained considerable, it never regained the bounds that it had enjoyed in earlier periods.

On the other hand, much else that was basic to the system disintegrated. The fiscal policy, and the concepts of equalization on which it was based, gradually broke down. The dignity and influence of the rural leadership were steadily eroded and eventually destroyed. Lastly, the *li-chia* organization itself weakened and disappeared. The departure of these elements left a vacuum in rural administration which was never adequately filled, to the detriment of both rural society and the local administrative system. Why did the system break down, and why was it not successfully replaced?

9

The breakdown of the li-chia system

The breakdown of the *li-chia* system is a process which began soon after the death of Emperor T'ai-tsu and continued on into the early and middle Ch'ing periods. The death of the emperor himself contributed in no small part to its decline. Other factors to be considered are changes in the relationship of administrative policy to social and economic conditions, the perennial problem of the lack of unity in rural society, and the tendency of administrators to neglect, or take advantage of, this weakness.

The death of Emperor T'ai-tsu at the end of the fourteenth century meant the departure of the foremost and most dedicated exponent of the program of rural reform. The emperor lacked a body of followers trained in his viewpoint and devoted to its furtherance. He had had to rely for the maintenance of the *li-chia* system on the support of the bureaucracy, even though distrusting it as ignorant and unsympathetic. To resolve this problem he had virtually set himself up as arbiter of the administrative system, receiving information both from the bureaucracy and the rural leaders, weighing it and acting accordingly. He made himself the point on which the balance of the system depended.

No subsequent rulers had Emperor T'ai-tsu's personal experience of rural conditions or could share his same concern for them. Scarcely twenty years later the usurping Emperor Ch'eng-tsu (Yung-lo) moved the capital away from Nanking and back to his own base at Peking, where it had been located during the Yuan dynasty. This indicated a shift in imperial preoccupation away from internal administration and toward solidification of dynastic power in internal and external affairs. From the mid-fifteenth century on, the dynasty, in the opinion of the editors of the *Ming History*, concentrated on metropolitan affairs, at the expense of provincial affairs.[1] With this shift in imperial goals, the bureaucracy was in a position to regain influence as an agent of imperial power, at the expense of the much weaker and more dependent *li-chia* system.

These changes in imperial policy were accompanied by important changes in the state of the society and economy. In judging the performance of local administration or, for that matter, of rural society, it is necessary to take into account the interrelationship of administrative policy and social and economic conditions. The main function and responsibility of local administration was to implement imperial administrative policy. The success of its performance is, therefore, affected by the relevance of that policy to social and economic conditions. Where the policy is relevant, its administrators should, other things being equal, be expected to do an adequate job. But if the policy loses relevance, the task of the administrator is then made more difficult. Only if there is no change in the society or economy or in administrative policy, can any change in local administrative performance be pinned on local administration itself.

This may seem obvious enough, but there has been a strong tendency in analysis of Chinese history to concentrate analysis of administrative performance on factors intrinsic to administration. While this analysis has itself been thorough, other factors of possible significance have been less well explored. To balance this tendency, let us consider what changes took place in the interrelationship of state policy and social conditions, and what influence these may have exerted on local administrative performance.

First, let us consider the interrelationship of social conditions and Ming administrative policy, at the time when the latter was first formulated. The society and economy were then in a state of disruption. Many families had been scattered and depleted, and villages deserted. Prolonged fighting had reduced the size of the adult labor force and decreased the extent and quality of cultivation. Labor would be scarcer than normal in relation to land, and rural systems of distribution and interconnection disrupted. As is to be expected in a near-subsistence economy, the hardest hit by all this were the "small people"—those who had the least property and connections, and the least insurance against adverse conditions.

The *li-chia* system and its accompanying fiscal policies were designed in the light of these conditions. In line with its aim of achieving equity, its machinery was intended to assess land by productivity rather than acreage. The inclusion of property in labor service assessments made allowance for the high value of labor. By taxing poorer families in money rather than labor, it in effect transferred their levy onto the land, thereby spreading the exaction among the total household rather than limiting it to its most productive members. Thus taxes and services would be distributed according to means. A second objective was to restore organization to rural society. The *li* and *chia* would provide an unsettled and damaged society with the means to handle its own affairs, as well as participate systematically in the functions of the state.

But once peace and order were restored, the condition of the society and economy began to change. Life expectancy increased. The labor-intensive cultivation, required especially for rice culture, called forth a demand for labor and further promoted population increase. For a time, more efficient utilization of land and labor and reclamation of uncultivated land would balance this increase. But on existing holdings the increase in population would lead in due course to a decline in the relative value of labor to land. There would be a gradual decrease in the per capita size of holdings. With the division of inheritance this would lead to a decrease in the size of holdings per household.

None of these developments would happen quickly. But without unlimited supplies of land or means of improving agricultural technology or forms of alternative employment, these pressures would begin to build up as each household's per capita output advanced, levelled off and then declined. Meanwhile, systems of distribution would return to normal. The volume of exchange would build up. Rural markets would recover their unifying economic and social role in village life. Eventually they would expand and proliferate as new settlements were thrown off by the increase in households.

Given this type of change, the effect of the existing tax structure would be to work to the disadvantage of the poorer and less powerful households, and so defeat its original ends. As the ratio of labor to land changed in the direction of labor, the continued assessment of the labor service of poorer households in terms of land would tend to fall on the scarcer commodity, land, instead of on the now more abundant commodity, labor. The land was already bearing the land tax. The poorer household could reduce the burden of the land tax by subdividing ownership of its land; and the record suggests that this practice was followed. It could not reduce the labor service by this means. Thus as the marginal product of labor declined, the continuance of a double levy on the marginal product on the land would merely drive the poorer household more quickly down toward minimum subsistence levels.

By contrast, the more affluent or well-connected families were in a more favorable position to maintain their rate of marginal income or even take steps to improve it. They could increase the household's net income after taxation by buying untaxed land or by buying and renting out taxed land. Such steps would also help to retain a favorable ratio of land to labor (that is, to household population) for the land-owning household. They could reduce the weight of the labor service levy by hiring substitutes and thus indirectly shifting the burden onto the land (which remained for them a relatively abundant commodity). They could also reduce the relative burden of the levy by "merging" with households owing a smaller levy or none at all. Such mergers would also aim at cutting down the frequency of the rotational service, and at uniting a more powerful "household" behind the collector.

The practice of establishing quotas for district tax assessments played an important part in providing these opportunities. It was the practice for administration to determine revenue on the basis of estimated expenditure. District administrations then allotted the income requirements on the basis of the land and labor assessments. Once the district revenue levels had been established, there was considerable pressure on the part of both influential landowners and district administrators to prevent any increase in them. Often new land was not assessed, in order to encourage land reclamation, or it was assessed under the overall quota, rather than on the basis of its actual productivity. Moreover, household allocations were not adjusted to annual changes in levels of income, because the household and property assessments were only revised every ten years.

Even then, the quota system ensured that changes in assessments would represent adjustments in allocation rather than fluctuations in acreage or productivity per se. This applied to the labor as well as to the land assessments. Although labor service was calculated in terms of numbers of adult males required to perform government service, its assessment in terms of both manpower and property converted it from the outset into a unit of manpower rather than an actual adult male count. Once the quota of units was established, reassessment would also tend toward adjustments in allocation rather than in the overall number of units. Thus an increase in the amount of land or adult male labor could be achieved without necessarily involving a proportional increase in the land-tax or labor-service assessments.[2]

The establishment of fiscal quotas has an important bearing on the intrinsic competitiveness of a near-subsistence economy, such as that of rural China. This competitiveness is due to the high element of risk facing the producers in such an economy. Many factors contribute to that risk. Land and labor productivity is generally low. Transportation and communications are poor. Storage facilities are limited in space and efficiency. The rural market does not provide a fully self-regulating market system: supply cannot always adjust to demand nor demand to supply. Alternative means of production are limited. Above all, the risk of famine through drought, flood, or other causes of crop failure is always present, so that the producer can never be sure what the next season or next year will bring.

Under these circumstances the producer will be hesitant about tying up any of his limited surplus in capital investments necessary to improve his long-term productivity. Instead he will tend to maximize his returns while he can, so that he can increase his command over the limited means of production and distribution and spread some of his own risk onto other shoulders. The Malthusian tendencies implicit in near-subsistence economies will, at certain periods, contribute further to this competitiveness, as households strive to maintain their accustomed levels of consumption.

The quota system increases this element of risk. Assessments are based on estimated productivity and not on actual annual output. Thus even if the annual allocations should remain the same through the decade, there is no guarantee that they will correlate with household income. Under these circumstances alone, the household's *rate* of taxation is liable to fluctuate inversely with its income. But the annual allocations will not necessarily remain the same. Additional government expenses could increase them, especially if no general review of fiscal obligations was scheduled in the near future. So could the annual rotation in the tax-collecting personnel. Responsible local administrators would endeavor to see that the annual tax burden was adjusted broadly to the district's estimated overall income. But even then, no individual householder could be sure that that adjustment would equalize his allocation either to his own income or to that of other households.

Because of these conditions, a quota system will push the near-subsistence householder into a state of fiscal competitiveness. The fact that he cannot predict his future output with reliability affects his fiscal position as well as his overall economic position. His ability to meet his tax allocation could be undermined by any one of the various risk-inducing factors. It is true that if the whole, or a large part, of the district suffers a decline in output the magistrate would probably be able to obtain a tax redemption from his superiors. But if an individual household suffers decline, because of plant disease or because of personal illness or other loss of working capacity, it cannot expect any remission; at best it can only hope for it. Once again the household will be induced to cut down the source of the risk while it can. If successful in maximizing returns, it will move to increase its landholdings, thereby extending its income sources as well as spreading the risk. If it is not successful, it might try to reduce the fiscal risk by decreasing its landholdings or its adult labor force, or by decreasing the number of its consumers.

All of these actions will make the household more vulnerable to natural risks. Before taking such dangerous steps it will prefer to do everything possible to shift the risk by other means. A fiscal policy which substitutes absolute levels for relative rates of taxation will inevitably encourage this resolve. Since the administration will be primarily concerned with maintaining the overall levels, it will be less concerned with examining the state of their distribution, so long as those levels are achieved.

One of the most obvious methods of transferring the risks was by maintaining and utilizing personal connections. This could be done through extended families and clans, or through administrative personnel. Since natural risks are nonnegotiable, extended families and clans served to provide forms of mutual insurance. This institutional insurance was not dependent on individual survival and was also strengthened by shared property and family bonds.

Administrative risks, on the other hand, especially those involved by the quota system, were negotiable. Connections with administrators could enable the taxpayer to bring influence to bear on his allocation and conceivably reduce it. This form of connection, however, depended much more on the individuals involved and was much less reliable. The agent in the administrative office might retire, be removed, or disgraced. The influential relative might suddenly die. Under these circumstances the taxpayer must continue to maximize his advantage while he could or lose an opportunity which might never return. It is in this situation, of course, that corruption would tend to appear.[3]

The effect of these conditions is to set the people in competition not only against each other but also against the local administration. The economically and socially successful would gradually maneuver out of the tax system, leaving the local administration to collect the quotas from the less successful. In this situation, a weak administrator might resent the successful for having thus imposed on him, but he was more likely to put pressure on the less successful. A stronger administrator who tried to relieve the less successful and put pressure on the more successful would antagonize the latter by interfering in the struggle for survival and hindering their chances, just when those chances were most favorable.

A secondary effect is that the tax system, since it was also risk-inducing, would act as an additional disincentive to capital improvement, thus helping to prolong the conditions of instability and competitiveness. Consequently, this competitiveness, although it might take ruthless and reprehensible forms, was basically a product of the prevailing atmosphere of risk, rather than simply of quirks in human nature. Because they contributed to that risk, administrative policies were in part responsible for the antagonisms which developed between taxpayers and tax collectors.

In effect the fiscal policy itself contributed to the economic and social changes noted above. Its stimulus to competitiveness was an indirect influence. But the form of the land and labor taxes served to influence those changes directly. To begin with, the land tax was labor-intensifying. This is because it was based on a relatively fixed estimate of the productivity of the land, rather than assessed on the annual rate of output. While cultivatable land was not yet being worked at full capacity, an increase in labor would increase the total output and thus reduce the proportion taken by the fixed levy. Other things being equal, an additional input of labor would then increase the per capita income left after deduction of the land tax, until the point when the marginal product of the additional labor fell to zero. The poorer households, which in effect means those with poorer or less land, would reach this point sooner than the wealthier, and would, therefore, be disfavored by the terms of assessment as well as by the forces of competitiveness.

The labor-service levy, for its part, had a monetizing influence on the economy. We have seen that it was assessed on property as well as adult males and, therefore, calculated and apportioned in units of manpower.

The term used for this unit (*ting*) was the same as that for "adult male." This was because the tax was at first collected primarily in the form of physical labor; therefore, the levy was allocated to specific individuals. Nevertheless, the unit of assessment itself was from the start fiscal rather than physical. In addition, the levy was collected in money from poorer households. Thus the levy itself established both the principle of convertibility and the unit of exchange.

The pressure for conversion came from the more prosperous households who were taxed in physical labor. The reason for this pressure was that the higher the productivity of the household the greater the reduction in total income resulting from the loss in labor input, particularly where the assessment of that labor was inflated by the property assessment. By converting to a monetary payment, the wealthier household could reduce the inconvenience both to its adult males and to the management of its production. It could also endeavor to obtain a rate of exchange for its manpower assessment which would increase its net income.

It is impossible to say at this stage to what extent such endeavors were successful. Nevertheless, the pressures of fiscal competitiveness would certainly urge the household to make the attempt. So would the high value attached to leisure in an economy of low productivity. In any case, the wealthy proceeded towards monetization of the levy by hiring substitute labor, until the time came when the administration itself saw the advantages of a monetary collection. This conversion of the labor-service levy transferred the onus of the levy onto the land and thus caused it also to contribute to the competition for command over the means of production. Under these circumstances, the advantage again went to the households or groups which maintained for longer a favorable ratio of land to labor.

If the tax structure came to have an injurious effect on the weaker households, the reviving economy produced a similar effect of the tax structure. To begin with, the increase in population and the expansion of the marketing system would have a disintegrating effect on the structure of the *li-chia*. For a while, the revival of the marketing system might work to the advantage of the *li-chia* management. It would provide another institutional framework for the exercise of local leadership. Given that the heads of the *li* "neighborhoods" were picked on the basis of wealth, the revival of the market structure should be to their administrative as well as economic advantage. Its business transactions would provide more concrete evidence of household income, and this evidence would tend to become widely known throughout the standard rural marketing area.[4] Thus it would improve the basis for effective tax allocation by the annual *li-chia* heads.

The expansion of the system would in due course nullify this advantage. The increase in the number of households and the size of villages, the movement of the less advantageously located households in search of better prospects, and the establishment of new villages, would all go contrary to the rigid decimal structure of the *li-chia*.

The organization of the *li-chia* had provided against the possibility of decrease in the number of its households; it was not well designed to cope with expansion.[5] The establishment of new settlements would require an effort on the part of local administrators to go out and organize extra *li-chia*. Provided the quota levels were being maintained there would be little to encourage such an effort and much to discourage it. The expansion and proliferation of local markets would, in their turn, upset the balance of economic forces, and particularly of the leadership structure achieved while the market was in a state of equilibrium. Expansion would undermine the stability necessary for members of *li-chia* groups to calculate terms for maintaining reciprocality. It would create conditions for wider variations in material fortunes. The establishment of new markets would introduce new centers of local power.[6] By the time the local market system achieved a new equilibrium, the distribution of households and of wealth would be undoubtedly altered. This would upset the composition of the existing *li-chia*.

The weakening of the *li-chia* meant the weakening of the tax-collecting and tax-assessing machinery. Assessment and collection would correspond less and less to the actual distribution of wealth. At first the fixed-quota system would enable unit-assessment returns to assume a similar uniformity, as fluctuations in administrative expenditure could be met by adjusting the rates charged to the units of land and labor assessment. But the stabilization of the number of the land and labor assessment units meant a gradual growth in disparity between the amount of actual units and their fiscal counterpart. This disparity introduced opportunities for informal and irregular exploitation from all sides. To a certain extent it reduced the volume of administrative revenue per head of population, thus prejudicing the maintenance of expenditures on public services such as education and famine relief at a level proportionate to the increase in population. A decline in the flexibility and coverage of the assessment machinery would of course be detrimental to the already assessed households. Any reduction in property would also reduce their ability, or that of the collectors, to meet the assessments, unless these could be adequately relocated.[7]

Finally, a change in the ratio of land to labor involved a change both in the content of the revenue and in its seasonal availability. We have seen that the inconvenient and somewhat degrading physical forms of the labor-service levy would encourage the wealthier households on whom it fell to transfer the payment onto the land. However, the development or redevelopment of the land would of itself encourage this transfer, as long as it continued to result in an increase in total net income. Moreover, the development of the land, by providing the means of increasing the monetary income of the household, strengthened the household's negotiating position in the all-pervading fiscal competition. In addition, land, as has been pointed out, could be more easily withdrawn or hidden from assessment, by such means as purchasing land in different assessment areas or even in neighboring districts, not to mention more obviously fraudulent devices.

It might be expected that a fall in the marginal product of the land would reduce the advantages of labor-service conversion and, therefore, slow down the trend towards conversion. In the modern context of underdevelopment, analysts have argued that after the marginal product of labor falls to zero, any further supply of labor produces conditions of underemployment or outright unemployment. These conditions are "disguised" by a redistribution of man-hours so that each worker puts in a shorter working day. This then creates an unproductive labor surplus. Consequently, a household in these conditions would appear to be more able to afford a removal of, or levy on, its surplus labor than on its agricultural output, since the removal of the former should not effect the latter. In present-day conditions, this has been an argument for shifting underemployed agricultural labor into industry and communications.

The main objection to this argument is that the removal of the underemployed labor will involve the removal of some or all of its strongest members and will require considerable reorganization of the work of the remainder. If consumption levels are not equally reduced and no countervailing incentives provided, the loss of the labor potential will actually harm rather than help the household.[8]

In the context of the labor-service levy, other factors add to this objection. The physical service is personally inconvenient and frequently degrading. In addition, once the administration has itself monetized its labor-service needs by developing a hired labor service, it will itself continue the pressure towards monetization of the levy and undercut the option of deconversion. This is partly because the transference of the levy from labor onto land changes the conditions of its availability. This will have led the local administration to reform its arrangements for providing the necessary labor and for obtaining, accounting, and allocating its labor service revenues. Second, the increasing monetization of the levy is a concomitant of the general increase in the monetization of the economy. A rise in the flow of convertible revenues increases the means for adjusting and fluctuating revenues and disbursements. Administrators of all levels, well placed in their cities to observe the opportunities created by the economic change around them, would inevitably be encouraged to try to cash in on these advantages.

It will be evident from the foregoing that the administrative policies themselves did not stand still. Here let us note some of the more significant changes in revenue requirements and in the composition of local administration.

An early development was the conversion of official salaries. At the beginning of the Ming dynasty, salaries were defined and paid in bushels of rice with a supplementary allowance in paper currency. Moreover, the salary scales appear to have been substantial at all levels. The removal of the capital from the heart of the rice-producing area set off the trend towards conversion, first to paper currency, subsequently to bolts of cotton, silk, and ounces of silver.

A combination of factors, of which the inflation of paper currency appears to have been most conspicuous, led to a drastic decline in the real value of the converted salary from a cash equivalent of one thousand cash for every bushel of rice in the late fourteenth century to ten or less cash by 1471. Exactly what proportion of the salary was converted and thus devalued is unclear. In the early fifteenth century, rice still constituted 40 to 50 percent of the salaries of high officials and upwards of 70 percent in the case of low officials. But by the mid-fifteenth century, commentators were pointing out that the purchasing power of the salaries of regional officials was quite inadequate to meet their public and private expenses while in office and provide for any support in retirement. Faced with this situation, "those who preserved themselves by sinking into crime were many."

The conversions to silver appear to have improved the real value of salaries. But now all salaries included no more than one bushel (*shih*) of rice per month, or enough to feed three or four persons. All the rest was converted. These changes in the content of salaries inevitably induced officials to resort to fees, surcharges, or extortions to supplement their income, and thus preserve its real value. They also increased the pressure at all levels of administration to collect revenue in convertible currency, particularly silver.[9]

These and other changes in the fiscal requirements of the central administration led to considerable changes in the content and level of the tax revenue. During the later years of Emperor T'ai-tsu, the revenue had consisted only of rice and wheat, paper currency, and bolts of silk. Between then and 1502 the quota system prevented any major fluctuations in these items, except in the devalued paper currency; the level of the grain taxes, which constituted by far the major item, actually decreased slightly.

An increase in revenue was achieved by raising its content to some forty different items, some for substantial amounts, others of a trifling but still inconvenient size. These items included silk, cotton, and hemp in various stages of production, as well as many items charged in terms of units of currency. By the end of the sixteenth century, the number of items had increased further. In addition, the sixteenth century saw a rapid rise in silver payments, from some two million taels at the beginning to nearly twenty million by 1639.[10]

A corollary of this increase in taxation was a decline in the share officially available to local administration. This was despite the fact that the decline in the *li-chia* system was to give local administration a closer control over collection. The reasons have to do with the methods governing the assignment of revenue, and also with the increasing centralization of administration. Items were added according to the needs of specific receiving points, such as government granaries and treasuries. When a new need led the central administration to allot a new tax, the amount collected had to be delivered directly to the assigned receiving point. In effect, instead of simply increasing the overall amount of revenue to be handed up by local administration, the central administration controlled the nature, size, regional allocation, and specific delivery point of each new levy it required.

Continuing centralization placed further revenue demands on local administration. The posts of governor and governor-general were introduced and established during the dynasty, each bringing with them a substantial administrative entourage. The palace bureaucracy of eunuchs also increased into an organization of several thousand persons. Commenting generally on this centralization of revenue, Ku Yen-wu held that every levy, down to the minutest, had to be delivered up to higher levels, leaving local administrations without the means to finance their affairs.[11]

It would appear from this that local administration not only did not benefit from the additional levies as such, but that also it received increasing demands on its own share of the original quotas from the expanding higher echelons. These demands were no doubt informal as well as formal, and would have to be met, if not by an increase in the quotas, then by an increase in forms of surcharges.

These changes point to a shift in fiscal emphasis from the payer back to the receiver. Equalization of allocation might still be the administration's avowed policy, but collection and delivery had become its real objectives. This shift was a logical consequence of the nature of taxation in an authoritarian regime such as that of Ming and Ch'ing China, where taxation is a debt owed by society to its administration.

This condition compares with that in states where political control belongs to representatives of the taxpayer. There, taxation is in the nature of a loan, albeit a forced loan, for which administration must provide a return. Thus signs appear reading "*your* taxes at work for *you*." In the Chinese imperial state, the initial contribution came from the administration, not from society. The form it took was the provision of peace and harmony. The return was taxation. Even Emperor T'ai-tsu had stressed this when he told his peasants that they paid their taxes as a "recompense."

The emperor's judgment reflected the polarity between payers and receivers in Chinese political thought. The payers were paying for a necessary service which they could not provide through their own devices, just as a child could not fend for himself and so was obliged to serve those who did provide for his security. During his lifetime Emperor T'ai-tsu had in fact obscured this polarity by his strong association with the interests of the payers. Its reemergence after his death brought back into focus the primary function of taxation: that it was to recompense the receivers, not benefit the payers.

The processes of routinization, described by Weber, played their part in effecting this shift in emphasis. Emperor T'ai-tsu had provided in his person a remarkable effusion of charisma. He had thrown the bureaucracy off balance, rejecting its claims to special significance, doing away with its leaders, and undermining its security. Such was the effect of this onslaught that throughout the dynasty the bureaucracy never quite succeeded in regaining the preponderant influence in the conduct of state affairs. Nevertheless, among the people at large its legitimacy was deeply rooted through its long personification of the prevailing administrative power structure. Once Emperor T'ai-tsu had gone, this legitimacy was strong enough to restore this identity and allow officials to revert attention to the service owed them as the standard symbols of order. Seen from this point of view, the forces for routinizing equalization of taxes could not hope to compete in legitimacy with the forces for routinizing collection and delivery.

The changes which took place in the structure and composition of administration at first continued to obscure the inequality of this competition. The reduction of the posts of assistant officials continued through the dynasty, as is illustrated in Table 20. This appears to have been in part due to a reduction in the work required from them.[12] In addition, by the middle of the fifteenth century, the examination system was established as the main method of recruitment, and the method of appointment to magistrate by recommendation was abolished.[13] This reduced to a minimum the prospects of appointment and promotion through merit, which in T'ai-tsu's time had still given substance to the assistant offices. The path to success now lay through success in the examination system, and the assistantships no longer provided a hopeful stepping-stone.

In consequence these offices were neglected by the ambitious and fell into disrepute. Ming (as well as Ch'ing) district appointment lists almost always show much shorter lists of names and fewer details under these offices than they do under that of the head official. This is because either the names were lost, or the turnover in appointments was very slow, or because there were insufficient applicants for the available appointments. None of these reasons reflect well on the prestige or influence of the offices. Only in the case of important districts like Wan-p'ing were the offices

Table 20. Sample showing attrition of assistant district officials in Ming era

| | DATE OR REIGN ERA OFFICE ABOLISHED | | |
DISTRICT	ASST. MAGISTRATE	REGISTRAR	COMMENT
HOPEI PROVINCE			
Ch'ang li	continued	1529[a]	asst. magistrate abolished Shun-chih period
Ku-an	1561[a]	continued	registrar abolished Shun-chih period
Chiao-ho	1505	continued	
Wen-an	1553 (2)	continued	
ANHWEI PROVINCE			
Chi-hsi	1565	continued	one subdist. magistrate abolished 1615
Ch'i-men	1565	continued	registrar abolished 1646
Lu-chiang	1368–98[a]	1531	
Wang-chiang	1403–24[a]	1629	
CHEKIANG PROVINCE			
Hsin-ch'ang	continued	1492[a]	
Shan-yin	continued	c. 1600	
T'ien-t'ai	1579	1629	
P'ing-yang	continued	continued	lost registrar, 3 subdist. magistrates, and 4 *ta-shih* between end of Ming and beginning of Ch'ing eras[b]
SHENSI PROVINCE			
T'ung-kuan	1426–36	1426–36 1573–1620	lost 1 *hsun-tao*, 1426–36[c], other, 1573–1620; 1 restored by Ch'ing
San-shui	none	none	
Li-chüan	1522–66	continued	registrar abolished Shun-chih period; 1 *hsun-tao* abolished 1621–27
I-yuan	continued	1573–1620	
HUNAN PROVINCE			
Ning-yuan	1579	1639	
Yu-hsien	during Ming	during Ming	
Hsin-hua	1451	continued	registrar not appointed in Ch'ing
Li-ling	1629	continued	registrar abolished Shun-chih period

Table 20. (*continued*)

| | DATE OR REIGN ERA OFFICE ABOLISHED | | |
| | ASST. | | |
DISTRICT	MAGISTRATE	REGISTRAR	COMMENT
SZECHUAN PROVINCE			
Chang-ming	1465–87?	1522–66 (2)	
Hsin-tu	1375[a]	c. 1628[a]	
Ching-ju	none	1580	
Kuang-an chou	1628–43[a]	none	no asst. magistrate in Ch'ing
KWANGTUNG PROVINCE			
En-p'ing	none	none	*hsun-tao*, 1505[a]
Jao-p'ing	continued	1539[a]1545?	
Hsin-ning	none	1618	
Jen-hua	none	1578	1 subdist. magistrate late 16th cen.
KWEICHOW PROVINCE			
T'ien-chu	none	none	
Mei-t'an	none	none	records begin 1573
Sui-yang	none	during Ming	only 5 registrars listed in Ming, then abolished

SOURCES. Gazetteers of each of the above districts.
NOTES. Province titles are those of the present day.
[a] Indicated year of last registered appointment.
[b] *Ta-shih*: treasury or granary keeper (unranked).
[c] *Hsun-tao*: assistant director of schools.

evidently kept regularly filled and the names and professional qualifications of their incumbents preserved.[14]

In the smaller districts, where the offices were abolished from the start, the duties of the magistrate fell, in his absence, on the unranked "chief officer" (or in a few places on other unranked officers). A summons to Peking would keep the magistrate away for a long absence, and then, as one magistrate pointed out, the local administration would lack continuity and the people "not know awe." But his request that a "principal official" (i.e., magistrate, assistant magistrate, or registrar) be constantly available in distant districts, came up against the efforts of examination candidates to hold out for better prospects.[15]

This had two effects on the condition of the district officials. Apparently, it pushed up the age of district magistrates. A neighborhood elder complained in 1459 that "nowadays many of those appointed magistrates are elderly *chien-sheng* (Imperial Academy Students). By the time they have completed their (official) nine-year tour of duty, they are nearly seventy years old and also careless and avaricious." [16] Evidently provincial graduates were afflicted with the same malady, since only a year later it was ordered that any over fifty years old were not to be appointed magistrates but instead offered miscellaneous offices.

Second, the popular esteem of the assistant officials was severely damaged. A late sixteenth century censor noting this memorialized: "Although assistant magistrates are very inferior they are also near to the people. They have to be treated with propriety if they are to be charged with responsibility. Nowadays menial underlings revile them. They are no different from chair-bearers and only serve to defile the people." [17] Here were the beginnings of a major problem in Ch'ing local administration.

The decline of the rural administrative system had much more obvious repercussions on the balance of rural power. This decline was already under way in the early fifteenth century. At the top, several factors combined to overwhelm the principal tax collectors (*liang-chang*). The increasing cost and complexity of the system, and population density of the areas allotted to them, proved too great a strain on their capacities. They also were responsible for any failures in collection among the lower tax-collecting units. The removal of the capital to the north weakened or severed their former direct link with metropolitan authority. Officials searching for means of supplementing the meager salaries exploited their weaknesses. They in turn exploited, if they could, the weaknesses of their subordinates. Otherwise, they fled. By the 1450s the breakdown of the system of tax collectors was apparent. Consequently, it was formally abolished in many areas of central, northern, and southeastern China, and collection was put in charge of the *li-chia*. [18]

But by this time the *li-chia* was itself in a state of decline, as population movement broke down its rigid order and disrupted its rotational system. As the greater pressure of the increasing taxes and surcharges began to fall on smaller and weaker household properties, the collection of the required amounts became increasingly difficult for the fragmenting and contracting *li-chia* units. The weaker took refuge in flight, thus weakening the remainder. This desertion brought about, in Liang's memorable phrase, a "history of fleeing that was never heard of before." [19]

Meanwhile, the neighborhood elders were losing their prestige and their social and political functions. The reason for this appears to have been that the not inconsiderable power of the position attracted opportunists, and that their qualifications were not adequately assessed by the city-bound district official. Already in the 1420s a censor complained that in many districts the position was being filled by "evil" persons or by administrative servants and retainers, who were making false judgments, perverting the law, and oppressing the villages. A decade later another official claimed that pavilions erected for the hearing of rural litigation were falling into decay and that even small matters were being taken straight to the district office.

Clearly, the decay was still within bounds, for in the 1430s and 50s elders were still memorializing on the defects of tax collectors and magistrates, as they had been empowered to do.[20] But their influence could not survive without the support of the central government and the continuance of the institutional framework within which it was designed to operate. By the late sixteenth century Lü K'un, a distinguished governor, noted that their position had sunk to that of neighborhood tax collectors and office runners. They were "beaten in the morning and flogged at night." Everyone was ashamed to do the work.[21]

The decline in the rural administration was countered by an increase in the work of the magistrates. Some of this, such as the growing interference in tax collection, was partly self-induced. But the general breakdown of the comprehensive rural services left no one else but the magistrate to take over their administration. This meant that as systems weakened from district to district, single individuals became increasingly responsible for seeing to a spectrum of functions that had previously been carried out by scores and hundreds of different individuals.

Seventeenth-century accounts of the Ming period put it this way. The one magistrate had to see personally to the allocation, collection, and delivery of the land tax, the decennial revision of the tax registers, the adjustment of labor requirements to household property and manpower, and the allocation of the supplementary taxes. It was up to him to make allowances for changes in seasons, productivity, and income, and to "equalize" accordingly, and to request from his seniors general tax remission in case of serious crop failures. It was his personal duty to nourish the aged, sacrifice to the spirits, choose licentiates to be sent up to court, read the laws, inspect trade, manifest the good, and relieve the poor and the starved. He must thoroughly enforce arrests and attend to civil and criminal suits. This, of course, meant enquiring fully into their circumstances (rational and emotional), deciding according to the relevant laws and statutes, and allowing appeals to be submitted to higher judgment. He must also investigate the produce of the mountains, seas, and marshes (considered state property) and submit whatever would be of use to the state.[22]

Along with this encumbrance of administrative duties returned the personal responsibility for the morale of the people. The magistrate again became the standard by which public virtue rose or fell. As the famous late Ming magistrate Hai Jui put it, the essence of the magistrate's governing lay in remembering to be serious toward Heaven and diligent toward the people. All those shouldering the responsibilities of the people must embody the will of Heaven and grieve in their hearts. They must sympathize with the lonely and take pity on the hungry and cold. Even more, they must identify with the condition of the people, depriving themselves when the people were deprived and acting on the basis of their needs. Political goodness lay in embracing the many in the one, and in sincerely seeking this end.[23]

The striking passage from which this comes contains in it elements of both the old and the new in the administrative role. Recognizing that the initiative for rural order lay once more with the magistrate, Hai Jui first reemphasized the traditional bureaucratic imperatives: that the magistrate was the source and determinant of moral health, that with his power went this burden; that both were a function of his cosmic role as mediator between society and the natural order. Here is an effort to reassert a certain independence from the central power. The magistrate is not simply its political agent; as moral exemplar his influence, within its territorial limits, goes beyond the political order and enjoys a direct association with cosmic power.

However, Hai Jui also emphasized the necessity for the magistrate to identify and unify. This is in part a Confucian variant of the view implicit in the policies of Emperor T'ai-tsu, that the scattered rural society needed for its coordinators men who were a part of it, who if not "rooted" in it nevertheless "knew" it in its full spectrum. Certainly, it is an application of Sung metaphysical affirmations at the local level.

Clearly, Hai Jui saw that there was, in practice, a gulf between the many and the one, and that if political initiative lay with the official, then the health of society and state depended on his bridging that gulf, by bringing together the separate identities. To achieve this end Hai Jui stressed two points: first, "knowing" the district; second, similarity of experience, sharing and acting in concord.

But seeing the extent to which the power of the administrator and the weakness of the people could set them against each other, Hai Jui was forced to fall back on the time-honored symbol of authoritarian unity, the state and society as family and brotherhood. He included one new dimension. The people were not merely the children, but the magistrate's "kith and kin" children. Here was an effort to reinforce the concept of the unity between the many and the one, even if it remained on a hierarchial basis.

With this appreciation of the renewed responsibility falling on the magistrate, let us see what steps local administrators took to give practical expression to that responsibility.

10

REFORMS IN LOCAL ADMINISTRATION DURING THE LATE MING AND EARLY CH'ING DYNASTIES

The late Ming and early Ch'ing is a period of sweeping adjustment in China's social and institutional fabric, running across the dynastic divisions and developing independently of imperial initiatives. The critical factors in this transition were probably the growing productivity of the land in relation to labor, and the increasing regionalization of production and commerce as new cash crops and improved strains in staple commodities made their appearance. These in turn contributed to changes in the structure of society and its relation to the organization both of production and state administration.

How did local administration reflect and respond to these social and economic changes? It would be very valuable to know more of the basic data denoting this interaction between society and administration, as it seems to be at this time that the society assumed the essential features which characterized it down to the late nineteenth century. If so, this was a crucial time for administration to consider its options in the light of existing values and material conditions. It would also be a crucial period for understanding how and to what effect it exercised those options.

As an index to the question stated above, a bare outline can be presented of certain changes and reforms which took place in local administration. The composition of the subordinate administrative staff was substantially altered. Other institutions of rural administration were reintroduced. Finally, local administrators themselves instituted widespread reforms in fiscal policies.

Changes in the staffing of local administration

The late Ming and early Ch'ing period saw several important changes in the structure of local administration, reflecting an increasing differentiation of functions performed for central and local, and for public and private, interests. The central government increased its control over the appointment and conduct of local officials. Subordinate functionaries, although progressively cut off from access to administrative office, proliferated into large, entrenched, subadministrations, primarily representing local interests. Between these two forces emerged an intermediary group of professional private aides. These men often obtained their positions through lobbying at the provincial capitals and went out as representatives of provincial administrative interests. In general they served to coordinate the differing functions of local administration.[1]

The extension of central government control took place through more rigorous surveillance of official conduct and continuing attrition of assistant administrative offices. As one early Ch'ing official said of this centralization, the "meshes of the law became even finer and the blackness of the law ever stricter."[2] In 1451, 730 provincial officials were recommended for dismissal. Of that number, thirty-one were subsequently retained. In 1493, 1,400 local officials and a further 1,300 miscellaneous and unranking officials were recommended for dismissal. Ninety were subsequently retained. Several similar waves of dismissals occurred inbetween. Apparently local officialdom had become highly vulnerable to central power.[3]

In its first two hundred years, the Ch'ing government was to extend this power by developing a less arbitrary but more systematic and comprehensive control system. We shall examine in further detail this system, and its impact on local administration, in chapter 12. The Ch'ing government also took immediate steps to continue the Ming attrition of assistant district offices. In its third year of power at Peking (1646), it abolished the post of district registrar entirely. A few such posts were reestablished between 1670 and 1683. In the first two reign periods, many assistant magistracies were also abolished. When new districts were apportioned, only the offices of magistrate and jail warden were normally established. Under the Yung-cheng emperor, more offices of assistant magistrate and subdistrict magistrate were cut back. In the long Ch'ien-lung reign, there was a tendency to hold to the overall number of assistant positions, but in the next two reign periods (occupying the first half of the nineteenth century), many more of these offices were dispensed with, while certain districts were demoted to rural subdistricts, thus dissolving their administrative establishments.[4]

In contrast to this long-term consolidation of central control over district offices, the positions of subordinate functionaries lost meaningful access to centralized administrative appointment and came increasingly under the control of local interests. Early Ming policy had been motivated by abuses of local authority during the Yuan dynasty. In a decree of 1371 Emperor T'ai-tsu claimed that Yuan officials had not personally attended to legal cases, providing corrupt functionaries (*li*) with many opportunities to "oppress and harm." He prohibited officials from appointing copyists (*t'ieh-shu*) at will and ordered that quotas be established for the appointment of regular functionaries according to the amount of administrative business. Officials who appointed copyists in excess of need were to be punished.[5]

At this time the *li* offices—if not their personnel—still enjoyed some respect. They constituted one of the three regular paths to administrative office. Senior licentiates and licentiates who had been unable to maintain their qualifications under the examination system were placed in these offices.[6] Those entering administrative office from service as *li* functionaries obtained initial ranks comparable to those awarded to metropolitan examination graduates.[7] A major step in the degradation of the *li* offices occurred in 1409, when Emperor Ch'eng-tsu barred functionaries from appointment to offices in the censorate. The emperor claimed that these appointments in particular required men well-versed in constitutional principles and concerned for their personal integrity. If they appointed "knife and stylus" functionaries who knew only how to oppress, this would cause the people to "look lightly at the Court."[8] Thus one factor in the decline of these offices was their lack of effectual association with ideological study at a time when the government was particularly concerned to rebuild the ideological legitimation of the civil administration.

Another related factor, which must have reinforced the emperor's decision, was the gradual association of the functionary offices with services performed under the compulsory labor system. As early as 1395 a regulation was enacted stipulating criteria for selection as functionary under labor-service obligations. Those selected were to be agricultural people of "blameless families" (*shen-chia wu-kuo*). They should be literate and not less than thirty years of age.[9] Clearly such people were of a different order of experience and competence from licentiates who had struggled on and finally failed under the examination system. Subsequent regulations elaborated conditions under which men of households owing labor-service contributions (*ting*) were liable for work as functionaries.[10] Other regulations attempted to cut back the number of functionary positions throughout the empire to one chief functionary (*ssu-li*) and two functionaries in charge of documents (*tien-li*) per office (*fang*).[11] Functionaries were held to nine-year terms of service. Those over fifty years of age by the completion of this term were disqualified from applying for administrative office and returned to commoner status.[12]

At the beginning of the Ch'ing period the situation was roughly as follows. Through commutation of labor service payments officials were hiring commoners as clerks. The multiplication of district office business under the Single Whip reforms (see under Reform of Fiscal Policy in this chapter) attracted the services of a great many more clerks than allowed by the quota for functionary-clerks. One mid-seventeenth-century authority stated that probably more than a thousand clerks were employed in a district. In addition, clerks were becoming entrenched in their positions. Ku Yen-wu complained of fathers transmitting their offices to sons and elder brothers to younger brothers, and held that all the authority of the officials was being completely given over to the clerks.[13]

More significant, perhaps, was the gulf which had emerged between the officials and the clerks. In terms of status, the work of clerks was now indelibly associated with the demeaning labor-service requirement. As the editors of the Ch'ing *T'ung-k'ao* pointed out, whereas formerly the job had been carried out by scholars and not regarded as base, now it was staffed through a form of induction and therefore called a labor-service.[14] Second, the degradation in functionary status and proliferation in numbers of clerks effectively barred the overwhelming majority of clerks from hope of access to any administrative service. At the level of district administration, clerical service was localized. Clerks represented local interests, while officials came in as powerful but marked outsiders.

Early Ch'ing legislation made no attempt to reverse these historical trends. After an initial period in which functionaries were established according to the amount of official business, quotas were established in 1668. Prefects were provided with between seven to twenty-four documentation clerks, department magistrates with between six to twelve, and district magistrates with between two to twelve. Assistant officials were assigned substantially fewer numbers of recorder clerks (*tsuan-tien*).[15] Appointment to these posts required the issuance of a certificate bearing the name, age, and date of entry to service of the recipient. His qualifications were to be guaranteed by a neighbor, friend, or relative and certified by the local official before he could assume his job. As of 1667 officials were forbidden to appoint civil or military licentiates to the quota positions. Terms of service were set at five years, and between 1655 and 1790 entry to administration for those qualifying under the clerical examinations was reduced to the lowest administrative rank.[16] From 1647 district magistrates were assigned twelve *shu-pan* (clerks "inducted" under the labor-service system), and small and specific quotas of similarly "inducted" doormen, treasury clerks, granary clerks, treasury janitors, grain measurers, horsemen, guards, lictors, lantern carriers, sedan, parasol and fan bearers, and jailers.[17] Initially, small stipends were provided for all these clerks and runners. But in the 1660s these stipends were expropriated to help finance the campaigns against Ming rearguard forces. After the completion of these actions, runners holding quota positions regained their wages but clerks did not.[18]

Finally, clerical conduct was made an important aspect of Ch'ing disciplinary regulations. Local officials were ordered to choose for clerical service men over the age of twenty who were "well mannered and respectful." They were prohibited from permitting clerks to serve in excess of the regular quotas and supplementary quotas for copyists, and they were penalized for any failure to control infractions of duty by clerks.[19]

The enlargement of official, and degradation of clerical, responsibilities created serious gaps in communication and control between the district official and his subordinate functionaries. In the emergence of the Ming–Ch'ing private secretarial (*mu-yu*) system, officials found one vital means of dealing with this problem. Under earlier dynasties, *mu* were assistant officials holding established administrative positions. The Ming–Ch'ing system grew up outside the established administrative order. During the Ming dynasty, *mu* first appeared as aides to officials holding military and frontier commissions. Apparently because military officials were unskilled in documentation, subordinate Board officials were sent out in 1425 to the regional military commissions to assist commanders in handling documentary communications. But by the sixteenth century, other military and frontier administrators were themselves "inviting" officials and scholars to assist them in administrative management.[20] Biographies of Ming secretarial aides indicate that those preparing for this service studied such subjects as military methods, laws and regulations, taxation, and river administration, over and above the classics and history.[21]

There is no evidence yet that *mu* private secretaries had percolated down to district administration before the end of the Ming period. But by the mid-Ch'ing, the private secretarial system had become a well-established and indispensible feature of all levels of provincial administration. The main stimulus for this development came from the many and complex legal and fiscal responsibilities placed on Ch'ing district officials. As we have seen, the secretaries who advised in these areas became the most prestigious and well paid of all private aides. Early titles of secretaries were derived from administrative titles of earlier dynasties and confirm that they were employed initially to aid in the drafting and transmission of reports. Significantly, the titles of secretaries of law and taxation had no such institutional precedent, suggesting that the importance exerted by law and taxation in Ch'ing local administration was itself without obvious precedent.[22] In any case, mid-Ch'ing legislation, while distrusting secretarial conduct, admitted that the affairs of provincial officials were "complex and many," and that under the circumstances they could not but invite secretaries to help in managing those affairs. The Court contented itself with ineffectual efforts to inhibit secretarial missions between different administrative offices.[23]

These developments pushed the focus of identification between local society and the state away from the magistrate and down towards the clerks and runners. The magistrate's ability to maintain this identification had always been challenged by his alien origin; regionalization of local fiscal and economic conditions would increase the challenge. In this situation, length of tenure became a crucial factor. The Ming nine-year term of office would give officials time to develop an informed relationship with their districts, provided that they retained enough energy, skill, and administrative support for this purpose. But the conditions of tenure already found in the early Ch'ing precluded such a time span. The secretaries, for their part, were identified with local and regional officials and were not usually natives of the districts in which they worked. The clerks and runners, however, were not only local agents but also knew a good deal about the operation of state regulations. This helped to make them accessible and useful to the vast mass of local society as intermediaries with the state, whereas the magistrate could more readily act for the limited group of examination candidates and graduates, whose aspirations he shared. For the masses he was in danger of becoming as distant and unknown as they were for him.

The professionalization of local administration also undermined the public relationship between local society and the state. In the case of the magistrate, the imposition of the examination system as the predominant pathway to appointment was bringing into office a group of men forced by long experience to have to consider their own interests.[24] The stringent surveillance of official performance added fuel to this preoccupation, forcing officials to view the public interest in terms of its contribution to self-preservation. Protecting the official's public record became a major duty of secretarial service. In addition a special group of private servants came into service, one of whose primary functions was to supply local and regional officials with private incomes.[25] Clerks and runners, above all, were notoriously believed to be living off corruption. They would gobble up punishment like "delicious vegetables" so long as they were profiting from office.[26]

These pressures impaired the efficiency of local administrators by bringing their self-interest into conflict with the values instilled in them. Given the Confucian emphasis on the role of the official as public moral exemplar, this conflict would have serious repercussions both for the individual magistrate and for rural society. If the magistrate could not bring full moral conviction to the administration of rural society, rural institutions must at least themselves supply moral leadership. Otherwise, the people would be left without adequate guidance. From this standpoint the decline of the *li-chia* system, in combination with the professionalization of local administration, posed not only a fiscal but a moral threat.

The revival of the Pao-chia and Hsiang-yueh

By the early sixteenth century, there were signs of a major crisis building up in the economy and society. Economic and fiscal pressures were depriving the poor of ownership of the land. "Guest households" (*k'o-hu*) were becoming a widespread phenomenon in the south and east and providing easy victims for landlords and loan sharks. The rich, meanwhile, were living (or claiming to live) outside their registered areas as a means of evading tax requirements. Moral standards suffered in the scramble for success or survival, and the rural institutions designed to maintain them were themselves crumbling because of the flux and drift of the people.

Local administration was ill-equipped to bring these conditions under control. Its fiscal requirements were damaging its relationship with rural society. Its leaders were losing physical touch with the countryside. Its records no longer reflected the actual distribution and condition of population and resources. To a large extent it no longer even knew where the people were or where they were from. Under these conditions impoverishment and oppression were rising and provoking the classic response of banditry. By the early sixteenth century banditry, reinforced by anti-dynastic rebellion, had become in parts of the south a major political challenge.

These conditions brought to the forefront the philosopher and political administrator Wang Yang-ming. Wang's significance as a philosopher is well known. He is also important as the precursor of the rural administrative institutions of the Ch'ing dynasty. In the Ch'ing period these institutions functioned for the most part as imperially sponsored control systems. However, as shaped by Wang they were designed for the more positive aim of giving practical expression to his philosophy and providing a solution to the pressing social problems of his day.

Wang's approach to rural administration was deeply rooted in his personal life as well as in his outward observations. He was a man of restless intellect. Although born to comfortable circumstances, he experienced extremes of cruelty and deprivation. For defending at court two unjustly sentenced officials he was flogged almost to death. He was then banished for three years to what was to him a barbaric and hostile environment. On top of this he had applied himself to the teachings of Chu Hsi as well as those of Buddhism and Taoism, driving himself to exhaustion and sickness, and yet had found them all unsatisfactory. This social and intellectual isolation threw him back on his own resources and led him into an intensive examination of the inner life and its relationship to the outer world.[27]

Wang's findings can be summarized as follows. In line with the general Neo-Confucian view he held that man naturally formed one body with Heaven, Earth, and all created things. The world was one family, the country one person. Human nature was inherently good. Humanity (*jen*) was the constituent by which man united himself with other entities. The mind was the instrument which gave expression to that unity.

Wang regarded the mind as formed of Heavenly principle; its basic substance was thereby inherently "clear" and good. When substance was in a state of repose, there was no existence of good or bad as distinct phenomena, but only absolute good. Differentiation of value came through activity. Badness constituted deviation from absolute good, through obfuscation of the natural clarity of the mind. Wang attributed badness to poor education, not to basic flaws in human nature; he rejected any notion that habit could deprive the mind of its innate knowledge.[28]

If human nature was inherently good, Wang assumed that the mind must prefer to become absolutely good in activity as it was in tranquillity. Confucianism held that the mind should seek this ideal as an essential preliminary to the ordering of the state. Consequently, learning how to "abide in the highest good" had become the primary business of the *chüntzu*. Wang himself gave special emphasis to the method of attaining full self-realization. Orthodox Neo-Confucianism taught that this lay through the extension of knowledge and the achievement of sincerity. Wang developed the view that the extension of knowledge itself proceeded through the unification of knowledge and action. Action, since it was in activity that value differentiated; therefore without action the innate knowledge of value would remain unrealized. Knowledge, because without it action would fail to differentiate between bad and good. For Wang, the obscuring of reality by confusion over value made the correct extension of knowledge a matter of urgent personal and public interest. In line with this he made the "extension of innate knowledge" into his cardinal doctrine.[29]

Wang developed his philosophy as a guide to individual practice and to social action. Here we must limit ourselves to its social application.

As a social philosopher Wang emphasized magnanimity towards others, combined with the removal of "selfishness" as the key to mental health. He was alarmed by the increasing polarization of society into rich and poor, landlords and tenants, oppressors and bandits, and characterized it as a serious and long-standing matter, a "defect" to be "exposed as soon as possible," a "sickness" that must be cured. But he regarded this social harm as a product of misapprehension, not of any inherent moral or natural dichotomy. Accordingly, he believed that it should be dealt with through developing greater awareness of objects of consciousness and greater personal restraint. In particular, he urged affectionate closeness (*ch'in*) as the completion of social knowledge, thereby returning to the original connotation of *ch'in-min* as "being close to the people," rather than to Chu Hsi's view of it as *hsin-min* or "reforming" them. In short, he upheld the Confucian belief that man was capable of mastering the struggle for survival through moral solutions, and his anxiety over social conditions hardened his resolve to take action.

As an administrator Wang was famous for his suppression of rebellion and banditry, and for his reconstitution of the *pao-chia* and *hsiang-yueh* rural control institutions.[30] Wang's attitude towards bandits was like his attitude toward weeds. If they must be removed, then remove them. But they too were made of Heavenly principle and, in substance, free of taint. Consequently, administration should try to win them over, while taking steps to protect nonbandits against personal injury. Most of all, it should encourage a sense of identification among the people, and between the people and their administrators.

Wang's policy towards bandits was to hold out the promise of rehabilitation. In proclamations he pointed out that they were no worse than others. Weeds among the hemp, he said, citing Hsuntzu, grow straight without help. White sand among the mud will also look black.[31] He also made clear his view that administration was in part to blame for any accumulation of bad practice. He warned people not to hold the evil of others against them but to concentrate on their own failings. He also warned "reformed" people (*hsin-min*) not to relax simply because they had been pardoned. They must renew themselves through hard work and honest practice, if they were to avoid bringing on self-destruction.[32]

To provide villagers with a means of self-defense, Wang reinstituted the *pao-chia* or watch-group system. He described its intention as the elimination of banditry and the restoration of "peace and nourishment" to ordinary people. More specifically, it was intended to check the whereabouts of people and assure the provision of mutual aid in case of attack. All families were to organize in groups of ten. They were to write down such details as the size of their households, guests if any, *li-chia* heads, and *ting* obligations. "Guest households" were to indicate their district of original registration, local business, labor service, and land occupied. Every day each group was to hand round a note informing its members of the movement and business of its members. Each family was to take charge of this daily service in turn. Suspicious activities were to be reported to the officials. If anything was concealed, all families were responsible.

For defense purposes each natural village (*hsiang-ts'un*) was to have a watch-chief. He had to be someone trusted and acknowledged by all, and his appointment was to be recommended by the magistrate and confirmed at the circuit level. His function was solely to lead the villagers in protecting themselves from bandits. Each village or isolated household was to set up a drum. When a drum was struck warning of attack, all surrounding villages or households were to come to the rescue. All persons who were late or absent were to be reported to the officials by their watch-leader and group and heavily punished.

Wang did not conceal the fact that he was far from happy about the *pao-chia* system. He tried to inject some positive morality into his *pao-chia* regulations. In his philosophy he had urged practice of the established familial and social attitudes as a means of "knowing" them, reducing selfishness, and unifying the individual's humanity with that of others. In his regulations he also urged their practice. He added the duty to cooperate with the state, preserve a livelihood, be considerate of others, avoid rushing into litigation, encourage good and dissuade bad. At the same time as governor he lamented that his government had not yet proved its "good intentions" and dismissed all this exhortation as "mere words." The *pao-chia* system itself appeared, he admitted, like "official harassment." Unfortunately, it was necessary "to preserve peace for the good." But despite its utility, Wang could not avoid associating it with his "inadequacy" and his shame that good government was "not yet in flower."[33]

Without doubt Wang attached much more importance to his revival of the *hsiang-yueh* or rural district pledge system. Its function, in his words, was to bring harmony into rural administration, spread confidence among the people and above all foster the expression of *jen* humanity towards others. Wang urged the people to forget their differences and concentrate on what drew them together. To this end he established the *hsiang-yueh* as a system run by the people themselves, merely laying down its guidelines and providing for a minimum of official intervention.

The *hsiang-yueh* were intended to encompass a wide variety of activities, ranging from moral inculcation to mutual aid and social entertainment. Each was to have a staff of seventeen officers and to keep three registers, one for recording the name and business of each member, the others for recording good and bad actions. Meetings were once a month. Those absent without reason were to be fined one tael of silver by the group (a heavy fine).

The main business of the meetings was to review social conduct. Wang urged the leaders to put their effort into arousing the good side of each person. When faced with error they must try to discuss it indirectly, so as to avoid humiliating and cornering the individual. In case of disputes or vendettas, the leader must resolve them by arbitration. Wang urged people to avoid letting private gain conflict with the public interest. Transients must honor their tax obligations, instead of returning to their native districts at collection time. Rich households and merchants must not seize goods of debtors, acting inhumanely and driving them into robbery. Rural administrative personnel were not to exact fees in the course of official business. If any flouted these obligations, the leader should then report the matter to the officials. However, the whole emphasis is on internal cooperation and control within the group, rather than control from outside.[34]

By these principles Wang hoped to restore to rural society a sense of social responsibility to itself. It is noteworthy that he too believed that it was for the villagers, wherever possible, to manage their public affairs. He mainly tried to supply them with organization and purpose. However, in one important respect his systems differed from his teachings. Where his philosophy left the assessment of moral improvement to the individual alone, his systems provided for group assessment and a public record to back it up. By these means they might give weight to public opinion as well as maintain objective standards.[35]

Once the *pao-chia* and *hsiang-yueh* had been reestablished, other officials began to introduce them in other provinces and districts. In so doing they did not necessarily provide these systems with the same form or even spirit as that incorporated in Wang Yang-ming's. For example, those introduced in Shansi by Lü K'un in the late sixteenth century provided a case of much closer integration of defense and admonition. Their primary function appears to have been the protection of property. Ownership of property was the basis for membership, and wealth an important requirement for leadership. Leadership was not rotational and was to be properly deferred to.

Lü K'un's regulations placed much more emphasis on exposing bad behavior than on inculcating good. Much of this behavior was defined as behavior contrary to the preservation of property. Offenders were to be stigmatized by having large character signs placed outside their doors reading "bandit," "idle bully," "villain," and a number of other opprobrious terms, for offenses such as breaking off heads of grain, idleness, falsely concealing land tax, cheating over property, or loose living. The *hsiang-yueh* itself was to provide group security directors to report on robbery, drill the watchmen, and lead them against attackers. Since the function of the watch-groups was to "protect the wealth of the rich," the rich were warned not to shirk their leadership.

A feature of Lü K'un's system was the conservatism of its administrative thinking. It banded together possession with leadership. It also placed a premium on elite status. "Of old," said Lü K'un, "getting a thousand good people was not like getting one worthy prefect or magistrate."[36] Accordingly, he emphasized official supervision of the control systems. He exempted degree-holders from enrollment in the *hsiang-yueh*. By contrast the ordinary people were treated as potential lawbreakers, to be bound over and placed on probation to keep the peace. This distinction no doubt reflected a growing disparity in wealth and opportunity, and an awareness that this brought about differences in political identification. Certainly this system, compared with Wang Yang-ming's, accepted difference as a political fact and made no point of trying to reduce it. Instead it limited itself to developing an administrative alliance between power-holders and landholders. From this viewpoint, Lü K'un's system, although distinctly partial, appears more in tune with the trend of the times than does Wang Yang-ming's.[37]

Reform of fiscal policy

The most familiar reforms in late Ming local administration are the reforms which took place in fiscal policy. As they have been widely discussed elsewhere, the present account will be limited to a note of their salient points and their effect on the efficiency of local administrative management.[38]

The immediate causes for fiscal reform may be recapitulated as follows. Magistrates were finding it necessary to produce more revenue. The breakdown of the tax-collecting machinery and the flight of the poor from the land were putting pressure on the district office to take over the management of tax collection. Its fiscal registers, however, had become confused and artificial. All that most could show was a steady decline in acreage and labor-service assessment, static or declining income figures, and plentiful evidence of evasion, subterfuge, or impoverishment. The complexity and confusion of the assessment system, the number of different levies, and the numerous and widely varying delivery points, all made the management of tax collection and delivery an unpromising and time-consuming job.

This state of affairs laid the fiscal system wide open to exploitation by local record keepers and tax collectors. In areas substantially affected by these problems, administrators felt a pressing need to simplify the tax system, bring it to bear on the existing distribution of wealth, and enable the magistrate and his assistants to exercise greater personal supervision over its management.

The reform of fiscal policy began in the early sixteenth century and continued through the next two hundred years. The changes were initiated by local administrators and constituted an effort to adjust fiscal policy to local economics conditions. Thus, they varied greatly in detail and in timing from place to place. In the main, the reforms were initiated earlier in the more advanced economic areas of the east and southeast, which bore a greater share of the overall fiscal burden. They are generally referred to as the "Single Whip" reforms, a play on homonyms for "combine" and "scourge," which says much about the popular opinion of Ming fiscal policy.

The reforms were aimed at simplification and unification. Land rates were equalized, land taxes combined, and collection limited to specified periods. Labor-service assessments were equalized and monetized, and conversion rates fixed. The labor-service assessments were gradually apportioned on the basis of land ownership and in consequence amalgamated with the land tax. Rates were chosen which would meet the revenue requirements of sixteenth- and seventeenth-century local administration. Taxes were increasingly collected in silver, and paid directly by the taxpayer to the district office.

Many advantages resulted from these reforms. For the administration, the amalgamation of the labor-service with the land tax cut down the loss of labor-service revenue through the flight of the poor households from the land. The land could not flee. Charging taxation to the land rather than to the household undercut the evasions formerly practiced by wealthy households. The limitation of fiscal assessment to two standardized items, land and adult males, greatly simplified the problems of assessing fiscal obligations and reduced the opportunities for exploiting the former differentials in assessment. Combination of items and collection periods reduced the problems of both collecting and paying. Direct payment to the district office cut off the surcharges taken by rural tax collectors. Payment in silver provided revenue in a form far more convenient for meeting local administrative expenses and for transporting the income required by higher authority.

As for the tax payers, those who lacked land were thereby freed from labor-service payments. Opportunities for oppression by wealthy landowners and collectors were greatly reduced. More efficient assessment brought about a wider more equitable distribution of the tax burden. In effect, the trend toward taxation of land improved fiscal efficiency by placing the tax burden on the unit on production most suited to meeting existing fiscal requirements.

These advantages, all obvious and undeniable, brought considerable short-term relief to existing fiscal conditions. Partly because of this, and because of the air of reform and rationalization prevading the Single Whip movement, commentators have tended to concentrate on the advantages and avoid the less obvious disadvantages of the Single Whip reforms. Nevertheless, the disadvantages, in the long run, far outweighed the advantages of the reforms.

In the first place the reforms greatly increased the work of local administrators. By taking over the management of taxation, they created the need for subadministrations large enough to handle the volume of business involved. Attempts were made to limit the expansion of the Yamen staff by placing quotas on the numbers of clerks, runners, and other underlings and demanding a regular (usually five-year) turnover in personnel. But the increase in business caused by increase in population alone rendered these quotas meaningless. Consequently, the quotas were swelled by the accumulation of informal underlings, brought in to process and profit from the work of the district office.

Moreover, by accepting in principle the demise of rural fiscal administration, the reform also buried the principle of rural judicial administration. That administration, where it was not assumed by private agencies, also fell to the lot of the district office and contributed further to the expansion of the Yamen staff. It was influences such as these which led to the professionalization of the subbureaucracy, both formal and informal, and developed it into a potent force in district administration.

The effects of this administrative impact are already fairly clear. The balance of power in the district office was tipped in favor of the underlings. They were far more numerous, more entrenched, and more informed about the local situation. Yet they emerged as a dangerously disconnected group, cut off from the officials and secretaries by social and educational barriers and from the rural people by their urban life and work. Having set off the expansion of the subadministration, the reform created the problem of how to finance it. There had been no need to finance the *li-chia* personnel. They served on a rotational basis. Nor were the neighborhood elders financed, since they did not need to spend all their time handling litigation.

The district office establishment was, however, a full-time professional staff. Its income could only come from its office activities. The problem of financing was recognized to the extent that salaries were provided for some clerks and runners on the office quota. But these salaries, once established, were fixed and fixed at an extremely low level. In addition, the maintenance of the quota principle in fiscal administration ensured that there would be little outward means either of adjusting salaries to the cost of living or of producing for the increasing numbers of informal underlings.

No administration ever faced up to the problem of financing the subbureauracy. This was partly because of the resistance both from local landowners and local administrators to increasing the level of the overall tax quotas. In addition, there was an evident reluctance to consider financing menial service, more especially that provided by the runners, which had an obligatory origin, and whose performers labored under social and political restrictions. We have seen in chapter 1 that the subbureaucracy supplied itself through the exaction of fees. The tax-paying public had always been vulnerable to the imposition of fees by tax collectors. But the impersonality of centralized fiscal management increased this vulnerability. For the rural populace, particularly those lacking in influence and unaccustomed to seeking any dealings with the district office, the new tax managers were virtual unknowns on whom they could exert little leverage.

Moreover, many taxpayers found it inconvenient to make the trip to the district office and preferred to wait for the office runners sent out to round up payments, even though these runners required fees for this service. Fee-paying thus became an intrinsic feature of tax collection and also of litigation, and came to replace taxation as one of the chief scourges of the countryside. All this was a direct product of the unification of district tax management.[39]

Second, the reforms put greater pressure on the fiscal capability of the magistrate. As long as administrative revenue had been drawn by a variety of collectors from a variety of widely different sources (as was the case when it included grain, several forms of cash crops, currency, and physical labor), a loss of revenue in one category would not necessarily involve a loss in others. The unification of revenue into monetary payment, and its imposition primarily on one unit (land) and one level (the primary cultivator) of production, meant that the administration, more than ever before, was putting its fiscal eggs in one basket.[40]

Once given this unification, then the operations of the various levels of administration became increasingly dependent on the revenue-collecting capability of one group of individuals, the district magistrates. Moreover, these operations were increasing, through the formalization of new levels of provincial administration and the expansion of the local subbureaucracies. It is hardly surprising, therefore, that under the Ch'ing, revenue-collecting capability became one of the key tests of official competence.

It is doubtful if the Single Whip reforms really helped the magistrate to withstand the increase in pressures which it placed upon him. Since the reforms took the form of adjusting local fiscal procedures to local economic conditions, their effect was to bring about a considerable divergence in fiscal patterns, from province to province and even from district to district.

As a result of this, the alien origin of the magistrate came to be a considerable inconvenience. Coming in as an outsider, the magistrate would have to set to and discover how the land in his district was rated and assessed, how the labor service was assessed, on what basis and to what extent the land and labor taxes were combined. He would need to know to what extent the *li-chia* still functioned as a tax-collecting service and to what extent it had been replaced by other tax-collecting systems, what the latter were and how they functioned. He would need to know how far the formal tax revenue balanced district expenses after the transmission of revenue to higher authority. He would have to learn about the nature of local economic conditions to know when and where to press hardest for revenue, and when to ease the pressure. He would need to know about the relevance and equitableness of the assessment information at his disposal, about backlogs in tax payments, and about surcharges and levels of surcharges customarily acceptable in that district. He would have to learn about the degree of fiscal pressure to be expected from higher authority and the degree of cooperation to be expected from his subbureaucracy, as well as from the wealthy citizens of the district, whoever they might be.

In seeking this information, the magistrate could anticipate little cooperation from his clerks, who tended to be somewhat possessive about the fiscal records in their keeping.[41] He could hope to counter this through the employment of secretaries for taxation, more especially if they were well informed about the fiscal conditions of the district concerned. His chief problem, however, was in adjusting himself to the significance placed on fiscal management and learning how to master it in its local setting. Here the question of prior administrative experience and duration in office once again became crucial. Only magistrates who survived the first year or two in office could be confident of gaining the knowledge and experience necessary to counteract the pressures placed on their fiscal capability.

Last, the reforms helped to intensify the fiscal competitiveness already substantial throughout the countryside. The demand for specie meant that taxes could no longer be paid directly from the subsistence economy. Although taxation was assessed on the basis of productivity, that is, at the stage of primary production, the taxpayer was now obliged to *sell* his produce to be able to pay his taxes. Thus his fiscal solvency now depended on his ability to sell, as well as on his ability to produce. This situation obviously favored those more strongly placed to sell their produce, through proximity to the market, extent of land owned, type and quality of crops produced, size of net surplus, or influence within the market system.

The by-products of this fiscal pressure would not necessarily be harmful. It would, for example, encourage migration to remoter areas less accessible to tax assessment. There is plenty of evidence of peasant cultivation of untaxed land during the Ch'ing dynasty.[42]

At the same time, the policy would contribute to the spread of landlordism. The smallholder unfavorably situated toward the market would argue that in case of inadequate income he could scarely hope to reason with the unknown agents of an impersonal bureaucracy, who were themselves under pressure (usually physical) to make him pay. But by converting to tenant status he could normally hope to pass his fiscal obligations to the landlord and enter into a personal and contractual relationship with the agent to whom he owed rent. In case of inadequate income, this would hopefully afford him some leverage in obtaining rebate.[43] It goes without saying that because of the pull of ancestral loyalty, poorer families had strong reasons for preferring not to migrate, even though this weakened their chances of obtaining a fair bargain for their land and ultimately of maintaining their occupancy.[44]

Moreover, the conversion to taxation of land, while reducing the opportunities for tax evasion, increased the advantages of tax evasion. Once the labor-service tax was amalgamated in the land tax, the landowner who evaded the land tax also freed himself from the labor-service tax. The official land figures, being reported in fiscal rather than physical area units, do not directly indicate the overall extent of the evasion practiced. However, the fact that they were fiscal and not physical units indicates, as Ho has pointed out, that evasion could also be practiced by obtaining favorable rates of conversion from physical to fiscal acreage.[45]

The steps thus taken by more powerful landowners to reduce their share of the fiscal burden have been sharply criticized. However, in judging their motivation two factors, apart from the general pressures of fiscal competitiveness, should be taken into account. In the first place local landowners, no matter how powerful, were not formally represented in district administration. If high degree-holders or officeholders elsewhere, they could and did exert influence. But they could not make administrative decisions affecting their own local government. Their tax evasions may have been motivated solely by self-interest. On the other hand there may have been an implicit resentment against surrendering taxes to the management of a stranger appointed from outside, particularly one whose administrative skill and integrity might themselves be questionable. If so, this resentment was disloyal, and given the Confucian emphasis on loyalty, would seldom if ever rise to the surface in educated households. But it was not necessarily without practical foundation.

The attitude of the wealthy landowners can be judged more clearly in the light of the growing disparity in economic wealth and social influence noticeable during the late Ming and Ch'ing. Given the complexity and incompleteness of the early Ming and subsequent land and population surveys, this divergence in landholding can only be indicated in crude orders of magnitude. Official acreage figures for the last decade of the fourteenth century give averages of seventy-five fiscal *mou* per household, or thirteen *mou* per capita, for the whole country. It is virtually certain that any under-registration of the population is more than balanced by the under-registration of land and by the size of the conversion factors between physical and fiscal *mou*. Therefore, the actual average distributions were likely to have been greater than those indicated above. Moreover, Emperor T'ai-tsu's abduction of some 45,000 landowners from the lower Yangtze area affected a control of big landowning that was not to be repeated until recent times.

Subsequent trends in land tenure were, on the one hand, toward estates of several thousand or tens of thousands of *mou*. For the majority, however, they led toward the fragmented and scattered smallholdings of the nineteenth and twentieth centuries, of around five to thirty physical *mou* per family.[46]

The accumulation of a large estate did not necessarily give the right or the power to exert political influence. The accumulation of land along with a high examination degree did. The final establishment of the examination system, therefore, had important influence in consolidating the gulf in means and status between the haves and the have-nots in Ming–Ch'ing society and signaling the "rise" of the scholar-gentry as a distinct social class. The concept is an elusive one, as has also been shown in other cultures. Nevertheless, the presence of a distinctive gentry class or group of classes is a dominant feature of late Ming and Ch'ing society.

In the context of local administration, this class or group of classes was in an anomalous position. It did not wish to mix with the poor and illiterate masses in rural control institutions. This appears to be the case whether or not the landowner himself possessed a high degree. Even Lü K'un's effort to make rural leadership palatable to landowners lacking high degrees does not seem to have borne fruit.[47] On the other hand, the gentry had no other means of access to formal participation in local administration. This left it with little alternative to seeking its own ends. Sometimes these ends coincided with the public interest, as when the gentry engaged in financing construction works. Sometimes they contravened it, as when gentry "assisted" the task of tax collection, lining their own pockets in the process. However, the most conspicuous features of the late Ming and early Ch'ing gentry are the gentry's public apathy and its general disassociation from local administration. Centralization laid the basis for this attitude. Fiscal reform reinforced it.[48]

In the light of hindsight, it seems evident that the failure of the Single Whip movement was a failure to relate fiscal policy to its likely long-term impact on social and economic conditions. Hence its mistakes and misapplications. It sought monetary revenue yet it taxed output at a premonetary level. It sought to increase revenue, yet it failed to provide any economic or administrative incentives. It sought more fiscal equity, but it eventually resulted in more inequity.

This points to the fact that it was a locally initiated, piecemeal reform. Unlike the reforms of Emperor T'ai-tsu it was based on no master plan for society. In the late sixteenth century it was motivated strongly by the personal desire of Emperor Shen-tsung (Wan-li) for large increases in Court income.[49] Its objectives were primarily administrative and methodological, and confined in each instance to limited areas, in many cases to single districts.

Thus there was a surprising lack of interregional coordination of fiscal policy to the Single Whip movement. It was essentially a localized land-based reform. In its original development it showed little coordination with other province-wide or state-wide sources of revenue, and little coordination with other administrative objectives. It is inappropriate to pass judgment on this fiscal shortsightedness, particularly since even now extremely little is known about the ways in which fiscal policy can interact with traditional, or in modern terms underdeveloped, economies and societies. Yet its contribution to the divisiveness in Ch'ing society and local administration can hardly be doubted.[50]

PART III

11

CONFLICTS BETWEEN "PUBLIC" AND "PRIVATE"

By the middle of the seventeenth century, political commentators were fully aware of a deep-seated malaise in state and society. It was recognized before the Manchu invasion that the trouble had to do with the relations between state and society; that elements of the two were at serious odds with each other and were pulling in opposing directions. Then the Ming dynastic regime was overthrown by rebel armies, and subsequently a political order of around 150 million people was placed in subjection by an alien military despotism of a few hundred thousand. This double disaster exposed the weakness of that order and showed how very damaging the conflict between state and society had become.

The issues at stake were framed and thereafter fought out as a conflict of public versus private. To see the significance of this formulation we should briefly review its origins and development.

As found in Ch'ing institutional writings, the distinction between "public" and "private" (*kung* and *ssu*) is a Legalist rather than a Confucian issue. The Confucian position, as stated for example in Mencius' description of the Well Field system, carefully delimits the public and private orders.[1] Under this system the ruler was said to enjoy one-ninth of the arable land, from which his income derived. The possessors of the remaining land must first cultivate the ruler's fields. When that work was completed, they could then attend to their private business.[2] By this system *kung* means what belonged to the ruler, and public and private were demarcated territorially as well as functionally. The private or popular constituted the predominant share.

At this time *kung* also meant "duke" and referred to the ruler of a major domain enfeoffed by the Chou dynasty kings. The Confucian view of *kung* is limited to this feudal sense because its view of "public" was social rather than statist. Its primary concern was with the preservation of people through good government. Allegiance was conditional and was couched in human terms; it was to the individual ruler, not to the state, and certainly not preeminently to dukes. In sum, in the Confucianism of the Four Books *kung* represents the governmental establishment, but cannot be said to mean "public" in the sense of representing the people or body politic a whole.[3] Indeed, apart from Mencius, the difference between *kung* and *ssu* is not a major concern of these works.

On the other hand, the issue is of major significance in the writings of the Legalist school and the authoritarian wing of the Confucian school. These writings postdate the Four Books. In their time the personal loyalties and structural boundaries of the feudal system had long since lost their hold. Yet the surviving states of the late Chou dynasty had by then accumulated a long inheritance of separate institutions and culture, and a growing consciousness that this inheritance had over the years amalgamated to form something politically distinct and different. The further the Chou dynasty progressed, the clearer it became that the overthrow of a state meant not only the replacement of one group of rulers by another but the subversion of its long-established cultural identity. The ruler was the preeminent symbol of that identity, and the concept of *kung* extended to include it. The defense of the one became indistinguishable from the defense of the other.

Legalist writings are predicated on the generalization of the concept of *kung*. Their aim was to spell out the political implications of this condition. In them *kung* represented the common interest and was the concern of all. Legalists, therefore, concentrated on the defense of the common or "public" interest. They demanded unconditional loyalty and the most stringent sanctions against any behavior subordinating "public" to "private." As the ruler could no longer embody the public interest in its full dimensions, allegiance could no longer be secured only in terms of human bonds. Since that allegiance was vital to political strength, law was brought in to secure the public interest. "Private" became synonymous with "illegal" and could no longer coexist with "public."[4]

It was this position which had led the Legalist minister Shang Yang to abolish the Well Field system in the state of Ch'in. This decision had a dual objective. In terms of possession it converted a system of communal ownership of cultivation into a system of private ownership, with the object of harnessing private incentives to the greater service of State policy. In terms of authority it extended the rights of the ruler over the wealth and strength of the entire domain. It abolished the territorial distinction between public and private (i.e., governmental and common) land and recognized the domain only as public. Shang Yang therefore coupled this reform with the establishment of a "prefectural" system of administration, designed to place authority over the people and their land exclusively in the hands of the state government. The subsequent conflict between "public" and "private" ensued from this decisive change in policy.[5]

The Ch'in unification of empire under Legalist principles gave general currency to the preemption of private by public. Moreover, the vast power gathered up by the emperor made it possible to identify the public interest with his interest, instead of the reverse.[6] Confucianism was obliged to come to terms with this distasteful state of affairs. It succeeded in exacting a price, by insisting that the emperor be held personally responsible for the operation of power.[7] It also insisted that even if authority be centralized, its benefits should be dispersed. It did not succeed in restoring legimacy to the concept of private. Nevertheless, down through the generations, leading philosophers and statesmen continued to regret the passing of the Well Field system, and some of them never lost hope that it might some day be brought back to life, and with it a reduction in centralized state expropriation of authority. This continuing commitment was due not simply to a nostalgia for the past, but to the deep-seated Confucian concern over the welfare of the people. Confucian writers saw that free-market ownership of land led almost invariably to the oppression of the weak by the strong, and that a centralized and exclusive public administration appeared unable or unwilling to contain this trend.[8]

A partial Confucian revival was achieved with the general establishment, under the Sui and T'ang dynasties, of the Equal Field system. Under this system land was owned in common. Each cultivator was entitled to receive a hundred *mou*, just as had been thought the case under the Well Field system. Equally, he was to be secure in his possession of land for his lifetime. After his death it was to be redistributed. However, the system was not genuinely Confucian, since land was owned and distributed on the authority of the centralized state, and not on that of local communal groups. In the event, the machinery required for the management of land distribution proved too complex for the resources of centralized administration. Private ownership was restored and became henceforth the prevailing mode of tenure. In the late T'ang dynasty it was also accompanied by a sweeping encroachment on public authority by private sources of power. Since the central government remained politically responsible for public welfare, the recentralization of power became the ultimate consequence of the breakdown of the Equal Field system.

During the Sung, Yuan, and early Ming, the battle lines were drawn up between public and private, which were to provide the extended confrontation apparent in the late Ming and early Ch'ing. As the previous chapters have indicated, the state moved to clamp down on the private domain by further centralizing authority. Meanwhile, the private domain began to develop an institutional formation through the emergence principally of the lineage system. In the Sung, the encroachment of public on private remained limited, and efforts to increase it were staunchly curtailed. Nevertheless, there is an awareness, even in the writings of Chang Tsai, that the Confucian position had been long since subverted.[9] The distinction between the two domains was increased during the Yuan by the association of the public with a regime of barbarians with whom the literati found it very difficult to cooperate.

The centralizing policies of the native Ming dynasty served only to sharpen the growing confrontation. Through the *li-chia* system emperor T'ai-tsu himself attempted to reduce the dichotomy between public and private by including the people in public administration. In this major effort the public (in the sense of communal) interest was eventually defeated by the private. The state also attempted to consolidate its control of administration by centralizing official appointments and narrowing down the locus of public responsibility. Private influence reappeared through the emergence of private administration aides and through the growth in influence of the clerks and runners, only a small portion of whom were on the public quota. Thus in this area also the state suffered a pronounced setback.

However, the state also extended its control over administration by consolidating the examination system as the gateway to appointment. Here the public (in the sense of state) interest proved far more successful. Except through the purchasable statuses of senior licentiate and Imperial Academy student (*kung-sheng* and *chien-sheng*), private influence was largely eliminated. Moreover, the influence of private wealth was minimized by limiting the access of those with purchased statuses to inconsequential offices.[10]

In estimating the relative composition and strength in the late Ming of public versus private, it is necessary to distinguish between central and local administration. The central administration had gained greatly in the control of officialdom and had not lost nearly so evidently in the fiscal struggle. It retained the right to general taxation and was exacting what it needed in revenue.

The real loss was suffered by local administration. It was milked of its revenue by the central authorities and deprived of adequate income by powerful private interests. Its expedient of squeezing the poor or powerless was subject to diminishing returns and, moreover, was contrary to the feelings of any administrator susceptible to the Confucian position.

That is why the Single Whip reform was a locally based reform. It was an effort by local administrators to give vent to a Confucian policy within an increasingly Legalist institutional situation. But by placing public taxation on land in general, it preserved the Legalist principle of central authority over the product of the entire domain. Thus, it resulted in bringing local administration directly into conflict with the more powerful private elements in rural society, at a time when these elements were beginning to feel the full effects of the exclusiveness of the public examination system.

By the end of the Ming dynasty, the magistrate consequently found himself at the center of the tangled conflict between public and private. As an official he had been accepted into the now exclusive public sphere and appointed its chief representative in the private domain. His duty to collect the state's taxes, suppress private disturbance of public order, and prevent private incursion into public administration made him the frontline protagonist of the public cause. As if that were not enough, his distant provenance heightened his "public" image and increased the division between the official and the local people.

At the same time he was, both as an individual and as an official, illprepared to represent the official cause. His low rank limited his share of public authority. He was usually distant in location as well as rank from the center of public authority. The increase in superior regional offices increased that distance. It enlarged the weight of public vigilance on the office of magistrate, as if in admission that the public loyalty of its incumbents was suspect.

This position was justifiable, for despite the Legalist function of his office, the magistrate, nevertheless, remained Confucian in training. His education consciously influenced him to want to balance the welfare of the people against support of the state interest. Moreover, the magistrate was himself a private individual, with a household and an ancestral line to support. In the eyes of his private circle, his appointment actually enhanced his commitment to the private domain.[11] Thus, the conflict between public and private involved the late Ming magistrate both on the personal and on the official level.

After the downfall of the Ming dynasty, this personal and political dilemma was openly debated, in particular by the noted commentator Ku Yen-wu. Ku, who traveled extensively through China, gave particular attention to the troubles of local administration. He attributed them to the loss of authority by prefects and magistrates. He agreed that under the imperial system the emperor, as Son of Heaven, held the authority. But he interpreted "holding authority" as meaning that the Son of Heaven entrusted it to men, although it reverted to him. In this way all officials high and low shared this authority and were thereby able to order their affairs. As a result authority was extended out across the people and more greatly honored. But since the Chou dynasty, emperors had no longer "entrusted" authority. They had kept it all at the top. Since one man could not attend to everything himself, authority had shifted to the law, and laws had proliferated to uphold and protect it. These had deprived officials of initiative and put it in the hands of underlings (clerks) in a position to become familiar with and manipulate the laws. Authority had in fact been usurped by underlings and was no longer honored by the people.

As a result of these conditions, local administration had been deflected from supporting society to managing bureaucracy. Administrative financing had been geared only to central government needs. The prefects and magistrates, for whom it was urgent to be close to the people, had no authority with which to give effect to that closeness. The people no longer knew who were their real masters.

Ku had various recommendations for dealing with these conditions. He wanted to reduce all the official rules and investigations and make length of service the test of official advancement. He would have abolished the senior provincial officials and raised the rank of magistrate from seven to five. He would have chosen as magistrates men from *within* the same province as the district to which they were appointed. Once appointed they would have their residence and affiliations moved to the district under their management. Ku would then have the appointment made permanent and hereditary, barring serious disgrace. Official advancement would then be in grade rather than office. He would allow the central government to appoint assistant magistrates but empower the magistrate to appoint his other assistants, as had been the case during the Han dynasty. Once the magistrate had been chosen Ku urged that the government should trust him and not try to divide up and check his authority. Let him get on with his real job of making people equal to and content with their lot.

Ku's proposals involved a substantial transmission of authority back to private keeping, and he did not hesitate to say so. He claimed that there would always be private interest and that it would always command the strongest loyalties. "The people of the Empire," he said, "all cherish their families and all give private [consideration] to their sons. These are their constant feelings. The mind will never be as much for the Son of Heaven or the people as it is for itself. . . . The sages recognized and made use of this, employing the private [order] of the Empire to accomplish the public [order] of the One Man; and the Empire was kept in a state of order."

Ku's recommendations aimed at reconciling public and private interests, instead of building barriers between them. He claimed that if the magistrate was given a permanent stake in his district, then he would really identify with it and treat its people as his children. He would labor to defend their interests and preserve stability. To give substance to this localization of initiative, Ku stressed the need to cut down the profusion of administrative documentation, reducing the considerable expense which this entailed and giving the magistrate more time to attend to agricultural production. He urged decentralization of fiscal administration, to make sure that local administration was adequately financed. He also urged the rationalization of delivery of surplus funds to higher administration. He concluded that only by giving local officials this measure of authority would the people know that the officials and not the clerks were the real masters.[12]

Ku's ideas, like those of his contemporary, Huang Tsung-hsi, represent an attempt to find a Confucian resolution of the antagonism which had developed between society and state. The fact that this internal struggle had debilitated the country and made it vulnerable to outside aggression proved to them that each side was too strong to be submerged by the other. Greater internal autonomy appeared the only solution. This suggestion had been proposed without effect by earlier Confucianists; the collapse of Ming authority appeared to confirm the error of overcentralization and vindicate the Confucian position.

In their readoption of feudal administrative forms, the Confucian proposals appear retrogressive. This is principally because no institutional models genuinely reflecting Confucian political values had existed since the Chou dynasty. The Chou dynasty still provided the only tangible indications of how a Confucian state would be run. It is not impossible that had these ideas taken effect, other ways might have developed of expressing the meaning of public and private along less exclusive lines, which would have appeared more in keeping with the fluid society and economy of mid-seventeenth-century China.

The weakness of Ku's position is, however, that it did not question the basic location of authority. The Son of Heaven continued to be accepted as the ultimate source of authority and responsibility. This being the case, there is no adequate explanation why the Son of Heaven should not continue to demand rights over all resources available for supporting that authority. This position was not lost on the Manchus, who as foreign conquerors had every reason to demand the means to protect their hard-won authority. Their victory revived the power of the state over the domain, and so renewed the struggle between public and private. As a result, local administration continued to be caught in the middle of this conflict.

12

CONTROL OF LOCAL ADMINISTRATIVE AUTHORITY

The principal object of Ch'ing imperial policy before 1850 was to assert central authority over the state and society. There is a substantial increase of central control over regional and local administration. Emperors scrutinize administrative problems and performance, poring over documents and inspecting conditions and administrators with their own eyes. There is a great deal of administrative legislation designed to force administrative performance into line with imperial interests, and a constant outflow of edicts aimed at bringing further pressure on administration and society to cooperate with imperial policies.

At the same time, the Ch'ing emperors were sensitive to the influence of Confucian values and to the relative strength of existing social and institutional forces. They attempted to gild their essentially Legalist policies with a Confucian image. They maintained administrative and ritual institutions acceptable to the Confucian Way. They upheld the Chu Hsi interpretation of Neo-Confucian philosophy and widely supported scholastic research.

A particular feature of Ch'ing dynastic policy is the effort to distribute the benefits of authority. The government quickly cut back state taxation to the level at which it had stood before the extra levies of the Wan-li era, and frequently remitted taxes for entire provinces and regions thereafter. With the exception of the Ch'ien-lung emperor, the emperors themselves were personally abstemious. They gave close attention to penal administration and frequently issued amnesties or reduced or remitted individual penal or administrative sentences. As a further concession to

Confucian susceptibilities, they accorded privileged treatment to degree-holders and their families in the enforcement of law and security. But although they were generous with the benefits of authority, they were against any dispersion of authority itself. From the viewpoint of local administration it was this restriction of authority which counted upper-most.

The impact of the disciplinary system

The Ch'ing emperors moved from the outset to bring local administration into line with imperial objectives. They accepted the Legalist position that this could not be done simply through the influence of one man. They consequently spun out an ever-expanding network of regulations, checks, and counterchecks, all aimed at defining and imposing the will of public authority.

The Disciplinary Regulations constituted the warp of this policy.[1] They defined in unsparing detail the distinction between public and private in every aspect of administrative conduct. Each offense was characterized according to whether it was a public or private offense. "Public" was defined as an offense committed in the course of either public or private affairs which was not done with intent, that is, not with intent to harm the public interest. Neglect by an official to investigate the carryings on of his family retainers was offered as a typical example of a public offense arising from the pursuance of private affairs. "Private," by contrast, involved deliberate intent. Screening a subordinate official was given as the most typical form of the intrusion of private in public administration. Thus public and private offenses were differentiated in both public and private affairs.[2]

Great weight was attached to understanding the administrative significance of this distinction. Nineteenth-century compilations of these Regulations open with two edicts on this matter from the Chia-ch'ing emperor. In them he noted that the public offenses were manifold and complex. They could not help but trip up some genuinely worthy officials. Unworthy officials, however, would be skillful in evading them. High provincial officials must take this into account in judging the records of local officials. The emperor specifically ordered that public offenses should not be taken into account in assessing local officials for promotion to important posts.

These edicts are followed by all the regulations indicating the different effect of public and private offenses on the punishment as well as the cumulative record and general prospects of an official.[3]

A special chapter was devoted to offenses involved in using administrative appointments for private ends. These included such offenses as offering presents to bribe or to "please" another official,[4] or paying friendly calls on metropolitan officials at the time of receiving provincial appointments.[5] Here the point was to insist that provincial officials contact metropolitan officials only through administrative channels. Provincial officials were also not allowed to send personal representatives to the capital after arrival at their posts. Offenders were to be dismissed. Metropolitan officials receiving such visits were to be dismissed. Newly appointed officials were also not permitted to receive friendly visits from examination graduates (gentry) or their representatives belonging to the locality in which the appointment was situated. Gentry were also forbidden to send representatives to prepare receptions for the official. After his arrival they were forbidden to present themselves as his "students" or propose "clan affiliations." (This refers to the practice of joining together lineages having the same surname but different ancestors. In the social sphere these practices had wide currency.) New officials accepting such contact were to be dismissed.[6]

Officials were also ordered to keep strict watch over their relatives, friends, family retainers, and personal aides. As of 1686 all provincial officials were allowed to bring to their posts only a certain number of family retainers, over and above certain immediate relations (brothers, wife, and children). For example, governors-general and governors were allowed fifty family retainers; magistrates were allowed twenty.[7] Any official who allowed his sons, brothers, relatives, or friends to [abuse their authority] in his office or to indulge in any deception was to be dismissed. If he failed to investigate their behavior, he was to be demoted one grade and transferred (a public offense). Similar regulations existed for covering the behavior of family retainers and personal servants.[8]

Finally, we may note a few regulations under this head dealing with the appointment of private secretaries. These functionaries, as Ch'ü has shown, could exert considerable influence on local officials through their professional experience and their influence in the conduct of official correspondence.[9] The recommendation of private secretaries was thus a convenient method by which provincial officials or secretaries could introduce private agents into local administration, keep a watch on what was going on there, and exercise pressure whenever convenient. To counter this it was regulated that if senior officials insisted on recommending secretaries or servants, or allowed their own secretaries or relatives to do this, the subordinate official was permitted to present a report of the facts, and the senior was to be dismissed. If the subordinate bowed to the pressure, employed those recommended, and did not report the facts, he was himself to be dismissed.[10]

The Disciplinary Regulations for civil officials were issued by the Board of Officials. Other copies were then reprinted by the provincial authorities. It is worth comparing the different format of the Board and provincial editions, as it helps to show the seriousness with which the Regulations were taken in the provinces.

The provincial editions were much smaller and handier in size. Where the print of the Board editions was somewhat ornate, that of the provincial editions was workmanlike and unpretentious. The provincial editions, unlike the Board editions, used different-size print for the characters specifying whether an offense was public or private. On this vital matter the reader could see at once what was involved, and where he stood. The provincial editions, while grouping together the clauses under each section, used a different page to introduce each section and a different stitched volume for each chapter heading, whereas the Board editions tended to run these together.

Finally, the provincial editions indicated in the margin both the chapter and section heading, whereas the Board editions indicated only the chapter heading.[11] Thus, the official using a provincial edition could very quickly find the chapter heading he needed, pick up a handy small-size volume, run through the table of contents and marginal annotations, and in no time find the relevant clauses. These clearly distinguished the offense, the specific punishment for each rank of official, and the public or private connotation on which his subsequent career might hinge.

In addition, separate chapters or sections were sometimes published separately in works dealing with specific aspects of administration. For example, the *Pao-chia shu* (writings on the *pao-chia* system) of Hsü Tung opens with a chapter giving the regulations applying to the administration of this system.

The Disciplinary Regulations are vivid proof that the Ch'ing emperors recognized the dimensions of the conflict between public and private and were determined to bring their officials into line on this issue. No official after reading them could be in any doubt as to where the lines were drawn, or on which side his duty lay. The emperors also saw that the conflict centered on local administration. They aimed the regulations largely at this level of administration and invariably made the punishments of magistrates heavier than those of their superiors. The regulations show that the emperors held the Legalist interpretation of public interest and were able to make this view the basis of their administrative enactment. This constituted part of the dilemma facing local administrators: that behind every edict and essay urging them to be Confucianist lay a regulation warning them to be Legalist.[12]

The Ch'ing emperors utilized a number of different techniques for enforcing these regulations on local administration. In the first place, special regulations required that magistrates inform their superiors of the state of their fiscal, judicial, and security administration and of new developments in these sectors. The regulations imposed time limits on the delivery of this information; they also required superiors to keep informed on such matters.[13] For general surveillance of administrative performance, the Ch'ing regimes carried out triennially the examination of character (*ta-chi*) and administrative capability (*k'ao-man*) employed by the Ming. They enforced the annual examination of administrative accomplishment (*k'ao-ch'eng*) which had been practiced by the Sung. In addition, they made considerable use of the Imperial Audience (*yin-chien*).[14]

This looks like a formidable system of surveillance. Nevertheless, while it testifies to the importance attached by the Ch'ing to surveillance, it took the emperors many years to arrive at an arrangement capable of protecting their interest, without also bringing administrative initiative to a standstill.

In the triennial examinations they began by adopting both the *ta-chi* and *k'ao-man* categories. The former examination followed the Ming categories. The latter included four categories (integrity, ability, quality of government, and age), judged according to the Ming division into three levels of competence.[15] In 1662, the first year of the K'ang-hsi reign, the *ta-chi*, a virtual impeachment of character, was abolished, leaving only the *k'ao-man*, a much more neutral assessment. It was, however, stipulated that the *k'ao-man*, on which promotion or demotion depended, would only be carried out provided that the local official had fully collected his tax quotas. Three years later the *k'ao-man* was abolished and the *ta-chi* reinstated.

In 1670 this harder line was reinforced by a regulation punishing high provincial officials who recommended as "outstanding and distinctive" any subordinate who had not yet completed his tax quotas or cleared his robbery cases. This apparently gave too Legalist a connotation to "outstanding and distinctive." Consequently, three years later it was agreed that an official could only be recommended as "outstanding and distinctive" if he had both cleared his tax records and robbery cases and also disseminated education through his jurisdiction. It is worth noting that this concession to Confucian principles did not involve any surrender of Legalist priorities.

In the later years of the K'ang-hsi reign, certain other stipulations were added to these differing criteria of "outstanding and distinctive." It is, therefore, not surprising to find the Yung-cheng emperor noting in an edict of 1723 (the first year of his reign) that under the *ta-chi* only a small number of officials were being either characterized as outstanding or impeached under the "eight methods" (*pa fa*) for judging personal failure. Consequently, the *k'ao-man* was reintroduced as a means of evaluating the majority who were being neither recommended nor impeached.[16]

The Ch'ing emperors also paid a good deal of attention to the review of administrative accomplishment, using for this purpose the annual *k'ao-ch'eng* procedure of the Sung dynasty. In the Sung this review had been used as a general guide to promotion or demotion.[17] It was apparently not employed in the early Ming, because its criteria were not suited to Emperor T'ai-tsu's judgment of the performance required of local administrators. In the late Ming, the breakdown of the *li-chia* system made it necessary for local officials to play a much more active part in the conduct of local administrative affairs.

This led to the reintroduction of the Sung criteria for accomplishment into the existing *k'ao-man* evaluation of capability. In the early sixteenth century, the Board of Revenue ordered that in case of a *k'ao-man* assessment of local officials for change of appointment, the local official must report that he had collected the full amount of taxes required during his term of service. Only then was he permitted to hand over office to his successor.[18] As we have seen, the principle of reviewing the local official's fiscal and security record was also incorporated into the *k'ao-man* or modified *ta-chi* reviews of the early Ch'ing.

In consequence, the Ch'ing emperors used the annual *k'ao-ch'eng* review principally to bring pressure on local officials to get through their administrative business. The review concentrated on two aspects—tax collection and the arrest of robbers. The review of tax collection was under the management of the Board of Revenue. The *k'ao-ch'eng* regulations stipulated the procedure and time limits for the completion by the districts of the annual collection and forwarding of taxes, the auditing of the fiscal accounts, and the review of the accounts at the prefectural and provincial levels before their submission to the Board. Under these regulations, rewards and penalties were laid down according to the degree of success or failure in fulfilling the annual quota. Between the Shun-chih and Yung-cheng periods, imperial policy shifted toward reducing the rewards and increasing the penalties. This reflected the increase in the confidence of the regime as it extended its sway over Chinese society, and its preference for demanding, rather than cajoling, its rights over the general wealth. In the late eighteenth and early nineteenth centuries, when the tide was running against the State, the regime was obliged to increase the fiscal rewards considerably.[19]

The review of robbery cases was under different management. The exact procedure has yet to be established. The *Collected Institutes* of the K'ang-hsi period notes that the state established methods (*fa*) for the arrest of robbers, and that its regulations on this matter were very strict. Both civil and military officials were subject to the *k'ao-ch'eng* review procedure. If there was any necessity for disciplinary action, the offense was deliberated and the punishment determined by the Board of War and carried into effect by the Board of Officials. The Yung-cheng edition, under the same heading, says much the same, except that it specifically limits its allusions to disciplinary action to that required against military officials. Both accounts come under the heading "Arrest of Robbers" in the Institutes applicable to the Board of War.[20] There appears to be no further discussion under this heading of the procedure for the annual review of robbery cases, and no discussion under other relevant headings has yet been located.

From the regulations which do ensue it is clear that the terms laid down closely resemble those for the fiscal review. A regulation of 1663 required local officials "in accordance with regulations for the completion of tax collection," to close all outstanding cases requiring the arrest of bandits (or robbers), before they could be considered for promotion or transfer.[21] Subsequent regulations laid down time limits given to civil officials for the arrest of robbers and indicated the rewards and penalties applicable to various levels of success or failure. In this case both the rewards and the penalties were higher in the earliest years of the regime, when suppression of banditry was still a major necessity for dynastic policy.[22]

Of the three reviews discussed above, the *k'ao-ch'eng* led the way in the imposition of state authority on local administration. It took place three times as often. More to the point, it was much more tangibly connected with the dynastic effort to assert the right of the state to take from the general wealth, and to suppress private raids on property and disturbance of public order. Once again the pressure of this review was aimed primarily at district officials. The Ch'ing regime accepted the decline of the *li-chia* as an instrument of public policy. They knew that it still existed in one form or another in many parts of the country, but they were unconcerned to bring it under their direct control.[23] Instead, they followed the late Ming trend and put their fiscal pressure directly on the local magistrate. In public security they made, as we shall see, a much greater effort to exert control over the rural countryside; their pressure on the magistrate in this aspect of administration was part of their general anxiety to preserve peace and order.

In fact the main significance of the Ch'ing *k'ao-ch'eng* review is that it did deal only with the protection of the public interest. Unlike the *ta-chi* or *k'ao-man* reviews, or the *k'ao-ch'eng* of the Sung dynasty, it was unconcerned with matters of importance to Confucian teaching. Moreover, it was able to bear more heavily on local administration because its criteria were tangible. Although its sanctions were not particularly harsh or immediate, they were the more effective for being the less avoidable.

What effect did the Ch'ing disciplinary system have on local administrative performance? Much has been made of the Ch'ing official's ability to respect the letter while defying the spirit of Ch'ing legislation. There is no doubt that despite the thoroughness and severity of the laws and regulations, private considerations did exercise a powerful influence over conduct in Ch'ing public administration. Nevertheless, the evidence tends to show that in its curtailment of administrative initiative and prospects, the disciplinary system was regarded on all sides as too severe and too effective rather than the opposite.

The steady penalization of the magistrates of Wu-hsien and Ch'ang-chou districts (see chapter 4) provides a good case in point. These two districts belonged to the rice-rich prefecture of Su-chou (or Soochow). Su-chou, Sung-chiang, and certain other prefectures in southern Kiangsu were noted for having the highest rates of taxation in the country. In the early K'ang-hsi period several high provincial officials pointed out that district magistrates of these prefectures never obtained a full collection in any year. Under the existing *k'ao-ch'eng* regulations, they were all impeached and none could hold their posts for more than one or two years. The officials could not believe that the law (*fa*) of the Ch'ing court was only severe toward these prefectures or that the magistrates employed in them were entirely men of mediocre talent. It transpired that the high rates of taxation had been imposed by Emperor Ming T'ai-tsu as a punishment on these areas for resisting his bid for power. There had been some reductions since his day, but in the late Ming and early Ch'ing the rates still remained exceptionally high.[24]

The monetization of a substantial proportion of the tax levy had not alleviated the situation at all. The governor of Kiangsu noted in a memorial of 1665 that the rate of conversion for high grade rice (*pai-mi*) had been set in 1655 at two taels per bushel (*shih*). The current market rate in Wu-hsien for this grade of rice was not over eight- or nine-tenths of a tael. Consequently, monetization of the tax was forcing the people to pay out the equivalent of two bushels for every bushel originally levied.[25] He and other officials also pointed out that the area was vulnerable to floods, drought, and piracy. In good years the grain was cheap, in bad years scarce. This was why officials still defaulted on their quotas, even though pressing the collection without cease.[26]

The Ch'ing emperors responded characteristically to this problem by issuing frequent remissions for the area. In the eighteenth century, some of the districts concerned were divided, which had the effect of halving the fiscal and other administrative responsibilities of their magistrates.[27] In the late eighteenth and early nineteenth centuries, apparently the district tax quotas themselves were very slightly reduced.[28] This might appear to explain the declining trend in impeachments noted in Table 17. But this does not take into account all the other matters on which an official could be impeached. In the seasonal registers of officials it was especially noted of Wu-hsien that besides being a very important district (which already indicated that it had many overdue taxes), its taxes were heavy, its litigation troublesome, and its official delegations incessant. The possibilities for impeachment in these conditions still remained prolific.

The *k'ao-ch'eng* regulations for the suppression of robbery also began soon enough to take their toll on local administrators. In 1681 Yü

Ch'eng-lung, the highly respected governor-general of Chihli province, sent in a memorial stating that many of his subordinate officials had had their careers held back because of acts of robbery committed by unemployed bannermen. He requested an extension of the deadline for the arrest of robbers, saying that the officials had been long without promotion, and that this was to be pitied.

The K'ang-hsi emperor had recently returned from a tour of the province. He noticed that the more populous areas were vulnerable to robbery and admitted that the disciplinary regulations were "too severe" and were making trouble for both the officials and the people. He ordered his ministers to debate the matter. Subsequently, a censor suggested that the arrest of robbers be made the responsibility of military officials. The emperor opposed this on Confucian grounds, saying that the suppression of robbery was inseparable from the provision of prosperity and contentment. He added that if the responsibility for arresting lawbreakers was divided from that for trying and sentencing them, the culprits would be able to claim that they were worthy people who had been arrested under false pretenses. This implied that the civil official would not have the authority to question the military official directly on this point. It also pointed to the fact that the arrest was considered the crucial step in determining guilt. Therefore, it should be in the hands of those responsible for managing civil order.[29]

The K'ang-hsi emperor was right in noting that the *k'ao-ch'eng* affected the people as well as the officials. The Kiangsu authorities had spoken colorfully of the effect of the tax deadlines on the pressures exerted by local officials and their agents. "Rich became poor and poor fled." "Pressing and shouting went on every day." By the end, "nothing was left of the fat and blood of the small people."

High metropolitan officials also pointed out the social effects of the regulations for the arrest of robbers. Cases of robbery would be misreported as other crimes, such as petty larceny or vendettas, which did not involve deadlines, and which enabled the official to look for different and more accessible culprits (if he chose to take action at all). A recent case was cited of a magistrate who, when notified of a robbery, reacted by questioning the deprived owner under torture and putting the screws on his young daughter. Under the shock of this humiliation the grandfather committed suicide.

In an attempt to explain this behavior, the president of the Board of

Punishments noted that the human attitude toward the disciplinary regulations was always to avoid the heavy and settle for the light. Why, in the case of regulations for the arrest of robbers, should officials do exactly the reverse? After "deep reflection" he concluded that it was the only possible reaction. He pointed out that the regulations required magistrates to arrest all robbers involved in each reported case. If they missed only one, they would still have their salary and promotion stopped, and if they failed to catch him they would eventually be demoted and transferred. But, he argued, it was virtually impossible to achieve complete success in arresting robbers. Robbers came together from different districts, planned and committed their crimes, and then scattered in all four directions. Some would subsequently be killed or die. Dead robbers could not be brought back to life, much less arrested. The robbery regulations could not be met and, therefore, the magistrates took action which could be squared with other regulations, even if it involved them in duplicity and oppression.[30]

Despite such commentaries, the Ch'ing emperors were not disposed to reduce the regulations as such. The Yung-cheng emperor, while admitting that the robbery regulations were very hard to fulfill, said that if they were made too generous then district officials would not put their heart into the arrest of robbers. Policemen runners (who performed the arrest) would trifle with the law and nourish lawbreakers, and robbery would become more prevalent.[31]

Instead, the emperors preferred to provide other regulations ameliorating the professional consequences of public offenses. In 1662 the K'ang-hsi emperor ruled that all officials with four recordings of merit (*chi-lu*)—the equivalent of one advancement in grade (*chia i chi*)—could redeem one demotion in grade with only two recordings of merit. Similar allowances were made for the commutation of fines. The following year the emperor ruled that officials who got into trouble because of public offenses, or those who were demoted or dismissed because of failure to complete their tax quotas, would be entitled, after restoration to office, to recover all recordings of merit and advancements in grade earned during their previous term of service.[32]

The emperors also endeavored to restore the morale of downgraded officials by means of personal interviews. Audiences were a means of looking over newly appointed officials and honoring exceptional performance. Their application to the demoted and dismissed appears to have

been started by the Yung-cheng emperor. In 1726 he ordered that all
officials impeached under the triennial *ta-chi* review should, unless they
had been stigmatized as avaricious and cruel, be sent up to the Board of
Officials for an Imperial Audience as soon as their transfer of office had
been cleared.[33] He also stressed that this regulation was to be honored
permanently.

In 1729 the emperor extended the use of the Audience to officials
impeached under the Disciplinary Regulations in the normal course of
events. He reasoned that officials dismissed because of public offenses
were still serviceable to the state. Because of the regulations their dismissal
was unavoidable; but he did not want them to give up hope for the rest
of their lives. He ordered that they also be sent up for Audiences so that
he could show his "love for human talent" and his "sympathy with the
feelings of subordinates."

The emperor noted with some frankness that there were usually many
cases of impeachment and dismissal of provincial officials, and that often
these officials had been dismissed on previous occasions. He ordered the
Board to check into any earlier cases of dismissal, stating that he would
not interview officials who had been previously dismissed for private
offenses, or those whose subsequent dismissal was comparable to their
former dismissal. If the circumstances of the later case differed and were
still public in nature, then the official was to be interviewed. In keeping
with his well-known distrust, the emperor ordered the Board to send up
a check list of the complete record of the officials in question. Shortly
thereafter this procedure was also applied to officials penalized with
demotion and transfer.[34]

This use of the Audience was undoubtedly a shrewd move to retain the
loyalties of public-minded officials. It reinforced the imperial proscription
of private influence, but condescension toward public error. On the other
hand, the Ch'ing reluctance to dilute the base of public authority itself
created its own problems. Two of these were the tendency among local
administrators to do only what they thought their superiors expected of
them, or to refuse to have anything to do with matters outside their own
immediate jurisdictions. In the early nineteenth century (and very likely
well before then) these problems were clearly visible and were being openly
debated.

Shortly after the suppression of the White Lotus rebellion, a censor
returning from a tour of the countryside wrote: "The trouble with today's

prefects and magistrates is in knowing there are superiors and not knowing there are the people." He made this judgment in the course of an attempt to diagnose conditions for restoring social equilibrium. The censor Ku Yun-sheng, like others before him, settled on "nourishing the people" as the "urgent business," and saw that those placed to do this were the prefects and magistrates. He described their craving for superior approval as taking the following forms. First, when submitting judicial sentences, they considered only the likely reaction of their superiors and not the feelings of the people. Second, when handling official delegations they deferred only to the desires of their superiors and took no account of the people's strength. These attitudes paid off because they could then earn the ratings of "practiced and accomplished," or "diligent and capable." Thus it could happen, said Ku, that mediocre officials were sent up to the capital as "outstanding" at the very time when delegations were arriving to appeal against their harassment.

Ku went on to refer to the ways in which superiors took advantage of these attitudes. Despite all the regulations to the contrary, local officials were being forced to accept secretaries and servants recommended by senior officials—even though these appointments used up all their salaries—for fear of otherwise being framed for punishment. When these nominees committed any offenses the local officials found they could not "aim at the rat without fearing for the vase." Ku also accused provincial officials of exploiting the official transportation facilities far beyond their actual needs, leaving local officials actually no option but to extract the required animals and conveyances from the local populace. He described this as a burden on both farmers and traders. He urged that if the business legitimately needed extra facilities, these should be hired and any losses compensated.[35]

Ku's memorial is noteworthy for its effort to get at the factors causing local administrative misconduct. Like many other contemporary critics, he saw the faults of local administrators. But unlike unemployed scholars such as Hung Liang-chi, who tended to condemn local malpractices without analyzing their causes, Ku reported genuine difficulties. Thus, his basic advice was not to be more severe with local officials but instead to "show magnanimity in the examination of officials." On the other hand, Ku's analysis was not calculated to win high favor and did not, in its turn, come to terms with conditions affecting administration at the provincial level. The Chia-ch'ing emperor evidently did not know how to handle it. He merely took the line that "we should permanently prohibit" any abuses of the regulations.[36]

The reluctance among local administrators to show concern for the problems of neighboring districts seems to have been fairly common and to have enjoyed the support of local opinion. For example, it was considered an achievement for a magistrate to succeed in driving groups of troublesome beggars and vagrants out of his district. The fact that this merely drove them into some other district was not a matter for local concern.[37] Magistrates also appear to have been slow to arrest criminals escaped from other districts, despite regulations requiring them to do so if notified of the presence of fugitives from justice.

In the early nineteenth century, the rationale behind this indifference was vigorously defended by Chou Hao, a magistrate of Yin (Ningpo) district in eastern Chekiang. In 1807 there was a serious drought and food shortage in the adjacent districts. Yin alone had a good harvest. When outside traders came in to buy grain in Yin, Chou issued an order banning sales to outsiders, and promising penalties for all offenders. The traders appealed to the provincial authorities, who severely reprimanded Chou.

Chou did not accept this rebuke. He was already fifty-three years old and had ten years as an efficient and respected magistrate behind him. He rejoined, "A governor takes the whole province as his family. An intendant takes three prefectures as his family. A prefect takes six districts as his family. A magistrate takes one district only as his family. If the people of that one family are anxious about lack of provisions, how can I give priority to their neighbors?" He then pointed out that the traders could buy at the market town for distributing Su-chou rice, which was nearer to them than Ningpo was. If they bought in Yin they would raise the local prices and in effect take away the food from the mouths of his people. The price of rice in Yin had been very expensive that spring, and there were thousands of poor people. After saying this, Chou issued a second order explaining the reasons for his ban and ordering the poor to cooperate in obstructing outside "troublemakers" and the rich, in return, to cooperate in maintaining the needy. The editors of the Yin gazetteer commented with evident approval that there was a great deal of disturbance that year in neighboring districts. Yin alone was without trouble!

Having taken this stand Chou Hao drew up a long indictment of the treatment of district magistrates by their superiors. He said that district magistrates should be appointed and promoted on the basis of talent and not on order of arrival in the province or length of service. Unless men were matched with posts the talented would lose interest and the untalented get into trouble. On this point Chou protected his provincial superiors and blamed the central government for its inflexible regulations. He dismissed the argument that without such regulations governors-general and governors might indulge in private interests, saying, "this ignores the fact that these officials are court appointed and relied on as pillars of state. How can they still question their public [spirit] or quality of government?" Chou pressed this further, saying either the governors were public minded or they were as corrupt as they chose to be, in which case they should not be looked on as pillars of state.

Chou too urged his superiors to be magnanimous in the administration of the disciplinary penalties. He agreed that magistrates were less than perfect and that there must be proscriptions (*ch'u-fen*) to hold them accountable for their behavior. But nowadays, he said, there were proscriptions for virtually everything. They were intended to prevent neglect and deception. They resulted in provoking magistrates to become skillful at evading them. Chou said, "this is simply to hate our dirtiness but prevent us from cleansing ourselves." He cited examples of proscriptions which undermined the good intentions of magistrates and said that if they were lifted magistrates would be happy to avoid getting themselves into incriminating situations.

In the rest of his statement Chou urged that authority over affairs be entrusted to magistrates. He said that at the present time magistrates were unable to deal with even the most trivial affairs on their own responsibility, but had to use up their time compiling registers and reports for their superiors. Among other recommendations he demanded the abolition of contributions by magistrates to their seniors, as being beyond their means. Like Ku Yun-sheng he also held that magistrates should be evaluated by how they treated the people, not their superiors.[38]

It took strong pressures to produce such a critique, and it is worth summarizing what they were. The position of magistrate carried great responsibility but little independent authority. The official had to do all the taking from the people and yet lead in soothing and nourishing them. The magistrate himself was the lowest of officials of high degree and administrative consequence. Promotion was hard to get, and its prospect faded with every year. Despite advancing in age and social seniority the magistrate was expected to go on deferring to administrative seniors. He handed out contributions but could not allay the anxieties of investigation and impeachment. He was punishable for taking action and punishable for not taking action. Since the regulations were so all-embracing he could seldom escape the dilemma: was it better to conceal, and possibly risk his reputation, or expose, and probably risk his career?

Evidence and logic continued to point strongly to the former choice. Wang Chih-i, governor-general of Fukien and Chekiang from 1810 to 1817, noted in a memorial that thirty-nine out of a possible sixty-two magistrates serving in Fukien had incurred demotion and dismissal, or stay of promotion and further disciplinary action, through failure to satisfy the (recently tightened) *k'ao-ch'eng* requirements. He said that the magistrates were worried about the disciplinary proscriptions and that each of them had many times reported falsely that they had completed the *k'ao-ch'eng* requirements. He calculated that magistrates received their first impeachment within several months of arriving at their posts, and that subsequent impeachments followed each other in succession. Obstinate households knew that the official would have to quit his post before long and that therefore it was to their advantage to resist payment. Clerks and runners also knew this, and as the deadlines approached would stop pressing collections. Unlike many high officials, Wang had been a magistrate himself and knew the conditions at first hand. He reiterated the argument that regulations begat evasions and urged that the deadlines be relaxed.[39]

All this suggests strongly that when magistrates and emperors urged officials not to be deflected by the public offenses they were in fact fighting an uphill battle. A public offense was still an offense, involving embarrassing and frustrating penalties. The pressures to avoid them came from both the public and the private domains. These pressures might have been compensated by the provision of local initiatives in the public domain. It has been said that these were minimal, and we must now see what is involved in this charge.

13

SURVEILLANCE OF RURAL LIFE

The Ch'ing emperors took an active interest in all aspects of local administration which they considered important to the health of their empire. In the next two chapters we shall consider their influence over rural administration and district government finance.

The pao-chia system

For the Ch'ing rulers the most significant of the rural control institutions was the *pao-chia* or watch-group system. At the time of the Ch'ing takeover this system was far from universal. It also existed in a number of different forms, depending on the circumstances under which it had been introduced. Its functions included bandit suppression and household surveillance, by means of placards and mutual guarantees. It also manned security services such as the night watch or gate duty.

From the first, the Ch'ing were attracted by its bandit suppressing and surveillance functions. As the dynasty progressed, they found in it the means for implementing other policies in which they were interested. Consequently, their *pao-chia* enactment began at a very early stage and proceeded with considerable vigor throughout the eighteenth and early nineteenth centuries. Repeatedly the emperors insisted that it be used to uncover robbers and to examine population movement.[1] This stress on security is an outcome of the dynastic position as military overlord. Unlike the late Ming, the Ch'ing could afford to be, and were, forebearing in fiscal exaction. They could not afford to neglect security.

As a result of this preoccupation with security, Ch'ing *pao-chia* enactment concentrated on three objectives: setting out the methods for the
implementation of surveillance, making the system universal, and pinning
responsibility for its operation firmly on local administrators.

As to implementation, the emperors were concerned to establish the
household and watch-groups and use them to register and guarantee the
numbers and movements of adult males. An important edict of 1709
ordered all districts to establish in rural subdistricts and district cities
groups of ten households, with leaders for each group of 10, 100, or
1,000. Each household was to be given a placard on which to write the
names and numbers of its male adults. Similar cards were to be issued to
guest houses, temples, and monasteries. On these they were to write down
the names, numbers, destination, and provenance of all travelers. Guest
houses were also to record the occupation of their guests. No households
were to take in strangers or suspicious persons without questioning them
carefully. When it transpired that local officials "dreaded the trouble-
someness" of this arrangement, the Yung-cheng emperor brushed aside
this complaint and himself issued an edict enforcing the card system.[2]

The second major function required of the groups was to guarantee and
be liable for each other's security. Group leaders were to submit monthly
bonds to this effect.[3] Finally, they were required to bring to light all
fugitives from justice. They were not required to arrest them. This
remained the direct duty of the district official and his police officers.[4]

The emperors issued many edicts requiring the extension of the system
over the entire country and over all elements of the population. These
included Manchu bannermen, aborigines, squatters and transient groups,
fishermen and other fringe inhabitants, office underlings, clans, and all
ranks of the gentry.[5] In the interests of including the gentry, the emperors
sacrificed leadership to universality. The gentry were exempted from
leadership of the *pao-chia* groups or service on guard duties. In fact,
the edicts do not go deeply into the attributes required of group leaders
and are more concerned to stress the duties incumbent on all households.
Consequently, the main burden for the management of the system was
placed directly on the local officials themselves. Many regulations were
passed severely disciplining local officials who failed to implement the
system. In addition, its involvement with the disclosure and suppressing
of robbery made it highly relevant to the *k'ao-ch'eng* review and provided
officials with a further powerful incentive for putting it into action.

Given this kind of pressure from the top, it is at first sight surprising to find a steady stream of documentation claiming that the system was not being effectively carried out. Nevertheless, while these claims require careful interpretation, it is clear that they were in many cases justified.

There are several reasons for this ineffectiveness. The basic one, however, is that the *pao-chia* was unmistakably a "method" or *fa*, and thus a product of the Legalist outlook. The word "Legalist," in its Chinese context, means "a proponent of methods." Methods were the Legalist means for making the public right prevail. As such they are essentially means justified by ends. From the Confucian point of view, the use of "methods" is undesirable on several counts. It represents a political intrusion into social affairs. It means that the state is going out and forcing the people to participate in administration. The Confucian viewpoint, expressed many times in the Four Books, is that the ruler should stay still and attract the people in toward him. To Confucianism a method is, as it were, mindless and mechanical. It requires action, whether or not that action is based on perception of "humanity" and whether or not it is in the interests of the actors. Because of its denial of individual values it is always supported by punishments. But the mind of the people is vulnerable to methods. People can be exploited to resist them out of self-interest or to give way to them out of fear. Thus to Confucianism methods all too often merely provide opportunities for exploitation by self-seeking elements.

All this is part of the general conflict between public and private. The significance of the Ch'ing *pao-chia* system is that it constituted the operation of the policy of method in its most undisguised form. It pried into the affairs of the people, requiring them to count each other, watch each other, guarantee each other, and disclose each other. It put the all-important universality ahead of leadership. It put uppermost the provision of general public security. It led among other things, to much exploitation by office underlings, village thugs, and other opportunists; and it may be asked whether as a method it provided more, or less, in the way of general peace of mind. Ch'ing officials did not, of course, enjoy the luxury of being able to raise this question. They were ordered to carry out the system. The operation of the *k'ao-ch'eng* system made it unwise not to do so. Once again they were caught between the dictates of their training and the dictates of state policy.

Under the influence of these conflicting forces local administrators engaged at first in an acerbic debate over the merits of the *pao-chia* system. Some critics of Wang Yang-ming had said that the system aggravated the people without providing any benefits in return. Fortunately, they added, the districts were not really carrying it out.[6] Some early Ch'ing administrators also saw it as a means for underlings to oppress the people, and therefore refused to operate it effectively.[7] Others criticized it as impracticable, more especially in the more densely populated areas of the east and south. Huang Liu-hung, opposing this viewpoint, gave two different reasons for its poor operation in these areas. The complexity and heaviness of the taxation preoccupied the attention of magistrates and left them no time for the control of robbers and fugitives. Second, the gentry of the big clans and large families immediately resisted the promotion of any policy inconvenient to them and thereby prevented it from getting going.[8] A few writers simply pointed out that the systems of Kuantzu and Shang Yang were among the progenitors of the *pao-chia* and that these systems had the effect of "enriching and strengthening"—a famous Legalist catchphrase. This was a way of implying that such systems differed from the principles for which Confucianism stood. Not surprisingly, this comment was infrequent.[9]

The more common tendency in Ch'ing administrative writing was to look for reasons to support the *pao-chia* system. One argument advanced in times of trouble was that it served to bring peace to the people. This was undoubtedly a valid objective. Nevertheless, its proponents knew that they were obliged to show how the coercive methods of the *pao-chia* could achieve this end. Their principal argument was that the absence of the *pao-chia* system was more harmful to the people than its presence. One said that human feelings would be satisfied by its convenience.[10] Another claimed that it could cut off robbery at its roots.[11] From a Confucian viewpoint such arguments are dubious, and it is clear that their proponents recognized this, for they tended to take refuge behind the assertion that maintaining peace and calm was the overriding objective of administration. "Your duty," as one of them said to his administrative readers, "consists in pacifying the people, and that is all."[12]

The defenders put a good deal of energy into showing that the *pao-chia* system had its Confucian antecedents. Much was made of the rural administrative structure described in the *Chou li*. Many writers seem to have felt that the mere mention of this structure was as far as they needed—or were able—to go. Some went further and likened the watch-group leaders to the *shih ta-fu* who appear as knightly gentry in feudal times or as junior judicial officers in the ritual texts.[13] One writer went further still and in addition likened the governors to the "pastors" (a term which stood for provincial administrators, both of a prehistoric era and also of the Han dynasty) and the district magistrates to the feudal lords.[14] This was attributing to the watch-group leaders a prestige and an affinity with their superiors which they did not possess. Seventeenth- and eighteenth-century China was not lacking in men who saw the pointlessness of trying to give bureaucratic institutions a feudal gloss.[15]

There were also many references, some of them glowing, to Wang Yang-ming's part in the emergence of the *pao-chia* system. The advantage of Wang was that he could never be accused of being a Legalist at heart. However, the great difference between Wang and the Ch'ing apologists is that Wang did not present the system as anything other than a distasteful and hopefully temporary necessity. Since Wang's reputation as a philosopher was in eclipse throughout most of the Ch'ing dynasty, it is doubtful if his association with the *pao-chia* did much to further its cause among those who were already skeptical about it.

The Ch'ing apologists became more frank when they appealed to the self-interest of administrators. They claimed that the districts were too large and populous for one man to supervise effectively by himself, and pointed out that if he did not, he would soon fall foul of the disciplinary system.

Yeh P'ei-sun, who while treasurer of Hunan drew up an influential set of methods for implementing the *pao-chia*, argued that a single magistrate, no matter how talented, could hardly know all that was going on for better or for worse within his district. Yet the purpose of "establishing offices and dividing duties" had been precisely to cause the affairs of each one district to be known. Yeh added that all sorts of undesirable people and goings-on existed in rural areas, such as heterodox teaching, robbers and bandits, village thugs, private minting and melting down, dens of gambling and prostitution, escaped murderers and fugitives, not to mention proscribed articles such as gambling apparatus and heterodox books. All these were matters for which there were prohibitory regulations. When magistrates failed to investigate any such matter and were at once trapped in disciplinary enquiries, it was all because the *pao-chia* system had not been carried out. The result was to bequeath an act of wrongdoing to their descendants. The blame for this, said Yeh somberly, was not light. But if the official carried out the *pao-chia* thoroughly, criminal acts would be forthwith exposed; criminal intentions would lie dormant and change. How could there then be any serious cases requiring the penalization of the official? "This," said Yeh triumphantly, "is the height of effectiveness!"[16]

In the conditions of late eighteenth-century administration Yeh's argument and his subsequent proposals were full of sound practical sense. It must also be one of the most unalloyed appeals to the self-interest of administrators to appear in imperial Chinese administrative writing. Yeh's statement received wide approval and in 1813 was endorsed by the Chia-ch'ing emperor.[17] Wang Feng-sheng, himself a noted exponent of the *pao-chia* system, repeated the above argument almost verbatim.[18]

There also existed a more subterranean appeal to self-interest, which evidently carried greater conviction. This was that as long as the *pao-chia* system had to be enforced, it might as well be utilized to fulfill the *k'ao-ch'eng* fiscal and robbery deadlines. The existence of this attitude is indicated by numerous edicts and memorials, which denounce this use of the system and stress that it was to be used only to investigate and disclose the whereabouts of robbers.[19] Evidently this perversion was widespread and continuing. It should be remembered, however, that if local officials had not been under strong pressures both to fulfill the deadlines and to carry out the *pao-chia*, it is questionable whether they would have seen any advantage in thus exploiting it. In the first place they had other fiscal and security agents at their disposal. Second, such a misuse of what was already an imposition could only stir up popular resentment and run the risk of backfiring.

The introduction of the so-called village constables (*ti-fang* or *ti-pao*) indicates that this danger was appreciated. These agents are found as early as the late seventeenth century.[20] Present knowledge indicates, however, that their use gained currency during the eighteenth century. Their advantage to officials was that unlike previous rural fiscal or security agents they were not drawn from any obligatory roster or supposed to meet any general standards of character and means. They were simply rural agents appointed by, and personally responsible to, the district official. They were used to perform all the more disagreeable administrative tasks, such as pressing tax collection, investigating homicides, or arresting thieves. This reduced the magistrate's dependence on the *pao-chia* personnel for the performance of these mandatory duties. It also provided him with agents on whom he could exert as much pressure as he needed, without directly irritating the villagers.

Some officials attempted to make the *pao-chia* more attractive by providing it with tangible benefits. Yü Ch'eng-lung, under the influence of the *Chou li*, included in his *pao-chia* regulations methods for watch-groups to "nourish" and "aid" improverished member families.[21] Yuan Wen-kuan arranged for the watch-groups in his district to provide mutual support in case of serious disease, as well as the required mutual guarantees and guard duties. He also had the *pao-chia* personnel attend the bi-monthly lectures on the imperial Sacred Edict and laws relating to public morals.[22] Huang Liu-hung gave attention to the civil defense functions of the *pao-chia* and made a point of choosing robust and able-bodied persons to head the watch-groups and drill the watchmen.[23]

Several factors prevented the early Ch'ing *pao-chia* from being developed more generally along such lines. It appears to have been extremely difficult to obtain reputable persons to serve as watch-group leaders. The gentry, who were the natural leaders, were exempted from serving as such. Others who valued their reputations were understandably reluctant to go through the expense and inconvenience of delivering the guarantees or bonds of good order, and then be held to account if any undesirables appeared in the midst of their groups. Many complaints attest that as a result the leadership of these groups often fell into the hands of opportunists.[24] Moreover, ordinary people feared to submit reports on criminals. It was essential for the magistrate to overcome his anxieties for his own career and make it clear that he would welcome and follow up such reports. Otherwise those who submitted information ran the triple risks of running up expenses with the underlings, being belabored and possibly beaten by the official, and being victimized by the criminals on their return home. As often as not the criminals were likely to be nearer to home than the district officials. Under these circumstances, villagers had to be very certain or desperate before exposing themselves by visiting the district office.[25]

The Ch'ing emperors, for their part, continued to have their own ideas about how the *pao-chia* should be used. In the middle and late eighteenth century, it was given the function of measuring the size of the total population. Before this the only way of estimating population size lay through reference to the fiscal registers, which recorded each five years the number of adult tax-paying units. In 1713 this number had been fixed as a permanent quota at the number of units registered in 1711. Thenceforth these registers no longer provided any connection with the increase or decrease of the total population. Subsequently, it was discovered in times of dearth that the numbers of those applying for relief in a given area could substantially exceed the anticipated total population. The Ch'ien-lung emperor became aware of this problem as early as 1740.[26]

As Ho has shown, it took time for the government to change from a fiscal to a demographic concept of population eumeration. In 1775, as the result of another crop failure, the emperor issued an edict ordering provincial administrators to see that henceforth local officials registered annually the actual numbers of the population. "Then," he noted, "I will be able to see whether the provinces are really enrolling and inspecting the *pao-chia*."[27] The quinquennial *ting* registers were abolished and the annual population count was thereafter based on the *pao-chia* household placards.

This reform altered and may have confused the character of the *pao-chia* system. As a means for household enumeration it came under the purview of the Board of Revenue (literally Board of Households). The Board of Revenue was concerned with fiscal planning rather than with security problems. It is not unlikely that the demographic function of the *pao-chia* became strengthened at the expense of the security function.

After the outbreak of the White Lotus rebellion, the Chia-ch'ing emperor issued an edict in 1799 stressing the security function of the *pao-chia* and accusing local officials of having come to look on it as a mere formality.[28] Where the Ch'ien-lung emperor had regarded the population count as a means of preparing for relief requirements, the Chia-ch'ing emperor saw it rather as a means of "depriving evil-doers of their hiding places." In subsequent edicts, the emperor ordered local officials to go out into the villages and make personal inspections of the population surveys, exact security bonds, enforce mutual surveillance, and punish watch-group heads who guaranteed rebels and other criminals.[29] A few public-spirited magistrates, such as Liu Heng and Wang Feng-sheng, followed this up by instituting careful population checks. Otherwise this repressive posture failed to achieve any lasting results.

Nor did it give way to any fresh thinking from the center of authority. The Tao-kuang emperor continued to regard the *pao-chia* as the means for "preventing villainy from sprouting." In 1850, when robbers were causing trouble in every province, secret society rebels harassing Hunan, and the Taiping rebellion beginning to drive forward in Kwangtung and Kwangsi, the emperor issued an edict complaining that all this was happening because the *pao-chia* method was not being carried out. He accused local officials of giving "weed" people nothing to respect or dread, and ordered them to carry out the system according to his earlier but ineffectual commands.[30] There could be little room for constructive local initiatives under this kind of direction.

The hsiang-yueh

The Ch'ing emperors were not unaware of the ideological poverty of their *pao-chia* policy. They tried to compensate for this by converting the *hsiang-yueh* or rural district pledge system into a vehicle for displaying their view of public morality.

The initial Ch'ing policy for the *hsiang-yueh* was to reactivate it as it stood, or appeared to stand. The Shun-chih emperor adopted the six maxims of Emperor Ming T'ai-tsu and in 1659 issued a statement ordering local officials, along with families and elders, to expound and clarify them. The *hsiang-yueh* specifically was charged with this function. Its leaders were to convene the men of the *hsiang* and nominate "exemplary and studious" licentiates of over sixty, or failing that "virtuous and reliable" commoners of over sixty or seventy. Twice a month these men were to explain the maxims and admonish the people. Meanwhile the *hsiang-yueh* was to continue to distinguish good and bad conduct, note this in its registers, and cause the people to exert themselves.[31]

It soon became apparent that neither the system nor the maxims were having any effect in warning or ordering the "stupid and obstinate." The main reason was that the six maxims bore little relevance to existing conditions or to the objectives of Ch'ing policy. They had been designed to underwrite the leadership of the communal *li-chia* system. The Ch'ing emperors needed something to underwrite their own leadership. In an edict of 1670 the young but able K'ang-hsi emperor noted the continuance of wastefulness, cheating, litigation, and other symptoms of social disorder. In particular he charged large and wealthy families with oppressing the orphaned and widowed, perverted senior gentry with "settling matters by force," evil-minded junior gentry with hanging around district offices, and "verminous" underlings and village thugs with cheating and harming the well-intentioned and good. The emperor declared that the existing policy of the state had been to add daily to the laws and punishments. He affirmed, in Confucian vein, that education must precede punishment so it would reduce it. He issued his sixteen maxims on this basis.[32]

The aim of this enactment was to promote and explain the form of society necessary to the functioning of administration as then constituted. Essentially, it urges people to live in harmony with their relatives and neighbors, to maintain a viable income, and to fulfill the requirements of the government. As to the latter, it calls for prohibiting the concealment of fugitives, desisting from false suits, paying up taxes, and uniting the *pao-chia* security system. It includes prescriptions aimed to promote study by *shih* (here, scholars), to stamp out heterodoxy, and to make the penal laws more widely known. In most of the explanations there is the implied or stated objective of avoiding trouble with the authorities. While the maxims begin on a positive note, their preventative and negative character becomes increasingly clear as they proceed. The impression which they leave is one of stern admonishment.[33]

The sixteen maxims or "Sacred Edict," and their subsequent elaboration, reveal the problem which the government had in explaining its case to the people. Already the enactment had grown from the twenty-four words of Emperor Ming T'ai-tsu's six maxims to the one hundred and twelve of the sixteen maxims. Within a short while provincial officials began producing exegeses, one of which the K'ang-hsi emperor approved for distribution to all local jurisdictions, rural district, and villages.[34] In his old age the emperor issued an edict intended to put more stress on the familial values propounded in the first maxim.[35]

The Yung-cheng emperor, in the second year of his reign, issued his own 10,000-word official amplification. It is moved by a sense that physical factors, such as density of population, contributed to social unrest. The emperor urged the people to be tolerant of the requirements of the state and the rights of others. As well as emphasizing the bonds of filiality and loyalty, he advised the people to study and fear the laws. What is the use, he implied, of risking all for small gains? Rest content with your lot. When you get angry, consider the consequences. A loquacious official in the salt administration contributed a highly colloquial commentary to the amplification, which was itself to gain wide currency. Much of it reiterates the laws available for punishing behavior out of step with the maxims.[36]

Taken in isolation, much of what the maxims and amplification say appears to be sensible. But as an administrative policy it was basically unsound. For material supposed to educate and transform there was too much emphasis on law and retribution. Where a Confucian treatment would have played on good intentions and shame, this one played on fear. The imperial system lost sight of the village initiatives intended for the pre-Ch'ing restraint systems. In it initiative came only from above. In addition, the imperial system became simply a monologue by the emperors for their people. The local administration served to echo the imperial viewpoint and see that it got reiterated. The Ch'ing emperors were right in seeing that their case had to reach down to the people. With a modern communications system they might have achieved some success. It was unrealistic to expect local administrators and scholars to go all out in propagating their case. Too many differences in intellectual and social viewpoint were involved.[37]

As it was, the *hsiang-yueh* system of Wang Yang-ming had itself been criticized because the initiative behind it came too much from above. A magistrate who served in a district in Kiangsi between 1666 and 1676 noted this situation and its consequence: that the implementation at the local level had not been vigorous. Because of this the institution had become a "thing of the past," and the local people had been left to their violent practices. Nevertheless, the magistrate praised Wang's methods of rural administration as well-intentioned (*liang*) and providing a combination of "inwardly the sage's and outwardly the king's teaching." He denied that the people were to blame for their wild behavior and expressed the desire to put Wang's methods into practice, so that he could be an "elder" and give the people an example to follow.[38]

In this context, the provision of the sixteen maxims actually supplied new initiative to magistrates looking for a basis on which to exert moral pressure. A gazetteer of another Kiangsi district noted that a magistrate who served from 1656 to 1662 was carrying out Wang's *hsiang-yueh* method, and described it much as it is described in Wang's own writings. But it commented that the rural leaders were using the system not to unite but to stir up conflict. Consequently, the eighteenth-century editors asked that only the sixteen maxims and amplification be used. The system should not be concerned with registering personal reputations; it should incite the virtues of public-mindedness (*kung*) and loyalty.[39]

It appears then, that the initiative to turn the *hsiang-yueh* into an official lecturing system came from district officials as well as from the emperors.

This, accordingly, is what it gradually became. The name was in due course changed to "*chiang-yueh*" or "expound and restrain."[40] The Yung-cheng emperor changed the composition of the personnel. He ordered the appointment of one old and accomplished senior or ordinary licentiate as leader and three or four conscientious and careful persons as monthly aides.[41] Twice a month these were to assemble rural leaders and recite and expound the maxims and amplification. Those effective over the space of three years were to be recommended for an Audience and other marks of distinction. Local officials who failed to implement the lecture system were to be impeached and disciplined. Candidates for the degree of licentiate were obliged to learn the entire work by heart. Subsequently, the Ch'ien-lung emperor ordered selections from the Penal Code to be read at the close of each lecture session.[42] He ordered district officials to tour all the places selected for the exposition of the imperial word and to put real effort into the operation of the system. District magistrates were expected to lead the lecturing in person in the district capital.[43]

It was one thing for district officials to seek a basis on which to exert moral initiatives. It was another thing to be obliged to do so twice a month, and according to cut-and-dried formulas. Magistrates found out soon enough that they had more pressing business to attend to, such as dealing with criminal cases and collecting taxes. Thanks to the disciplinary system, their careers and economics means depended on these matters. They did not depend on the lecturing system. Consequently, the *hsiang-yueh* as a lecturing system came less and less to occupy the interest of magistrates. We have seen, for example, that in the seventeenth and eighteenth centuries it was still of concern to Kiangsi local officials. By the early nineteenth century it was no longer mentioned in Kiangsi district gazetteers. The subject was quietly dropped.[44] This does not mean that the centralized lecturing system was completely discontinued, either there or elsewhere, but it no longer held any genuine opportunities for local initiative and any real interest to local administrators.

14

Impact of fiscal policies

Such were some of the limits placed on the magistrate's ability to provide for the people. By contrast, when it came to taking from them, as in collecting taxes and financing administrative expenses, magistrates holding substantive appointments found they were able to exercise considerably broader initiatives. Nevertheless, the Ch'ing emperors were far from sympathetic to these initiatives. Their policy was to keep taxation low and issue remissions wherever possible. They were repelled by administrative exactions of informal fees and surcharges.

Several considerations influenced these attitudes. There was an underlying feeling that the wealth taken administratively from the people became the property of the central government. The Ch'ing rulers, in return, were sensitive to the fact that their revenue came from the countryside. With the example of the late Ming surcharges before them, they did not want their own taxation to become a source of unnecessary irritation. By the early eighteenth century, they were developing an awareness that the population was increasing out of proportion to its means of support. Since government income now came largely from land rather than households, they felt it all the more important to hold down the level of taxation and restrict the arbitrary exactions of local administration. This does not mean that the Ch'ing rulers were unconcerned with the fiscal solvency of local administration. But they were more concerned to adjust revenues to the solvency of the central government and the tax-paying public.

Because of this, Ch'ing fiscal policy for local administration was to restrict what it could control and denounce what it could not. As we have seen, the government was determined to check closely into the tax collection procedures and insist on full collection of the authorized quotas and delivery to it of the required sums. Unauthorized exactions it prohibited and penalized. Those which appeared to have gained widespread popular acceptance were brought under central control. As a result, local officials found out that in this, as in so many other areas of administration, authorized practices were removed from their control. Those which they could control remained unauthorized and reprehensible.

The Ch'ing regime began at a very early stage to put the squeeze on local government financial administration. Despite evidence that the Single Whip method of collecting in money was beginning to drive the poor off their land and increasing opportunities for corruption by local underlings, it approved, in principle, of the reforms. Unstandably, it viewed the previous system, with its many different items and separate levies, as "complex and mystifying." The advantage for the Ch'ing of the Single Whip method was that it was "simple and to the point:" its method of paying was "convenient" and its records "easy to examine."[1]

As a result of the *k'ao-ch'eng* system and a vigorous land reclamation policy, the regime was able, without affecting the level of the quotas, to raise the level of land-tax income reaching the central government from 21 million taels in 1651, to 30 million in 1725.[2] The government also instituted a drive to increase the registration and assessment of male adults. In 1661 central government income from this source was only about one-seventh of that from the land tax.[3] As might be expected, the government announced rewards for local officials who increased their male adult registration, and heavy punishment for those who only assessed the "small people," leaving the "big families" untouched. At the same time it published deadlines for the arrival of the *ting* registers at the Board of Revenue and promised disciplinary action against officials whose registers arrived late. Under this kind of pressure, the total for male adult units was increased by nearly four million between 1661 and 1724.[4]

The central government also took steps to reduce the salaries and allowances of local officials. The Ch'ing salary structure, like its predecessors, was based on the rank of the official. Under the initial salary structure the district magistrate, at rank 7A, received a basic annual salary of 27.46 taels. He also received four separate allowances for wages, stationery, furnishings, and entertainment of superiors, amounting to 96 taels. This gave him an official personal income of 123 taels. The department magistrate received 145 taels.[5] But during the Shun-chih and early K'ang-hsi periods, the allowances were whittled down and abolished. The basic salary structure was revised upwards, giving the department magistrate 80 taels and the district magistrate 45 taels. This then became their total official income. As these income levels were based on *rank* and not on *office*, they no longer bore any relation to the expenses and responsibilities of the offices in question.[6]

As well as reducing the official incomes, the central govenment took steps at this time to increase its share of the total tax revenues. This decision was made necessary by the alarming and prolonged rebellion of the Three Feudatories. The K'ang-hsi emperor admitted that under the stress of military expenditures he had required the delivery of all sums that would normally have remained in the provinces. It had also been necessary to put pressure on local officials to collect the entire tax quotas without fail.[7]

Under the stress of these many-sided pressures, local officials had maintained themselves by a number of financial practices, some overt and "customary," some deceptive. The most significant of these was the overt practice known as "meltage and wastage" (*huo-hao*). On this procedure Ku Yen-wu commented: "The taxes of the district are troublesome. They are collected household by household and paid coin by coin. One cannot take all these little bits and hand them on up to the prefecture. There is no alternative to melting them down. When there is melting there is wastage. This only amounts to 1 or 2 percent. But coarse, greedy persons make use of the practice to cook up all sorts of tricks. Each transmits his methods to the next, so that officials come to take a profit of two or three parts in ten, and clerks, one or two; the people pay fifteen for every ten of the state." Ku ended by noting that the practice could not be stopped because it contributed to the income of the senior provincial officials.[8]

The initial Ch'ing policy toward this practice was to prohibit it. When an official requested in 1649 a *huo-hao* collection of 3 percent per tael, an edict rejected this as covetousness.[9] In addition, an order was published in 1665 during the minority of the K'ang-hsi emperor permitting *li-chia* heads or "small people" to lodge complaints against district officials, who with the connivance of their superiors made "private allocations" over and above the established tax quotas.[10]

Neither of these orders could have been effective. In 1685 a censor complained that district officials in Shansi were collecting a *huo-hao* surcharge of up to 30 or 40 percent. The K'ang-hsi emperor himself noted twelve years later the collection of surcharges of 20 or 30 percent in Shansi and Shensi.[11]

But the emperor was sensitive to the problems of local financial administration. In an edict of 1687 he admitted that there had been a very great deal of cancelation of salaries as a result of troubles involved in managing public affairs. Noting that the original purpose of the provincial salaries had been to "nourish honesty, " he ordered all canceled salaries to be restored.[12] In addition he declined a suggestion to legitimize the *huohao*, holding that the existing salary levels were stingy, and that if the (local) authorities lost this surcharge they would oppress the people but have nothing to set aside for local public expenditures. He recommended a level of 10 percent for a *huo-hao* surcharge on the regular tax.[13]

The emperor's most famous fiscal reform was the freezing of the maleadult tax on the basis of the 1711 returns. The figures reaching the central government since 1661 had been showing a much greater rate of increase in the numbers of registered male adult units than in the income accruing from the *ting* tax. This was because male adults could be assessed on the basis of several different grades. Since 1685, however, the rate of increase in registered male adults had itself been dropping off.[14]

After receiving the 1711 returns, the emperor's first reaction was to conclude that local officials were concealing the actual rate of increase in male adults. He ordered the provincial authorities to impeach at once all those guilty of committing this deception. He also ordered that no further rewards be offered to officials if the male adults added to the registers were lower grade and those removed because of age were upper grade, even if the amount of the increase had hitherto warranted a reward.[15]

But the actual increase in income from the *ting* tax was itself financially inconsiderable. This led the emperor to the conclusion that the income from the tax could not be substantially increased. Therefore it was impracticable to continue to press local officials on this issue. He noted that there had been a long period of peace and that the overall population was "multiplying daily." It was not possible (meaning proper) to raise the assessments of the presently registered male adults. Although the actual number of male adults was increasing, the cultivated land (on which their income depended) was not yet itself growing in area. Here the emperor was implying that since the *ting* tax was now very largely assessed on the basis of the land, an increase in the *ting* tax could only be made effective by an increase in the cultivated area. The increase in the number of male adults was no longer the principal factor on which an increase in the *ting* tax could be achieved. As a result there was little to be gained fiscally by striving to increase the number of registered male adults.

The emperor had already noticed on his tours that only a few male adults were paying the *ting* tax. Others had suggested that their tax-free status was due to the "abounding grace" of the emperor and said that freedom from the labor services had enabled them all to enjoy peace and happiness. The idea that the limitation of the tax would cause social rejoicing obviously appealed to him.

He further noted that the state treasuries were presently full, despite recent tax remissions of up to 10 million taels, and held that the state had all the income it needed. Finally he allowed that local officials who concealed the actual number of male adults only did so because they feared to increase the taxes. "Don't they know," he chided, "that I, too, have no wish to add to the taxes? I only wish to know the actual numbers." [16]

On the basis of this reasoning, the emperor enacted in 1713 that the *ting* be fixed permanently at the level obtaining in 1711. Males who came of age after that date were to be registered only as a guide to their actual number. They were not to be assessed for taxation. [17] In 1716 the emperor agreed that the *ting* assessment should go with the land, not with male adults as such. If an assessed male adult sold his property, the new owner was to assume the *ting* assessment. It was no longer to go with the male adult himself. Regulations were also provided for replacing the already assessed male adults when these reached the cut-off age of sixty. [18]

As might be expected, the freezing of the *ting* tax excited considerable enthusiasm. As it was binding, it constituted a concession of principle to the tax-paying public. In effect the state was terminating its rights of exaction over the totality of an element of its wealth and strength. It was limiting itself to a given proportion. The rest was liberated from the public sphere. From this viewpoint the remark of Kung Tzu-chen that this decision "marked the end of two thousand years of government oppression" is hardly an exaggeration. [19] But as we have seen, the emperor's decision was based principally on the solvency of the central government and the tax-paying public. As far as local administration was concerned, the emperor's primary thought was to take some unnecessary pressure off local officials. He did not apparently consider that the freeze, based as it was on overall annual increases of only a few thousand taels, could possibly affect local government financial resources.

Nevertheless this freeze of the *ting* tax helped in due course to precipitate a financial crisis, which in turn led the state to take over control of the *huo-hao* surcharge. The financial administration of Shansi province provided the catalyst for this chain of events.

It happened that the northern and northwestern provinces were far behind the southern in the Single Whip amalgamation of the land and labor (*ti-ting*) taxes. This was especially true of Shansi. As well as paying a substantial land tax, it owed far the largest *ting* levy of any province.[20] While the reasons for Shansi's backward fiscal condition cannot be explained here, they had to do with the fact that many of its people were engaged in trade, much of its land was barren and its people poor, much of its soil was sandy and alkaline, and a fair proportion of its land tax was still collected in "original kind" (bushels of grain).[21]

In the early eighteenth century Shansi was manifesting the classic conditions of economic crisis found in the southeast by the early sixteenth century, and described by Shen Pang in Chihli at the end of the sixteenth century. The rich were gaining possession of all the land. The poor, who had hardly enough land "to stick the point of an awl in," were burdened with a great deal of labor services. *Ting* were failing and affecting households, households failing and affecting *chia*, *chia* failing and affecting *li*. In times of deficiency the "mat-hut dwellers" (the poor) were drifting away. Thus it is not without significance that it was in Shansi and Shensi, the provinces with the highest per capita *ting* rates, that the high *huo-hao* surcharges had been noted in the late seventeenth century.[22]

In the last years of the K'ang-hsi reign, Shansi experienced several harvest deficiencies.[23] In 1723, the first year of the Yung-cheng reign, No-min, a Manchu with no prior experience of provincial administration, was appointed governor of Shansi. He discovered that local officials had been fulfilling the tax quotas by raiding the official granaries and treasuries, which were thus unable to help in the food crisis.

No-min responded by instituting a thorough purge of local officialdom and requesting the Board of Officials to send out "worthy and capable" administrators. He also had the sense to see that something had to be done to put the financing of local administration on a sounder basis. So he included among his recommendations a request that the income from the *huo-hao* be delivered to the provincial treasury. It should then be used to make up existing deficits and to "nourish the honesty" of local officials by supplementing their salaries.[24]

Although this recommendation has been associated with No-min, it seems that it came from the provincial treasurer Kao Ch'eng-ling. In contrast with No-min, Kao had spent all his career in provincial administration, serving with distinction as magistrate in Yunnan and rising through prefectural appointments in other provinces. He had held office as provincial judge in Shansi before becoming treasurer. He had experienced the problems of local administration in differing areas and at different levels of authority.

Kao pointed out that the *huo-hao* was a part of the tax-collection procedure. He argued that since the people themselves regarded it as a contribution to the public sector (*feng kung*), therefore it belonged, in effect, to the wealth and revenue (*ts'ai fu*) of the Court (i.e., government). Accordingly it should be handed up to the provincial treasury so that the senior officials could disburse it where it was most needed. Kao suggested a surcharge of one-tenth and repeated No-min's proposals for its distribution. He also recommended that all the other high provincial authorities calculate the annual *huo-hao* levy of their provinces and use it to cover supplementary salaries, public expenditures, and compensation of deficits.[25]

In making these proposals, Kao specifically blamed Shansi's troubles on the *ting* levy. He based his position on a statement in the *Book of Documents* that taxes were fixed according to the land.[26] Kao argued, in a personal Audience, that the fortunes of men rose and fell. The product of the land remained constant. In saying this, Kao was reflecting the standard viewpoint of the economic conditions of a traditional economy. In this viewpoint it is not assumed that the product of the land will, or could, increase. It has a regular level of output which will be normally maintained. On the other hand it is not subject to the long-term vicissitudes of human talent and fortune. Consequently the land could bear a quota system; men could not.

As Kao put it, the tax on grain was easy to complete; the silver levy on adult males was subject to much deficiency. Kao described the conditions of economic competitiveness discussed earlier and pointed out that they applied whether or not the harvest happened to be good. The labor charges fell on the poor, who could not pay them. Officials were punished for not collecting what could not be paid. Kao cited the current silver revenues from the Shansi land and labor taxes, which showed that the income from the labor tax constituted the remarkably high proportion of 22 percent of the total silver income from these taxes. He requested that the labor tax be allocated to the land, thus reducing the pressure on the poor and removing the (existing) cause for deficits in the state taxation.[27]

Kao's arguments convinced the Yung-cheng emperor. Although knowing that local officials viewed the *huo-hao* as an "accomplished" (and therefore legitimate) precedent, his initial reaction, on ascending the throne, had been to prohibit it as a predatory exaction.[28] He now saw that it was needed both to finance provincial public expenditures and to "nourish the honesty" of officials.

The preoccupation with "nourishing honesty," while primarily associated with the supplementary provincial salaries introduced by the Yung-cheng emperor, stems from a deeply rooted political premiss. This is that "conscientiousness, trust and a 'heavy' salary are the means for a ruler to encourage his officers."[29] In the Sung dynasty officials were provided with official fields in order to "nourish honesty."[30] An early sixteenth-century Ming commentator noted that the initial Ming salaries for magistrates had been sufficient to "nourish their honesty" and cover their expenses. Following the repeated commutations of later reigns, both metropolitan and provincial officials had actually failed to be paid their salaries. In this situation, he concluded, it was hard to prevent covetousness![31] Wang Yang-ming, commenting on these conditions, had himself invoked the principle of conscientiousness, trust, and a heavy salary.[32] The heavy salary had not been forthcoming, and the practice of *huo-hao* had begun in the late Ming period. Nevertheless the principle of nourishing honesty remained alive and had been of concern to the K'ang-hsi emperor.

The problem facing the Yung-cheng emperor was to weigh the benefit of nourishing the honesty of officials against the harm of increasing the state's exactions from the people. In principle it seems to have been easier on the mind of the early Ch'ing emperors to accuse their officials of greed and corruption than to bear the burden of raising the state's share of the people's wealth beyond existing rates. As the Yung-Cheng emperor said, "I do not wish that in the departments and districts a single speck should be taken from the people." But if the surcharge in question was clearly necessary to provincial solvency and was already regarded as public levy, this left the way clear for ridding it of corrupt practices and putting it on a regular basis. The emperor now declared that the current informal system of collecting the *huo-hao* incited greed and dishonesty. Moreover, as practiced it meant that the district officials were nourishing their superiors. "How much better," exclaimed the emperor, "to have superiors nourish the district officials!" Consequently, the emperor approved the conversion of the *huo-hao* into a public levy to be used for encouraging honesty and aiding public expenditures. Any surplus was to be retained for aiding local public business.

Having taken this bold decision, the emperor laid down several significant stipulations. Against the advice of his ministers, he refused to allow Shansi to be used as a test case. He declared flatly "in the affairs of the Empire there are only two possibilities: either it can be done or it can't." But in deference to those who feared that the policy looked like a "method," with all that connoted, he expressed his "deepest desire" that it should only run for a limited period. After the deficits had been cleared, treasuries filled and officials made good, the *huo-hao* should be gradually lightened and abolished. Consequently, he stated that provinces which could carry out the policy should be permitted to do so. Those which could not should not be forced to. Finally he warned that once the *huo-hao* had been made public, officials should not be permitted to contrive other items by which to exhort from the people.[33]

On the basis of this policy, official surcharge rates were established for each province. They were mainly of the order of one-tenth of the existing tax rate, though in a few northern and southwestern provinces they rose to one-sixth or one-fifth. In Kiangsu and Chekiang they ranged down to one-twentieth or one-twenty-fifth.[34] The government also pressed ahead with the reassessment of the *ting* levy, which had brought about the crisis in the first place. In nearly every province its amalgamation with the land tax was completed by the end of the Yung-cheng reign. In Shansi alone the amalgamation could not be completed until the early nineteenth century for the reasons indicated above.

The conversion of the *huo-hao* enabled the government to arrange substantial supplementary provincial salaries (see Table 2). Except on the busiest districts these should for a time have gone far in encouraging fiscal honesty. However, the emperor's hope that the conversion of the *huo-hao* would solve the general financial problems of local administration soon proved shortlived.

The reasons for this letdown are not hard to find. In the first place, the centralization of the *huo-hao* surcharge deprived local administrations of initiative and flexibility in adjusting local revenues to the public and private expenditures of each local administration. Circumstances fluctuated from year to year and from administration to each succeeding administration. Fixed rates did not provide for such fluctuations. Second, the policy did not provide adequate guarantees that provincial administrations would hand down the supplementary salaries as specified. Inasmuch as the *huo-hao* was to be divided between provincial administrative expenditures and official supplementary salaries, the provincial administrations gained the initiative as to how the income would be divided and how much would in fact go back to the districts.[35]

Third, the provision of fixed rates took no account of secular changes in the cost of living. In fact the cost of living rose steadily through the eighteenth century.[36] On present evidence it seems that the more agriculturally and commercially developed regions of the south and east were more affected by this divergence in costs and earnings than were districts off major arteries of communication. Whatever the regional differences, local administrators soon found or increased other ways of supplementing local income.

Some would say that the real trouble lay in the lack of integrity of local officials. But this explanation, although germane, is by itself inadequate. Administration, in China or anywhere else, is capable of functioning without corruption if its administrators are adequately financed and given genuine initiative and purpose. Control and surveillance may be necessary. But they are no substitute for trust and adequate provision. To say this is not to condemn Ch'ing administration as shortsighted. It should be clear by now that that administration was well aware of these issues. Its problem was that under the existing system of authority it could find no way of resolving them.

This basic administrative predicament may be further observed from the evolution of another "customary practice" known as *p'ing-yü* or "weight surplus." This referred to the fact that silver coins brought by taxpayers into the district office might weigh slightly more than the required amount. The silver ingots sent up to the higher authorities would not. The *p'ing-yü* constituted the difference in weight between these two amounts.

In 1737 the governor of Szechuan sent in a memorial notifying that apart from the *huo-hao*, districts were also collecting and retaining six-tenths of a tael per 100 taels (0.6 percent) in *p'ing-yü*. This filled the new and youthful Ch'ien-lung emperor with disgust. He pointed out that because the public expenditures of Szechuan had been inadequately financed it had been provided with a (high) surcharge of 25 percent. Out of kindness to the villages he had on his accession reduced it to 15 percent. On hearing of this next exaction he could "not overcome a feeling of horror." The *huo-hao* had been requited to officials precisely to prevent covetousness. If officials were to be allowed to go on picking out further items, why should they not go on and on adding charges on the small people?[37]

Nevertheless by the next year the emperor overcame his horror. He converted the *p'ing-yü* to a public surcharge, and declared that it was to be retained in the provincial treasury to be used on "public affairs." The level was first fixed at twenty-five taels per thousand (2.5 percent), and later reduced by half.[38]

The fiscal course of events described above included major decisions involving much mental stress. It is worth reviewing the motivations behind these decisions, as well as their implications. The emperors, apart from the K'ang-hsi emperor, could not tolerate exactions not specifically approved and controlled from the top. These exactions are usually described as being "pocketed" by local officials and clerks, because they were used to meet the personal expenses of those administrators. As such they were private. In this respect there is no difference in principle between either the "customary" practices or outright corruption. Both were private, and viewed as such by all levels of officialdom.

The reason for regarding the customary practices as private would seem to stem from a basic resistance to extending the scope and legitimacy of "public" expenditures. The emperors themselves were anxious to hold back public expenditures. However, the emperors, as holding the ultimate responsibility for administrative performance, obviously could not tolerate a combination of corruption and insolvency. If the private practices could not be suppressed, they could be made public. But "making public" meant bringing under imperial control and raising the price of imperial responsibility. The central government would therefore establish certified rates and put their management under the level of provincial administration closest to the central government and most easily supervised by it. It was not considered that independent initiative and control by local administration could be contained within the public sphere. Independence ran the risk of going private and out of control.

Thus there were forces trying to resist and reduce both public and private in imperial administration. These dual forces were expressed by officials as well as by their rulers. When the K'ang-hsi emperor proposed to tolerate collection of *huo-hao* he was opposed by the governor to whom he made this suggestion. When the Yung-cheng emperor proposed to make the collection of *huo-hao* public, he also was opposed by his advisers. The official position was simply that the surcharge should not in principle be collected at all. In the latter case officialdom was trying to hold back the increase of public authority over the people. That also was why local officials, although constrained to increase the registration of male adults, had minimized the public income accruing from the increased registration. At the same time officials had elected to serve the public cause. Consequently they were bound to resist administration from financing itself through any other than accepted public sources.

Such conflicting forces led to a deadlock difficult to resolve within the terms of the conflict. The K'ang-hsi emperor attempted to deal with it by permitting reasonable private collection, and by reducing the public share. But the first was bad for official morale. The second decreased revenue sources from which local government could receive income through either official allocations or informally accepted customary surcharges. The Yung-cheng emperor attempted to break the deadlock by reducing the private share and insisting on greatly increasing public collection. This provided substantial salaries but created its own problems by cutting back local initiatives. It was also a drastic solution. It was viewed as temporary; it became permanent.

But when need for revenue steadily rose none of the subsequent emperors dared take comparable steps. They preferred instead to raise the pressure on local officialdom as a means of increasing central revenue.[39] They left the problems of local income unsolved, despite the conflict of interest which this created.

Consequently local officials continued to find ways and means of financing their affairs. One such practice was known as "weighting the steelyard" (*chung-teng*). In Szechuan this practice brought in as much as one-tenth of a tael per tael. The Ch'ien-lung emperor attacked officials who made use of it as "degenerate."[40] Another very common practice was known as "official price" (*kuan-chia*). This consisted in setting official prices for commodities required by administrative offices regardless of the current market prices. Some officials defended the practice openly.[41]

Another common practice was to manipulate currency exchange rates. Many smaller taxpayers brought in their dues in copper coin. The rates were assessed in silver, and the payment had to be converted to silver for delivery to the superior authorities. The district office could set its own exchange rates regardless of current market rates. Or it could simply demand payment in copper cash when cash was expensive in relation to silver. The central government had unwittingly laid the ground for this abuse by decreeing that where the amount owed was less than one-tenth of a tael the tax could be delivered in either copper or silver.[42] In addition to such surcharges, district office personnel contrived to charge fees for every imaginable service.

Finally if none of these measures raised sufficient funds, local officials could connive at malpractices in tax collection. Acting officials may well have been obliged to do so, as the price of maintaining the cooperation of local underlings and gentry.[43]

Such practices were inevitable. With the rise in the cost of living and the increasing importance of reliable secretarial services, the salaries of private secretaries alone could use up the district official's entire supplementary salary. As the outspoken Chou Hao pointed out, the official also had to take care of his father and mother, his wife and children, the wages of his personal servants, the expenses of traveling on official business, the entertainment of superiors, presents for friends and fellow officials, and fees to superior offices for auditing district records and processing documents and registers. All these cost several times the amount of the supplementary salaries. In addition (the Yung-cheng emperor's wishes notwithstanding), local officials continued to have to offer many customary contributions to superior officials. As Chou said, if given time they took from the people. If pressed they raided the treasury.[44] Given the risks of the latter, the former was an obvious and irresistible alternative.

Thus in fiscal affairs the local official had little alternative than to exercise personal initiative. But this initiative was of no lasting advantage because it either strained his resources or took him into the forbidden territory of the private domain. It cannot therefore be thought that the practices arising from this initiative helped to invigorate or satisfy the aspirations of local officials. On the contrary, their only effect was to disturb or demoralize.

15

SOCIAL CONFLICT: THE PROBLEM OF LITIGATION

In addition to the pressures of the central government, local administration also came under considerable pressure from the general populace. While the central government pressed its interests by forbidding, constraining, and depriving, the population—or more often pressure groups in the population—maintained their interests by defying or importuning local administration.

The relative power of groups within the populace has been indicated at length in several recent studies, particularly those of Chang on the gentry and of Hsiao on rural China. They show that the Ch'ing central government determined to make substantial inroads into popular life and independent organization. They also show that many sections of the populace were capable of counteracting these inroads. The sources of power of these groups are complex and as yet far from understood. But undoubtedly organization and identity of interests played an important part in shaping their behavior.

The gentry, itself a conglomeration of groups, was united by a sense of status and vocation. Those who held senior degrees and examination status were also supported by the acquisition of wealth. However, the political strength of the gentry came principally from the ramifying contacts provided by the examination system, contacts which could connect them with members of provincial administrations or the central government itself. In addition, the clans provided in the east and south a multitude of social pressure groups, combining wealthy and indigent through physical and territorial cohesion.

At the lower end of the economic and social spectrum were large groups of transients and migrants, such as the "Shed" people and the Hakkas, identified through their segregation from native inhabitants. Many groups of roving beggars or outright bandits existed. They drew cohesion from their mobility and inaccessibility, and also from their relative desperation.

The secret societies formed another major series of groups. They regularly exerted local influence through control of local marketing systems and extortion of dues. They were united by a variety of anti-dynastic credos and came out in open hostility in times of unrest or revolt.

The administrative system itself provided groups whose members were ready to turn against it. The "rapacious" clerks and "verminous" runners were the most numerous of these elements. The personal servants, though fewer in number, were a source of frequent subversion. Leaders of rural control groups were also noted for a tendency to "misuse" their influence.

Finally, attention may be drawn to the so-called "village thugs" or bullies. These were an unending source of malediction in official writing. Whether the term is a catch-all or represents groups defined by specific characteristics of age, wealth, domicile, or occupation, is presently hard to determine.

Two major implications for administrations arose from this array of diverse and fluid, but often interlocking groups. First, nearly all these groups or clans used their power to check or undermine the encroachment of the central government. They resisted tax collection and rural organization. They hindered and disregarded law enforcement. They corrupted government administration. These moves were all part of the general conflict between government and society over the division of control over the public wealth and strength.

For the central government the overriding task was to bring these groups to heel and assert its right to authority over the entire domain. Its constant concern was how to maintain this authority once established. The variations in pressure which the central government brought to bear on local administration have to do principally with the scope of the resistance which it sensed in the local populace. They applied only secondarily to the state of local administration itself.

In the early Ch'ing period, the basic political struggle was between the central government and the powerholding groups within the populace, not between central and local administration or between local administration and the people.[1] In this general political conflict, local administrators were theoretically cast as agents of the central government. In practice they often found themselves as hostages of both sides. Yet they were bound to represent the public cause, however difficult and compromising this might be. Otherwise they were disloyal and would be cast aside. A great deal of the abuse of power by local administrators arose from the dilemmas created by this conflict.

At the same time the social power groups, and indeed the whole of the populace, were constantly divided among themselves. This was a function of the endemic competitiveness in the private life of society. Ch'ing government was well aware of this turmoil, but unlike Emperor Ming T'ai-tsu, it had no coherent policy for dealing with it. The government could not approve of social competitiveness because of the friction and conflict it stirred up. This conflict was a potent source of individual economic failure; it contributed to fiscal and judicial maladministration, and thereby resentment against the government itself. Yet the government was unable to solve the problem of competitiveness. It could only issue rebates and amnesties, exhort and chide, demand checks and controls, and when necessary suppress and punish. All these procedures were merely attacking the problem from the outside. They failed to get at its roots.

This inadequately controlled or channeled competitiveness was responsible for a great deal of the crime and litigiousness which plagued Ch'ing administration. The central government knew how to deal with crime. It insisted on suppressing it. It also took seriously its duty to prevent crime with moral education. In its careful system of judicial reviews and frequent amnesties, it projected an attitude toward the treatment of crime which compares favorably with conditions prevalent in the eighteenth- and early nineteenth-century West. The Ch'ing record on crime is marred by the abuse of crime prevention by local administrations. But this happened because the imperial regime insisted on assuming responsibility for the state of public order. Because it felt its capability implicated by crime, it insisted that its agents resolve crimes. But this was an outcome of the general conditions of public authority, and not simply of attitudes toward crime.[2]

The imperial government had no such clear-cut policy toward litigation. In principle the government disapproved strongly of this practice and would have liked to have put a stop to it. But it did not actually prohibit it. The people for their part litigated insistently. With the breakdown of the system of neighborhood jurisdiction, the first official court before which they could press their claims was that of the district magistrate. The Ch'ing government made no provision for the pressure of litigation on public administration, other than to prohibit and penalize the practices of bringing false charges, or taking suits to higher courts before they had been adjudicated in the magistrate's court.[3] Thus it actually required magistrates to process and judge all litigation brought before public authority. It did not make provision for the time and effort which this adjudication might involve.

There is little doubt that this double imposition by the people and the government strained the capabilities and goodwill of district magistrates. These officials were already under pressure from all the sanctions imposed by the central government. To be required to hear all manner of pleas and suits ran counter to their order or priorities. Nor suprisingly, the common reaction of officials was negative to litigation. It took time from other business on which their record depended. It often confronted them with complex issues requiring a forensic skill for which they were not prepared. They also had the same reasons as the emperors for disapproving in principle of litigation. Inevitably, these conditions led to much backlogging of cases, or to hasty analysis and inappropriate judgments. They also inspired direct antipathy between the people and their local judges. The latter were put out by the excessive and untoward nature of the litigation. The former, when faced with costly delay or misjudgment, developed a resentment or contempt for public justice. In sum, few matters could cause more trouble between the local officials and the people than the treatment of litigation.

The problem caused by litigation was in the first place conceptual. There is no clear definition of what litigation (*sung*) constituted, other than that it involved conflict. The *Chou li* commentary states that litigation concerned disputes over property, as opposed to disputes of a criminal nature, the proceedings for which were called by a different term (*yü*). The *Li chi* commentary says, however, that criminal disputes were also called *sung*. One early source distinguished *sung* as involving small affairs and *yü* as involving large. Another gave the term *sung* an essentially moral connotation, by saying that it concerned conflict between the "crooked and straight."[4]

Such differences of opinion would have provided Western jurists with an exegetic field day. The Chinese reaction, however, has been to avoid such a response. No doubt this attitude has been influenced by the treatment of the term in the *Book of Changes*. In that highly allusive document, *sung* "conflict" is interpreted in a manner that is both somber and ambivalent. The classic views "conflict" as meaning "not to be in affectionate closeness" (*ch'in*). It comments that the hexogram is made up of the strength of Heaven and the danger of water. Danger and strength produce conflict. This conflict must not be allowed to become permanent. At the same time the passage defines conflict as "sincerity which is obstructed." It implies that action should be brought before a great man, holding that a cautious halt half-way will bring good fortune. Only going through to the end brings misfortune.

In its line by line interpretation of *sung* the implication of danger comes out strongest. One may not prolong the conflict. One cannot engage in conflict; one returns home and gives way, so as to avoid implicating others. One turns back and submits to fate. One changes, becomes peaceful and perseveres. Thus there is good fortune and nothing lost. To contend before the great man brings supreme good fortune, because he is in the middle and upright. But to press the matter to a conclusion will fail to command respect and, by implication, will cause lasting resentment.

The image that remains is of Heaven and water going in opposite and divisive ways. The weight of the advice is against taking action. Thus, the classic comments, the *chüntzu* in all his doings considers the beginning.[5]

This view of *sung* is reinforced by other statements from Confucian literature. Confucius himself said, "as to hearing litigation I am as good as another. What is necessary is to cause there to be no litigation." The *Chou li*, in its more authoritarian way, spoke of the minister of justice as prohibiting litigation.[6]

The Ch'ing rulers reflected this unease over litigation. The K'ang-hsi emperor criticized officials who liked to receive suits. He said that while they should value probity it was still more important to value social harmony. "If you like to receive suits, many will be brought by trouble makers. Then, even if you hear and settle them at once, the whole livelihood of those against whom the suit was brought will still be spent. How will the people bear it?"[7]

In the Sacred Edict and Amplification, the emperors attempted to dissuade the people themselves. Practice harmony in the villages, said the Edict, so as to put an end to conflict and litigation. Put an end to false pleas, so as to preserve the good and the well-intentioned. Settle animosities so as to value life. The Yung-cheng emperor maintained that discord generally arose from small matters. He admitted that those who sustained injuries obviously must bring pleas, but implied that most suits were irresponsible or false and thereby contrary to the laws. But the emperor also stressed that the Edict said "put an end" and not "prohibit." Prohibition would have implied that the control of litigation was up to the officials."Put an end" admitted that it was beyond official control, and could only be restrained by public opinion.[8]

Unfortunately for the government, the cases brought before the courts often did not arise from small beginnings. Many involved disputes over property, particularly over the disposition of estates. In the eighteenth century, when the population was expanding rapidly in relation to the arable area, and especially in relation to established rice- and wheatland, conflict over estates was inevitable. But inheritance disputes were often extremely difficult to resolve because of the complexity of the rites of succession.

The point may be illustrated by the following case, which came before Wang Hui-tsu in 1776. It involved, in Wang's words, a "cunning rogue" named Shu Ch'iu. Feng Yü, a member of a collateral branch of Shu's sib, who was of the same generation as Shu's father but younger, died leaving a daughter and a substantial estate of 270 *mou*, but no son to inherit it. Shu decided to claim the inheritance for himself. The clansmen found that Feng Yü's elder brother had had one son (who would have had prior claim over Shu), but that he naturally could not abandon his own line. Feng's wife had already died and his daughter already married.

The clan held that there ought to be a male inheritor but did not specify whom. However Wang, as a secretary, divided the estate as follows. He recommended that one hundred *mou* be allotted to the married daughter, twenty to funeral expenses and the remaining one hundred and fifty be set up as sacrificial land, for the purpose of maintaining sacrifices for Feng's father.

Shu thereupon appealed to the prefect. The prefect considered that, since Feng had left property, an heir should be established. Shu was in the correct line of succession and therefore had not made a "false" plea. If the authorities found fault with Shu because he had "instigated" litigation, and had the (married) daughter taken over much of the property, the soul of Feng would be associated with only general sacrifices (there would be none to him specifically). This was not the right way to restore a line of succession broken by the absence of an heir, and was correcting a fault with a fault. Consequently, the prefect ordered the district authorities to look into the regulations with a view to determining the succession.

Wang did this and rejoined that the regulations did not specify that there *must* be a successor. They merely stated that in the case of one who died without a son it was *permissible* that a patrilineal male of the next generation receive the inheritance. The regulations indicated the order of priority for inheritance, and said that it was permissible to appeal to the authorities to establish an heir if there were no close relatives. But such a one must correspond to the correct mourning sequence (i.e., be only one generation down) and be "worthy, capable, and well loved by the close relatives."

From this Wang concluded that the succession should be determined in the interests of the principal who had left no son. If the principal had not himself established a succession, it was not for the authorities to let anyone else interfere. As far as receiving a succession was concerned, it was receiving the ancestral hall which was important, not receiving the estate. Receiving the ancestral hall meant having served the parents in their lifetime and mourning them in death. In other words the adopted heir and the senior relatives were bound by ties of mutual affection. This was not the case with Feng and Shu. As Feng and his wife had not established an heir they would know nothing of the why's and wherefore's of their "successor"; the successor could not be moved by feelings of mutual affection and could only be coveting their estate.

Wang added, "in natural relationships there is none surpassing father and son. To call another man father is not a fortunate thing." The son who was to become heir to another definitely should receive the permission of his own father. For that reason the *Li chi* held that an orphan did not become the descendant of another.

Shu's father had been dead many years. If Shu was not the choice of Feng, or the specific recommendation of the clan, and did not have his own father's permission, he was in effect abandoning his own father for the sake of another's wealth. If he could not be filial to his own parents, how could he be expected to be filial to those who had not chosen him?

On the other hand, said Wang, the affection of living parents, if not lavished on a son, is lavished on a daughter. The Fengs would have wished their daughter to receive an inheritance. As to the sacrifices, these could correctly be performed by Feng's nephew in the name of Feng's father and his nephew's grandfather. By this means Feng's inheritance would contribute to his father's sacrifices and he would not be cut off from this service. Wang therefore maintained his original allotment and with these arguments convinced the perfect.[9]

This case produced an unexpected sequel. A certain Mrs. Huang, who had been widowed for four years and who had no son, was supporting herself and two daughters off forty-two *mou* of land. The clan elders took advantage of the ruling in the Shu Ch'iu case to request that the land left by the heirless Mr. Huang be transferred to the clan temple as sacrificial land. The elders of Mr. Huang's branch of the clan should be authorized to collect the rent and Mrs. Huang prevented from making any private sale of the property.

Wang was startled by this and argued that the purpose of transferring land for sacrificial use had been to prevent unfilial contests for succession. It was not intended to open the way for clans to seize property. It happened that just then Wang's employer was recommended for a prefecture and granted an Audience. He was absent for nine months, during which Wang waited for his return in his native district. In that time an acting magistrate granted the request of the clan. He transferred the land to the custody of the branch temple, allotted Mrs. Huang a modest annual income of thirty bushels of rice, and ordered the tenants not to pay rent privately to her.

After Wang was able to return to the district he reversed this ruling. Instead he allotted the temple five *mou*, thus indicating that the clan case was not entirely without foundation. But he held that a widow was entitled to receive her husband's estate and pointed out that Mrs. Huang had proved herself capable of supporting her family. As the proposed income would have been insufficient to provide for the expenses of upbringing, marriage, sickness, and dowry, she and her daughters should retain control of the remaining land to dispose of as they pleased. To allow the head of the clan to take over the land was not in keeping with either law or social custom and would merely cause the widow to cherish grievance.[10]

The above cases, and many more like them, were motivated by economic pressures. Wang's judgment on the basis of traditional morality may seem old-fashioned. However, this morality continued to exert a powerful influence. When in conflict with economic pressures it was itself a source of litigation.

For example, one case, which dragged on for eighteen years, involved a wealthy widow who had borne her husband a posthumous son. The son died when he was seventeen, before coming of age, and one month before his marriage. The clan proposed to exercise their right to choose an heir for the husband, a choice which the widow could not have controlled. The widow, however, wished to choose an heir for her own dead son. At issue, besides a rich inheritance, was the question whether an heir could be established for an unmarried person. Evidently district administrations had found the case a tough one to handle (because of the influence and wealth of the disputants) and had preferred to refer it back to the clan. In due course the widow nominated an heir for her son, but the clan opposed him on the grounds that he was not in the right generation to succeed her husband. After further years of indecision, the widow reopened the case when she felt herself nearing death.

Wang, who had lost his own father when a child and who was devoted to his mother, sided with the widow. He sensed the effort which she had put into the upbringing of her child and the grief caused by his untimely death. To establish an heir for the son might not be provided for by law, but, as Wang put it, "it was the only [solution] in accordance with human feelings." Wang secured his opinion with a statement from the *Li chi* that "the descendants of one who dies before attaining his majority should put on their mourning garments and mourn him." If such a one was without a succession, who, said Wang, could constitute his descendants? What the laws had not forseen could be followed according to the rituals. Wang also emphasized that the widow had been faithful to her husband. What could be better than giving the son a successor, thus fulfilling the intention of the virtuous wife? She had chosen a "grandson" who was presently alive. Let him be selected.

Wang's decision had serious consequences. Because he had "abandoned the laws to follow the rites," his fellow secretaries were sure he had been bribed. The magistrate was also "very startled" and many times referred the decision back to Wang for revision. Wang told him, "it is not hard to decide against the clan. But as father and mother of the people, you cannot order a faithful widow to bear a grievance to the end of her days." He refused to alter his opinion and offered his resignation.

Then the provincial governor ordered the district to send up the entire record on the case. The secretaries were all very agitated, but Wang said, "I have nothing to hide!" The governor happened to be Ch'en Hung-mou, an official of the highest repute. It transpired that some licentiates of the clan, dissatisfied with Wang's ruling, had lodged an appeal against it. After reading the documents Ch'en approved of Wang's opinion and "severely punished and demoted" the appellants. The magistrate, summoned to the governor's office, was able to leave "highly satisfied." [11]

These cases help to illustrate the extent to which society pressed its conflicts on administration, and the trouble which administration had in resolving them. In theory society was not supposed to press its claims on administration. Clan regulations also took this view and threatened sanctions against members who took suits to the district court without first obtaining a hearing before the clan officials.

But when clans were themselves parties to disputes it was obviously difficult for them to provide adjudicators who were "in the middle and upright" (as opposed to leaning on one side). Moreover, clan courts could not cater very well to inter-clan disputes, let alone to those between any of the millions who were without organized clan affiliations. The district magistrate, as an outsider, was the most obvious arbitrator. In any case clan members themselves viewed him as such and were ready to insist that he play this role. Moreover, they would bring all their available pressure to bear, particularly on temporary officials. The stakes could be high, and bribery was expected. Appeals to higher courts were not uncommon. Wang speaks of one case in which every year for ten years the disputants appealed from the district to the prefecture to the circuit to the province, without achieving any result. [12]

Local administrators in return, were reluctant to handle such cases. They would have preferred that the disputants settle them out of court. It is true that litigation brought in valuable income and was encouraged by office underlings on these grounds. But the officials themselves had also to weigh the consequences of their decisions. They might contravene the law. Or they might stir up resentment and opposition. Either eventuality could lead to further trouble.

In this respect the ignorance of the laws among officials was a special handicap. It will be noticed that two of the above cases were in fact resolved through reference to ritual prescriptions, not to the laws of the state. This is because of the importance attached to the satisfaction of human feelings and the reestablishment of social harmony. It might be thought that officials, being thoroughly trained in matters of ritual and human feeling, would have been able to arrive at ritually based solutions without needing the assistance of legal secretaries. But the truth seems to be that ignorance of the laws made officials afraid to turn to the rituals, even though ritual teachings were canonical and held to provide the moral basis underlying the laws. Only those who were thoroughly acquainted with the laws were able to have confidence in relying on the rituals.

These conditions called for men who, while turning themselves into legal specialists, retained a basic Confucian orientation. Such a commitment was not required of legal specialists, any more than legal specialization was required of officials. Under these circumstances it is not surprising if officials should have lacked confidence in arriving at judicial decisions.[13]

In due course the central government found it necessary to bring pressure to bear on local officials to deal with pending litigation. A regulation required magistrates to give decisions on legal disputes within twenty days. In 1810 penalties of a relatively light nature were prescribed for failure to meet this time limit.[14]

The government also put pressure on magistrates to deal with all those who "fomented" litigation. These consisted of notaries (*sung-shih*, often referred to in Western language texts as "pettifoggers" because of the perjorative official usage of the term *sung-shih*), clerks or scribes (*tai-shu*, office employees designated to take down the depositions of plaintiffs), and also the above-mentioned "village thugs" or bullies. Apart from the clerks, these were all private operators, who assisted illiterate or uniformed people in drawing up suits. They had existed in the southeast for many years. A late Sung author wrote of "several hundred specialists" opening litigation schools in the Kiangsi of his day, so as to teach the people how to "reply to the law point by point."[15]

The Ch'ing government objected to litigation specialists because they thrived on drumming up business which the government was trying to suppress. However, the government was particularly incensed by the notaries. Many of these were licentiates who, in its view, should have been supporting the state's objectives instead of flouting them.

Accordingly the government moved to make local officials responsible for litigation specialists. It could not prohibit the actual drawing up of suits, but it ordered in 1725 that suits were only to be transcribed according to the actual circumstances of the charge. Those who magnified or belittled the circumstances were to be punished according to the law against false pleas. Local officials were given moderate penalties for neglecting to investigate, or for condoning, the activities of notaries.[16] The Board of Punishment also recommended that local officials be ordered to examine the pleas drawn up and sealed by the authorized office clerks (*tai-shu*). Those who collaborated with notaries should be punished according to law. "Perverse" lesser gentry who fomented litigation should be given double the punishment.[17]

Among the local officials themselves, even those who were experts in legal administration exhibited an attitude of unease towards litigation. Wang Hui-tsu, speaking as an official, held that magistrates must hear suits. "Those in authority over the people," he pointed out, "clothe themselves in taxes and feed off levies. What is there that is not taken from the people? Therefore, the way in which they repay the labor of the people is in settling disputes and in leading the people according to what is right."[18]

Wang himself made a point of acting on this view, and took pride in his ability to bring disputes to a harmonious end. Nevertheless, he felt bound to find a broader justification for accepting litigation than the mere provision of a public hearing and an authoritative decision for two parties' at dispute. He found this in the general educational value of public hearings. By hearing cases, he claimed, the spectators could deduce the rights and wrongs in comparable cases. Then those who had not brought suits could be warned off; those who had could desist. Therefore, the official should explain the reasons for a flogging "over and over again" and show the full significance of social values in his judgments.

But Wang preferred arbitration to public hearings. "In hearing a case one acts according to the law; in arbitrating, according to feelings. With the law you have to distinguish between "clear and turbid." With feelings . . . there is nothing to bar a compromise . . . . Then those in the wrong can avoid the law of the public court." This, he concluded, must be why the Chou administrative system provided for an "arbitrator."[19]

Comparable opinions were expressed by Mu-han and Liu Heng. Mu-han held that in the ordinary world (as opposed to the world administered by sages) it was impossible to cause the people to be without litigation. "Of course," he added, "those officials who are weak and apprehensive and those who are stubborn and opinionated can cause the people to be without litigation. But how can we talk of them? If you willingly let cases accumulate, this is not being the father and mother of the people; it is being the bandit-enemy of the people." He insisted that magistrates must hear and settle cases, so as to convenience the people and "help somewhat" to put an end to litigation.[20]

Liu Heng was another noted legal expert and unflagging auditor of disputes. To avoid obstructions by "verminous clerks" he dispensed with the services of a gate porter. When he heard the gate bell ringing, signifying the presence of a plaintiff, he at once went out and heard the matter on the spot. He advised the people against bringing small cases to court, saying "even if you feel one hundred percent in the right, restrain your anger . . . and at most take the case to the clan for settlement. Even though you suffer some loss, this is far better than taking it before the official. If you only feel fifty or sixty percent in the right, then let the matter rest."[21]

These skilled judges all distrusted litigation because of the harm it could do both to the people and to local officials. They saw it as a "snare," leading people toward disgrace and ruin. It was expensive, time-consuming, and would merely wipe out the livelihood of small cultivators. It could bring criminal implications and disgrace, since anyone bringing an unsubstantiated accusation ran the immediate risk of fifty blows of the bamboo for bringing a "false" plea.

More generally, there was little doubt in the minds of these officials that litigation involved distinguishing between "right and wrong," "crooked and straight," "clear and turbid." The penal laws and statutes were very comprehensive when it came to defining and punishing crooked and turbid behavior. Consequently, litigation could, and did, involve criminal punishment. In principle the punishments of the penal law were supposed to be "bright" and "educative." In practice they involved wearing halters or undergoing naked floggings in public. They might also involve "punitive interrogations" in public. These magistrates knew that such punishment could very well turn the victim into a laughing-stock and be the source of lasting resentments and social strife.

They also saw litigation as "entangling" the officials. Litigation exposed officials to fears of delays and deceptions by their office staff. Such fears were not unfounded though they may have been exaggerated. Among many deceptions practiced by office underlings was one known as "cutting out and pasting in." The clerk would cut out a key word in the written plea, on which the interpretation of the case depended. He would then reinsert the same word in such a way that the excision was almost, but not quite, unnoticeable. The idea was to let the sharp but unwary official think that the document had been tampered with and conclude that the plaintiff had bribed someone to dress up his case. Magistrates had to be experienced in such tricks and know how to circumvent them. Otherwise, they would get involved in miscarriages of justice and inflict unjust punishments.[22]

Litigation also brought with it the risk that dissatisfied parties would spread rumors and anonymous accusations against the presiding official, or they might appeal and involve him in difficulties with his superiors. Perhaps worst of all, from the viewpoints of the experts, was the strain which litigation placed on the judgment of the official. In their picture the magistrate as judge was ringed by ill-wishers, observing all his mannerisms, conscious of his difficulties, and waiting to exploit every mistake. It was easy to act too quickly, or not quickly enough.

The strain imposed by litigation came out in the virulent antipathy which magistrates expressed toward notaries and other "fomentors" of suits. Mu-han branded them as "ulcers." They "perverted the truth," "stirred up mischief" and fomented suits out of trivialities; then they "harassed with talk of loss" or "swindled with talk of certain victory," "suppressed the truth," "trumped up falsehoods," "ruined families and squandered inheritances." Wang Hui-tsu grouped bullies and notaries with robbers, bandits, and villainous beggars. He held that clerks relied on them as their "stomach and heart."[23]

These are harsh words. The picture is also one-sided: we do not know what notaries thought of magistrates. It is possible to make out a case of sorts for them. They were persons of some educational experience, as is indicated by their ability to phrase and write down formal pleas. A good number were licentiates. How were they to make a living? The state had nothing to offer, beyond despised positions as office underlings. Litigation was not prohibited and was admittedly inevitable. Why not turn one's education to advantage and profit from this money-making activity? This is an unflattering rationale. But it serves to show that even the litigation experts were symptoms of a problem, rather than its cause.

Nevertheless the notaries and bullies represented a threat to the equanimity of local officials. They forced activity in an area lacking any clear guidelines and full of hazards and pitfalls. As individuals they were hard to identify; while some were "openly malignant," many operated under cover. Plaintiffs refused to disclose their names and would merely say they had been helped by "passing fortune-tellers."[24] In short, they were influential and hostile, and they were impossible to repress. The Yung-cheng emperor's charge that officials conniving at notaries did so out of "fear" carries conviction. For local administrators, the threat of entanglement was the predominant association with litigation. Their tendency to let cases pile up should be seen in this light.

Moreover, on this matter they appear to have been impervious to imperial pressure. The Chia-ch'ing emperor complained that litigation should be heard and settled speedily so as to prevent delay and entanglement. "Already I have often sent down edicts to this effect; but officials in the provinces let matters drift and pretend not to hear. Either they sink themselves in pleasure and are lazy about hearing and deciding, or they take precautions against reopening cases, hoping to avoid entanglement. Thus notaries presume on their cunning, confound right and wrong, and brew small into big. Appeals to higher authority and to the capital daily increase in multitude." All this, said the emperor, was because "worthless district officials nurture perverse customs," which he denounced as "loathsome."[25]

The passage implies that local magistrates were at fault for equivocating over right and wrong. As a diagnosis this is hard to doubt; it seems to point to the crux of the dilemma facing Ch'ing magistrates. These officials were becoming uneasy about the relevance of their values. Under the impact of the disciplinary system the test of what was right was increasingly becoming the test of what served the public interest. How well, and how much longer, could this be squared with the values instilled through the long Confucian training, which itself contained the seeds of conflict? Even the most reflective magistrates preferred arbitration to legal proceedings, because it relieved them from having to make orthodox value judgments. Less responsible men, by prevaricating or by relying rigidly on the laws, simply evaded the challenge to their values.

This behavior has been condemned. But the institutional system itself is hardly free of implication. It placed magistrates under mounting pressure to exert control, and yet at the same time deprived them of the authority to do so according to their convictions. This was threatening to take the humanity out of local administration and invalidate the cultural role of the magistrate.

16

GOVERNMENT BY MEN: THE STRUGGLE TO UPHOLD
POLITICAL HUMANISM

The problem of authority in Ch'ing local administration lends force to the plea for administration by men rather than methods. This idea, first voiced by Hsuntzu, is a recurrent theme in Ch'ing administrative writing.

It was originally provoked by Shang Yang's determination that government by method should be universally enforced to eliminate independence in subordinate administrators and unite the body politic under one all-powerful ruler. What Shang Yang valued uppermost in officials was consistency; what he distrusted most was integrity. To stress that his policies involved the overthrow of existing values and systems he denounced such values as "evil" and preferred to employ the "wicked" rather than the "good." When methods were clear, he said, there would be no need for intelligent and thoughtful officials. Officials would not be "depraved"— meaning, maintain their own "private interest" over the people; the "worthy" would be put aside and the "wicked" obtained for administrative service.

This position had been too radical for Hsuntzu. He had rejoined that methods could not act of themselves. The preservation of order depended on getting the right men. While methods were the starting point to administrative order, the *chüntzu* was its fundamental principle. No matter how well the methods were drawn up, if there were no *chüntzu* to adapt and apply them, methods themselves would lead to disorder.[1]

Of course, when it came to the employment of officials, none of the Ch'ing emperors subscribed to the opinions of Shang Yang. But they did believe in methods. Their advisers, in return, questioned whether methods could be pressed without undermining morale and penalizing the worthy. On these grounds they had opposed the conversion of the *huo-hao* surcharge into a public levy. For similar reasons they rejected the establishment of extra offices in local administration, and regretted the heaviness of the disciplinary regulations.

On the question of the *huo-hao* surcharge, the ministers said outright that it was not a way which could be maintained on a regular or long-term basis. "Wherever methods have been established to carry out government, how can things go for long without malpractices? Hitherto 'administration has been by men, not by methods.'" The ministers reinforced this claim with a quotation from the *Doctrine of the Mean* saying: "The government of Wen and Wu (founders of the Chou dynasty) is displayed in the records of wood and bamboo. If such men are preserved, their government will flourish." They left unsaid the antithesis: "If such men are lost their government ceases. . . . Therefore the carrying out of government depends on men."[2]

The emperor responded sharply, "I say there is administration by men *and* by methods." He continued with the insistent Legalist argument that methods were designed to suit the needs of the times. When a person was sick, one gave him medicine to get well. When he had recovered, then one stopped it. The analogy is appropriate, for the emperor fully hoped to end the treatment, as happened in other instances. In this case, however, the treatment went on without achieving any lasting cure.[3]

As well as opposing methods as superfluous or corrupting, officials also held that they deflected attention from the prerequisities for sound administration. During the Yung-cheng reign, a censor recommended the establishment of ranking officials at the *hsiang* or rural subdistrict level. This would have given on the average four extra officials per district. He suggested that they be chosen from degree holders native to each *hsiang*.

The emperor was rather taken with the idea. He saw that the business of district magistrates was "really very complex and manifold." When they had different tasks in different areas, they could not "divide themselves in two." The addition of an official would reduce delays and errors and leave a regular colleague in charge whenever the magistrate was promoted, was transferred, or left office. (It seems that the emperor was thinking in terms of one additional assistant rather than four). The danger in having two people to make up one administrative function was that there would be no clear division of responsibility or authority, and business might end up being delayed after all. With this in mind the emperor handed the suggestion over to some of his most trusted metropolitan and provincial officials for their consideration.

These advisers rejected it as of no advantage whatsoever. They held that the district magistrate already had enough ranking assistants. They disapproved of the appointment of natives, saying that the laws of avoidance had been established precisely because, when officials were given office near to their native place, it was easy for them to turn public office to private advantage. The employment of local degree-holders or elderly commoners would introduce all the evils which the laws of avoidance had been designed to prevent. The advisers admitted that such people would have the advantage of "really knowing a *hsiang* and its undesirable inhabitants." But could they genuinely be counted on to act justly and according to the facts?

"First employ those who have office," said the advisers, drawing on the opinion of Confucius himself.[4] This meant "employing" the existing assistant officials and the heads of the rural control institutions. If the magistrate was competent, the assistants would help him to get things done. If he was not, then *hsiang* officials, no matter how worthy, would not be able to be master of their affairs. If unworthy, they would simply aid an evil cause.

The advisers admitted that there were failings in the conduct of district business by underlings and heads of rural control institutions. But, they argued, we cannot dispense with these persons. We already have plenty of regulations for holding them to their duties; there is no question here of having neglected methods. If subordinates did not carry out orders vigorously, it was because their superior official did not direct them conscientiously. "This," they affirmed, "is a human failing. What has it to do with methods?"

The point was to cause officials, high and low, to be *sincere* and to put real heart and effort into their work. We already have good laws and institutions, said the advisers; so let us not cause confusion by altering methods simply for the sake of expediency. "From old there is the saying that 'administration is by men, not by methods.' This is something that cannot be changed." The advisers concluded that even though district administration was "complex and manifold," the important thing was simply for the magistrate to "grasp the essential" (a basic Confucian premiss); then it would not be difficult for them to regulate their duties.

This opinion carried the day. No *hsiang* appointments were created. Significantly, a local official later criticized the opinion as unsound, and held that the idea of appointing *hsiang* officials was a very good one.[5]

The most prevalent of all the methods were the penal laws and regulations. By the time of the Ch'ing dynasty, officials had long since accepted the inevitability of the laws. Canonical documents sanctioned the principle of administrative enforcement of punishment. The position established in a (spurious) passage in the *Book of Documents* is that punishments were established to assist in the inculcation of civilized standards, so that through punishment there might come to be no punishment. The Ch'ing emperors affirmed this view of punishment.[6] Consequently, officials promoting judicial administration were able to argue that its practices belonged within canonical concepts of administration.

For example, Mu-han supported his case with citations from the Books of *Odes* and *Documents*, the *Chou li* and the *Han shu* (History of the former Han dynasty). He cited statements from the *Analects*, out of context, to imply that Confucius himself regarded the conducting of trials and administration of punishments as part of the task of government, but pointed out that there was more to judicial administration than applying the "bright" and educative punishments.[7]

Yuan Shou-ting, who was as much an advocate of Confucian principles as any Ch'ing administrator, held that just as early penal regulations were based on ritual prescriptions, so too was the Ch'ing penal code. He described it as a "great embankment designed to shore up the drifting current of the people" and bring about the "humanity" and "justice" of Mencius. Therefore officials must study the laws (literally "methods and orders") and take them as a "guide." Then they could be officials.[8]

But there was a distinction in attitudes toward punishment and penal laws. Punishments were constant; they were also canonically limited in type and number. Penal laws, being methods, were expedient; but they were not limited in type or number. The Confucian position was that penal regulations were no substitute for moral power, and that Confucius himself disapproved in principle of regulations. While Mu-han might argue that Confucius regarded penal regulations as a fact of administration, his contemporary, Liu Pao-nan (who also served as a magistrate and wrote an influential commentary to the *Analects*) was nearer the truth in inferring that Confucius preferred the moral power of the former kings to the (assumed) profusion of regulations and penalties in the governments of his day.[9] In view of this, the Ch'ing proliferation of binding, and apparently permanent, regulations was a source of justifiable anxiety to officials, particularly since so much of this legislation applied to the control of administration.

It is thus no surprise to find that Wang Chih-i, in his memorial regretting the severity of the disciplinary regulations, should have opened it with the words, "your servant reflects that, from old, administration has been by men, not by methods." Wang argued that unless methods could be universally enforced, the more comprehensive they were made, the more they would be evaded and the worse would be the laxity in administration. Thus deliberating methods could not be compared in importance with care in employing the right men. The Chia-ch'ing emperor accepted this argument and admitted that "methods were unable to cause action by themselves."[10]

The aversion among Ch'ing officials and scholars to methods was sufficiently strong so that it was hard for them even to accept the role of private secretary as a valid lifetime career. In the Ch'ing period, private secretaries played a vital role in local administration and were influential in other levels of administration. The legal secretary in the district office was second only in importance to the magistrate; his influence far outweighed that of ranking assistants. But private secretaries rose to office as the practitioners of methods. They served as a buffer, protecting the Confucian role of the official against the accumulated laws and regulations. For that reason competent secretaries found themselves pursued by officials with offers of employment at salaries sometimes comparable with those of magistrates themselves. But as experts in methods, they themselves had trouble in obtaining satisfaction from their role, and their performance could not excite the interest of biographers.

This applied even to distinguished secretaries like Wang Hui-tsu. He served as a private secretary for thirty-three years. He wrote in his autobiography that when he received his first appointment he did not really want the job of secretary as a profession. In his handbook on the function of private secretaries he wrote, "If a scholar, because he cannot get himself into administration, therefore assists others to administer, it is because he has no other option."[11] The modern editors of the gazetteer of his native district gave one line to his long career as a secretary, but two pages to his four years as a magistrate. Of the former, they noted that he studied the sayings of the Legalists (or methodists) and entered many district offices as secretary. They explain that he did this to get money to nourish his mothers (his real mother was his father's concubine). Nothing else is said, even though Wang was still working as a secretary ten years after the death of his stepmother. [12]

The key to the silence is in the word "Legalists." Some biographical accounts say specifically of distinguished secretaries that they studied the arts of Shen (Pu-hai) and Han (Feitzu). [13] In Wang's case the slur of Legalism is excused on Confucian grounds. Fortunately he achieved an official career, so his record as a Legalist could be hurriedly passed over.

In fact Wang's career as a secretary is extremely interesting, because he determined to play the role according to Confucian principles. Not only did he consider feelings and circumstances and give judicial decisions according to the Rites; he wrote that, as a legal secretary, whenever he was assisting on a case, no matter whether great or small, he always sat quietly for a while, put himself in the position of the criminal, and reflected about it as if he were his "father and mother." [14]

This resistance to methods and to Legalism is in keeping with the general resistance to encroachment by the public domain. Methods represented an assertion of the authority of the public domain over the private. As an assertion of authority, they enjoyed no justification other than expediency. In return for the benefits of expediency, "methodism" had introduced an era of permissive social competitiveness and exploitation and, from the Confucian viewpoint, driven out humanism. Consequently, the distrust of existing methods reflected a distrust of the moral basis of public authority.

This distrust was furthered by the conviction that the "humanity" essential to sound administration could never be attained by means of coercion. The existing system of "public" authority had been grounded on the use of force. It had originated in the system of "overlords" or "hegemons," first established in the early seventh century B.C. The power of the Chou dynasty kings having waned, a number of their subordinate feudal rulers grouped together under an agreed "overlord" as a means of resisting the encroachment of border states indifferent to the integrity of the declining Chou order. Subsequently the system was used largely as a means of containing the power of the stronger feudal rulers and introducing some rules into the conduct of interstate relations. The first overlord was duke Huan of Ch'i. His chief minister, who solidified his political power, was Kuan Chung.

The significance of the overlord system was that it was an expedient which took the place of kingly authority and maintained itself on the balance of competing state power. The authority of the overlord was grounded on a guarded and conditional recognition of his physical force. Thus Mencius wrote: "The one who by means of force pretends to humanity is an overlord; an overlord must have a large state. The one who by means of moral power carries out humanity is a king; a king does not depend on size . . . king Wen made do with a state of a hundred *li* (thirty-five miles)." [15]

This comment seemed germane to the conditions of administration in the early Ch'ing empire. Few states could have been larger. Few administrations and societies had been more subject to coercive regulations.

A high official of the time, who was a lifelong student of Mencius, considered the rise of the overlords, and Kuan Chung in particular, as forming the root of the trouble. "Kuan Chung," he wrote. "is the beginning of the [system of] overlords and the means by which the kingly way was cut off." The official, Jen Ch'i-yun, cited the opinion that the one who by means of force pretends to humanity is an overlord, and commented, "Mencius hated their pretense; he did not hate their humanity . . . *But now we hate the humanity which they pretended.*" Instead, claimed Jen, people revered Kuan Chung above all others and desired after the methods which he had established. Jen listed a number of eminent statesmen, including Wang Yang-ming, and commented, "These men all possessed the force to move Heaven and Earth." But, he said with some truth, they drew their policies deeply from those of Kuan Chung. Thus, he insisted, "If we say we wish to restore the kingly way, we must start at Kuan Chung, where Kuan Chung departed from it." [16]

This was a fairly drastic judgment; but in terms of Confucian ideology, it was not unsound. Confucianism held that the legitimacy of the king arose from his acceptance as sovereign by the people. It insisted that popular sanction was won only by moral power and never by coercion. From this standpoint, "public" authority was synonymous with arbitrary power. It was not based on popular acceptance; dukes and other state rulers were appointed by kings and were their feudal subordinates. Their authority stemmed only from that of the accepted king, and his only from the people. By the same token, the philosophy of Legalism, for which Kuan Chung provided the prototype, was the philosophy of force. Its laws

and methods were instruments of coercion, based on the will of the overlord, not of his subjects.

In this connection, it is worth emphasizing that the objection to methods
is specifically an objection to Legalist methods. There was no objection
to the methods of the kingly way, because this way was based on an
accepted (and acceptable) mandate. With the usurpation of "private" by
"public" this mandate was overruled.

It is for this reason that it has been considered preferable here to refer
to *fa* by the more inclusive term "methods" rather than, as is usually the
case, "law." The idea of law, particularly in its Anglo-Saxon context, is
that it is something which contains and checks the sovereign authority.
The law is an expression of the will not of the sovereign but of the sovereign
and his subjects. The sovereign authority is itself subject to the law.

With "Legalism" the reverse is the case. *Fa* became the instrument of
the sovereign and a denial of the authority of subjects. It is understandable,
therefore, that if "Legalism" undermined the right of the private domain,
its opponents should have resisted methods and insisted on the principle
of administration by men. In this they were not unsuccessful; for while
imperial rulers went on establishing methods, they also accepted and did
not try to deny this opposing principle.[17]

Under imperial rule, the effective administrator of the people was one
who could maintain a balance between the dictates of methods and of
Confucian administrative norms. Among the latter, none exceeded the
principle of closeness. Its connection with administration is summarized
in the passage from the Doctrine of the Mean alluded to above. It said:
"Government depends on men. Obtaining the men is by means of character; cultivating character is by means of the way; cultivating the way is by
means of humanity. What is humanity? It is men! Showing affection to
relatives (*ch'in ch'in*) is its great [principle]."

"Being close to the close" remained the principle underlying humane
administration. The principle of closeness to the people (*ch'in min*) survived Chu Hsi's reinterpretation of it as "reforming" them (*hsin min*).
Wang Yang-ming stressed closeness. Hsü Tung, the compiler of the
Writings for District Magistrates, also affirmed that "*ch'in min* should
definitely not be altered to *hsin min*. It means what it says and should be
truly carried out."[18]

District magistrates of the early Ch'ing era were unable to maintain a
balance between Legalist and Confucian priorities. On the one hand, their

authority was eroded by the steady encroachment of the public domain. But more important to their self image, they were losing the means and the will to be close to the people. Their exclusive status and wealth alone divorced them from the masses. Because they were posted to an alien environment, their immediate means of identity lay with other degree-holding gentry. Most magistrates did not stay long enough in any one post to develop broader social identifications. In the struggle between the central government and social power groups, they were required to work for the public or government cause. While in office, they had their own private interests to serve. The population expansion of the early Ch'ing produced too many people to be known by fifteen hundred district administrators. It created social stresses which isolated officials were unable to manage.

In fact it was apparent to contemporary officials that Ch'ing magistrates were close neither to the people nor to public authority. Under the circumstances it is not surprising that they had trouble in fulfilling the growing demands of their role.

MAGISTRATES OF WU-HSIEN, CH'ANG-CHOU, AND
YUAN-HO DISTRICTS

The following list is compiled to give evidence about the career patterns of magistrates serving in the three districts of Wu-hsien, Ch'ang-chou, and Yuan-ho, all rated "most important" and under Su-chou prefecture in Kiangsu province. The gazetteer for Wu-hsien lists the magistrates for the three districts side by side on the same page instead of consecutively, as would be the order in most prefectural lists (and as in the Su-chou prefectural gazetteer). It is thus possible to see at a glance to what extent a magistrate moved between districts. The Wu-hsien gazetteer is also unusually informative about prior or concurrent appointments and subsequent appointment or fate. It indicates whether the current appointment was acting or substantive, the date and month, and sometimes day, on which the appointment was taken up, and the date of termination in case of promotion or demotion.

The present list is limited to those magistrates serving between 1723 and 1850, for whom there is information about more than one appointment. Where prior or subsequent appointments are said to be held in other districts under the same prefecture, the information has been cross-checked, where available. It has not been crosschecked if the appointment was outside the prefecture. Spot checks indicate that such crosschecking would increase the number of magisterial appointments held by these officials. But this is a task that could be more conveniently accomplished by computer analysis, and the present list is compiled primarily to suggest what might be accomplished by such analysis.

The items to note are: 1) whether or not a magistrate held any office before being appointed to the office of magistrate; 2) whether or not a magistrate held an acting appointment before going on to a substantive appointment, and if so, for how long; 3) the duration of the substantive appointment; 4) the number of substantive appointments and whether or not they were within the same prefecture; 5) the reason for the termination of substantive appointments, when given (on this point the list declines after the middle of the Ch'ien-lung period); 6) any correlation between rank and subsequent performance. An appointment interrupted for two to four months in the middle of a year usually indicates that the magistrate was seconded to help adjudicate the provincial examination.

All districts are in Su-chou prefecture and all prefectures in Kiangsu province unless otherwise indicated. The dates of service are given according to the Chinese calendar. A repeated figure in the month series refers to an extra month, necessitated from time to time in the lunar calendar (this does not apply to the figure 11). *A* indicates an acting appointment, *S* a substantive. The terminal date for the appointment, other than in cases of promotion and demotion, is approximate and represents the date of arrival of the successor. But districts of this importance were very unlikely to be left for any length of time without an incumbent in charge. As an indication of this, an acting magistrate who served for only seven days is included in the gazetteer lists.

Terminal dates for reign periods are as follows:

	Chinese	*Western*
Yung-cheng (YC)	1–23	1723–1735
Ch'ien-lung (CL)	1–60	1736–1795
Chia-ch'ing (CC)	1–25	1796–1820
Tao-kuang (TK)	1–30	1821–1850

1. Ch'a Yung-ch'ing: prefect.
   YC 1/9–2/2, magistrate of Ch'ang-chou (A).

2. Li Shih-chin: *chien-sheng* (CB).
   1st-class asst. prefect of Ch'ang-chou in charge of coastal defense.
   YC 2/12–3/2, magistrate of Wu-hsien (A).
   YC 10/7–12/7, magistrate of Yuan-ho (A).

   YC 11/2–11/2, concurrently magistrate of Wu-hsien (A).
   YC 12/7–12/9, subprefect of T'ai-hu subprefecture (s).

3. Hsu Yung-yu: *chin-shih*.
   Magistrate of Wu-chiang.
   YC 3/7–3/11, concurrently magistrate of Ch'ang-chou (A).

4. Chang Fu-ch'ang: *chü-jen*.
YC 3/11–4/2, magistrate of Yuan-ho (s).
YC 3/11–4/? concurrently magistrate of Ch'ang-chou (s).
Impeached and dismissed.

5. Chiang Chih-wei: *chü-jen*.
YC 4/2–6/2, magistrate of Yuan-ho (s).
Promoted to Dept. magistrate of T'ai-ts'ang independent dept.

6. Cheng Chi: *chien-sheng*.
Asst. magistrate and acting magistrate of Chen-che.
YC 4/10–4/11, magistrate of Wu-hsien (A).
YC 5/33, magistrate of Chen-che (s).
Degraded same year.

7. Ch'a I-jen: *chien-sheng*.
YC 4/11–5/7, magistrate of Wu-hsien (s).
YC 5/10–6/5, magistrate of Wu-hsien (s).

8. Lo Chi-hung: *chü-jen*.
YC 5/7–5/10, magistrate of Wu-hsien (A).
YC 5/10–6/5, magistrate of Ch'ang-chou (s).
Impeached and dismissed.

9. Shih Ai: *lin-kung*.
YC 6/2–8/6, magistrate of Yuan-ho (s).
YC 6/5–6/10, concurrently magistrate of Wu-hsien (A).

10. Chu Erh-chieh: *lin-kung*.
YC 5–6, magistrate of Chia-ting.
YC 6/6–6/8, concurrently magistrate of Ch'ang-chou (A).

11. Hsu Liang-mo: *chien-sheng*.
2nd class subprefect in charge of grain.
YC 6/10–6/12, magistrate of Wu-hsien (A).

12. Wu Tung: *sheng-yuan*.
YC 7/3–8/4, magistrate of Wu-hsien (s). Degraded and transferred.
YC 8/6–9/11, magistrate of Wu-hsien (s).

13. Wang Ch'en-chün: *chien-sheng*.
Magistrate of Pao-shan (under T'ai-ts'ang chou).
YC 7/7–7/77, concurrently magistrate of Ch'ang-chou (A).

14. Liu Shao-ch'i: bannerman *chien-sheng*.
2d-class asst. prefect of Ch'ang-chou in charge of arrests.
YC 7/77–8/2, magistrate of Ch'ang-chou (A).

15. Lin Ying: *kung-sheng*.
Asst. magistrate of Li-yang (under Chen-chiang prefecture).
YC 8/2–10/4, magistrate of Ch'ang-chou (A).
Promoted to magistrate of Shu-yang (s) (under Hai-chou).

16. Chu K'uei-yang: *chien-sheng*.
Asst. magistrate of Hsien-yang.
YC 6, promoted to magistrate of Hsin-yang, where served till YC 8.
YC 8/4–8/6, concurrently magistrate of Wu-hsien (A).
YC 8/6–10/7, magistrate of Yuan-ho (s).
YC 9/11–10/1, concurrently magistrate of Wu-hsien (A).
YC 10, prefect of Huai-an (A).

17. Li Pi-ch'eng: *chü-jen*.
YC 10/1–11/2, magistrate of Wu-hsien (A).
Transferred to T'ai-chou (YC 11–12).

18. Shen Kuang-ts'eng: *chien-sheng*.
YC 10/4–12/8, magistrate of Ch'ang-chou (A).
Transferred to magistrate of K'un-shan (A), where succeeded, YC 13.
YC 13/2–CL 3/7, magistrate of Ch'ang-chou (s).
Transferred to magistrate of Shan-yang (in Huai-an prefecture).

19. Chang Jo-hsi: *chien-sheng*.
    YC 12/7–CL 5/3, magistrate of Yuan-ho (s).
    CL 1/6–1/8, concurrently magistrate of Wu-hsien (A).
    CL 3/8–3/11, concurrently magistrate of Wu-hsien (A).

20. Ting Ch'uan: *chü-jen*.
    Magistrate of K'un-shan, YC 8.
    Succeeded, YC 12.
    YC 12/8–12/11, magistrate of Ch'ang-chou (A).
    Degraded and transferred.

21. Hu Ying-k'uei: *pa-kung*.
    YC 12/11–13/2, magistrate of Ch'ang-chou (A).
    YC 13/2–CL 1/6, magistrate of Wu-hsien (A).

22. Ch'en Chih-wei: *pa-kung*.
    Prefectural commissary of records (*ching-li*, rank 8A).
    CC 1/8–3/8, magistrate of Wu-hsien (A).

23. Wei Che-chih: *pa-kung*.
    YC 3/8–6/9, magistrate of Ch'ang-chou (s).
    Left to attend audience.
    YC 6/10–7/10, magistrate of Ch'ang-chou (s).
    YC 7/5–7/9, concurrently magistrate of Wu-hsien (A).
    Promoted to dept. magistrate of Hai-chou independent dept.

24. Huang Chien-chung: *pa-kung*.
    CL 3/11–5/3, magistrate of Wu-hsien (A).
    CL 5/3–8/4, magistrate of Yuan-ho (s).
    CL 6/8–6/10, concurrently magistrate of Ch'ang-chou (A).
    Degraded and transferred.

25. Chin Ping-tso: *pa-kung*.
    CL 5/10–7/5, magistrate of Wu-hsien (A).
    CL 7/9–7/10, magistrate of Wu-hsien (s).

Transferred to magistrate of Shan-yang (under Huai-an prefecture).

26. Wang Yun-chien: *pa-kung*.
    Magistrate of Chin-kuei (under Ch'ang-chou prefecture).
    CL 7/10–8/3, magistrate of Ch'ang-chou (A).

27. Feng Ching-ts'eng: *chü-jen*.
    CL 7/10–8/3, magistrate of Ch'ang-chou (s).
    Left because of illness.

28. Chiang Shun-chiao: *pa-kung*.
    Magistrate of Wu-hsi (under Ch'ang-chou prefecture).
    CL 8/3–10/6, transferred to magistrate of Wu-hsien (s).

29. Wang Ting-yuan: no degree.
    Clerk in the Historiographical Commission in Peking (*kung-shih*).
    Asst. magistrate of Ch'ang-chou.
    CL 8/4–9/3, magistrate of Yuan-ho (A).

30. Chang Yueh-mo: *chien-sheng*.
    Asst. magistrate of Yuan-ho.
    CL 9/3–13/9, promoted to magistrate of Yuan-ho (s).

31. Ch'en Hsun-hsiang: *chin-shih*.
    Magistrate of Ch'ang-shu.
    CL 11, demoted and transferred; attended Audience; still employed as magistrate.
    CL 11/33–11/10, magistrate of Ch'ang-chou (A).

32. Chin Hung: *chin-shih*.
    CL 10–11, magistrate of Kan-ch'üan.
    CL 11/10–12/6, transferred to magistrate of Ch'ang-chou (s).
    Promoted to subasst. salt controller.

33. Cheng Shih-ching: *chin-shih*.
    Magistrate of Chin-kuei (under Ch'ang-chou prefecture).
    CL 12/6–13/4, transferred to magistrate of Ch'ang-chou (s).
    Retired for mourning.

34. Fang Lu: rank not indicated
    1st class asst. dept. magistrate of Hai-chou.
    CL 14/1–14/9, magistrate of Ch'ang-chou (A).

35. Li Kuang-tso: *chin-shih*.
    CL 14/9–18/6, magistrate of Ch'ang-chou (s).
    CL 16/8–16/9, concurrently magistrate of Yuan-ho (A).
    CL 18/11–19/4, magistrate of Ch'ang-chou (s).

36. Li Yung-shu: *pa-kung*.
    Magistrate of Ch'ang-shu.
    CL 17/4–18/2, transferred to magistrate of Yuan-ho (s).

37. Ch'en Yen: *chien-sheng*.
    CL 18/7–18/10, magistrate of Wu-hsien (s).
    1st class asst. prefect in charge of grain.
    CL 19/4–19/8, magistrate of Ch'ang-chou (A).

38. Chu Shao-wen: *chien-sheng* (CB).
    CL 18/9–19/4, magistrate of Yuan-ho (s).
    Promoted to 1st-class asst. prefect.

39. Lin Jo-shu: banner; *chien-sheng*.
    CL 18/10–19/4, magistrate of Wu-hsien (A).
    CL 19/4–19/8, magistrate of Yuan-ho (A).
    CL 19/8–21/5, magistrate of Ch'ang-chou (A).
    Left to attend Audience.
    CL 21/9–24/8, magistrate of Ch'ang-chou (s).

40. Sun Yao-te: *chü-jen*.
    CL 19/8–24/11, magistrate of Yuan-ho (s).
    Left for mourning.
    CL 24/8–24/10, concurrently magistrate of Ch'ang-chou (A).
    CL 26/12–27/5, magistrate of Yuan-ho (s)

CL 28/4–29/3, magistrate of Ch'ang-chou (s).
CL 29/6–30/4, magistrate of Ch'ang-chou (s).
Promoted to dept. magistrate of Ch'u-chou independent dept. (under Anhwei province).

41. Cheng Yü-hsien: *chien-sheng*.
    Magistrate of T'ao-yuan (s) (under Huai-an prefecture).
    CL 24/10–28/1, transferred to magistrate of Ch'ang-chou (s).
    Impeached and dismissed.

42. P'an Hsun: no rank indicated.
    1st-class asst. prefect in charge of grain.
    CL 28/1–28/4, magistrate of Ch'ang-chou (A).

43. Hsu Chih: no rank indicated.
    CL 29/8–29/11, magistrate of Wu-hsien (A).
    CL 30/4–31/2, magistrate of Ch'ang-chou (A).
    Impeached and dismissed.

44. Chou Feng-ch'i: *chü-jen*.
    CL 29/4–31/4, magistrate of Yuan-ho (s).
    CL 31/2–31/3, concurrently magistrate of Ch'ang-chou (A).
    CL 31/8–32/6, magistrate of Yuan-ho (s).
    CL 32/8–33/6, magistrate of Yuan-ho (s).

45. Kuei Chung-fu: *chü-jen*.
    CL 31/3–32/4, magistrate of Ch'ang-chou (s).
    Other appointments as magistrate.
    Promoted to dept. magistrate.

46. Huang Ping-ching: *chin-shih*.
    CL 32/6–32/8, magistrate of Yuan-ho (A).
    CL 33/6–34/4, magistrate of Yuan-ho (s).

47. Chu Pang-li: banner; no rank indicated.

CL 33/12–34/1, magistrate of Wu-hsien (A).
CL 34/10–37/8, magistrate of Wu-hsien (A).

48. Sun Ju: no rank indicated.
CL 37/8–38/4, magistrate of Wu-hsien (s).
CL 38/10–39/9, magistrate of Wu-hsien (s).

49. Yang Yi-lun: no rank indicated.
CL 38/4–38/10, magistrate of Wu-hsien (A).
CL 40/4–41/12, magistrate of Wu-hsien (s).

50. Shih Shang-ch'ueh: *chü-jen*.
CL 34/5–35/4, magistrate of Ch'ang-chou (A).
Apparently magistrate of Yuan-ho in CL 34 (no precise dates, almost certainly an acting appointment).

51. Chao Chün: *chü-jen*.
CL 38/10–38/10 (8 days), magistrate of Wu-hsien (A).
CL 39/9–40/4, magistrate of Wu-hsien (s).

52. Li Feng-ch'un: no rank indicated.
CL 46/6–47/6, magistrate of Wu-hsien (A).
CL 47/10–51/8, magistrate of Wu-hsien (s).
CL 51/10–52/2, magistrate of Wu-hsien (s).

53. Wang T'ing-fang: *pa-kung*.
CL 46/5–46/8, magistrate of Ch'ang-chou (A).
CL 47/6–50/8, magistrate of Yuan-ho (s).
CL 50/11–52/3, magistrate of Yuan-ho (s).

54. Li Ying: *chü-jen* (?).
CL 47/5–47/6, magistrate of Yuan-ho (A).
CL 47/6–47/10, magistrate of Wu-hsien (A).

Listed in gazetteer of Wu-chin (under Ch'ang-chou prefecture) as native of Chekiang (this implies he held office in Wu-chin).

55. Ko Chien-ch'u: *chü-jen*.
CL 48/5–48/10, magistrate of Ch'ang-chou (A).
CL 50/7–50/7 (23 days), magistrate of Ch'ang-chou (A).
CL 50/8–50/11, magistrate of Yuan-ho (A).
CL 53/10–56/5, magistrate of Ch'ang-chou (s).
CL 57/5–58/2, magistrate of Ch'ang-chou (s).

56. Yuan Ping-i: *chin-shih*.
CL 48/10–50/7, magistrate of Ch'ang-chou (s).
Promoted to dept. magistrate of T'ai-chou dept. (under Yang-chou prefecture).

57. T'ien Wen-lung: no rank indicated.
CL 50/7–53/10, magistrate of Ch'ang-chou (s).
CL 58/2–59/?, magistrate of Ch'ang-chou (s).

58. Ching Pien: *chien-sheng*.
CL 52/3–53/5, magistrate of Yuan-ho (s).
CL 53/10–58/2, magistrate of Yuan-ho (s).
Listed in gazetteer of T'ai-ts'ang dept. as being native of Kwangsi; implies held office in T'ai-ts'ang.

59. Liang Lan-sheng: no rank indicated.
CL 60/22–CC6/7, magistrate of Ch'ang-chou (s).
CC 1/5–1/6, concurrently magistrate of Wu-hsien (A).

60. Shu Huai: *chin-shih*.
CC 1/7–8/11, magistrate of Yuan-ho (s).
CC 11/4–12/6, magistrate of Wu-hsien (s).

61. T'ang Chung-nien: *chin-shih*.
    CC 4/7–7/1, magistrate of Wu-hsien
    (s).
    Promoted to dept. magistrate of
    Hai-chou independent dept.

62. Chu Hsi-chueh: *chü-jen*.
    CC 7/1–8/2, magistrate of Wu-hsien
    (A).
    CC 9/6–10/4, magistrate of Yuan-ho
    (A).

63. T'ang Tao: *chü-jen*.
    CC 8/2–8/10, magistrate of Wu-hsien
    (A).
    CC 8/11–9/2, magistrate of Yuan-ho
    (A).

64. Chao T'ang: no rank indicated.
    CC 8/8–8/11, magistrate of Ch'ang-
    chou (A).
    CC 10/5–12/1, magistrate of Ch'ang-
    chou (s).

65. Liu Kuei: *pa-kung*.
    CC 10/4–10/6, magistrate of Yuan-
    ho (A).
    CC 12/1–12/11, concurrently magis-
    trate of Ch'ang-chou (A).

66. Chao Jih-hsu: *yin-sheng*.
    CC 12/1–12/10, magistrate of
    Ch'ang-chou (A).
    CC 16/3–19/5, magistrate of Ch'ang-
    chou (s).
    CC 20/4–21/5, magistrate of Ch'ang-
    chou (s).

67. Chou Tai-ling: *chü-jen*.
    CC 14/1–14/10, magistrate of Yuan-
    ho (A).
    CC 15/2–17/6. magistrate of Yuan-
    ho (s).
    CC 18/7–21/6, magistrate of Yuan-
    ho (s).

68. Chu Shu-chi: *chü-jen*.
    CC 18/10–24/?, transferred by
    imperial order to magistrate of
    Wu-hsien (s).
    Promoted to 1st-class asst. prefect
    in charge of grain.

69. Wan Ch'eng-shao: no rank indi-
    cated.
    CC 20/3–20/4, magistrate of Ch'ang-
    chou (s).
    CC 21/5–21/7, magistrate of Ch'ang-
    chou (s).
    CC 21/9–23/6, magistrate of Ch'ang-
    chou (s).

70. Li Ching-yi: *chü-jen*.
    CC 21/6–23/6, magistrate of Yuan
    ho (A).
    CC 23/6–25/7, magistrate of Ch'ang-
    chou (s).
    CC 25/11–TK 2/6, magistrate of
    Ch'ang-chou (s).
    TK 2/33–2/4, concurrently magis-
    trate of Wu-hsien (A).

71. Ho Shih-ch'i *chin-shih*.
    TK 5/7–7/55, magistrate of Yuan-ho
    (s).
    TK 7/6–8/5, magistrate of Yuan-ho
    (s).
    TK 11/7–12/7, magistrate of Yuan-
    ho (s).

72. Yang Ch'eng-chan: *chin-shih*.
    TK 8/5–10/8, magistrate of Yuan-ho
    (s).
    Promoted to 1st-class asst. prefect.

73. Hsiung Chuan-li: *chin-shih*.
    TK 9–12, magistrate of Wu-hsien
    (s).
    Later promoted to 1st-class asst.
    prefect.

74. Ch'en Yu-ch'eng: *pa-kung*.
    TK 10/8–11/7, magistrate of Yuan-
    ho (s).
    TK 12–15, magistrate of Ch'ang-
    chou (s).

75. Ching Shou-ch'un: *chü-jen*.
    TK 15–18, magistrate of Ch'ang-
    chou (s).
    TK 15/7–15/10, concurrently magis-
    trate of Yuan-ho (A).
    TK 18/?–19/?, magistrate of Ch'ang-
    chou (s).

(The Ch'ang-chou list declines in this period; no name intervenes between Ching's first and second appointments.)

76. Shen Ping-yuan: *chü-jen*.
    TK 15/10–16/7, magistrate of Yuan-ho (A).
    TK 18/7–18/10, magistrate of Yuan-ho (A).

77. Lien T'ing-huang: *pa-kung*.
    TK 16/7–17/8, magistrate of Yuan-ho (s).
    TK 20/?–23/?, magistrate of Ch'ang-chou (s).
    TK 23/?–23/?, magistrate of Wu-hsien (s).

78. Hsiao Ch'ung: *chü-jen*.
    TK 17/8–18/7, magistrate of Yuan-ho (s).
    TK 19/?–19/?, magistrate of Ch'ang-chou (s).

79. Wang Hsi-chou: *chin-shih*.
    TK 19/?–19/?, magistrate of Wu-hsien (s).
    TK 19/9–21/8, magistrate of Yuan-ho (s).
    TK 28/?–30/?, magistrate of Wu-hsien (s).

80. Chang Chih-kao: *yu-kung*.
    TK 21/10–21/10 (10 days), magistrate of Yuan-ho (s).
    TK 23/?–27/?, magistrate of Ch'ang-chou (s).

81. Tung Yung-wei: no rank indicated.
    TK 22/8–23/9, magistrate of Yuan-ho (s).
    TK 23/12–26/?, magistrate of Wu-hsien (A).
    TK 24/7–25/9, magistrate of Yuan-ho (s).

APPENDIX II

CAREER PATTERNS OF MAGISTRATES OF T'AN
AND SHEN CLANS

In this appendix the subjects of career patterns is illustrated
through the use of clan genealogies. As is well known, the clan system was
strong in southern and eastern China, and the clans living in a historically
minded society were highly conscious of their own heritage. There are many
such genealogies in existence. Most, though not all, deal with the external
participation of the clan in society at large. Among those which do are the
genealogies of the T'an and Shen clans. The T'an clan, entrenched in
Kwangtung and strong in other southern provinces, was a large and rami-
fied group with several thousand degree- and officeholders in its records.
The Shen clan shown here belonged to Hsiao-shan district in eastern
Chekiang and was a much smaller and more compact group. It was,
however, located in one of the leading areas for the production of degree-
holders and officials.

The interest of the genealogical tables is in the comparatively firm
picture they give of the career achievement of the individual. They provide
the date of his degree, if *chin-shih*, *chü-jen*, or *pa-kung*, and a fair record
of his subsequent administrative career. They have two drawbacks. They
do not necessarily give the whole record. Through an examination of the
biographies of those magistrates of the T'an clan who had biographies,
several more posts were found which were not listed in the career tables.
Second, they do not usually give the dates or periods of the appointments.
It has generally been necessary to consult the gazetteers of the district

prefectures or provinces in question, where these are available, to obtain this information.

The points to note are: 1) the type of degree or examination status; 2) whether or not the magistrate held any office before being appointed as magistrate; 3) the period between the date of the degree and the date of the first recorded magistracy; 4) the number of magisterial posts held and the time span involved; 5) the subsequent career; 6) the correlation between the type of degree and achievement in the office of magistrate; 7) the correlation between both of these and the subsequent career.

T'an Clan

1. T'an Yuan-yang: 1756, *chü-jen.*
1766, asst. director of schools.
Later promoted to magistrate of Fu-ch'eng.

2. T'an Tzu-t'ung: 1844, *chü-jen.*
Brevet 1st-class asst. prefect.
Expectant magistrate.

3. T'an T'ing-chan: 1678, *chü-jen.*
Father was prefectural director of schools.
1691–94, magistrate of T'ai-p'ing.

4. T'an Lung: 1726, *chü-jen.*
1750–52, magistrate of Kuang-shan.

5. T'an Chao-chi: 1732, *chü-jen*; 1733, *chin-shih.*
1740–43, magistrate of Lung-ch'uan.
1742, magistrate of Sui-ch'ang (A).
1743–49, magistrate of Ch'ang-hsing.
Magistrate of Tzu-hsi.
Promoted to 2d-class secy. (rank 6A) of the Dept. of Waterways and Dykes, Board of Works.

6. T'an T'ing-tsuan: 1771, *yu-kung*; 1774, *chü-jen.*
Son of No. 5.
Magistrate of Nan-lo.

7. T'an Ta-ching: 1774, *chü-jen*; 1775, *chin-shih.*
1786–88, magistrate of Ju-kao magistrate of Wu-chin.
1791, magistrate of Feng-hsien.

Promoted to dept. magistrate of Lo-p'ing dept. (name not listed in Yunnan gazetteer list).
Transferred to 2d-class asst. prefect of Chin-hsing prefecture.
1800–1, concurrently magistrate of P'ing-hu (A).
Won popular title T'an "of the clear skies" from people of Ju-kao.

8. T'an Yi: 1789, *chü-jen.*
Magistrate of Yang-so.
1809, magistrate of Lin-yi.

9. T'an Yu: 1736, *chü-jen*; 1737, *chin-shih.*
1748–51, magistrate of Yang-wu.

10. T'an Hsiang: 1693, *chü-jen.*
1712, magistrate of Tzu-ch'uan.

11. T'an Yu: 1821, *chü-jen.*
from Hsu Shensi t'ung-chih: 1836/5, magistrate of Yen-chou (A).
1836/7–1837/1, magistrate of Yen-ch'ang (A).
from clan list: 1837–39, magistrate of Lueh-yang, also magistrate of Wu-pao.

12. T'an Shao-t'ai: 1654, *chü-jen.*
Father was Board dept. director.
1648, dist. director of schools.
1670–74, magistrate of Yü-t'ai.

13. T'an Chia-yuan: 1663, *chü-jen*.
    Brother of No. 12.
    Magistrate.

14. T'an Chih-tao: 1651, *chü-jen*.
    Magistrate of Yung-fu.

15. T'an Lien: 1713, *chü-jen*; 1715,
    chin-shih.
    Father was dist. director of schools.
    1725–30, magistrate of Kuan-hsien.
    1735, magistrate of San-t'ai.
    Died in office while seconded from
    San-t'ai as provincial asst. exam-
    iner, aged 51.

16. T'an Hung: 1759, *chü-jen*; 1760,
    chin-shih.
    son of No. 15; 1769–70, magistrate
    of Chen-yuan.

17. T'an Yuan-ti: 1682, *sui-kung*.
    Dist. director of schools, concur-
    rently dist. administrator (A).

18. T'an Hsing-hsueh: 1654, *pa-kung*.
    1673, magistrate of Chien-shih.
    Appointed dept. magistrate of Ta-
    chou.

19. T'an Kuang-lun: 1765, *pa-kung*;
    1768, *chü-jen*.
    Magistrate of T'ung-shan.
    Promoted to 1st-class asst. prefect of
    Shih-nan prefecture.
    Praised as virtuous administrator.

20. T'an Chao-yen: 1786, *chü-jen*; 1796,
    chin-shih.
    Magistrate of Chao-ch'eng.
    Retired because of mourning; did
    not wish to return to official
    service.
    1818, director of schools, Kuang-
    chou prefecture.

21. T'an Chiao: 1813, *chü-jen*.
    Magistrate of T'ien-li and Ting-pien.

22. T'an Hai-kuan: 1834, *chü-jen*.
    1861–68?, magistrate of Nei-chiang.
    Magistrate of Shih-fang.
    Promoted to 2d-class asst. prefect.

23. T'an ch'ih
    1882, Magistrate of Shou-kuang.

24. T'an Ch'eng: 1760, *chü-jen*.
    1769, dist. director of schools.
    1773, dept. director of schools.
    1780, dist. asst. director of schools.
    1784–85 magistrate of Ch'ing-chien
    (A).

25. T'an K'o-tse: 1744, *chü-jen*.
    Magistrate of Ch'eng-hsien.

26. T'an Kao-chieh: 1818, *chü-jen*.
    Magistrate of Ch'ang-ho.

27. T'an Tsai-fen: *lin-kung* in Ch'ien-
    lung reign.
    Dist. director of schools in two dif-
    ferent districts; concurrently ad-
    ministrator of Sui-yao t'ing (A).

28. T'an Chung-ting; 1699, *chü-jen*.
    1715–21?, magistrate of Ho-chiang.
    Retired for mourning.

29. T'an Chih-chi: 1741, *pa-kung*.
    Brother of No. 30.
    Magistrate of Ch'ing-h'o.
    from Li-yang district gazetteer:
    chiao-hsi (government instructor).
    1762/7–1763/6, magistrate of Li-
    yang.
    Impeached and dismissed.

30. T'an Chih-kang: 1753, *chü-jen*.
    Brother of No. 29.
    Dist. director of schools.
    Magistrate of Chin-hsiu (biography
    has Li-yang).

31. T'an Jen-hao: 1789, *pa-kung*.
    Magistrate of Hai-feng.

32. T'an P'ei-tzu: 1837 *pa-kung*.
    1844, Dist. director of schools.
    Recommended for dist. magistrate.

33. T'an Feng-hui: 1768, *chü-jen*.
    1795–97, magistrate of Ch'ien-yang.

34. T'an Hsiang-ching: 1777, *pa-kung*.
    Dept. magistrate of Ching-chou.

Biography adds: 2d-class asst. prefect for Pao-ting prefecture, went to An-chou (in Pao-ting).
Transferred to magistrate of Wu-ch'iao dept.
Magistrate of Ching-chou (A).
Died in office.

35. T'an Yung-yu: 1794, *chü-jen*.
Magistrate of Hui-hsien.

36. T'an Shu-liu: 1807, *pa-kung*.
1838, magistrate of Pi-shan.
Transferred to dist. director of schools (s).
Noted for integrity.

37. T'an Shang-wu: 1713, *chü-jen*.
1727–28, magistrate of She-hsien.
1729, Dist. director of schools.
1730, another appointment as dist. director of schools.

38. T'an Ch'ang-ming: 1732, *chü-jen*.
Dept. director of schools.
1759–63, magistrate of Fen-t'ai.

39. T'an Jen-yuan; 1763, *chü-jen*.
Magistrate of Chu-chi

40. T'an P'eng-hsiao: 1800, *chü-jen*; 1808, *chin-shih*.
1810–? selected and received magistracy of Kan-yu.
Retired for mourning.
1821–22?, appointed magistrate of Shao-wu when mourning completed.

41. T'an Yi (T'an Meng-ch'ien): 1807, *chü-jen*.
Late in Tao-kuang reign, magistrate of Ta-yu.

42. T'an Hsiang: 1816, *chü-jen*; 1817, *chin-shih*.
Brother of No. 41.
Board 2d-class secy.
Dept. magistrate of Wei-ming dept.

43. T'an Huan: 1648, *chü-jen*.
Dist. director of schools.
1671, magistrate of Kao-yao.

1672, dept. magistrate of Te-ch'ing dept. (A).

44. T'an Che-p'u: 1768, *chü-jen*; 1772, *chin-shih*.
1784–87, magistrate of Nan-ling.

45. T'an Hsun-shih: 1777, *chü-jen*.
Chia-ch'ing period, magistrate of Yu-tz'u.

46. T'an Chih-sui: *chü-jen*.
1799, magistrate of P'u-t'ai.
1807, magistrate of Ling-hsien, also magistrate of Chia-yang.
1811, magistrate of Tan-hsien.
1815, magistrate of Ch'ang-shan.

47. T'an Wen-mu: *chü-jen*.
1801, magistrate of Yang-hsin.
1802, magistrate of Chin-hsiang.
1803, magistrate of Fan-yang.
1809, magistrate of Chi-mo.
1815, magistrate of Chang-ch'iu.

48. T'an Wei-yi: *chü-jen*.
1663, magistrate of Yung-ming.

49. T'an Shang-kua: *chü-jen*.
1781, magistrate of Ch'eng-wu.

50. T'an Tsai-sheng: 1690, *chü-jen*; 1700, *chin-shih*.
1707–11, magistrate of Hsu-p'u.

51. T'an Chien-lung: 1744, *chü-jen*.
1767, magistrate of Hsin-an (A).
1768, magistrate of Lung-men.

52. T'an Chih: *sui-kung*.
1680, magistrate of Ch'u-chiang.

53. T'an Kuan-ch'eng: 1657, *chü-jen*.
Magistrate of Huo-ch'iu.

54. T'an Yu-te: *chin-shih*.
1761–62, magistrate of Lin-kao.
1769, 1st-class asst. dept. magistrate of Sui-yao independent dept.

55. T'an Chen: *chü-jen*.
1805, magistrate of Lan-shan.
1818, magistrate of T'ao-yuan.
1824, 1st-class asst. prefect of Yung-shun prefecture.

56. T'an Ching-p'in: *chin-shih*.
1826, magistrate of Lu-chi.

57. T'an Piao: *chü-jen*.
1729, magistrate of Yu-hsien.

58. T'an Chih-hung: *chü-jen*.
1747, magistrate of Shou-chang.

59. T'an Ts'ung-chien: 1654, *chü-jen*;
1655, *fu-pang*.
from biography and gazetteers:
1662–66, magistrate of Ling-ch'iu.

Retired for mourning.
1672–75, on returning to service,
magistrate of Lou-hsien.
Transferred to magistrate of Meng-
chin.
1685–87, promoted to dept. magistrate of Chin-ning dept. (Yunnan)
for services rendered during rebellion in Kiangsu.

60. T'an Ch'ung-yi: *chü-jen*.
1782, magistrate of An-jen.
Magistrate of Heng-shan.

Shen Clan

1. Shen Fang.
Magistrate of Hsing-p'ing.

2. Shen Wen-shin: SC period, *kung-
sheng*.
Magistrate of Wan-an.

3. Shen T'ing-kuei.
Magistrate of Shen-yu.

4. Shen Shih-pen: 1678, *fu kung-sheng*;
1678, *chü-jen*; 1685, *chin-shih*.
1692–97, magistrate of P'ing-shan.
Magistrate.
Promoted to dept. director of the
dept. of selection, Board of
Officials.

5. Shen Ming-piao.
Asst. magistrate of Lin-kuei.
Promoted to 1st-class asst. magis-
trate of Ch'uan-chou.
Seconded as magistrate of Yung-fu
(A).

6. Shen Ch'ing-piao.
Magistrate of Lin-yi.

7. Shen Yuan-hung: 1723, *chü-jen*
(33d name); 1733, *chin-shih*.
1741–45, magistrate of Lin-ch'u.

8. Shen Yuan-ch'i: 1768, *chü-jen*.
Selected through the *chien-hsuan*
procedure as magistrate (but no
record of any subsequent appointment).

9. Shen Chen-shih: 1717, *chü-jen* (99th
name).
Son of No. 4.
Magistrate of K'ai-hsien, promoted
to dept. magistrate of Sung-ming
dept. (Yunnan).
1749–52, dept. magistrate of Pin-
chou (Shantung).

10. Shen Hsun.
Grandson of No. 4.
Expectant magistrate.

11. Shen Su-han: 1759, *chü-jen* (89th
name).
Expectant magistrate.

12. Shen Hao 1774, *chü-jen*.
1787, selected under the ta-t'iao
procedure as probationary magistrate.
1791, magistrate of Lai-yang.

13. Shen Chia-hsing.
Magistrate of Wang-chiang (A).
Magistrate of Hsi-ming (A).
Asst. magistrate of Kuei-ch'ih.

14. Shen T'ing-kuei: 1813, *pa-kung*.
Dist. director of studies.
Promoted to magistrate of Hua-
yang.
Magistrate of Chiang-chin.
Magistrate of T'ung-hang.
Promoted to dept. magistrate of
Tzu-chou independent dept.
Prefect of Sui-ting prefecture (A).

15. Shen Yi.
    Prefectural commissary of records.
    2d-class asst. prefect (A).
    Magistrate of Chi-chi.
    Transferred and sent out to Kiangsi.
    Prefectural commissary of records.
    Magistrate of Te-hua (A).

16. Shen Ch'ing-li.
    Awarded Blue Feather.
    Brevet 1st-class asst. prefect.
    Expectant prefectural comm. of
       records.
    Through military merit successively
       guaranteed district, then dept.
       post.
    Dept. magistrate of Po-chou dept.
    Transferred to dept. magistrate of
       Shou-chou (A).

17. Shen Chan.
    Expectant magistrate.

18. Shen Hsi-keng: 1808, *chü-jen* (206th
       name).
    Selected under the *chien-hsuan*
       procedure as magistrate.
    Director of studies at Imperial
       Academy (Rank 8a).
    Promoted to 1st-class asst. pre-
       fect.

19. Shen Chih-lin.
    Magistrate of Yang-hsien.

20. Shen Yu-fen.
    Awarded Blue Feather.
    Brevet 1st-class asst. prefect.
    Expectant magistrate in Shantung.

21. Shen Tsu-pei.
    Brevet 1st-class asst. prefect.
    Selected (*chien-hsuan*) as magistrate
       in Kwangsi.
    Magistrate of Lo-ch'eng (A).
    Magistrate of Yi-ming (A).
    Magistrate of Lai-p'u (A).
    Magistrate of Lin-chuan (A).
    Magistrate of Kuan-yang (A).
    Magistrate of Lu-chuan (S).
    Transferred to magistrate of Ling-
       yun (S).

22. Shen Chin: 1844, *chü-jen* (19th
       name).
    Brevet prefect.
    Asst. police magistrate of Peking
       (rank 7B).
    Expectant 1st-class asst. prefect in
       Fukien.
    Magistrate of Fu-ting (A).
    Dept. magistrate of Yung-ch'un
       independent dept.

APPENDIX III

CAREER PATTERNS OF MAGISTRATES OF LI-YANG
AND CHIN-SHAN DISTRICTS

This appendix again presents career patterns compiled from district gazetteers, but the information differs from that given in Appendix I. Li-yang and Chin-shan were "medium," Board-appointed districts (also in Kiangsu province). Many of their magistrates were holding their first substantive office. Some of them returned several times after brief secondments. Many others only held acting commissions, either as probationary or as subordinate assistant officials.

In this appendix, years in office are given according to the Western calendar, in order to correlate with the degree dates. (In the original record, degree dates appear according to the sixty-year cycle system; years in office according to the reign period.) The months, however, remain the months of the Chinese calendar. They are left in to give a more precise breakdown of the length of terms of service. *A* means acting, *B* Banner, *M* Manchu, *C* Chinese.

It is regrettable that both appendices I and III deal only with districts in Kiangsu. But this province produced by and large the most systematic, informative, and accurate district gazetteers. Most gazetteers would not provide nearly as much information as is shown below (the district of origin, indicated in the original gazetteer lists, is omitted here). They would give only the name of the official, his district of origin, degree—if they had recorded it—and the year in which he arrived in office. Many are clearly defective even in the information which they do convey. As it happens, the second editions of the Li-yang and Chin-shan gazetteers are also much less informative than the first, although by general standards they are accurate and full enough. The record that follows is taken only from the first editions.

Magistrates of Li-yang District

NO. NAME	DATE OF DEGREE	DEGREE	PERIOD IN OFFICE	TYPE OF APPT.	QUALIFICATIONS, REASON FOR LEAVING OFFICE AND SUBSEQUENT APPOINTMENT
1. Yen Ch'i-han		*chin-shih*	1723/7-10		transferred to Ying-shang
2. Shao Hsi-kuang			1723/10-1726		demoted and transferred
3. Chang Ts'eng-shih		*chü-jen*	1727-1728/4		resigned
4. Kao T'ing-hsien		*chü-jen*	1729/2-1730/3		transferred to Hsin-yang; promoted to 1st-class asst. prefect
5. Liu Hua		*chien-sheng*	1730/3-1731/5		transferred to Ch'ang-shu
6. Tsou T'ing-mo		*chien-sheng*	1731/6-1731/11	A	left for Audience
7. Hui Tung		*pa-kung*	1731/11-1732/4	A	transferred to Chao-wen
Tsou (2)			1732/4-1737/2		transferred to Ju-kao
8. Wu Hsueh-lien			1737/2-1744/2		retired ill
9. Shen Yu-ying	1723	*chü-jen*	1744/3-1745/2	A	probationary magistrate; left office
10. Ch'ien P'u		*chien-sheng*	1745/2-1745/7	A	had purchased rank of 1st-class dept. magistrate; left office
11. Li P'u (CB)	1732	*chü-jen*	1745/8-1749/1		selected through *t'iao* procedure as magistrate; impeached and left office
12. K'ung Ch'uan-tsu (CB)		*chien-sheng*	1749/1-1749/4	A	had purchased rank as 2d-class asst. prefect; and served as 1st-class asst. prefect in charge of coastal defense; left office
13. Liu T'ing-kuang	1726	*chü-jen*	1749/4-1751/11		selected for magistracy; impeached and left office
14. T'ien Mao-fang		*pa-kung*	1751/11-1752/4	A	government instructor; probationary magistrate; left office
15. Huang Li-yin	1742	*chin-shih*	1752/4-1752/9		selected for magistracy; impeached and left office
16. Ts'ui Fang-hui		*chü-jen*	1754/9-1754/10		left office
17. Min Lien	1723	*chü-jen*	1754/10-1758/12	A	selected for magistracy; probationary magistrate; impeached and left office
18. Ch'iu Shen-tsao		*pa-kung*	1759/1-1759/66	A	government instructor; left office

	Year	Degree	Dates		Notes
19. Ch'eng-hai (MB)			1759/66–1762/7		clerk in Board of Revenue; selected for magistracy; retired ill
20. T'an Chih-chi	1741	*pa-kung*	1762/7–1763/6	A	government instructor; probationary magistrate; impeached and left office
21. Wu Hsien	1756	*chü-jen*	1763/6–1763/10	A	selected through *chien-hsuan* procedure as magistrate; left office
22. Wu Tan	1751	*chin-shih*	1763/10–1764/6		transferred to meet avoidance laws
23. Li Pen-shu	1724	*chü-jen*	1764/6–1764/7		diverted from metropolitan position and sent out to provincial post; transferred from T'ai-hsing; died of illness in office
24. Yang Mao-ch'ien		*pa-kung*	1764/7–1764/9	A	took examination for office; appointed asst. magistrate of Li-yang; left office
25. Liu En-hsun	1753	*chü-jen*	1764/7–1765/7		selected through *chien-hsuan* procedure as magistrate; seconded to assist exams
26. Li Chih-ch'iu			1765/7–1765/9	A	asst. magistrate; left office
Liu (2)			1765/9–1768/7		seconded to assist exams
27. Lo Ching			1768/7–1768/9	A	asst. magistrate; left office
Liu (3)			1768/9–1770/7		seconded to assist exams
28. Li Chung-yen		*pa-kung*	1770/7–1770/9	A	took examination for office; appointed asst. magistrate of Li-yang; left office
Liu (4)			1770/9–1771/3		demoted and transferred
29. Miao T'ing-jen			1771/3–1771/6		prefectural commissary of records; left office
30. Wei Ch'i-jui	1761	*chin-shih*	1771/6–1771/7		selected for magistracy; seconded to assist exams
Miao (2)			1771/7–1771/9		left office
Wei (2)			1771/9–1773/9		impeached and left office
31. Lin P'ei-hsuan			1773/9–1773/11		left office
32. Wang Shih-feng	1756	*chü-jen*	1773/11–1774/6		meritorious official; served as copyist and evaluated for administrative office; seconded to assist exams

continued

Magistrates of Li-yang District *(continued)*

NO. NAME	DATE OF DEGREE	DEGREE	PERIOD IN OFFICE	TYPE OE APPT.	QUALIFICATIONS, REASON FOR LEAVING OFFICE AND SUBSEQUENT APPOINTMENT
33. Ma Li			1774/7–1774/9		clerk; took examination for office; appointed asst. magistrate; left office
Wang (2)			1774/9–1777/7		retired ill
34. Chang Tung			1777/7–1777/7	A	magistrate; left office
35. Sung Kuan-kuang		pa-kung	1777/7–1778/2	A	left office
36. Kuo Chan-hsuan			1778/2–1779/7		seconded to assist exams
37. Chiang Pien			1779/7–1779/8	A	left office
Kuo (2)			1779/8–1780/7		seconded to assist exams
38. Wang Liang			1780/7–1780/9	A	left office
Kuo (3)			1780/9–1782/7		transferred to Tan-t'u (A)
39. Ko Chien-ch'u			1782/7–1783/3	A	left office
Kuo (4)			1783/3–1785/10		transferred to Tung-t'ai (A)
40. Wan T'ing-wu	1771	chü-jen	1785/10–1786/4	A	left office
Kuo (5)			1786/4–1787/4		transferred to Wu-hsi
41. Huang Yü-hu	1771	chü-jen	1787/4–1788/7	A	selected through *ta-t'iao* procedure as probationary official; seconded to assist exams
42. Pien Chien-lung (CB)		chien-sheng	1788/7–1788/9	A	asst. magistrate; left office
Huang (2)			1788/9–1789/55		left to care for parents
43. T'ang Tao	1780	chü-jen	1789/55–1789/11	A	left office
44. Chang Ching-pang	1779	top chü-jen	1789/11–1794/7		seconded to assist exams
45. Huang T'ing-shou	1789	chin-shih, chien-sheng	1794/7–1794/8	A	served in imperial cataloguing office; evaluated for office; asst. magistrate; left office

Name	Degree year	Degree	Tenure	A	Notes
Chang (2)			1794/8–1795/6		retired ill
46. Liu Hsiu-ch'eng			1795/6–1796/3	A	prefectural commissary of records; asst. magistrate; left office
47. Li Yen-teng	1771	*chü-jen*	1796/3–1796/11		selected through *ta-t'iao* procedure as probationary official; transferred to Tan-t'u
48. Chou Wei	1777	*chü-jen*	1796/11–1798/7		selected through *ta-t'iao* procedure as probationary official; seconded to assist exams
49. Sung Chun	1779	*chü-jen*	1796/7–1798/9	A	selected through *ta-t'iao* procedure as probationary official; left office
Chou (2)			1798/9–1800/7		seconded to assist exams
50. Li Shao-lo	1780	*chü-jen*	1800/7–1800/9		selected through *ta-t'iao* procedure as probationary official; left office
Chou (3)			1800/9–1801/7		seconded to assist exams
51. Chang Ping-nan	1788	*chü-jen*	1801/7–1801/8	A	selected through *ta-t'iao* procedure as probationary official; left office
Chou (4)			1801/8–1802/10		left on special assignment
52. Feng Hsiang			1802/10–1803/8	A	left because of mourning
53. Liu Kuei	1801	*pa-kung*	1803/8–1803/10	A	left office
54. Hou Ch'i-yuan	1768	*chü-jen*	1803/10–1807/10		selected through *chien-hsuan* procedure as magistrate; retired ill
55. Liu Ta-chang			1807/10–1807/10	A	asst. magistrate of Li-yang; left after seven days
56. Li K'o-shih	1779	*chü-jen*	1807/10–1809/6		selected through *ta-t'iao* procedure as probationary official; impeached and left office
57. Chin Wen-chun	1783	*chü-jen*	1809/6–1809/8	A	selected through *ta-t'iao* procedure as probationary official; left office
58. Li Ching-yi	1794	*chü-jen*	1809/8–1811/3		government instructor; transferred to Ch'ang-shu
59. Ch'en Hung-shou	1801	*pa-kung*	1811/3		end of list in this edition of gazetteer.

Magistrates of Chin-shan District

NO. NAME	DATE OF DEGREE	DEGREE	PERIOD IN OFFICE	TYPE OF APPT.	QUALIFICATIONS, REASON FOR LEAVING OFFICE AND SUBSEQUENT APPOINTMENT
1. T'ang Chih-cheng	1720	*chü-jen*	1726/2/8–7/21		retired ill
2. Chang An-kuo		*chien-sheng*	1726/7/22–27/11/7		concurrently 2d-class asst. prefect in Chiang-ming prefecture; after three months empowered by Board to become *hsien* administrator
3. Ai Yuan-fu			1727/11/17–12/20	A	concurrently asst. magistrate in Shang-hai
4. Huang Ming-ho	1705	*chü-jen*	1727/12/21–28/8/22		died in office
5. Hsiao T'ing-jui	1714	*chü-jen*	1728/9/22–29/4/17	A	concurrently magistrate of Shu-hsien
6. Wen To		*chien-sheng*	1729/4/18–8/2	A	
7. Lu Hung-chang		*chien-sheng*	1729/8/3–1730/6/26	A	
8. Kao Che-lai		*kung-sheng*	1730/6/27–1732/9/18		
9. Sun Chien-lung	1713	*chin-shih*	1732/10/2–1733/2/26		
10. Liu Shao-chou (B)	1723	*chü-jen*	1733/2/27–35/4/8		left because of mourning
11. Chang Tiao	1730	*chin-shih*	1735/44/1–5/10	A	
12. Ch'en Hsüeh-shan	1730	*chin-shih*	1735/5/11–12/19	A	
13. Wang Tao		*sui-kung*	1735/12/20–37/6/3		instructor in Yellow Banner
14. Wang Shih-chin	1717	*chü-jen*	1737/6/4–38/2/19	A	concurrently magistrate of Shu-hsien
15. Li Hung-ju	1714	*chü-jen*	1738/2/20–7/1		transferred to Tan-t'u
16. Ch'iu Wen-shih	1724	*chü-jen*	1738/7/2–39/2/25	A	
17. Hu Chü-t'i		*chien-sheng*	1739/2/25–3/14	A	concurrently magistrate of Shu-hsien.
18. Hsu Kuo-ching (B)		*chien-sheng*	1739/3/15–40/6/16	A	
19. Chang Lei	1724	*chin-shih*	1740/6/17–66/16	A	left because of mourning
20. Wang Ssu-en		*pa-kung*	1740/66/17–41/2/21	A	transferred to Ching-ch'i (A)
21. Feng Tsung-shu	1708	*chü-jen*	1741/2/22–7/14		retired ill
22. Chang Tan-lien			1741/7/15–10/20	A	
23. Ch'ang Wan	1730	*chin-shih*	1741/10/21		The first edition ends at this point. He subsequently served, with three brief interruptions, until 1752/2.

APPENDIX IV

BIOGRAPHICAL NOTES ON CH'ING ADMINISTRATIVE WRITERS CITED IN THIS STUDY

Ch'en Hung-mou (1696–1771), a student of Sung philosophy, became a *chü-jen* and *chin-shih* in 1723. After appointments in the Han-lin Academy and as department director in the Board of Officials, he was sent out to the provinces in 1729 as prefect and, concurrently, censor. He rose rapidly to intendant and provincial treasurer, but was demoted in 1737 for requesting the abolition of taxes on newly cultivated land in his native province of Kwangsi. A year later he was reappointed to office as river intendant, and from 1740–1763 served as governor in Kiangsi, Shensi, Hupeh, Honan, Fukien, Kiangsu, governor-general of Kwangtung-Kwangsi, and again governor of Kiangsu and Hunan. He subsequently rose to grand secretary. *Eminent Chinese*, pp. 86–87.

Ch'eng Han-chang (1762–1832), became a *chü-jen* in 1792 and was selected as magistrate in the *ta-t'iao* selection of 1801. Dismissed from his first appointment in Kwangtung for covering up for his predecessor, he rehabilitated himself in coastal service against pirates and was awarded an imperial audience. Between 1809–1813 he served as magistrate of several independent departments but was again dismissed for failing to investigate deficits incurred in subordinate districts. After carrying out a successful land survey, he again received an imperial audience. He subsequently served as prefect, intendant, provincial judge, and provincial treasurer. He was governor of Honan, Kwangtung, Shantung, and Kiangsi. In 1824 he became acting vice-president of the Board of Works in charge of water conservation in Chihli, and in 1825 governor of Chekiang. His request to retire being rejected, he was transferred to Shantung. In 1827 an irregularity in his management of salt administration in Chekiang was uncovered. He was impeached and demoted to assistant department director of the Board of Punishment, a fall of three full ranks. In 1828 he became provincial treasurer of Fukien and retired ill the same year. *Ch'ing-shih*, 4602.2–4603.3; *Ch'ing-shih lieh-chuan*, 35/22a–26b; *Kuo-ch'ao ch'i-hsien lei-cheng*, 196/3a.

Chu Tse-yun (1666–1732), a noted student of Neo-Confucian philosophy, apparently never held administrative office. *Ch'ing-shih*, 5154.6–5155.1 (there are many other biographies of him in leading biographical sources).

Fang Ta-chih (n.d.), a junior licentiate (*fu-sheng*), volunteered in 1855 for military service under Hu Lin-i. He was recommended for appointment as district magistrate and was appointed to Kuang-chi district. Despite the loss of his district to the rebels he survived the war and subsequently rose from prefect to intendant, provincial judge, and provincial treasurer. *Ch'ing-shih*, 5132.8–5133.3.

Ho Ch'ang-ling (1785–1848) became a *chü-jen* in 1807 and *chin-shih* in 1808. From then until 1821 he held various metropolitan and educational posts. He then went out to the provinces as a prefect, rising rapidly to intendant, provincial judge, and provincial treasurer of several provinces, during which time he helped to survey a sea route for grain transportation and compile his celebrated collection of essays on practical administration (the *Huang-ch'ao ching-shih wen-pien*). From 1836 to 1845 he served as governor of Kweichow. He was promoted to governor-general of Yunnan-Kweichow but was rapidly demoted to provincial treasurer of Honan for failing to suppress a Muslim uprising. He retired almost immediately on grounds of illness. *Eminent Chinese*, pp. 281–82.

Hsieh Chin-luan (1757–1820), the son of a *chü-jen* who became a district director of education through the *ta-t'iao* system, himself became a *chü-jen* in 1788 and was ranked second class in the *ta-t'iao* of 1801. He served as district director of education in several different districts, including Taiwan. *Ch'ing-shih lieh-chuan*, 67/39a and *Kuo-ch'ao ch'i-hsien lei-cheng*, 258/1a–b.

Hsu Tung (1792–1865), the compiler of the original *Mu-ling shu*, was a *chin-shih* of 1822. He received appointment as a second-class secretary of the Board of Works, from which he was promoted to Board department director. He began his compilation of essays on local administration on the grounds that: *a*) the affairs of the empire originated in the departments and districts, therefore they were the first place in which to seek good order; *b*) the larger compilations by Lu Yueh and Ho Ch'ang-ling (see *Eminent Chinese*, pp. 35 and 282 on the former), although excellent, were not specifically about district administration or for district magistrates, therefore there was need for a work specializing on this subject. After completing this major source in 1838, he followed it with a similar collection on the management of the *pao-chia* system. From 1841 to 1849 he served as prefect of several prefectures in Shensi. During this time he was noted for effective implementation of *pao-chia* and of dyke reconstruction and grain distribution. For this he was evaluated as "outstanding and distinctive" in the triennial review of 1847. He retired on grounds of illness. Subsequently he helped to organize *t'uan-lien* militia in Chihli against the Taiping forces and to repair the provincial capital, for which he received further imperial commendation. He was later requested by the emperor to return to service but declined because of his health and age. *Ch'ing-shih*, 5122.9–5123.1; *Ch'ing-shih lieh-chuan*, 76/17a–b; *Ta-ch'ing chi-fu hsien-che chuan*, 16b–19a.

Liu Heng (1776–1841), one of the outstanding magistrates of the Ch'ing period, was a second-class senior licentiate (*fu kung-sheng*) of 1800. After serving a term as government instructor in one of the schools for bannermen, he was eventually called up for selection in 1813 and sent out to Kwangtung as magistrate. While in acting positions he distinguished himself for restoring order in economically depressed districts troubled by banditry and suicide. He was given a substantive appointment but was obliged to return home in 1819 to mourn his father. On returning to office in 1823, he received a district appointment in Szechuan. Once again he succeeded in winning back the allegiance of bandit and secret society groups driven to robbery by poverty and hunger. In another district he staved off drought by timely embankment repairs and, when appointed to the province's capital district, he reduced the burden of government by cutting back the number of office runners from 7,000 to 100. As a magistrate he was distinguished for his determination to deal directly with the people and for his professional legal competence. Between 1827 and 1831 he rose from magistrate of an independent department to prefect, within Szechuan, and to intendant in Honan. He resigned on grounds of illness. *Ch'ing-shih*, 5122.0–5123.1; *Ch'ing-shih lieh-chuan*, 76/7b–9a; *Kuo-ch'ao ch'i-hsien lei-cheng*, 214/5a; *Kuo-ch'ao hsien-cheng shih-lueh*, 54/8a–9b.

Ting Jih-ch'ang (1823–1882), editor of the *Mu-ling shu chi-yao*, was a *chien-sheng* who began his career by purchasing the rank of expectant director of schools. In 1854 he became expectant magistrate and in 1859 received his first appointment at that rank. He was dismissed from another magistracy for losing the district city to the Taiping forces but restored his reputation in personal service under Tseng Kuo-fan and Li Hung-chang and was responsible for arranging the effective disbandment of the Ever Victorious Army. For his success in dealing with foreigners, he was appointed intendant of the Shanghai region, in which office he founded the Kiangnan arsenal. He rose to governor of Kiangsu, director-general of the Foochow arsenal, and governor of Fukien. For a brief period he held titular rank as governor-general. He was noted for his promotion of modern economic development and for his efforts to revitalize local administration after the conclusion of the massive Taiping rebellion. He completed the *Mu-ling shu chi-yao*, with its extensive editorial commentaries, in 1869, while governor of Kiangsu. See *Eminent Chinese*, pp. 721–22.

Tung Kuei-fu (n.d.), a *chin-shih* of 1805 became a bachelor and later compiler of the Hanlin Academy. His official career was cut short by illness, and he subsequently taught at a local private academy. *Ch'ing-shih lieh-chuan*, 67/27b.

Wang Feng-sheng (1776–1834), author of several highly valued works on local administration, was the son of a *chin-shih* who rose to the metropolitan office of deputy commissioner of the transmission office (rank 4A). He himself failed in several attempts to pass the examinations. A *chien-sheng*, he purchased in 1805 the rank of probationary second-class assistant prefect and was sent out to Chekiang. He obtained a substantive appointment at that rank after fifteen years. In the intervening period he served as acting magistrate of several districts, including P'ing-hu (1814–1816 and twice in 1818) and Lan-ch'i (1819). In the Tao-kuang period he rose to prefect, intendant, and finally in 1829 acting salt controller of the Liang-huai region. He was removed from office soon afterwards for mishandling the punishment of a prominent salt smuggler but was retained as an adviser and acting administrator in salt administration and embankment construction under several high officials, including T'ao Chu. *Ch'ing-shih*, 4618.1–7; *Hsu Pei chuan chi*, 34/11a–12b; *P'ing-hu hsien-chih*, 12/15b. Dr. Thomas Metzger kindly elucidated Wang's experiences in salt administration.

Wang Hui-tsu (1731–1807), who was also one of the most noteworthy local administrators of the Ch'ing period, was the son of a jail warden. He obtained his *chü-jen* in 1768 and *chin-shih* in 1775 after many failures at both examinations. From 1786 to 1790 he served as district and department magistrate in Hunan. His vigorous efforts to collect taxes from defaulting landowners in Tao-chou stirred up influential opposition, and his enemies managed to get him impeached and dismissed over a legal technicality. After that he never returned to administrative service. He was noted for his long career in secretarial service and for his highly practical and widely circulating works on local administration. In his old age he wrote down a long and detailed autobiography remarkable for its close scrutiny both of himself and of the world around him. See *Eminent Chinese*, pp. 824–26.

Yuan Shou-ting (1705–1782), an orphan at the age of two, rose rapidly from *sheng-yuan* in 1724 to *chü-jen* in 1726 and *chin-shih* in 1730. Sent out to Hunan, he first assisted in the compilation of the provincial gazetteer and then served with success as district and department magistrate. At the age of thirty-seven he retired to care for his foster parents, and while in retirement served as head of a private academy. In 1756 he resumed his public career and, after serving twice in districts in Chihli, was promoted to second-class secretary of the Board of Rites. In 1757 he again retired on grounds of illness. *T'u-min lu*, introductory biography, and *Kuo-ch'ao ch'i-hsien lei-cheng*, 144/23a.

Yuan Wen-kuan (n.d.), a *chü-jen* of 1750 and *chin-shih* of 1754, received his first appointment as district magistrate of T'ung-kuan from 1763 to 1765. There he was noted for school-building and for preparing a new edition of the district gazetteer. He was promoted to department director of the Board of Rites, and in 1773 returned to the provinces as a prefect. But after one year he was banished to a garrison area in Kweichow for "failing in an investigation." He employed his time there as principal of a private academy. In 1792 he was released and returned home. His writings do not seem to have gained currency outside T'ung-kuan. *Fu-chou fu-chih*, 54/30b; *Shih-nan fu-chih*, 19/26b–27a.

Yü Ch'eng-lung (1617–1684), a *kung-sheng* in 1639, received an appointment in 1661 as magistrate of a derelict district in Kwangsi. After getting its reconstruction under way, he was promoted in 1667 to department magistrate in Szechuan. He rose gradually through intermediate provincial offices and became governor of Chihli from 1680 to 1682 and governor-general of Kiangnan-Kiangsi from 1682 to 1684. He died while in office. Praised by the K'ang-hsi emperor for outstanding uprightness, he also earned the popular accolade of Yü "of the clear skies." He was noted for his frugality. *Eminent Chinese*, pp. 937–38. Yü is to be distinguished from his namesake and contemporary, whose career resembles his closely. See *Eminent Chinese*, pp. 938–39.

NOTES

1: POWERS OF THE DISTRICT MAGISTRATE

1. *Yung-cheng shang-yü*, ts'e 18, 8th year, 3d month, 4th day (April 20, 1730), p. 4.

2. Hsu Nai-p'u, *Huan-hai chih-nan wu-chung*, compiler's preface, dated 1859.

3. Tan Hsiang-liang, in his preface to Fang Ta-chih's *P'ing-p'ing yen*.

4. *T'ung-tien*, 34/2211.2.

5. *T'ung-k'ao*, 85/5619.2 and 5620.1. The functions of the assistant officials are also described in the *T'ung-tien* and *T'ung-k'ao*. According to the former, the function of the assistant magistrate and registrar was to "divide management of matters concerning grain, horses, tax collection, population registration, and police, as a means of assisting their magistrates." The jail warden's function was to "superintend the inspection of prisons. If there is no assistant or registrar, he also performs their functions." The sub-district magistrate's function was to "superintend the arrest of robbers and bandits and the interrogation of fraudulent persons. He is to be established at all department and district passes, fords, and strategic places." *T'ung-tien*, 34/2211.2–3. The *T'ung-kao*, 85/5620.2, adds that the assistant magistrate and registrar divided superintendance of water conservancy.

6. Wu Ching-tzu, *The Scholars*, pp. 570–72.

7. Wang Hui-tsu, *Hsueh-chih i-shuo*, No. 41, p. 13; see also Yuan Shou-ting, *T'u-min lu*, 3/1a–b.

8. Ping-ti Ho, *Studies on the Population of China*, pp. 33, 107, 109, 112, 115, 118, 120; Ch'ü, *Local Government*, p. 38.

9. The whole subject of manipulation in tax collection is treated at length in Kung-ch'üan Hsiao, *Rural China*, ch. 4; see also Ch'ü, *Local Government*, ch. 10.

10. Wu Ching-tzu, *The Scholars*, p. 86, gives an illustration of this condition.

11. Chung-li Chang, *The Income of the Chinese Gentry*, pp. 26–28.

12. Many examples of the independence of southern clans are cited in Hsiao, *Rural China*, chs. 8–10. Clan efforts to preempt litigation in particular are dealt with in Liu, Hui-chen Wang, *The Traditional Chinese Clan Rules*, pp. 152–58.

13. See Chang, *The Chinese Gentry*, pp. 56–62 and 66–70.

14. See Wang Hui-tsu, *Hsueh-chih i-shuo*, No. 64, pp. 21–22. The case is also cited in Ch'ü, *Law and Society in Traditional China*, pp. 212–13, where it is translated in full. Ch'ü also mentions other cases in which magistrates took advantage of supernatural influences. See also Tsao Hsueh-chin, *Dream of the Red Chamber*, translated by Chi-chen Wang, p. 39; Van Gulick, *Dee Goong An*, pp. 201–2; Wang Hui-tsu, *Ping-t'a meng-hen lu*, A/19a. On the threat of supernatural action against injustice, see Ch'ü, *Law and Society*, p. 211.

15. A good example is Yuan Shou-ting's *T'u-min lu*, written in the second half of the eighteenth century. The subject will be developed in greater detail in chapter 5.

16. This summary is based on A. F. P. Hulsewe, *Remnants of Han Law*, and Etienne Balazs, *Le Traité Juridique du Souei-chou*.

17. The military had a similar set of regulations, under the management of the Board of War. The term "disciplinary" is used here to distinguish the penalties and their management from those of the penal laws and statutes. Both use the same term (*tsui*) in referring to offenses. But the *ch'u-fen* were limited to administrative sanctions and provided rewards as well as penalties. As administrative sanctions they applied to rank and degree holders, even though the offenses themselves were concerned with control of conduct of unranking subordinates and the people at large.

18. *TCHT:KH*, 11/1a–b.

19. *Ibid.*, 11/2a.

20. *Ibid.*, 11/4a–b.

21. *LPCFTL*, 25/7a, and 41/12a, 18b–19a, 20a, 24a; 42/41a.

22. *Ibid.*, 1b, 17a, and 16/11a, 18a; 41/12a, 48/9b; 25/8b.

23. *TCHT:KH*, 11/1a–b. Officials who were demoted but retained in office became eligible for reinstatement (*k'ai-fu*) after three years service without fault. If dismissed but retained in office, they became eligible after four years. *TCHT:CC*, 8/7a.

24. *LPCFTL*, 24/2a.

25. *Ibid.*, 50/1a, 2a; *TCLL*, 36/14a–b.

26. *TCLL*, 37/2a. Similarly, if an official maliciously tortured an innocent person, and death ensued, his punishment was execution following the Autumn assizes. *Ibid.*, 36/8b.

27. *TCHT:KH*, 11/2b. See also Ch'ü, *Local Government*, 122–24.

28. For example, in the case (note 22 above) in which a magistrate unjustly sentenced someone to death, and the sentence was executed, the official in charge of hearing the retrial was punished by demotion four grades and transfer. The provincial judge received demotion three grades and transfer. The governor and governor-general received demotion two grades and transfer. If a magistrate tortured a person falsely accused by a policeman and death ensued, the magistrate's punishment was dismissal, the prefect's demotion two grades and transfer, the intendant's demotion one grade and transfer, the provincial judge's demotion one grade and retention in office, and the governor and governor-general's loss of one year's nominal salary. *LPCFTL*, 42/22a.

29. Balazs, *Traité Juridique*, p. 167, note 237.

30. *TCHT:KH*, 11/3a, 4b.

31. These are detailed in Ch'ü, *Local Government*, p. 222.

32. *LPCFTL*, 21/12b–13a.

33. According to the *T'ung-tien*, the function of the prefect was to "control the districts subordinate to him . . . he is in charge of all subordinate officials of the prefecture and investigates and assesses them." *Ibid.*, 34/2210.1. The function of the intendant included "assisting the provincial judge in the assessment of officials." *Ibid.*, 2210.1. That of the provincial judge included "superintending the criminal cases and impeachments of the whole province. He promotes discipline and purifies local administration." *Ibid.*, 2209.2. The governor "examines the administration of all officials"; the governor general "examines and assesses officials" *Ibid.*, 2205.3.

34. Wang Hui-tsu, *Hsueh-chih i-shuo*, No. 29.

35. In Appendix I, virtually every individual listed. In Appendix II such individuals as Nos. 5, 7, 15, 19, 21, 22, 34 in the T'an clan list and 4, 5, 14, 21 in the Shen clan list. The Manchu magistrate Mu-han wrote that he served for over twelve years in several

districts in Chih-li province, during the Tao-kuang reign (1821–1850). Mu-han, *Ming-hsing kuan-chien lu*, preface, 1b.

36. See examples 20, 40 and 59 in the T'an clan list, Appendix II. See also chapter 3 on appointment procedures and p. 264, note 17.

2: QUALIFICATIONS OF THE DISTRICT MAGISTRATE

1. There is a considerable Western-language literature on the examination system. In English see Chang, *The Chinese Gentry*, Part III, "The Examination Life of the Gentry of Nineteenth-Century China," and Ho, *The Ladder of Success*, passim. In French see Etienne Zi, *Pratique des examens litteraires en Chine*, and Li Chow Chung-cheng, *L'examen provincial en Chine sous la dynastie des Ts'ing*.

2. For this reason, some writers prefer to regard "licentiate" as a status rather than a degree proper. However, in a few cases licentiates appear as magistrates, more especially in the early reigns, and from the middle of the nineteenth century. Both were periods when the pressure of events prevented a strict application of rules for appointment. See Table 4, *sheng-yuan*, and Ch'ü, *Local Government*, p. 20, Table 4.

3. The numbers are from Chang, *The Chinese Gentry*, Part II, "A Numerical Analysis of the Gentry of Nineteenth-Century China."

4. *Eminent Chinese of the Ch'ing Period*, biographies of Chang Ch'i, Ch'ien T'ai-chi, Liang Yu-sheng, Pao Shih-ch'en, Shen Te-ch'ien, Wang Hui-tsu; Chang, *The Chinese Gentry*, p. 171.

5. Ch'ü, *Local Government*, p. 20.

6. The classifications of every district are recorded in the seasonal registers of officials. See below p. 47.

7. Hsu Ta-ling, *Ch'ing-tai chüan-na chih-tu*, chs. 2 and 3.

8. "The general aim [of the examination system] is to obtain genuine talent for the use of the State (*kuo-chia*)" *T'ung-chih*, 72/7175.2. "The reason for the selection of *pa-kung* . . . is to reach the talent not yet being selected through the provincial and metropolitan examinations." *TCHTSL*, ch. 1098. The edict from which this comes is quoted more extensively in Chang, *The Chinese Gentry*, p. 27, note 103.

9. *TCHTSL*, ch. 72.

10. Ch'ü, *Local Government*, pp. 212–13, notes 26 and 27.

11. A check of the forty oldest magistrates in the list against a seasonal register for the year 1833 showed that all but two had either been in office or were still in office in that year. At least six of these men were already dead by 1836.

12. These calculations come from Chang, *The Chinese Gentry*, Part II, "A Numerical analysis."

13. Table 9 shows that some of the provincial graduates were selected by the *ta-t'iao* system (on this, see chapter 3). This system was designed to speed up the prospects of employment for able and intelligent provincial graduates. It would be interesting to know to what extent it was successful in doing so. A nation-wide *ta-t'iao* selection of provincial graduates took place in 1853. An examination of the list produces the following findings: 187 were sent out for employment as probationary or "immediate employment" magistrates; their average age was forty. The degree dates are shown for 134 of them. They indicate an average wait of eleven to twelve years between graduation and selection.

To place these findings on a par with those in Table 8 it would be necessary to add the time between selection and achievement of office, whether acting or substantive. The *ta-t'iao* list does not provide this. Even so, it could scarcely have involved as much as eight or nine years. Thus this particular *ta-t'iao* selection evidently was successful in selecting provincial graduates at a noticeably younger age than they could have otherwise expected. But this selection cannot be regarded as representative of the *ta-t'iao* selections in general. Already the Taiping rebellion was in full swing. There are no candidates in this list from Hupei province. Between one-fifth and one-quarter of them come from Yunnan and Kweichow. This is a disproportionate percentage of the total for two otherwise minor provinces. (Without them the average age rises one year.) A satisfactory result will have to await analysis of earlier lists, if such are available. See *Ta-t'iao nien-p'u* for the year 1853.

14. See Chang, *Chinese Gentry*, p. 106; *TCHT:CL*, 5/2a–b; Hsu, *chüan-na chih-tu*, passim. Wu Ching-tzu, *The Scholars*, pp. 461 and 478, contains opinions impugning appointments other than through the examination system.

15. On this subject see Ch'ü, *Local Government*, pp. 22–32.

16. On this subject see K. W. Swart, *Sale of Offices in the Seventeenth Century*. This study deals with every major European country, as well as the leading Eastern empires.

17. *T'ung-k'ao*, 50/5321–2; Hsü, *Chüan-na chih-tu*, passim.

18. Ho, *Ladder of Success*, pp. 111–14.

19. Chu Yun, *Ssu-ho wen-chi*, 15/13a–15b, citing the reaction of Mrs. Wang to the success of her legal son Wang Hui-tsu. See also Ho, *Ladder of Success*, pp. 27 ff.

20. Ch'ü, *Local Government*, p. 112. Chang's estimates of the salaries of private secretaries appear too low. Chang, *Income*, ch. 3.

21. Chang, *Income*, ch. 4.

22. Ho, *Ladder of Success*, p. 116, Table 11.

23. Hsu, *chüan-na chih-tu*, section of tables. To these prices must be added numerous fees and expenses involved in traveling to Peking to make the payment at the Board of Revenue and have it processed.

24. Hsu, *ibid.*, pp. 44, and 89–90.

3: THE PATH TO OFFICE

1. This account is limited to the appointment of district magistrates. No attempt is made to cover the general structure of the appointment system. For this see items vii and viii below. The information is taken primarily from the following sources: i) The *Collected Institutes (Ta-Ch'ing hui-tien [TCHT])* of the various reigns; ii) *The Statutory Amendments to the Collected Institutes (Ta-Ch'ing hui-tien shih-li [TCHTSL])*; iii) *Seasonal Registers of Officials (Chin-shen ch'üan-shu [CSCS]* or *Man-Han chueh-chih ch'üan-shu [MHCCCS])*; iv) *The Appointment Regulations of the Board of Officials (Li-pu ch'üan-hsuan tse-li [LPCHTL])*; v) *The Rules for Examinations (K'o-ch'ang t'iao-li [KCTL])*; vi) *Ch'ing Administrative Terms CAT* (translation by E-tu Zen Sun of the *Liu-pu ch'eng-yü chu-chieh*).

For general purposes the first two groups of sources have proved the most useful. The unfortunate lack of page numbers in the otherwise excellent *Shih-li* makes this source less convenient as a reference work. The Appointment Regulations, while the most detailed of primary sources, is apparently a late work, dating from 1886. The Rules for Examinations has a particularly useful account of the special selection system (*ta-t'iao* or "great selection") for provincial graduates. Some seasonal registers give useful summaries of the appointment procedures current at the time of writing in their introductions. In this account, that for 1764 has been used as a reference (*MHCCCS*). The seasonal registers also state how each district rated under the fourfold classification system. They and the

Chia-ch'ing and Kuang-hsu editions of the *Collected Institutes* also indicate which districts fall under which method of appointment.

There are no detailed accounts of the general appointment system in Western-language literature. In Chinese and Japanese a detailed and scholarly account is: vii) Oda Yorozu, *Ch'ing-kuo hsing-cheng fa*, the first volume of which was translated into Chinese in 1906 (*CKHCF*). A concise but reliable summary is: viii) Hsu Dau-lin, "Ch'ing-tai k'ao-shih yü jen-kuan chih-tu" in Chang Ch'i-yun, *Chung-kuo cheng-chih ssu-hsiang yü chih-tu shih lun-chi*, Vol. III, article 8.

2. *LPCHTL*, han-kuan, 3/4b–5a. See the following examples. From district director of schools (rank 8A): Appendix II, T'an clan, 12, (17), 24, (27), 30, 38, 43; Shen clan, 14. From assistant magistrate (rank 8A): Appendix I, 6, 15, 16, 30; Appendix II, Shen clan, 5. From prefectural commissary of records (rank 8A): Appendix I, 22. From assistant director of schools (rank 8B): Appendix II, T'an clan, 1, (24). From government instructors (*chiao-hsi*): Appendix III, 14, 18. From metropolitan clerks: Appendix I, 29. Appendix III, 32.

3. *TCHT:CC*, 7/2b. The number is only 936 in *TCHT:KH*, 9/2b.

4. *TCHT:KH*, 8/11a–12b; *CKHCF*, 3/88; *CAT*, No. 18.

5. *TCHTSL*, ch. 60.

6. *TCHT:CC*, 6/37b, 38b; *TCHT:KH*, 8/12a–14b; *TCHTSL*, ch. 60. Numbers 46 and 60 in Appendix I appear to break this rule. The latter had obtained his *chü-jen* degree sixteen years before his *chin-shih* and could have served in office in between degrees. The former obtained his *chü-jen* only one year before his *chin-shih*. Unless his second appointment should be "acting," not "substantive," he could hardly have served the formal qualification. For dates of *chü-jen* degrees, see degree lists in *Shun-t'ien fu-chih* (for 46) and *Chin-hsien chih* (for 60). See also *LPTL*, 6/13a for exceptions to the general rule.

7. *CSCS* for 1745 under the provinces indicated.

8. As, for example, the reclassification of P'u-t'ien district, Fukien province. This district, originally classified as "frequented" and "troublesome," was a "medium-important," Board-appointed post. In the 1880s the governor-general informed the Board that it was difficult to administer, giving several reasons (among them the sub-stantial increase in its population). He and his immediate subordinates feared that a Board-appointed official would be unable to make a success of the appointment. They recommended that P'u-t'ien be reclassified as a "most important" and "transfer" post. It would then be controlled by the regional authorities, who would find a man whose local experience and qualifications were up to its demands. In return they offered to have another allegedly less exacting post reclassified from a "transfer" to a Board appointment. Between autumn 1884 and spring 1885 this proposal was carried out. See note in *CKHCF*, 3/93, which follows *HCCSWHsuP*, 17/8a–b. Other examples can be found by comparing CSCS for different years.

9. *TCHT:CC*, 6/35b; *TCHT:KH*, 8/14b; *CKHCF*, 3/88.

10. *TCHT:CC*, 6/6b; *TCHT:KH*, 7/6b; *CKHCF*, 3/35–36, 92–93; *CAT*, No. 2506.

11. *TCHTSL*, ch. 72.

12. *CKHCF*, 3/90.

13. *TCHT:CC*, 7/2b. *TCHT:KH*, 9/2b, which shows one less Board appointment than in the previous source. See also Ch'ü, *Local Government*, p. 22, Table 5, which indicates that the overwhelming majority of the department as well as district magis-trates were Chinese. See also chapter 4 on promotion of metropolitan officials and promotion to department magistrate.

14. Ch'ü, *ibid.*, p. 22.

15. *TCHT:CL*, 5/8b; *TCHT:CC*, ch. 9; *MHCCCS*, 13a, 14a; *TCHTSL*, ch. 44; *LPCHTL*, han-kuan, 2/45b–47a.

16. *TCHT:CL*, 5/8b–9a; *TCHT:CC*, ch. 9; *MHCCCS*, 13a; *TCHTSL*, ch. 44; *LPCHTL*, han-kuan, 2/55a–b.

17. *TCHT:CL*, 5/9a; *MHCCCS*, 13a; *CKHCF*, 3/79. This account reduces the monthly selection system to its essentials. In addition, the order of selection on each monthly list was arranged according to five or more selection procedures (depending on the rank of the office) as follows:

1) Immediate Selection (*chi-hsuan*). For officials whose special circumstances entitled them to the first available post at the appropriate rank.

2) Regular Selection (*cheng-hsuan*). In the early nineteenth century the regular selection for district magistrates applied in the even months to the five metropolitan graduates, five provincial graduates, four contributors, and three officials who earned promotion. Regular selection in the odd months applied to the four officials who had completed mourning, two officials restored to office after disciplinary action, four contributors, four metropolitan graduates, four provincial graduates, and one metropolitan official who had earned promotion.

3) Selection by Insertion (*ch'a-hsuan*). This procedure contained various provisions. For example, after ten provincial graduates had been appointed district magistrates in even months, two provincial graduates and two senior licentiates who were government instructors were to be inserted. New metropolitan graduates picked by the emperor for immediate employment were to be inserted at the rate of two per month after the regular metropolitan graduates. The two educational officials who had completed the necessary terms of office were selected by the insertion procedure. In 1830 some of these went on to the regular selection, bringing the number on regular selection for magistrates posts in even months up to twenty three.

4) Selection by Substitution (*ti-hsuan*). This included the provincial graduates to be substituted if, for example, not enough contributor officials registered for appointment in time to fill the quota allotted in any one month. If not enough new metropolitan graduates were available to fill the quota allotted for selection by insertion, the selection by substitution provided metropolitan and provincial graduates to take their places on the even and odd months respectively.

5) Selection by Withholding (*tso-hsuan*). For provincial officials who had recovered from illness, transferred nearer to their homes to provide terminal care for parents, or completed mourning for parents, and who were returning to duty at their original posts. According to the *TCHT:CC*, magistrates in the above situations need not, if authorized by imperial rescript, return to their original posts. They then were placed on the odd-month regular selection quota for restored officials. *TCHT:CC*, 9/4b–15b.

18. *TCHTSL*, ch. 43 (among many sources to this effect).

19. *CKHCF*, 3/82.

20. *TCHT:CL*, 5/7b.

21. *TCHTSL*, ch. 44. Huang Liu-hung, *Fu-hui ch'üan-shu*, 1/3b–4a.

22. *TCHT:CL*, 5/7b, 8b; *CKHCF*, 3/77–78. If a candidate was absent for good reason, a Board official drew for him. If a candidate drew an appointment from which he was barred by the avoidance laws, he drew another lot, and his previous lot was resealed and put back in the lottery holder.

23. *TCHT:CL*, 5/9a–b; *LPCHTL*, han-kuan, 2/110b–111a.

24. *TCHTSL*, ch. 72.

25. *TCHTSL*, chs. 43, 72.

26. *TCHTSL*, ch. 72.

27. *TCHT:CC*, 6/6a–b; *TCHT:KH*, 7/6a–b; *CKHCF*, 3/34–35.

28. *TCHTSL*, ch. 72.

29. *TCHTSL*, ch. 73. The order of provinces is indicated, for example, in a regulation of 1765 as Chihli, Kiangnan, Shantung, Shansi, Honan, Shensi, Kansu, Chekiang, Kiangsi, Fukien, Hupei, Hunan, Szechuan, Kwangtung, Kwangsi, Yunnan, Kweichow. The distant provinces were the last six along with Fukien.

30. *TCHT:YC*, 11/6a.

31. *TCHTSL*, ch. 73.

32. *TCHT:CL*, 5/2a.

33. *KCTL*, 52B/8a–b.

34. *Ibid.*, 2a, 9b. The provinces divided as follows: eight large (Chihli, Kiangsu, Anhwei, Kiangsi, Chekiang, Fukien, Hupei, Hunan), seven medium (Shantung, Shansi, Honan, Shensi, Kansu, Szechuan, Kwangtung), and three small, (Kwangsi, Yunnan, Kweichow).

35. *Ibid.,* 2a–3a, 9b–10b, 3b–4b, 5a–b.

36. *LPCHTL*, han-kuan, 4/24b–25a.

37. *TCHT:CC*, 6/6a, 13a; *CKHCF*, 3/90–92; *LPTL*, han kuan 6/39–40, 68–69.

38. *TCHT:CL*, 5/2a–b; *TCHT:CC*, 6/10a–b; *CKHCF*, 3/10–11, 34–35; *LPTL* han-kuan 6/38a.

39. *TCHT:KH*, 7/12a–b.

40. This account is based on Hsu, *Chüan-na chih-tu.*

41. For department magistrate the costs in 1774–1776 included 6,020 taels for a senior licentiate or Imperial Academy student, 1,600 taels for a district magistrate, 2,200 taels for someone awaiting selection or substantive appointment as district magistrate. For senior licentiates and Imperial Academy students the costs of appointment as district magistrate between 1774 and 1850 were as follows: 1774, 4,620 taels; 1798, 5,090 taels; 1801, 4,620 taels; 1803, 4,070 taels; 1814, 4,070 taels; 1819, 1826, 1833, 1841, 1850, 3,700 taels. Hsu, *ibid.*, section of tables.

42. According to the *LPCHTL*, officials sent out as probationers also had to be over twenty years old. *LPCHTL*, han-kuan, 2/111a.

43. Senior licentiates and Imperial Academy students could also sit an examination to qualify for office. Those who had obtained their status by purchase were graded into two classes. Those passing first class were qualified as district registrars, the second class qualified as department jail wardens. Their names were entered in the monthly lists for these offices and they were called according to their examination order. *TCHT:CL*, 5/2a–b; *TCHT:KH*, 9/12a–b. As Table 1 indicates, the number of positions available within these offices was very limited.

44. *LPTL*, han-kuan, 3/16a. By a regulation of 1739, those whose purchased rank (brevet) was lower than that of the office to which they had been given acting appointments had to put in the same time to qualify for a substantive appointment as officials qualifying for "preferment" posts, that is, five years. *TCHTSL*, ch. 60.

45. *CKHCF*, 3/34–36.

46. *CKHCF*, 3/91.

47. It is difficult, in view of this, to go all the way with Ch'ü's statement that "nearly all newly appointed magistrates were inexperienced" (Ch'ü, *Local Government*, p. 95). Ch'ü based his remark on the point that talented men were unwilling to accept positions as subordinate district officials because of their inferior status and slight chances of

promotion. Thus, he argued, there was little possibility of recruiting magistrates from those who had started their careers as subordinate officials (Ch'ü, *ibid.*, pp. 94–95). In effect this is true, though not exactly for the reasons stated, but because the appointment system itself did not provide for broad recruitment from this source.

Ch'ü also argued that magistrates came to their position untrained in its technical administrative routine and had to learn through trial and error. Thus their need for secretaries. All this is true of those receiving a substantive position as magistrate as their "first appointment" (*ch'u*). It would not apply to all those being reappointed or sent out from the capital to their first substantive provincial appointment, such as Hanlin bachelors (i.e., a *pu* appointment). Nor does it apply to those being promoted (*sheng*), "preferred" (*t'i*), or transferred (*tiao*). It does not apply to department magistrates. It is true of those holding acting office (*shu*) who were on a "deputy" (*ch'ai-wei*) or "probationary" (*shih-yung*) appointment and had not held any previous acting appointments. In the early nineteenth century, the former included new metropolitan graduates for employment as magistrates, rehabilitated officials remaining in the province in which they were serving; the latter included provincial graduates in the first class of the "great selection," first-class senior licentiates examined and sent out as district magistrates, and, as indicated in the text, contributors. (Cf. *TCHT:CC*, 6/6a; the *TCHT:KH* list is somewhat larger, *ibid.*, 7/6a–b.) On the other hand, it is not true of those holding acting office who concurrently held substantive office elsewhere. As suggested in Appendix I, this could involve a considerable number of those holding acting office, more especially in the more important districts.

Thus the problem of lack of training—and it was a real problem—referred primarily to those on "first appointments" and to some on acting appointments, and not to all.

48. Rough calculations of the overall numbers of district secretaries are based on Wang Hui-tsu's statement that more than ten were needed in a district where the administrative load was heavy, while in a less busy district only two or three secretaries were needed to handle all secretarial duties. Taking the 350 or so "important" and "most important" districts (*hsien*), adding 70 such departments, and multiplying by ten arrives at 4,200 secretaries. Between two to three secretaries for each of the remaining 1,080 districts produces an average of 2,700 secretaries. By this calculation the total is of the order of 7,000.

On the basis of Wang's assessment, Chang Chung-li took seven as the average number of secretaries at the prefectural and district level, arriving at a total of 12,200 for the 1,743 prefectural and district posts in 1880. This would mean 11,000 district secretaries, which would seem too high a figure for the eighteenth century. Whether Wang's assessment was relevant one hundred years later is also, of course, debatable.

The figure of 7,000 assumes that the districts with heavy administrative loads were the same as those classified as "important" and "most important" which is very likely a conservative assumption. But Ch'ü is right in arguing that since magistrates paid secretaries out of their own pockets the tendency would have been to keep the number at a minimum (Ch'ü, *Local Government*, p. 97). Thus 7,000 seems reasonable as a minimum estimate. In the post-Taiping era, reconstruction, the extension of government activity into commercial enterprise, and the larger population, are all likely to have resulted in a greater number of secretaries.

49. Chang, *Income*, p. 86.

50. The function of the private secretaries is described in Ch'ü, *Local Government*, ch. 6.

51. Regulations provided for the examination of secretaries for appointment to

office. But they were evidently seldom utilized in the eighteenth century. Cf. Ch'ü, *ibid.*, pp. 111–12. In the turmoil of the mid-nineteenth century, the appointment system came to rely much more on recommendation. Several eminent men, such as Tso Tsung-t'ang, Ting Jih-ch'ang, and Hsueh Fu-ch'eng, who began their administrative careers as private secretaries, rose to official appointment at this time. See Chang, *Income*, pp. 83–84 and their biographies in *Eminent Chinese*.

52. See Chang, *Income*; Appendix III, throughout.

53. E.g., Liu Heng, Liu Pao-nan, Ting Jih-ch'ang, and Wang Hui-tsu. Liu Heng, who was distinguished as a legal administrator in the early nineteenth century, was the author of several handbooks for magistrates. Ting Jih-ch'ang, a distinguished governor during the T'ung-chih restoration (1862–1874), obtained imperial consent in the 1860s to edit a summary of the *Writings for Department and District Magistrates* (Mu-ling shu), a substantial collection of essays by local and regional Ch'ing officials compiled in the early nineteenth century by a junior metropolitan official. On Liu Pao-nan, an important early nineteenth-century scholar, see *Eminent Chinese*, pp. 528–29.

Although it is presently impossible to estimate how many secretaries rose into the administrative service at any given period, the fact that some did is beyond dispute. In view of this, Ch'ü's statement that "the experts" (i.e., private secretaries) "and the officials remained two distinct groups throughout the dynasty, with no possibility of interchange" (*Local Government*, p. 115) is exaggerated.

54. See their biographies in *Eminent Chinese*.

55. The formal review of probationers (*chen-pieh*) took place at the end of their probationary period, whenever that happened to be. The triennial evaluations (*ta-chi* in the case of provincial officials) took place in the following years: in the Yung-cheng period 1725, 1728, 1731, 1734; in the Ch'ien-lung period 1737, 1740, 1743, 1746, 1749, 1752, 1755, 1758, 1761, 1764, 1767, 1770, 1773, 1776, 1779, 1782, 1785, 1788, 1791, 1794; in the Chia-ch'ing period 1797, 1800, 1803, 1806, 1809, 1812, 1815, 1818; in the Tao-kuang period 1821, 1824, 1827, 1830, 1833, 1836, 1839, 1842, 1845, 1848.

56. Many of these handbooks are listed and summarized in Ma Feng-ch'en. *Ch'ing-tai hsing-cheng chih-tu yen-chiu ts'an-k'ao shu-mu*. The following represents a brief list of some of the most well known among them.

General Handbooks

Huang Liu-hung, *Fu-hui ch'üan-shu* (complete book of good fortune and benevolence). Late seventeenth century. The one Ch'ing handbook indexed in Morohashi.

Yuan Shou-ting, *T'u-min lu* (planning for the people), mid-eighteenth century.

Wang Hui-tsu, *Hsueh-chih i-shuo* (how to learn good administration), late eighteenth century.

Wang Feng-sheng, *Hsueh-chih t'i-hsing lu* (how to embody good administration), early nineteenth century.

Agriculture and Famine Control

Hsü Kuang-ch'i, *Nung-cheng ch'üan-shu* (complete book of agricultural administration), late Ming.

Wang Chih-i, *Huang-cheng chi-yao* (essentials in famine control), early nineteenth century.

Legal cases and handbooks

Lan Ting-yuan, *Lu-chou kung-an* (the cases of Lan T'ing-yuan), early eighteenth century.

Liu Heng, *Tu-lu hsin-te* (what to get out of studying the law), early nineteenth century.

—— *Shu-liao wen-ta* (questions and answers for officials in Szechuan), early nineteenth century.

Lü Chih-t'ien, *Lü-fa hsu-chih* (what to know about the law), early nineteenth century.

Mu-han, *Ming-hsing kuan-chien lu* (administration of law and litigation), early nineteenth century.

Post Mortems

Hsi-yuan lu (instructions to coroners), original version mid-thirteenth century. Translated in part by H. Giles (London, Bale, 1924).

57. The most well known is the *Ch'in pan chou-hsien shih-i*. Originally the Yung-cheng emperor commissioned two favored metropolitan officials, Grand Secretary Chu Shih and Senior President of the Censorate Shen Chin-ssu, to write a work on this subject. When illness and death prevented them from carrying out this task, it was entrusted to two favored provincial officials, T'ien Wen-ching, for whom the emperor created the post of governor-general of Honan, and Li Wei, for whom he created the post of governor-general of Chekiang. All had had long experience in provincial administration. See their biographies in *Eminent Chinese*. See also *Yung-cheng shang-yü*, ts'e 18, eighth year, 3d month, 4th day. The *Ch'ing shih* mentions, but does not describe, a work of the Chia-ch'ing period, *Ch'in-ting hsun-chih chou-hsien kuei-t'iao*. Ting Jih-ch'ang's edition of the *Mu-ling shu* (Mu-ling shu chi-yao) was also imperially sponsored.

58. Lu-Yueh, *Ch'ieh-wen chai wen-ch'ao* (essays from the Ch'ieh-wen study), late eighteenth century, on many aspects of private and public administration. Ho Ch'ang-ling, *Huang-ch'ao ching-shih wen-pien* (collected essays of the present dynasty on government), early nineteenth century, a famous work which produced several subsequent continuations. Hsü Tung, *Mu-ling shu* (writings for magistrates), early nineteenth century, specifically on local administration, as opposed to the previous work, which contains many sections on local administration, but is more general in scope.

59. The Yung-cheng emperor wanted a copy of the *chou-hsien shih-i* on every magistrate's desk, so that he could refer to it when reviewing the day's proceedings (see source note 57). Wang Hui-tsu advised one son, who intended to study for secretarial work, to read the Penal Code and the *Peking Gazette* (*Meng-hen lu-yü*, 25); he advised another, who was appointed a local official, to read the Penal Code and the *Instructions for Coroners*. (*Meng-hen lu-yü*, 5b.) Ho Shih-ch'i, a magistrate during the Tao-kuang period, urged magistrates awaiting substantive appointment to study the provincial annals and the Penal Code. *MLSCY*, 1/35b.

The late-nineteenth-century magistrate Fang Ta-chih produced the most elaborate reading list. It began with twenty handbooks, including those by Huang Liu-hung, Yuan Shou-ting, Wang Hui-tsu, Liu Heng, Hsü Kuang-ch'i, Wang Chih-i, Lan Ting-yuan, and one by the educationally minded eighteenth-century governor Ch'en Hung-mou, as well as the collections of Ho Ch'ang-ling and Hsü Tung. These, said Fang, would enable the reader to know the difference between gain and loss.

He then listed the *Collected Institutes*, the *Ta-Ch'ing t'ung-li*, and the *Hsueh-cheng ch'üan shu* (an official handbook for educational commissioners). These he equated with the *Chou li* (Chou dynasty institutes or Rites of Chou) "of Confucian times" (it was in fact written much later), as indicating the constitutional structure of the body politic.

Next he listed the Penal Code and the *Instructions to Coroners*, followed by two official compilations of legal cases and precedents and the *Disciplinary Regulations of the Board of Officials*. Read the latter, he urged, and you will commit few mistakes. He ended with the *Peking Gazette* and, to accord with the times, two works dealing with overseas affairs (the *Hai-kuo t'u-chih* by Wei Yuan and the *Ko-kuo t'ung-shang t'iao-yueh*). *P'ing-p'ing yen*, 1/12a–15b.

60. One way of doing this was to publish several handbooks in a joint edition. Hsü Nai-p'u's *Huan-hai chih-nan* (guide to the sea of officialdom) including works by Wang Hui-tsu, Liu Heng, and the *Chou-hsien shih-i* of T'ien Wen-ching and Li Wei. Another such compilation for secretaries (*Ju-mu hsu-chih wu-chung*, edited by Chang T'ing-hsiang) includes works by Wang Hui-tsu and three other writers noted for secretarial experience. Ho Ch'ang-ling devoted his section on private secretaries in the *Huang-ch'ao ching-shih wen-pien* to Wang Hui-tsu's *Tso-chih yao-yen* (essentials in aiding administration).

4: LENGTH OF SERVICE AND SUBSEQUENT CAREER

1. See Ch'ü, *Local Government*, p. 32. Further details are in *TCHT:KH*, 10/4b–8b.

2. Ch'ü, *ibid.*, pp. 33–35.

3. Chang, *The Chinese Gentry*, p. 53.

4. The ratios are Wu-hsien, 80–42, Ch'ang-chou hsien, 75–44, Yuan-ho 80–51, or 68–39 up to 1837.

5. *TCHTSH*, ch. 44. Yuan Shou-ting and Chu Shih were among the few who obtained this promotion.

6. *TCHT:CC*, 7/2b; 9/6b, 8a.

7. *LPCHTL*, han-kuan, 2/8a, 7a–b, 4a–5a.

8. *TCHT:CC*, 9/6a, 8b, 7b.

9. *LPCHTL*, han-kuan, 1/16a.

10. Among them were Ch'en Hung-mou, Ho Ch'ang-ling, Hsü Kuang-chin, Hsü Tung, Liang Chang-chü, and Yeh Ming-ch'en. Some who first came to provincial administration as intendants were Pi Yuan, T'ao Chu, and Lin Tse-hsü. Juan Yuan's first provincial position was as educational commissioner; Yin-chi-shan's was provincial judge. In the late seventeenth and early eighteenth centuries, the chances of promotion were more open. Yü Ch'eng-lung, his namesake Yü Ch'eng-lung, Chu Shih, and Shen Chin-ssu all rose to the top in provincial or metropolitan administration from district magistrate. T'ien Wen-ching, a comparatively unlettered man, began as assistant magistrate. In the late eighteenth century, one official who managed to rise high from the rank of magistrate was Wang Chih-i. After a checkered career he eventually became governor-general of Fukien and Chekiang during the Chia-ch'ing period. He had, however, held a junior metropolitan appointment before going out to the provinces. For Wang's career, see *Ch'ing shih*, pp. 4476–77. For the rest, see *Eminent Chinese*, or Appendix 4.

11. *TCHT:CC*, 6/36a; 7/2b.

12. For example, the cost of qualification for a prefecture was in 1774–76 10,300 taels for officials not qualifying directly for promotion and 13,300 taels for senior licentiates and Imperial Academy students. Among qualifying officials, the cost was as follows: board department director, 2,300 taels; magistrate of independent department, 3,640 taels; metropolitan sub-prefect and first-class assistant prefect, 4,500 taels. The additional cost for the odd-months list was 1,000 taels. As in the previously cited examples, the prices rose at the end of the eighteenth century and declined gradually during the nineteenth century. Hsu, *Chüan-na chih-tu*, section of tables.

13. *TCHTSL*, ch. 72.

5: INFLUENCE OF CLASSICAL THEORY ON THE ROLE OF MAGISTRATE

1. See *Analects*, 8/9; 12/7, 19; 15/1, 24; 16/9. *Mencius*, 1A6, 7; 1B4, 7; 3A3; 3B9; 4A10; 5A5; 6A7; 7A12, 13. See also the *Shu ching*, K'ang kao 4; Yao tien 2; P'an keng *passim*; Kao yao mo 16; T'ang shih 3; Wei tzu 2; Chiu kao 3, 11; Lü hsing 2.

2. *Shu ching*, Yao tien; Kao yao mo. *Mencius*, 3A4. Contrast the Taoist view of primordial bliss and natural harmony, when "men lived in common with birds and beasts, and were on terms of equality with all creatures as forming one family." From Legge's translation of *Chuangtzu: Sacred Books of the East*, Vol. XXXIX, Book IX, Section 2, "Horses Hoofs," p. 278 (Julian Press edition, p. 326). *Chuangtzu* adds that far from improving the world the sages merely disrupted it, perplexing the people, exciting their thirst for knowledge and pursuit of gain. *Ibid.*, pp. 278–80 (Julian Press edition, pp. 326–28). Cf. Waley, *Three Ways of Thought in Ancient China*, pp. 66–75 and especially p. 69.

3. For an account of the aristocratic usage of *chüntzu*, see Hsu, *Ancient China*, pp. 161–68. Many examples can be found in the *Shih ching*, e.g., odes 55, 167, 172, 213, 215, 216, 249, 251, 252.

4. See the following passages in the *Analects*: 4/2–5; 6/28; 8/6; 9/8, 28; 11/19; 12/1–2, 22; 13/19; 14/2, 5, 7, 30, 45; 15/8 (see also *Mencius*, 6A10), 32, 34; 17/6.

5. *Mencius*, 7A15; 6A4–6; 2A6; 3A4; 7A24; 4B14; 6B6; 4B28; 4A4; 6B8; 7A41; 5A7; 6B14; 6A16; 7B32; 7B37; 4A1; 6A4; 1B8; 2A4; 4A2, 3; 4A1; 6B9.

6. See Liu Pao-nan, *Lun-yü cheng-i*, note to *Analects*, 4/9.

7. Hsu, *Ancient China*, pp. 89–90, 98–99.

8. *Analects*, 4/9; 8/7; 12/20; 13/20; 15/8; 19/1 (for the different value to be set on courage by *shih* and *chüntzu*, see 8/2, 10; 15/1; 17/8, 23, and also 5/6; 11/25). *Mencius*, 1A7; 2A4; 5B6; 6B7; 7A9–10, 33, 37; 7B3.

9. *SPPY* text, introduction to chs. 1 and 9 (Biot, pp. 2, 171); chs. 10–12 (Biot, pp. 196–261).

10. See Elmquist, *Rural Controls*, pp. 339–43; Hsiao, *Rural China*, p. 569, note 6; p. 580, note 116; p. 625, note 138.

11. A recent translation by Sister Mary Lelia Makra views this classic as a work of enlightened morality. It is true that it is concerned with propagating private and public morality, but it is morality geared to the needs of imperial and universal authoritarianism. The *Hsiao ching* argues that the ancient kings brought order into the world, therefore the people willingly submitted (1; 7). Order was preserved by universal demonstrations of filiality, led by the ruler himself (2–6). Filiality is the constant norm of heaven, the justification of the earth, and the model of the people. In human conduct there is nothing greater than it (7; 9). When the former kings governed by filiality, no one dared act in a disorderly way (8). This means that those who are really filial will not be arrogant as superiors, refractory as subordinates, and contentious among equals (10). The interest of the classic is in political security. The virtues which it expounds are *ching* (reverence), *chung* (here loyalty), and *shun* (submissiveness). As Sister Makra's translation puts it, "to serve one's elders reverently paves the way for civic obedience" (5). "There is nothing better than fraternal love for teaching men propriety and obedience ... nothing better than propriety for giving security to rulers" (12).

The classic pretends to be based on Confucian conversations and teaching, but says nothing about the conditionality of power, which is a doctrine central to the authentic passages of the *Shu ching* (see Kao Yao mo 6; Kan shih 3; T'ang shih 1–2; P'an keng 3; Wei tzu; Ta kao *passim*; K'ang kao 6, 23; Chiu kao 11–12; Shao kao *passim*; Lo kao 13,29; To shih *passim*, etc.,—in fact it is the basic teaching of the Duke of Chou and appears in virtually all his speeches) and of course to Mencius (see 1B8; 2A4; 4A1–3; 6B9).

The *Hsiao ching* also says nothing about the rights of an official to preserve himself from an unjust ruler (see *Analects*, 18/1, 8; 5/22; 14/17–18; 15/36. *Mencius*; 2A2; 2A9; 4A14; 5B1; 6B6. Contrast the *Hsiao ching*, ch. 15). Where Confucius and Mencius argue that filiality is the attitude of mind through which a child learns the meaning of *jen* and *i*, the *Hsiao Ching* conveys no hint of this truly ethical teaching. It does not mention *jen*. In its view, what is right in public life is obedience to de facto authority (5; 8; 9; 10; 12; 13; 14; 17).

The *Hsiao ching's* disrespect for genuine Confucian teaching is highlighted by its appropriation of a famous passage in the *Tso chuan* extolling moral observance (*li*). By substituting "filiality" for "moral observance" it enhances the former with borrowed glamour, capping this by presenting it as the direct words of Confucius himself. (Cf. the *Tso chuan*, Duke Chao, 25th year, paragraph 2; Legge, pp. 704 and 708, column 2; Couvreur, III, 379; and the *Hsiao ching*, ch. 7.) The source of the original statement of moral observance is said to have been the famous minister Tzu Ch'an. It was not Confucius. In fact its alleged conversation between Confucius and his disciple Tsengtzu are foreign to the spirit of the authentic views of these philosophers and in places verge on the ludicrous.

There can be little doubt that the *Hsiao ching* was written as a means of justifying de facto sovereignty, by bringing existing philosophical concepts to its support. The fact that the early Han emperors were the first rulers to lack any pretense to a princely lineage and that they extolled filiality, particularly their own filiality, suggests that if they did not actually commission the *Hsiao ching* they must certainly have found it a gratifying work. The fact that the *Hsiao ching* was aimed at young readers—the new generation—adds to this suspicion. By providing a logic for unconditional loyalty— and an allegedly Confucian one at that—and by directing that logic at impressionable minds, the *Hsiao ching* could kill two valuable birds one with simple, well-aimed stone. It is hardly surprising that Neo-Confucian thinkers, although having to accept the *Hsiao ching* as part of the orthodox canon, looked on it with distaste. (Cf. Creel, Herrlee Glessner *et al.*, *Literary Chinese by the Inductive Method*, Vol. I. the *Hsiao ching*, p. 36; Legge, *Hsiao ching*, *Sacred Books of the East*, III, 459–60).

12. *Eminent Chinese*, pp. 902, 309, 327. An edition was also issued in 1656 under the name of the Shun-chih emperor (*ibid.*, p. 258). Cf. Legge, *Hsiao Ching*, pp. 457, 458, 461. The Yung-cheng emperor, believing that loyal and honest officials were produced from filial sons, assiduously promoted the *Hsiao ching*, ordering publication in Chinese and Manchu. See also Huang Pei, *A Study of the Yung-cheng Period*, p. 234. An edition was produced by his confidant, the Grand Secretary Chu Shih.

13. Yuan Shou-ting, *T'u-min lu*, 1/1a; T'ung-chih emperor in preface to *MLSCY*. Another writer affirmed the Mencian view that the people were the means by which Heaven established the supreme ruler. Hsieh Chin-luan, *Mu-ling shu*, 1/51b.

14. Yuan Wen-kuan in *T'ung-kuan hsien-chih*, 26/9b–10a; Ch'eng Han-chang, *MLSCY*, 6/16b–17b; Yuan Shou-ting, *T'u-min lu*, 1/1b.

15. See Ch'ü, *Law and Society*, pp. 129–33, and Hsiao, *Rural China*, pp. 373–75 and ch. 10. Hsiao's documentation is largely for the period after 1850.

16. Ting Jih-ch'ang, *MLSCY*, 3/1a. See also Wang Hui-tsu, "the way of the district magistrate has education and nurture as its joint base," *Hsueh-chih*, A/12. See also Tung

Kuei-fu, "all those who speak about local administration speak of nurturing and education; these are their constant words." Introduction, dated 1824, to Wang Feng-sheng's *Hsueh-chih t'i-hsing lu.*

17. Wang Feng-sheng, *Hsueh-chih t'i-hsing lu*, B/6a–7a; Wang Hui-tsu, *Hsueh-chih*, A/12.

18. Chu Tse-yun, *MLSCY*, 3/43a–44a; Ch'eng Han-chang, *ibid.*, 6/16b–17b; Ch'en Hung-mou, *ibid.*, 6/16a; Wang Hui-tsu, *Hsueh-chih*, A/12.

19. Yü Ch'eng-lung, *MLSCY*, 2/44b–45a; Chu Tse-yun and Ch'eng Han-chang *MLSCY*, 3/43a–44a and 6/16b–17b.

20. Ch'eng Han-chang, *MLSCY*, 6/16b–17b; Wang Hui-tsu, *Hsueh-chih*, A/12.

21. Ch'en Hung-mou, *MLSCY*, 6/16a.

22. Wang Hui-tsu, Wang Feng-sheng, Ch'eng Han-chang as cited.

23. *MLSCY*, 6/13b. So, too, Yuan Shou-ting insisted that "getting people by good government is not like getting them by good education. The difference between educating the people and flogging them is like that between heaven and earth." *T'u-min lu*, 3/23b–24a.

24. Ch'eng Han-chang, *MLSCY*, 6/16b–17b.

25. Yuan Wen-kuan in *T'ung-kuan HC*, 26/9b–10a; Ch'en Hung-mou in *MLSCY*, 6/16a.

26. Hsieh Chin-luan, *Mu-ling shu*, 1/51b. Possibly this particular judgment was a little too close to the bone, as the essay from which it was taken was not included in the *MLSCY* whereas others by this author were, to the accompaniment of considerable editorial stress.

27. Fang Ta-chih, *P'ing-p'ing yen*, 1/10a–b. Liu Heng, who rose from long experience as district magistrate to prefect and intendant, said on this theme: "The department or district magistrate, being close to the people, can do his utmost as things happen. The prefect (as a superior) is sufficiently distant from the people so that pacifying, and leading subordinates, is all he can do. He cannot compare with district magistrates for getting the people's business at first hand!" *Ch'ing-shih*, 5122.6; *Ch'ing-shih lieh-chuan*, 76/8b.

28. Yuan Shou-ting, *T'u-min lu*, 1/1a–b.

29. *Ibid.*, 1/3a–4b.

30. *T'i-hsing lu*, A/14b–15a; *MLSCY*, 6/15b. Cf. also Yü Ch'eng-lung, "The district officials are called the father and mother, the common people are called the child people. . . . One who looks after the people should also see to their hunger and cold, and toil over exhorting and transforming them. Everything proceeds from the avoidance of insincerity." *MLSCY*, 2/44b–45a.

31. Yung-cheng emperor (see chapter 1, note 1), Ch'eng Han-chang in *MLSCY*, 6/16b–17b.

32. *Ch'ing-shih lieh-chuan*, 76/7b–9a; *Kuo-ch'ao hsien-cheng shih-lueh*, 54/8a–9b (for Liu Heng). *T'u-min lu*, introduction, or *Kuo-ch'ao ch'i-hsien lei-cheng*, 144/23a ff. (for Yuan Shou-ting).

33. *Hsueh-chih*, A/1 and 9.

34. Yuan Shou-ting, *T'u-min lu*, 1/1a–b and notes 26–27 above. Wang Hui-tsu noted that the people, conversely, were close to the district capital but far from the provincial capital. This was all the more reason for the district magistrate to do his duty conscientiously. *Hsueh-chih*, A/19.

35. The *Hsiao ching* turns this round, making the father the basis for both love and reverence. The mother obtains love (*ai*) by extension, as the other parent. *Ibid.*, ch. 5.

36. *T'u-min lu*, 1/3a.

37. *Hsueh-chih,* A/12; See also Ch'eng Han-chang. "District magistrates are the officials close to the people. The official is high and the people are low, but their condition is easy to see. If I am not close to the people, who will be? If I then wish to be close and the people still doubt and fear and dare not be close, how much the more, if I am lazy and arrogant, oppressive and covetous, will the people lose hope and scatter." *MLSCY,* 1/21b–22b.

38. *Hsueh-chih t'i-hsing lu,* A/14b–15a.

39. Hsieh Chin-luan, *MLSCY,* 1/20b–21a. See also Wang Feng-sheng, *Hsueh-chih t'i hsing lu,* A/15a–b; Wang Hui-tsu, *Hsueh-chih,* A/12; Yuan Wen-kuan, *T'ung-kuan HC,* 26/10a; Ch'en Hung-mou, *MLSCY,* 6/13b; Fang Ta-chih, *P'ing-p'ing yen,* 1/55b.

40. *T'u-min lu,* 3/22b–23a.

41. *MLSCY,* 1/21b–22b.

42. *Hsueh-chih,* A/1 and 11.

43. Tung Kuei-fu in introduction to *Hsueh-chih t'i-hsing lu.*

44. Yuan Shou-ting, *T'u-min lu,* 4/14a–b; 3/3b–5a.

45. Wang Hui-tsu utilized this when he wrote: "Putting one's heart into the job is basic for good administration.... The administrator is called 'one who knows the district' or 'one who knows the department.' This means he must know the entirety of that one district or department. If there is one thing he doesn't know, even if he wants to put his heart into the job he won't be able to assure good order." *Hsueh-chih,* A/1. Much the same point had been made earlier by Hai Jui, a famous magistrate of the late Ming period. (See below chapter 9.)

46. Chu Tse-yun, *MLSCY,* 3/43a–44a; Hsieh Chin-luan, *ibid.,* 1/20b–21b; Wang Feng-sheng, *Hsueh-chih t'i-hsing lu,* A/6, 18 (also *MLSCY,* 7/37a–b); Wang Hui-tsu, *Hsueh-chih,* A/3, 19 and especially 20; Liu Heng as quoted in *Kuo-ch'ao hsien-cheng shih-lueh,* 54/8a–9b.

47. *T'u-min lu,* 1/2a.

48. *Hsueh-chih,* A/9.

49. Chu Tse-yun, *MLSCY,* 3/43a–44a.

50. *MLSCY,* 6/16b–17b.

51. *Hsueh-chih,* A/8.

6: Distinctiveness of ch'ing administrative theory

1. *Shu-ching,* K'ang-kao, p. 9.

2. Preface to *Sheng-yü kuang-hsun* (Amplification to Sacred Edict).

3. *Tso chuan,* Duke Ch'ao, 30 (Legge, 734.2, text 733.5–6). See also *ibid.,* Duke Hsiang, 25 (Legge, 517.2, text 513.3–4), "the people should be looked on as one's children." See also *Han shu,* ch. 89, "in his administration he looked on the people as his children."

4. *Shih ching,* odes 172 and 251. *Shu ching,* Hung fan, 24. See also *Shu ching,* T'ai-che, 21 (a spurious chapter), "Heaven and Earth is the parent of all creatures, and of all creatures man is the most highly endowed. The sincere, intelligent and perspicaceous (among men) becomes the great sovereign; and the great sovereign is the parent of the people" (Legge, pp. 283–84). *Mencius,* 1A4, 3A3.

5. Liang Chang-chü, *Ch'eng-wei lu,* 22/12b–13a, citing Wang Yü-ch'eng (954–1001), *Hsiao-hsu chi* (annotation by Wang, ch. 8, p. 96). According to an informant, Emperor Wen of the Han dynasty first referred to magistrates in this way.

6. Liang Chang-chü, *ibid.,* 32/26. Hai Jui, viewing the family symbol from the position of magistrate, not people, distinguished the Court, at the top, as "my father and

mother"; the top provincial officials, intermediate officials, and metropolitan and provincial officials, in the middle, as "my elder and younger brothers"; and the clerks, village elders, and common people, at the bottom, as "my children" (*tzu-hsing*). *Hai Jui chi*, p. 146.

7. *Shu ching*, Yao tien, pp. 2, 30.

8. *Mencius*, 7A45.

9. *T'ang Hui-yao*, 69/1217. The order goes on to urge that priority be given in the selection of magistrates to men of proven administrative merit.

10. *Tso chuan*, Duke Hsiang, p. 14 (Legge, 466.2–467.1, text 462.5 ff.).

11. *Analects*, 13/9; 5/15; 20/2; 13/29–30. On the last point, see *Mencius*, 6B8.

12. *Mencius*, 7A22; 3A3; 4B16; 7A14; 3A3; 1A7; 1A4; 3B9; 7A23; 4B7.

13. *Analects*, 4/15; 15/23.

14. Hexograms 11 and 12 (T'ai and fou). See Legge, *Yi King*, pp. 81–85, 223–24.

15. *Analects*, 13/1; 16/10. The *Tso chuan*, Duke Hsuan, 12 (Legge, 318.1 and text 313.3–5) states that the ruler of Ch'u, after subduing Yung, instructed his people daily, saying: "The people's welfare is not easily secured; calamity may come without a day's warning. You must be cautious and apprehensive, never giving way to idleness. . . . The people's welfare depends on diligence; with diligence there is no want."

16. *Analects*, 2/13; 14/29; 14/32; 15/18; 15/20; 4/11; 20/1.

17. *I ching*, commentary to Hsi-tz'u hsia, Legge, pp. 391–94.

18. *SPPY* text, 4/11a–b (Legge, I, 230); 20/9a–b (Legge, II, 446–48); 11/1b (Legge, II, 82–83). The idea of daily examination as a means of identifying deficiencies stems from *Analects*, 1/4. See also *Mencius*, 2A2; 4A4.

19. *MLSCY*, 6/16b–17b.

20. *Analects*, 19/10; *MLSCY*, 1/21b–22b; *Hsueh-chih*, A/9.

21. *Mencius*, 7B16; 6A9.

22. For the interpretations of *jen* by these authors, see Wing-tsit Chan, *A Source Book in Chinese Philosophy*, ch. 30–32 and also ch. 33 on Chu Hsi's summation of these interpretations. All three writers lived in the middle to late Sung dynasty (11th–12th century A.D.).

23. Chan, *ibid.*, p. 496. Ch'eng Hao also served as a district magistrate, among other positions.

24. *MLSCY*, 3/43a–44b.

25. *T'u-min lu*, 4/14a–b; Ho Ch'ang-ling citing Li Wen-chen in his *Hsiao-ching shu*, 1b–2a. See also Ho's comment that love (*ai*) is *jen*, *ibid.*, 4b. In contrast to this, Ch'eng I had insisted that it was wrong to equate love with *jen*. Love, he pointed out, was a feeling, whereas *jen* was nature. How could love be taken exclusively as *jen*? Chu Hsi also held that love was something produced by *jen*. He argued that it was acceptable to talk of *jen* as the principle of love, but not as its expression. Chan, *Source Book*, pp. 559 and 594–95.

26. On Confucian hostility to laws, see *Analects*, 2/3; 12/13; 13/18; and also 5/1; *Mencius*, 1A7; 3A3; 1A5. A selection of classical statements opposing and favoring law is given in Balazs, *Traité juridique*, appendix 9.

7: Centralization and diversification in Chinese political development

1. Chan, *Source Book*, pp. 284–85, 323.

2. *Ibid.*, pp. 463–64 and pp. 470–74 (chs. 11 and 22 from Chou's *T'ung-shu* or Penetrating the Book of Changes). The later thought is that of Ch'eng I, *ibid.*, pp. 550, 571.

3. *Ibid.*, pp. 467, 470 (chs. 4 and 11 from Chou's *T'ung-shu*).

4. These developments are well treated in Wang Gung-wu, *The Structure of Power in North China.*

5. A summarization of Chinese demographic history was made by Earl H. Pritchard in his "Thoughts on the Historical Development of the Population of China," *JAS*, XXIII (Nov. 1963), 3–20. Pritchard offered the following orders of magnitude: Sui, 46–54 million; T'ang, *642*, 42–50 million; *750*, 70–75 million; Sung, *980s*, 60–70 million; *c.1110*, something over 100 million; Chin and Southern Sung, *c.1195*, about 110 million; Yuan, *1390s*, at least 85 million; Ming, *1380s and '90s*, not less than 75 million; *1600*, about 150 million; Ch'ing, *1790s*, over 310 million; *1850*, 430 million. The late Ming and Ch'ing estimates follow those of Ho.

6. G. William Skinner, "Marketing and Social Structure in Rural China, Part II," *JAS*, XXIV (Feb. 1965), 208.

7. Skinner, "Marketing . . . Part I," *JAS*, XXIV (Nov. 1964), 18–20, 32–43.

8. See Ho, *Population*, chs. 8 and 9.

9. Louis J. Gallagher, *China in the Sixteenth Century: The Journals of Matthew Ricci, 1583–1610*, p. 12; Ho, *Population*, pp. 199–200.

10. Liu, Hui-chen Wang, *The Traditional Chinese Clan Rules*, chs. 4 and 5. Hsiao, *Rural China*, ch. 8.

11. The account which follows of pre-Ch'ing local government has been aided by the following secondary studies and sources. The major treatment is Yen Keng-wang's *Chung-kuo ti-fang hsing-cheng chih-tu shih* (History of the local administrative system in China). At the time of my research, the published volumes of this work reached up to the Northern and Southern dynasties. Mr. Yen has also written a brief account covering the whole imperial era, "Chung-kuo ti-fang hsing-cheng chih-tu," which describes the structure of local administration as it existed under each major dynasty.

In Western languages there are the following studies. For the T'ang, Robert des Rotours, "Les Grands Fonctionnaires des Provinces en Chine sous la Dynastie des T'ang," *T'oung Pao*, XXV (1928), 219–332. This extensive article identifies three periods in T'ang local administration: 1) the period of administrative centralization (618–705); 2) the period of the increasing power of provincial officials (705–56); 3) the period of the independence of the provinces (756–907). Much valuable material on developments during the Five Dynasties is contained in Wang Gung-wu's *Structure of Power*, cited above. For the Sung, E. A. Kracke, *Civil Service in Early Sung China, 960–1067*, and Chang Fu-jui, *Les Fonctionnaires des Song*, describe changes in the system and the offices identified with them. For the Yuan, Paul Ratchnevsky, *Essai sur la Codification et la Legislation à l'Epoque des Yuan*, may be consulted.

As for the Ming, Charles O. Hucker, "Governmental Organization of the Ming Dynasty" includes some material on the general structure of local administration. Paul Oscar Elmquist, *Rural Controls in Early Modern China*, describes the systems of local control tried out in the Sung, Yuan, and Ming dynasties. Important among these were the systems initiated by the first Ming emperor (Emperor T'ai-tsu) and by influential regional administrators such as the philosopher Wang Yang-ming and Lü K'un. General source accounts by dynasty or subject are available in successive institutional encyclopedias and summaries and in general histories for the successive dynasties. These also tend to concentrate on system and on imperial legislation. More informal notes on the evolution of local administration were compiled by Ku Yen-wu in his *Jih-chih lu* (Record of Daily Knowledge). The important changes that took place under the Single Whip Reform are set out in Liang Fang-chung, *The Single Whip Method of Taxation in China*, and in other books and articles by this author.

Since this research was undertaken, Hucker has edited a new volume, *Chinese Government in Ming Times* (New York, Columbia University Press, 1969), which contains an article on Ming local administration by Lien-sheng Yang.

8: CENTRALIZATION OF DISTRICT ADMINISTRATION UNDER THE SUNG AND
MING DYNASTIES

1. Ku Yen-wu, *Jih-chih lu*, 9/12–14.

2. The concept of "paring down" is quite often used of the central government policy toward local government. See *TSCC*, ming-lun, kuan-ch'ang, 645 hui-k'ao/8b.

3. *TSCC, ibid.*, 645 hui-k'ao/1b–8a; 656 hui-k'ao/6a–7a.

4. The subdistrict magistrate, an office established by the Liao dynasty, and located at strategic crossings such as certain fords, passes, or crossroads, also appears in the Sung. See *TSCC, ibid.*, 664 hui-k'ao/1a. However, even the smallest T'ang district was entitled to support a magistrate, assistant magistrate, registrar, security officer, recorder, secretary of finance bureau, secretary of law bureau, six jailers, four inquisitors, eight *pai-chih* (guards?), one director of markets, one master of great learning, one assistant educator, and several clerks. The six metropolitan *hsien* supported two assistant magistrates, registrars and recorders (with a substaff of six clerks), and six security officers, all ranking officials. In addition they had twenty-four secretaries for bureaus of merit, granaries, finance, defense, law, and public works with a substaff of forty-eight clerks. They also included fourteen jailers, eight inquisitors, eighteen *pai-chih*, one master of great learning, and one assistant educator. *Chiu T'ang shu*, 3255.3.

The difference between this complement and the staff of the Sung district is corroborated by local records. Thus San-yuan *hsien* in Shensi records itself as having had, during the T'ang period, virtually the full staff of a metropolitan-suburban district. Actually, it records three security officers where the system called only for two. For the Sung it records only a magistrate, assistant magistrate, registrar, and one security officer (admittedly it was then no longer in a metropolitan region). *San-yuan hsien-chih*, 5/5a–8a. This does not mean that the Sung district was necessarily lacking all the other subordinate offices. But at the very least their position was unclear, and the titles of their offices drop out of sight in the records.

5. *TSCC, ibid.*, 645 hui-k'ao/8b–10a, 645 tsung-lun/1b–3a. Kracke, *Civil Service*, pp. 93–95, 105–8.

6. Consider these passages: "When I was formerly among the people my heart always grieved whenever I set eyes on the orphaned or solitary, the hungry or cold, the troubled or the fallen. I have now already managed affairs on behalf of Heaven for over ten years. If there are any among the people who are still wandering, deserted or lost, this goes directly contrary to my original intentions. . . ." *Ming hui-yao*, p. 959.

"The energies of the people are all stricken. They are like birds first flying which cannot pluck up their wings, or trees first planted which cannot spread out their shoots. But while the pure (among administrators) can love others and restrain themselves, the covetous must squeeze others and fatten themselves. . . ." *Ibid.*, p. 858.

"In the newly submitted regions the people are exhausted and wasting away. If there is not the means to bring peace and nourishment to them, they will again go astray and lose hope. . . ." *Ibid.*, p. 730.

7. *HWHTK*, 3375.1; Paul Ratchnevsky, *Essai sur la Codification et la Legislation à l'Epoque des Yuan*, p. xxvii.

8. *Yü-chih ta-kao*, para. 1. See also *Ming hui-yao*, p. 858, edicts of 1368 and 1380.

9. *Ming hui-yao*, p. 730, edict of 1368, also edict of 1368 cited in previous note; also p. 864, editorial note. On these signs, see Shimizu Taiji, " Min no Taiso no takei 'hakuhi jisso' ni tsuite," *Shicho* (Tokyo) No. 68 (1959), pp. 19–28, noticed in *Revue Bibliographique de Sinologie*, V (1959), 116 where it is said that the term *pao-p'i shih-ts'ao* is thought to have referred to a kind of skin-stripping punishment introduced by Ming T'ai-tsu. However it is suggested that it was never officially used and was at most an extra legal expression of revenge against particularly venal officials by people who had suffered under them. Later the phrase entered the language as a warning against corruption.

10. Liang Fang-chung, "Local Tax Collectors in the Ming Dynasty," p. 252.

11. Liang, "Local Tax Collectors," p. 265; and *Ming-tai liang-chang chih-tu*, p. 63.

12. Liang, *The Single Whip Method of Taxation in China*, p. 7. Ho, *Population*, p. 26.

13. This explanation has bearing on the relationship of the "administrative" village to the "natural" village. Some authorities hold that the "administrative" villages, such as the *li-chia* or the *pao-chia* (principally a defense system) of the late Ming and Ch'ing, were heteronomous institutions designed to control the rural countryside. Their decimal structure ran counter to the natural configuration of the villages and thus impeded natural villages from developing as local centers of power.

In general the validity of this theory varies according to the institution and according to which emperor or regional official is concerned. However, there are several reasons why it bears qualification:

1) The most obvious function of the decimal structure is to arrange for rotational service, and to arrange it on a basis that was neither too frequent nor infrequent to be inequitable.

2) The institutional paradigms, primarily those of the *Chou li*, were based on decimal systems, the form which most readily suggested itself for Chinese rural administration.

3) It is doubtful whether the villages of rural China could exert sufficient strength on their own to constitute a threat to central power. They are small, scattered and hemmed in by poor communications. What natural strength there was in the rural countryside came from clans and secret societies, rather than from the villages (on this, see Skinner, "Marketing . . . Part I," p. 37, or Hsiao, *Rural China*, chs. 8–10). If a clan dominated a village or series of villages then it could, and in many cases did, constitute a strongly rooted rural power base, against which the artificial "administrative" villages would be at a considerable disadvantage, if indeed they were in opposition. However, the record suggests much more strongly that the villages were too weak rather than too strong, and that except in outlying areas the local bureaucracy could manipulate this weakness if it wished to. On the other hand it could not control outlying areas sufficiently closely to give the "administrative" systems much chance of success against the societal.

4) The "natural" villages differed greatly in size, ranging from the scattered farms of Szechuan to villages varying from under 10 to over 100 or 200 households. It would be impossible to provide any meaningful and viable organization of the smaller villages except on an artificial, inter-village basis.

5) The "administrative" villages, as long as they were functioning effectively, actually tended to strengthen the power of local village leaders, by providing an additional formal framework for the exercise of leadership. It was when their purposes and composition were distorted that the administrative villages became a burden, weakening the leaders and villagers alike. But this condition was hardly part of the original plan of the central authority. In sum, it is doubtful if the administrative villages can be viewed simply as a deliberate design by central authority to check the development of autonomous power.

By the same token, attempts to categorize *li-chia* as oriented toward the natural village because of its exploitative function, and the *pao-chia* towards the administrative because of its control function, require qualification in the face of the evidence. For one thing, their functions are not that easily contrasted. For another, we find the K'ang-hsi emperor informing local officials that it was more important to fit the *pao-chia* structure to the existing (i.e., natural) village configuration rather than force the organization of the latter into a rigid decimal structure. Ch'ing officials noted for *pao-chia* organization followed this flexible approach. Evidently the tasks of mutual surveillance and assistance against attack could more easily be carried out within the natural framework.

Conversely, Emperor Ming T'ai-tsu was anxious to maintain the decimal organization of the *li-chia*. This is because tax collection imposed more stringent, inevitable, and costly duties on collectors than did mutual surveillance. Rotation was, therefore, essential to keep the system equitable. Each *li* (neighborhood) included a reserve of "odds and ends" households (those which for various reasons were relieved of *li-chia* collection duties at the time of the formation of the *li-chia*), and these were to be used to replace defunct households. However, under the *li-chia* administrative superstructure were *tu* and *t'u* large and small land registration areas (or maps). A *li* was permitted to cross a *t'u* boundary if, and only if, it ran out of "odds and ends" households. But no *li-chia* was to cross the larger *tu* boundaries. The statutes explained that if a *tu* contained six-hundred households, five *li* were formed and the residual fifty households divided amongst the *li* heads to share in the service duties.

In sum, the *li-chia* and *pao-chia* were both administrative systems which were intended to establish relationships with the natural configurations: the *li-chia* by staying within landholding perimeters and sticking to small units (10 and 110), the *pao-chia* by keeping the size of its units (ideally 10, 100, 1000) relatively flexible.

On the organization of the *pao-chia* see *T'ung-k'ao*, 22/5051.3; *HCCSWP*, 74/24–8 (*pao-chia* regulations of Yü Ch'eng-lung); Liu Heng, *Yung-li yung-yen*, p. 88 ff. (cited by Hsiao, *Rural China*, p. 29). On the *li-chia*, see *TMHT*, 20/1a–3a. On the size of the natural villages, see Hsiao, *ibid.*, pp. 10–24; Skinner, "Marketing . . . Part I," *JAS* XXIV, 6–7. On the *tu* and *t'u*, see Hsiao, *Rural China*, Appendix I (the discussion is limited largely to 19th century conditions).

It may be noted that the present study prefers the term "neighborhood" to "village" for the *li-chia*, in order to bring out its administrative character.

14. In the same way, the emperor argued that the establishment of tax collectors saved the officials the trouble of attending to collection of taxes. Liang, "Tax Collectors," p. 251, citing the Great Ordinance (*Yü-chih ta-kao*).

15. *Chiao-min pang-wen*, translated in Elmquist, *Rural Controls*, pp. 277–301. Having been unable to see a copy of the original text I am indebted to Dr. Elmquist for permission to consult his dissertation.

16. *Chiao-min pang-wen*, para. 2.

17. The agents for inculcating the six maxims were the neighborhood elders. Twice a month they were supposed to proceed along the village pathways, to the accompaniment of a wooden-clappered bell, reciting them. See *ibid.*, para, 19; *T'ien-t'ai hsien-chih*, 3/5b–6a.

18. *TMHT*, 4/5a–7b; *Ming-shih*, 803.5 and 8. For the Yuan complement, cf. *TSCC*, ming-lun, kuan-ch'ang, 645 hui-k'ao/11a–b and 656 hui-k'ao/7a, or *HWHTK*, 3360.1–2, 3375.1. The Ming complement of educational officials was one director and three assistant directors per department (two or one in smaller departments). The *Hui-tien* notes that in many departments this staff was not fully established. Districts were

allowed one director and two assistant directors, (later reduced to one or none in smaller districts). See *TMHT*, as above. This staff was to run the schools for licentiates which the emperor ordered established in all local jurisdictions. See Ho, *Ladder of Success*, p. 171. These changes in the composition of district offices give further evidence of the emperor's desire to alter the emphasis of district administration, restraining its managerial and extending its educational function.

19. *Ming hui-yao*, pp. 734, 859; Chao I, *Nien-erh shih cha-chi*, 33/477.

20. *TMHT*, 9/3b–5a, 12/46a–47b. The term for "well-intentioned" (*liang*) has the more literal meaning of "conscientious," "attuned to what is right." It was used particularly by Wang Yang-ming, who took it from Mencius. On Wang see below, chapter 10, section on revival of the *pao-chia* and *hsiang-yueh*.

21. *Ming-shih*, 803.

22. *TSCC*, Ming-lun, kuan-ch'ang, 656 hui-k'ao/7b.

23. *Ming hui-yao*, p. 731. Another remarkable case was the promotion of a chief officer (recorder) to a position in the censorate, "for his grasp of current conditions."

24. *Ibid.*, pp. 853–54.

9: BREAKDOWN OF THE LI-CHIA SYSTEM

1. *Ming shih*, 803.9–804.0.

2. Ho, *Population*, ch. 2 and 6 are particularly valuable for an understanding of these conditions. The following figures for Shanghai district give an example of how the quota system tended to settle down and rigidify.

	SUMMER LEVY			AUTUMN GRAIN TAX		
DATE	LAND (*ch'ing*)	GRAIN (*shih*)	SILK (*liang*)	PAPER CURRENCY (*kuan*)	GRAIN (*shih*)	BEANS (*shih*)
1391	22,062	71,467	4,735	5,089	496,521	76,344
1403–24	21,109	67,226	4,973	6,528	437,453	58,877
subsequent	21,300–500			6,200–300		59,000
1426–35		57,731	4,991		335,372	
subsequent		57,800–900			330,000	
1436–49			5,045			
subsequent			5,000			
1465–87 & subsequent				5,938		

SOURCE. *Shanghai hsien-chih* (Chia-ching ed.) 2/5a–b.

3. For examples of some of the forms this corruption took, see Liang, *Single Whip Method*, especially pp. 12–13, or Ho, *Population*, pp. 11–17.

4. See Skinner, "Marketing . . . Part I," pp. 33–36, for the detailed information which every household possessed about the situation of other households within the marketing area. This seems to have been especially true of landlords. See also p. 20, note 52.

5. See chapter 8, note 13; see also Ho, *Population*, pp. 9–10.

6. Skinner cites two cases in which markets were deliberately established to combat the group dominating the existing market. In one case it was the manner of the tax allocations which was at issue. "Marketing . . . Part II," p. 202.

7. Many of these problems are graphically described by the late sixteenth-century official Shen Pang. Shen was magistrate of the metropolitan district of Wan-p'ing. On looking into the district records, he found that the area of registered land in the district had dropped, between 1566 and 1592 alone, from 3,427 *ch'ing* to 2,865 *ch'ing* (1 *ch'ing* = 100 standard *mou*). Where were the missing 600 *ch'ing*? Influential officials had, under various pretexts, obtained tax exemption for them, without the magistrate being able to do anything about it. This, hinted Shen, was tantamount to refeudalization. Already the ten biggest families had more land than the largest acreage registered for any single land registration area (given as 150 *ch'ing*), and still land was being "bestowed" without cease. By contrast, one particular urban ward with barely half a *ch'ing* was still allotted a *li-chia* collecting unit. This may refer to the practice found elsewhere in the sixteenth century of allotting *li* on the basis of land area rather than number of households (see Ho, *Population*, p. 28). Dismissing compromise solutions, Shen advocated bringing all tax-free land gradually back into fiscal service.

Turning to the *ting* (labor-service) records, Shen found for c.1573 a figure of 38,000 adult males (*ch'eng-ting*) out of a "total" population of 81,700. This did not of course represent the number of assessed *ting* (labor-service units) and within ten years the magistrate fixed that at 13,700 *ting* which, after allowing for exemptions, left 12,800 *ting*. During the next six or seven years, a valiant effort by two subsequent magistrates raised the total number of *ting* to 13,960 and of assessed *ting* to 13,400. This produced a revenue of 5,330 taels, a large portion of which went to administrative wage laborers not in the district's employ. (The land tax at this time amounted to 7,210 taels, but about 1,200 taels of this was delivered to its destination without passing through the control of the district office, leaving 6,000 from this source. Half of that sum had to be handed over to other offices in the metropolis.)

Discussing the difference between the 38,000 registered adult males and the under 14,000 labor-service units, Shen pointed out that the latter figure did not represent a reduction in the *ting* quota—which would have benefited the people—but a withdrawal from it—which harmed them. To add further exemptions to this huge withdrawal was adding insult to injury and harming both the people and their local administration. Moreover, the original figure of 38,000 adult males did not even represent the full adult male population. Meanwhile, of the so-called 14,000 remaining for assessment, many had fled or died, so that the actual number of male adults taxable for labor-service units was still less. They had fled, Shen calculated, because of lacking enough land to support the labor-service payments. But how was the magistrate to get labor-service payments out of land not having any *ting* (assessed males)? The only solution was to impose it on other *li-chia*.

He concluded: "I fear that the more the land quota decreases, the more heavy the labor-service assessment, and the more the fleeing and the extinction; and the population will gradually waste away." *Wan-shu tsa-chi*, pp. 44–50. Admittedly the problems of a metropolitan district were probably exceptional, but it was no doubt partly for that reason that Shen brought them out into the open. Many discussions in local gazetteers of these sensitive issues are by contrast oblique and cursory.

8. On this see Hla Myint, *The Economics of the Developing Countries*, pp. 29–37, 86–90.

9. The salary scales were as follows (B ranks omitted for the sake of brevity):

	1380		1392
RANK	BUSHELS (*shih*)	PAPER CURRENCY (*kuan*)	BUSHELS PER MONTH
1A	1,000	300	87
2A	800	300	61
3A	600	300	35
4A	400	300	24
5A	220	110	16
6A	120	90	10
7A	100	60	7.5
8A	75	45	6.5
9A	65	30	5.5
directors of schools	2 (per month)		
chief officer	3 (per month)		
misc. officials	2 or 3 (per month)		

At this time one *kuan* had a cash value of 1,000 *ch'ien* and a grain equivalent of one *shih*. Thus a magistrate (7A) received in the late fourteenth century 100 to 90 bushels of hulled grain plus currency worth a further 60 bushels.

How far would this salary go? To answer this question we must know the approximate weight of the bushel (here a unit of capacity) and average annual levels of consumption. During the Ming period, the official *shih* (bushel) equalled 10 *tou* (pecks). Grain was measured in *hu*, a unit of capacity measuring 5 *tou* (pecks). Its average weight during the Ming was 100 *chin* (catties, a unit of weight), which in both Ming and Ch'ing times weighed the same and equaled 1 *tan* (piculs). The *tan* at this time corresponded to 59.7 kilograms. Thus during the Ming, 1 *shih* (bushel) was the equivalent, if correctly measured, of 2 *tan* (piculs). At this point it should be stressed that these measurements are all according to officially designated standards. Local measurements varied widely. For the above information on measurements, see Wu Ch'eng-lo, *Chung-kuo tu-liang heng shih*, pp. 57, 68, 123, 175.

Ch'ing sources estimate average annual per capita consumption at 3 or 4 *shih* (bushels), or 358 to 478 kilograms. See Pao Shih-ch'en, *Keng-ch'en tsa-chu erh*, p. 311. (The figure of four is from Hung Liang-chi and was kindly supplied by Dr. Thomas Metzger.) This *shih* is actually 1 percent smaller than the Ming *shih*. Wu, *ibid.*, p. 57 and Table 6, facing p. 59.

Modern estimates appear to corroborate and fill out these figures. More detailed estimates were collected from two widely differing areas by Fei Hsiao-t'ung. In his study of rural economy in Yunnan, he put the average annual consumption of the adult male laborer at 7 piculs. He took this as the standard market picul (equivalent to 50 kilograms), on the grounds of its being the measure "chiefly in use at the present time." This gives a consumption of 350 kilograms. (The local Kunming catty weighed 740 grams. This would give a consumption of 518 kilograms.) Allowing for consumption adjustments on the basis of sex and age, he arrived at household consumptions of 28 piculs in one landowning household of six members and 40 in another of seven. (The conversion factors were: under six years, 2.5 piculs; six to ten, 3.5 piculs; eleven to fifteen, male 4.9, female 4.2; sixteen to twenty, 6.6 or 5.6; twenty-one to sixty, 7 or 5.6; over sixty, 5.6 or 4.9). See Fei, *Earthbound China*, pp. 51 and 85–86.

In his village study in the lower Yangtze, informants gave Fei different estimates of annual consumption, as follows: old man over fifty, 9 "bushels"; old woman over forty, 7.5; adult male, 12; adult female, 9; child above ten, 4.5. An "average household" consisting of an old woman, two adults, and a child consumed around 32 bushels annually. Fei does not say that by this "bushel" he meant a picul (*tan*), but from the differences in weight between the Kunming (Yunnan) catty and the weights of catties in the Shanghai–Hangchow region it is clear that he is speaking of piculs and that, if local piculs are meant, the weight of grain consumed was approximately the same as that in Yunnan or possibly less (depending on which of the many catties operated in the village which he studied). See Fei, *Peasant Life*, pp. 125–26. For regional differences in the gram equivalent of catties see Wu Ch'eng-lo, pp. 247–49.

From these various examples it can be inferred that Ming annual per capita consumption would not be above 3 or 4 *shih* (bushels), more especially in households not engaged in manual labor, unlike those on which Fei's estimates were presumably based. Early Ming households averaged around 4.1 to 4.6 persons. See Ho, *Population*, p. 7. Without estimating their age distribution or the effect of different occupations on consumption, one can still see that the magistrate received up to ten times more than was necessary to maintain his own immediate family in food. His household was probably larger than average in size. But if he also owned land, which would be almost certain, then his household expenditure on food could well be below 10 percent of his legitimate income. Given his limited duties at this time, his income would appear, on a prima facie basis, to have been not unreasonable.

Changes in salary conversion proceeded as follows:

REIGN	BUSHELS	CASH	PAPER CURRENCY UNITS	BOLTS OF COTTON	BOLTS OF SILK
Hung-wu 1368–98	1	1,000	1		
Yung-lo 1403–24	1		10		
Hsuan-te 1426–35	1		15		
1433			200		1
1436	1		15/20–25		

Salaries were now paid 30 percent in grain and 70 percent in paper currency for 6th rank and below, and 20 and 80 percent for 5th rank and up.

REIGN	BUSHELS	CASH	PAPER CURRENCY UNITS	BOLTS OF COTTON	BOLTS OF SILK
Cheng-t'ung 1436-49	1		25		
1471			200	1	
		2 or 3	1		
	1	(20 or 30)	10		
		200–300		1	
	20	(10–15)		1	
	30	(6–10)		1	

Salaries were now paid in two kinds: 1) original kind, consisting of monthly rice (one *shih* irrespective of rank), rice converted to silk, and rice converted to silver; 2) commuted kind, consisting of paper currency and rolls of silk and cotton cloth converted to paper currency. Some conversion values were as follows:

KIND	BUSHELS	SILVER (OUNCES)	PAPER CURRENCY (UNITS)	BOLTS OF COTTON	BOLTS OF SILK
original		0.6			1
	1	0.65			
converted	1		20		
	20				1
	10			1	

The lower the rank the greater the percentage paid in original kind. Thus rank 1 received 30 percent in original kind; rank 9B received 70 percent in this form. Sources comment that the above conversion rates were something of an improvement on those of 1471. It is not clear at exactly what date they apply.

For further but incomplete information see *HWHTK*, 3376.3–3377.1, which draws in part on the researches of Ku Yen-wu. A short article by Chao I on Ming salaries coincides with the *HWHTK* account almost verbatim. Its title "Ming Official Salaries were very stingy" emphasizes their condition by the middle of the fifteenth century. *Nien-erh shih cha-chi*, 32/473–4.

10. *TMHT*, chs. 24 and 25. Examples of changes in original levies are as follows:

	SUMMER LEVY			AUTUMN GRAIN TAXES		
DATE	RICE AND WHEAT (*shih*)	MONEY (INGOTS)	SILK (BOLTS)	RICE AND WHEAT (*shih*)	MONEY (INGOTS)	SILK (BOLTS)
1393	4.71[a]	39,800	288,487	24.73[a]	5,730	59
1502	4.63	56,800	194,000[b]	22.17	21,929	59
1578	4.60	57,920	206,200	22.03	23,660	59

[a] million bushels.
[b] This is a combined total. The *HWHTK* gives it as 202,050 bolts. The other *HWHTK* figures agree with the above. The addition of other cloth (mainly cotton and hemp) brought the total number of bolts up to 327,000 in 1502 and 339,470 in 1578. *HWHTK*, 2787.1; 2791.2; 2793.3.

Other large items in the taxes of the sixteenth century included 2.7 million ounces of silk in the summer levies of 1502 and 1578 (the data from Shanghai suggest that this item was already being levied in part at least by the end of the fourteenth century, see above, note 2); 26 million bundles of animal fodder in the autumn levy of 1502 (converted to 353,000 taels of silver in 1578); and 247,000 catties of spun cotton (244,000 in 1578).

As an example of additional labor-service levies, the Shanghai Gazetteer notes under 1520 the inclusion of further exactions outside the customary *ting* labor-service levies (now converted to silver payments) for the customary services. Among them were allocations for 300 sub-district guards, 400 commoner guards, salt office attendants, and many other personnel. All, it repeats, were "new levies." *Shang-hai hsien-chih*, 4/2a–b.

11. Ku Yen-wu, *Jih-chih lu*, 5/16–17. The essay from which this comes is cited by Lien-sheng Yang, in his *Les Aspects Economiques des Travaux Publics dans la Chine*

Imperiale, p. 11. The Censor Li Kuan noted in 1523 that the summer grain tax had decreased by over 90,000 bushels (*shih*) and the autumn grain tax by over 2.5 million bushels since the beginning of the dynasty. Yet the Court, civil, and military establishments had all expanded, and the increase in salary expenses were all drawn from this decreased income. He requested a return to the original quotas and expenditures—a hopeless request, it must be added. *Ming shih*, 825.0.

As to the trouble caused to local administration by the centralization of delivery see above, note 7. In one essay, Shen Pang refers to the problem of delivering 1,000 taels to two hundred and sixty-seven different receiving points. *Wan-shu tsa-chi*, pp. 48–50. There are actually two aspects to centralization of delivery: 1) delivery by rural tax collectors direct to the receiving points (the form of tax delivery emphasized by Emperor T'ai-tsu); 2) delivery by the district office direct to receiving points (not to the immediate higher authorities, i.e., prefect and provincial treasurer).

The lack of centralization in the delivery of tax funds may have especially affected the metropolitan districts and prefectures. In 1644 Yang Yin-tung, prefectural governor of Shun-t'ien (in which Wan-p'ing was located), noted that the forwarding of taxation was "very complex and confusing" and caused a great deal of trouble. In one district, a tax of 30 taels had to be forwarded in the form of 40 different items; one item amounting to 1.76 taels cost 20 or 30 taels to forward. He requested the government to group together all such items and have the districts remit each season directly to the prefecture, which would in turn arrange and forward them to the Board of Revenue. This would avoid incurring liabilities in subordinate offices. The proposal was discussed and carried out. *T'ung k'ao*, 5229.1; see also 5229.3 and 5230.1.

12. See *TSCC*, ming-lun, kuan-ch'ang, 641 hui-k'ao/8b. A passage in the T'ung-kuan gazetteer also infers this, citing a note from the eighteenth-century edition which remarked: "As for the offices of assistant magistrate and security officer, in T'ang and Sung times many *chin-shih* (metropolitan graduates) first served in these offices. . . . Their duties definitely were not light." Nothing, however, is said for the assistant offices in the Ming period, two of which ended in the early fifteenth century (see Table 20). The editor did, on the other hand, feel that the Ming introduction or increase of educational officials strengthened civil administration. *T'ung-kuan hsien-chih*, ch. 15. See also Ch'ü, *Local Government*, p. 258, note 8, citing the early Ch'ing official Li Kung on this point.

13. Ho, *Ladder of Success*, pp. 216–17; *Ming hui-yao*, p. 233. The date of abolition was 1442. See also Hucker, *Censorial System*, p. 35.

14. See Shen Pang, *Wan-shu tsa-chi*, pp. 24–26.

15. *Ming hui-yao*, p. 732; see also Ho, *Ladder of Success*, pp. 32–33.

16. *Ming hui-yao*, p. 733.

17. *Ibid.*, pp. 734–35.

18. *Ibid.*, pp. 954–55; Liang Fang-chung, "Tax Collectors," pp. 257–64, 267–68.

19. Liang, *Single Whip*, p. 17. See also Ho, *Population*, p. 11, and Shen Pang's comments in note 7 above. On the subject of the abandonment of property, the editors of the Wu-kung gazetteer (a district in Shensi) described the plight of the families assigned to staff the stations serving the shipment of horses and other animals (into China). The tour of duty was five years, and the families concerned all hired substitutes for the job. During this time they obtained no remission for their other land-tax and labor-service obligations. Consequently many of the households required to staff the stations ended by moving far away. Then the big families either seized their property outright, or (to get title to it) they made loud remarks about the anxieties of those who

moved far away. Then those households thinking of abandoning their land became frightened and instead thought themselves lucky to exchange it for some out-of-the-way and derelict property. *Wu-kung hsien-chih*, 2/1b.

20. *Ming hui-yao*, pp. 952, 733; Liang, "Tax Collectors," p. 257. See also Ku Yen-wu, *Jih-chih lu*, 3/72 (on *Hsiang-t'ing chih chih*). Conversely Emperor Hsuan-tsung (1426–35) complained of abuses in local judicial administration and said that in recent years multitudes of farmers had entered the capital daily to complain of injustice. Cited in Hucker, *Censorial System*, p. 259.

21. Lü K'un, *Shih-cheng lu*, 5/7a–b.

22. *Ming shih*, 803.7; *TSCC*, ming-lun, kuan-ch'ang, 645 hui-k'ao/11a–b.

23. *Hai Jui chi*, pp. 145–46.

10: Reforms in local administration during the late Ming and early Ch'ing dynasties

1. For a more extended analysis of the evolution of yamen organization see my article on "The Yamen as a Socio-Political System" in a forthcoming study on urbanization in traditional China, edited by G. William Skinner. This postdates the present discussion, except as regards the evolution of *li* functionary offices.

2. Li Kung (1659–1733). *Yueh-shih hsi-shih*, 3/3. The whole subject of the development of Ming administrative and penal law, although beyond the scope of this study, is highly relevant to an assessment of the problems inherited by Ch'ing local administrators.

3. *Ming hui-yao*, pp. 855–58.

4. *TCHTSL*, chs. 30–31.

5. Ch'üan Tseng-yu, "Ch'ing-tai mu-liao chih-tu lun," *Ssu-hsiang yü Shih-tai*, 31 (Feb. 1944), 31–32, citing Ku Yen-wu. I have not been able to locate the original.

6. See *TSCC*, ching-chi hui-pien, hsuan-chü tien, ch. 125, li-yuan pu hui-k'ao 5, under years Hung-wu 4, 16, 24, 26. The other two paths were by recommendation and by the examination system. See also Ch'üan Tseng-yu, pp. 31–32.

7. Ch'üan Tseng-yu, pp. 31–32, and *TMHT*, 8/1a.

8. Ch'üan Tseng-yu, pp. 31–32. Summarized in *Ming Hui-yao*, 892 and *TSCC*, Ching-chi hui-pien, hsuan-chü tien, 4a. See also Hucker, *Censorial System*, p. 58.

9. *TSCC*, *ibid.*, 3b.

10. See regulations of 1426 and subsequent years in *TSCC*, *ibid.* I regret that it has not been possible to examine this data in further detail.

11. *TSCC*, *ibid.*, 5a (for the year 1436). In line with this regulation, Shen Pang showed a distribution of thirty-eight *li* functionaries for Wan-p'ing (metropolitan) district. No office (*fang*) or section (*k'o*) listed more than one *ssu-li* or two *tien-li*. Three had only one of either. *Wan-shu tsa-chi*, 27 ff.

12. *TSCC*, *ibid.*, 3b (1398), 4b (1428).

13. For hiring of commoners, see *T'ung-k'ao* 21/5044.3–5045.1. For numbers of clerks, see Ch'ü, *Local Government*, p. 39, citing Hou Fang-yü (1618–1655). For Ku see *Jih-chih lu*, 3/78 and *Ku Yen-wu wen*, 11–12.

14. *T'ung-k'ao*, 21/5045.1–2. The editors pointed out that *li* were formerly appointed through the *pi-chao* procedure. This was one of two methods of appointment to office used under the eastern Han dynasty, and held in esteem because applied to men of "distinguished talent and reputation." See Morohashi, 38642.67, citing the *Wen-hsien t'ung-k'ao*.

15. *TCHT:Khsi*, 15/17a; *YC*, 21/16a.

16. *TCHT:Khsi*, 15/19a–21a; *YC*, 21/19a–23b; *T'ung-k'ao*, 21/5044.3; Ch'ü, *Local Government*, p. 43.

17. *TCHT:Khsi*, 36/27b, 28b–29a; *YC*, 54/23b ff. Shen Pang noted that Wan-p'ing had, in addition to its thirty-eight *li* functionaries, eighteen *shu-pan* likewise distributed in ones or twos among the various offices. He identified *shu-pan* as people owing labor service to the public domain. *Wan-shu tsa-chi*, 27 ff.

18. *TCHT:Khsi*, 36/27b, 28b–29a; Ch'ü, *Local Government*, pp. 45, 64–65.

19. *Hsin-tsuan LPCFTL*, 16/1a ff.; *TCHT:Khsi*, 12/13a.

20. Ch'üan Tseng-yu, p. 31.

21. *Shan-yin HC*, 1935, 14/20b, 21a, 39a, 15/5b, 10b.

22. One term used about secretaries during the Ming was *chi-shih*. See Feng Meng-lung (1574–1646), *Ku-chin t'an-kai*, 1/14a. This was the title of an office first established during the later Han dynasty for preparing the correspondence of princes, senior officials, and military leaders. See Liang Chang-chü, *Ch'eng wei-lu*, 25/11a.

Some of the Ch'ing terms for particular categories of private secretaries also have a distant origin. For example the term *cheng-pi* (used of secretary in charge of tax enforcement) comes from the *Chou li*, where it refers to the levying and auditing of taxes undertaken by the *hsien-cheng* (a low-ranking official having little in common with the *hsien-ling* or *chih-hsien* of later times than the name of the jurisdiction under his authority. See *Chou li*, ti-kuan, hsien-cheng, cited by Morohashi 10239.77). The term *shu-chi* (used of secretary of correspondence) is linked with *chi-shih* (see above). As *chang shu-chi* (in charge of correspondence), it refers to an office established during the T'ang dynasty under the *chieh-tu shih* or provincial military governors. In the Sung period, the office is said to have been a *fu* prefectural assistantship, ranking below *t'ung-p'an* (second-class assistant prefect). See Liang Chang-chü, *Ch'eng wei lu*, 22/8a. Morohashi (14294.87.2) also cites the *Shu-wu chi-yuan* on this term.

Ch'ing use of the term *mu* derives effectively from the Sung usage, when it appears in a variety of offices concerned with providing assistance, primarily of a secretarial nature, to chief officials, both in metropolitan and in provincial administration. See Chang Fu-jui, *Les Fonctionnaires des Song*, nos. 1279, 1280, 2021, 2065, 2812, 2949. However, apparently as a result of the early Sung policy of staffing local administration with central officials the term *mu-chih* or *mu-shu* came to refer generically to the assistant offices of a provincial department (*chou*) and is so used in the *TSCC*, e.g., ming-lun, kuan-ch'ang, ch. 641.

23. *TCHTSL:CC*, 76/13a–14b, for years 1740–41 and 1757.

24. See Ku Yen-wu, "*Chih-hsien*" (district magistrates), *Jih-chih lu*, 9/12–14. Ku argues here that in the Sung and Yuan periods metropolitan government was emphasized over provincial, so that worthy men came to despise the latter. The Ming gave primacy to the higher examination degrees over other channels of appointment, so that in official administration people regarded graduation (*ch'u-shen*) as the important thing.

25. See Ch'ü, *Local Government*, ch. 5, and Watt, "The Yamen as a Socio-Political System" (see note 1 above). The term for personal servants, *ch'ang-sui*, is said to have derived from the attendants of palace eunuchs during the Ming period. See Chao I, *Nien-erh shih cha-chi*, p. 537.

26. Ch'ü, *Local Government*, p. 67.

27. It is characteristic of Wang that, when his tutor told him that the finest manly accomplishment was to succeed in the examinations, he should have rejected this view in favor of the road to sagehood. Carson Chang, *Wang Yang-ming*, p. 2.

28. The meaning given by Wang to the term "innate knowledge" or "intuitive

knowledge" (*liang chih*) was been a matter of interpretation, and it was on this that his followers subsequently split and went astray. "Conscience" seems to be a close alternative. See Chang, pp. 24–28, 45–49, 64–67.

29. It is hard to accept Chan's comment that Wang's theory is "entirely subjective and confuses reality with value." *Source Book*, p. 655. Wang undoubtedly viewed reality as free of value distinctions while it was in a state of tranquillity. Thus he could write: "The spirit of life of Heaven and earth is the same in flowers and in weeds. Where have they the distinction of good and evil?" But he argued that activity automatically incorporated value, through the response of the mind to things and events. He says this explicitly when he stated: "(When) there is neither good nor bad: this is the substance of the mind. When there is both good and bad: this is the activity of the will." Chan inverts this order, translating it into "In the original substance of the mind there is no distinction between good and evil (or good and bad). When the will becomes active such a distinction exists." But Wang is not talking about the distinction between good and evil. He is stressing the difference between their existence and their nonexistence. (The insertion of "when" is indicated by Wang's view that tranquillity and activity are "matters of time." *Source Book*, p. 679.) In fact Wang elsewhere plays down the concept of good and evil as distinct entities. There is the "highest good" (*chih-shan*) which is "the original substance of the mind." When there is deviation from this original substance there is evil (or bad). Thus good and evil are one thing. *Ibid.*, p. 684.

Because Chan thinks that Wang confused reality with value, he has been led into a further obscuring of the distinction in Wang's mind between *shan* (good) and *liang* (innate, natural, instinctive). Where Wang writes "as for human nature (*hsing*) there is none that is not innate (*liang*)," Chan translates the second clause ". . . therefore there is no innate knowledge that is not good." This is as if Wang was implying that innate knowledge incorporated a value content. But Wang's theory actually requires, as he points out, that innate knowledge be without a value content, because it is absolutely quiet and inactive (or alternatively neither active nor inactive). *Ibid.*, pp. 683–84. It is activated knowledge which contains value.

But innate knowledge does have an awareness of value: "knowledge of good and bad: this is innate knowledge. Doing good, getting rid of bad, this is 'investigation of things' (*ko-wu*)." On this Chan writes, "it is difficult to accept his version of *ko-wu*, for if the term means to rectify the mind, why should it be *ko-wu* (to *ko* things) instead of *ko-hsin* (to *ko* the mind)?" Chan (who appears here to lean toward the standard Chu Hsi interpretation of *ko-wu*) explains this by saying that Wang's theory is based on the "shaky" grounds that "the mind and things are one." If this were so, then *ko-wu*, for Wang, would have to mean either to rectify the mind, or to investigate things, and that the individual engaged in *ko-wu* could adopt either approach since both were the same. But Wang does not adopt this viewpoint. He holds that both approaches are necessary, and that without coordinating them neither will succeed. *Ibid.*, pp. 681–83. This is what underlies his emphasis on the unity of knowledge and action. It must be added that on other points Chan himself hastens to Wang Yang-ming's defense.

30. As a provincial official, Wang is noted for his service as magistrate of Lu-ling district (in Kiangsi) in 1510 and as governor of Kiangsi from 1517–19. Shortly before his death he succeeded in ending bandit insurrections in Kwangsi. The biography of him in the Lu-ling gazetteer is disappointingly brief.

31. *Hsuntzu*, ch'üan-hsueh; see Dubs p. 33. This saying also appears in the *Ta-Tai li-chi* and in the *Shih-chi*.

32. See *Yang-ming ch'üan-shu*, pieh-lu, kung-i, pp. 352, 397, 399.

33. *Ibid.*, pp. 305–8, 410–11. The *pao-chia* regulations, from which the above is taken, have been partially translated by Elmquist in his *Rural Controls*.

34. *Yang-ming ch'üan-shu*, pieh-lu, kung-i, pp. 396–99. Most of the text for the above regulations has also been translated by Elmquist.

35. The subjectivization of standards practiced by his more extreme followers was the principle cause for the disrepute into which Wang's teachings fell in the seventeenth century.

36. Lü uses the term *shou-ling*, used generically of local administrators. The two words refer to the earliest local administrators under the imperial prefectural system. The *t'ai-shou* administered the *chün* or commanderies, the *hsien-ling* the (larger) districts, which were administratively under the *chün*. In Ch'ing writing, *shou-ling* refers to prefects and magistrates, just as *mu-ling* refers to departmental and district heads.

37. Lü K'un, *Shih-cheng lu*, 5/1–13b. Also translated by Elmquist.

38. See especially Liang Fang-chung, *Single Whip*.

39. The troubles engendered by the fee system are discussed at length in Ch'ü, *Local Government* and Hsiao, *Rural China*.

40. This discussion is concerned with the general picture, that is, the situation facing most magistrates in most districts. For the majority the land and labor tax, once amalgamated, constituted the most important part of the fiscal revenue. In the southeast, grain tribute continued to provide an important form of taxation. In certain areas the salt tax was also an important and irksome source of revenue. For other miscellaneous taxes collected by magistrates see Ch'ü, *Local Government*, ch. 8.

41. Ch'ü, *Local Government*, p. 38.

42. Ho, *Population*, pp. 116–18.

43. The way in which the Single Whip reform contributed to the growth of landlordism is well brought out in a passage from a gazetteer of 1593 cited by Ho. The reforms encouraged the poor to stay on the land, since they could now relieve themselves of any direct exposure to the tax burden by converting to tenancy. The fact that the poor would now stay on the land encouraged investment in land by the wealthier. As Ho points out, the ratio of population to land was not intensive enough at this time to make landlordism a serious problem. The problem would become serious with the increase in population. Ho, *Population*, pp. 224–25.

Meanwhile, landlords provided the poor with a buffer between both the state and the natural elements. They advanced working capital and financed construction costs. They could be more flexible about collecting rent than the magistrate could about collecting taxes: first, they were under none of the same legal deadlines and penalties pressing the magistrate (they were under some legal pressure to pay taxes, but they had a much smaller group to collect from and were in a better negotiating position than the magistrate was with his superiors, who were also under legal pressure to see that the taxes came in as required); second, they were closer to the tenants and more exposed to the influence of moral restraints; third, it was to their economic advantage to develop a working relationship with their tenants. Conversely, belief in the rights of private property seems to have encouraged tenants to feel an obligation to pay their rent. On this see Fei Hsiao-t'ung, *Peasant Life*, pp. 187–89. Clan rules also favored leniency to tenants. Hui-chen Wang Liu *Clan Rules*, p. 112.

It is thus no coincidence that amalgamation of the land and labor taxes began and proceeded furthest in the fertile southeast, and that tenancy also became most prominent in this region. This does not mean that landlordism in the southeast was the consequence only of fiscal reform. The fertility of the land and the increasing density of the population themselves contributed to the spread of tenancy. But the tax reform added further stimulus to this trend.

44. Visitation and upkeep of graves was an obligation strongly felt at all levels. The psychological harm caused by the forces which drove the poor off their land and thus prevented them for the rest of their lives from being able to visit the ancestral graves was pointed out by the editors of the *Wu-kung hsien-chih*, 2/1b. The right to visit graves could be a potent cause for litigation. A case on this issue which took ten years to solve is cited by Wang Hui-tsu in *Ping-ta meng-hen lu*, under the year 1758 (Ch'ien-lung 23).

45. Ho, *Population*, ch. 6, and especially p. 117.

46. The history of the changes in land tenure during the last hundred years is a subject of major importance for an understanding of the changing relations between society and state in imperial China. The evidence known to this writer suggests that the crucial period for the emergence of the distinct landholding strata of late Ch'ing and modern times is from the middle of the Ming through the early Ch'ing. In the absence of a systematic study, various pieces of evidence can be adduced to point out what was happening:

1) Between 1398 and 1645 the amount of registered land dropped by half. The major drop apparently occurred during the first hundred years of this period. The uncertainty is over the fact that official figures compiled in the late sixteenth century recorded a drop of 25 percent between 1398 and 1502 from over 8 million *ch'ing* to over 6 million. But a high official, Ho T'ao, stated in a memorial of 1529 that the loss was nearly 4 million *ch'ing*, adding that in the provinces of Hu-kuang, Honan, and Kwangtung over half the registered acreage had been "lost." The editors of the *HWHTK* accepted this earlier estimate for 1502. *HWHTK*, 2791.3; also cited in Ho, *Population*, p. 117. Since then the figures fluctuated and at one point (1602) rose above the 1398 level, only to fall back dramatically in 1645. The 1398 level was not reached again (in overall fiscal figures) until 1867. The figures have been tabulated in Ho, *Population*, p. 102, Table 21.

2) The land that went out of registration was evidently not that of the poor. This is clearly asserted by Shen Pang (see chapter 9, note 7). Ho T'ao, commenting more obliquely on the loss of land from the registers of the three provinces noted above, asserted that if it was not given away by provincial administrations, then it was concealed by "shifty persons," or abandoned to "plunderers or bandits." The implication in all cases is that the missing land fell under the control of families with "pull" or influence. This is not to say that the poor did not have their share of tax-free land. But the significant feature is that certain families now had sufficient influence actually to take land out of the registers, and that officials did not always feel strong enough to withstand this influence. According to the *Wu-kung hsien-chih*, these people were the *hao-yu* or *hao-min* "powerful and aggressive people" (households, families, clan branches, etc.) They were "cunningly evading the law," using their prestige to buy clerks and officials indiscriminately, and misrepresenting their means. It was through such activities that the Ming tax registers of the district had fallen into disorder. "None of this had happened in a day." *Wu-kung hsien-chih*, 2/1b–2a.

3) Under the influences of natural and fiscal competitiveness, the wealthy were not only maneuvering against administrative exactions but also directly waging economic warfare on the poor. This was noted in Wu-kung in Shensi in its discussion of Ming fiscal conditions (see chapter 9, note 19). In Kiangsi in the early sixteenth century, Wang Yang-ming was trying to urge *ta-hu* (large households) and merchants not to foreclose on debtors, seize their goods, ruin them, and drive them into robbery. Clearly this was

happening, and contributing to the serious bandit problem of that period. *Yang-ming ch'üan-shu*, pieh-lu, kung-i, 399.

4) The dominance of the examination system from the middle of the fifteenth century on sharpened these divergencies. Wealth became increasingly necessary to cope with the long training needed to establish a competitive position. Degrees set up a power barrier, greatly enhancing the influence of those who already had substantial economic means. They also set up social barriers. Kinship and legal privileges for relatives extended the influence of those possessing degrees and offices to relatives lacking these handles. The provision of purchasable degrees and titles from the middle of the fifteenth century on gave a further edge to wealth. All of these factors led to a steady decline in the social mobility of Chinese society, noticeably from the middle of the fifteenth century on and detailed in sharp outline in Ho's Table 9 in *Ladder of Success*, pp. 112–13 (especially col. A).

5) The separation of society into levels of means and influence based both on land and on degree status was already recognized in the sixteenth century as an accomplished fact. Lü K'un attempted a system of rural control which would take advantage of these differences. (See above pp. 150–51 and below, note 47). More importantly, the Single Whip reform accepted and greatly sharpened this separation by initiating a trend toward *differentiating taxpayers and non-taxpayers solely on the basis of landownership*. In so doing, it also helped to separate the local administrations from the large masses (more especially in the southeast) of the tenantry, and vice versa. Since the government saw taxes as a return on its effort to provide order, the political merit of tenants and other non-taxpayers was presumably less clearly defined than that of taxpayers.

Obviously one cannot distinguish merely between landholders and tenants. There are also many different levels of landholding. Given the economic, social, and administrative conditions and trends, the basic difference in landholders was between those who had enough influence to negotiate with local administrations and those who did not. Degree-holding or, for the less exalted, relationships with district office underlings, tended to secure the dividing lines established by differences in landownership.

The spread of tenancy in fact helped to alleviate (for a time) the economic struggle. By it the poor could signal their defeat, and surrender equality of economic status. Tenancy gave form to the social and economic differentiation of society which previous rural control institutions never could, and even established a basis for working relationships between rich and poor. Ch'ing administrative policy would, as we shall see, tacitly recognize this differentiation.

For pre-modern trends, see Ho, *Population*, ch. 6. Many writers have studied modern agrarian conditions and provided estimates of per capita land-holding. See R. H Tawney, *Land and Labour in China*, pp. 34–35, 40–41; Fei, *Earthbound China*, pp. 53–54; and *Peasant Life*, p. 192. The findings of Buck should be studied in the light of Ho's critique of them in *Population*, pp. 123–32.

47. Lü K'un tried to do this by prescribing rules of etiquette by which *hsiang-yueh* leaders were to be treated by officials. This would have brought them into a ceremonial as well as administrative relationship with officials. Ceremony was the vital constituent which attuned relationships to cultural values and gave them dignity. See *Shih-cheng lu*, 5/7b–8b.

48. The genuinely pathetic nature of this apathy is expressively revealed by Shen Fu (1763–c.1809) in his autobiography *Chapters from a Floating Life*. Wang Hui-tsu himself distrusted gentry who came to the district office on business and respected those who stayed aloof from it. *Hsueh-chih i-shuo*, A, essay No. 34, pp. 10–11. The contribution of

gentry to public affairs, both good and bad, is discussed by Chang, *The Chinese Gentry*, pp. 43–70.

49. Examples of these are given in Hucker, *Censorial System*, 158–59.

50. The influence of fiscal policy on near-subsistence economies is discussed by, among others, Bauer and Yamey in *The Economics of Under-Developed Countries*, pp. 82–84 and 194–201. In terms of their analysis, the amalgamation of the Ming land and labor taxes and the manner of its assessment defeated its monetary objectives by diverting the effort of the poorer households away from the monetary sector and back toward the subsistence sector. This is because the smallholder who converts to tenant status is not only relieving himself of the obligation to pay taxes but also cutting down the need to supply effort to the monetary sector (to the extent that he can pay his rent and supply his household needs in the form of primary products). In this way the tax would have a depressive effect on the supply of effort to the monetary sector.

In the case of the wealthier households, the amalgamated land tax affected not so much the distribution of effort between the market and subsistence sectors as the distribution of time between work and leisure. In economic terms, the tax exerted both an income effect (by falling on income from land presently owned and thus encouraging further effort) and a substitution effect (by taxing further investment in land and thus taxing the extra effort required to expand landholdings and compensate for the tax's income effect). Since land was the primary object of investment, the tax would reinforce other incentives to increase leisure and encourage landowners to transfer the management of the land to other hands. The maintenance of the quota principle guaranteed that as income increased, so would the substitution effect of the tax in relation to the income effect (this is provided that the landowner enjoyed the influence to keep his share of the quota and its accompanying unofficial fees stable). It is for reasons such as these that large portions of the late Ming and Ch'ing gentry class or classes appear to give little effort to economic as well as administrative management.

11: Conflicts between "public" and "private"

1. The following discussion has benefited from comments by an anonymous reader, some of the supporting material for which has been incorporated in note 3 below.

2. *Mencius*, 3A3. See Legge, pp. 242, 245. The earliest demarcation of land in this way appears to be in the *Shih ching*, Ode 212 (Karlgren, p. 166).

3. Instead, *kung* acquired the general meaning of "lord" or "ruler," applied to heads of state, alive or dead. See *Spring and Autumn Annals*, Ku-liang commentary, Hsi-kung 5th year, para. 9 (in the winter the men of Chin seized *Yü-kung* the ruler of Yü) and accompanying note: "People refer to all the rulers of states holding any of the five ranks as *kung*." For other similar usages of *kung*, see *Annals*, Huan-kung 12th year, Hsi-kung 8th year, Wen-kung 14th year.

4. The most eloquent defense of the public interest is by Han Feitzu (d. 233 B.C.) Han Feitzu argued that the relations between the state and society had changed drastically since the times of the sages or even of Confucius. Populations had grown much larger and states much bigger. Administrations had become much more impersonal and beyond the control of single individuals. Wealth per capita was much scarcer and the risk of ruin from either internal disorder or external invasion much greater. In this volatile situation, Han Feitzu insisted on total public commitment. He held that notions of private, while still valid for social purposes, were incompatible with political service. In such service, the only merit lay in what benefited the state. If the ruler assumed otherwise, private activities would prevail and the public interest be ruined.

In consequence, Han Feitzu deliberately polarized private and public: private scheming and public law; private family and (public) state; private and public minded; private and public interests. He defined private as meaning "encirclement" (*huan*)—that is, closed-in and exclusive—and public as meaning "opposed to private." To regard them nowadays as similar in interest (*t'ung li*) was disastrous. Han Feitzu did not condemn Confucian values as such. He advised the ordinary person to practice humanity and righteousness. He advised the state to reject them, and instead to strengthen its economic and military base and to prohibit private acts with public law. These ideas are found especially in ch. 6 "Having Standards" and ch. 46 "The Five Vermin" (both translated in Burton Watson, *Han Fei Tzu Basic Writings*).

For other Legalist views on this subject see the following:

1) *Shang chün shu*, ch. 18: "In a state in disorder there is among the people much private right (*i*, that is, control over what is right); in an army which is weak, much private valor. And this is how a state is dismembered " (See Duyvendak, JJL, *The Book of Lord Shang*, p. 290.)

2) *Kuantzu*, ch. 5, sec. 13: "If private feelings are put into action then public law is destroyed." Or ch. 17, sec. 53: "If among the people there is much private gain, their state is thereby impoverished."

For views from the more authoritarian wing of Confucianism, see the following:

1) *Hsuntzu*, ch. 2, "Self-Cultivation": "In anger he (the *chüntzu*) does not take away too much; in joy he does not give too much. He accepts law (*fa*) and prevails over his private (desires)." *Hsuntzu chi-chieh*, part 1, p. 23. It should be said that Hsuntzu views law (*fa*) as based on ritual (*li*) and ritual as the apex of the way and its moral power (ch. 1, "Encouraging Learning," p. 8). Thus the commentary interprets law here as ritual, i.e., the prescriptions arising from ritual. Hsuntzu follows the above statement from ch. 2 with a quotation from the *Shu Ching*, "The Great Plan." para. 14, "Have no likings but follow the king's way; have no aversions but follow the king's road," and says, "this refers to a *chüntzu*'s being able to let the public right (*kung i*) prevail over private desires."

2) *Hsuntzu*, ch. 12, "The Way of the *Chün*": "If the ruler does well in making clear the division of duties, arranging the order of the professions, measuring ability and confering office, then the public way will prevail and private gates (influence) be obstructed, public right will be clear and private affairs desist." *Ibid.*, part 3, p. 7.

3) Han Ying, *Han shih wai-chuan*, ch. 1: A loyal but human official goes out to die for his prince saying "'fear is my private (feeling); to die for my prince is my public (duty). I have heard that the *chüntzu* does not let what is private harm what is public.' Then he went out and died for him." See Hightower, pp. 29–30.

Many other statements, by these and other representatives of the Confucianist and Legalist viewpoints, exist on this theme. The above should help to show that the authoritarian Confucianists, although also holding that public should prevail over private. do so on different premises than those taken by Legalists.

5. As other writers have pointed out, it does not matter whether the system which Shang Yang abolished was the same Well Field system as that described by Mencius. What Shang Yang abolished was the right to private territorial jurisdiction. Undoubtedly that right existed in the feudal conditions of early and mid Chou; the Well Field system is its principal symbol.

6. This received its most radical expression under the Ch'in emperor's chief minister Li Ssu. He wrote that the real test of a ruler's power was his ability to monopolize the authority and the benefits of the Empire. See De Bary, *Sources*, pp. 155–58, citing

Shih chi, 87/13b–16b. Later writers did not forget how the founder of the Han dynasty and the second emperor and principal founder of the T'ang dynasty had looked on, and boasted of, the wealth and talent of the empire as their own possession. This may have been approved by the Legalist Shen Pu-hai, as Li Ssu claimed. It was going further than Han Feitzu permitted. He wrote, "The ruler must not (treat as) private his worthy and wise ministers and not treat as private his informed and capable officers (*shih*)." Ch'en Ch'i-t'ien, *Han Fei tzu chiao-shih*, pp. 28–29; also see Watson, *Han Fei Tzu*, p. 25. Watson's translation of *ssu* as "selfish," although acceptable, blurs the distinction made by Han Feitzu between public and private.

7. This was chiefly the achievement of the distinguished Han philosopher and statesman Tung Chung-shu.

8. For examples of this viewpoint see De Bary, *Sources*, citing the following: 1) Tung Chung-shu, pp. 232–34. Tung's remark that since the reforms of Shang Yang "the rich daily took over interlocking tracts of ground and the poor did not have the land to place the point of an awl in" became the favorite cliché for alluding to this symptom; 2) Wang Mang, pp. 240–41; 3) Chang Tsai, pp. 458–61. 4) His nephew Ch'eng Hao, pp. 455–56; Huang Tsung-hsi, pp. 594–97.

9. After maintaining that the Well Field system was the basis for nourishing the people and the only way of maintaining peace, Chang wrote: "Later generations (since the Chou dynasty) did not arrange the (people's) livelihood but merely exploited their strength. In addition, they perversely used the exalted position of the Son of Heaven to monopolize profit. The public domain thinks only of itself and the people only of the people (*kung tzu kung, min tzu min*), and they do not take any account of each other. If the people have enough, won't the ruler also have enough? If the people do not have enough, how will the ruler have enough"? See De Bary, *Sources,* pp. 459–60 and *Chang tzu ch'üan-shu*, 4/84. The undermining of the Confucian position is more frankly admitted by Chang's contemporary Su Hsun (see *Sources*, pp. 461–63). Even so, Su also deplored the passing of the Well Fields and wanted to restore a system "approximating" them. The resurgence of interest in the Well Field system during the early Sung is a product of the general revival of Confucian initiative associated with the Neo-Confucian movement. On this wave of revival, the Sung Confucianists reinvoked the Well Field system as the only one in which *jen* humanity functioned.

10. There remained the problem of private influence in recommendations for promotion, and many regulations were to be devoted to attacking this source of infiltration.

11. This is the effect of the subscriptions demanded from officials by clan organizations, some of which amounted to from one-eighth to one-quarter of the magistrate's formal and supplementary salaries. See Chang, *Income*, pp. 26–27, Tables 6 and 7. The importuning of subordinates, friends, and other officials also became a major problem after appointment. See below, p. 171.

12. Ku's diagnosis and proposals are put forward in nine essays on the prefectural (*chün-hsien*) system. See *Ting-lin wen-chi*, 1/6a–11a. Annotated and punctuated texts can be found in *Ku Yen-wu wen*. The quoted passage is from the beginning of essay 5. His critique on the loss of authority by prefectural and district officials is in *Jih-chih lu*, 4/15 ff. The first part of this is translated in De Bary, *Sources*, p. 611 under the title "On the Concentration of Authority at Court." Ku's own title is "*shou-ling*" (prefects and magistrates), and it is their authority which is his basic concern.

12: CONTROL OF LOCAL ADMINISTRATIVE AUTHORITY

1. The Regulations are found in the *Regulations of the Board of Officials* (Li-pu tse-li)

or in the *Disciplinary Regulations of the Board of Officials or of the Six Boards* (Li-pu or Liu-pu ch'u-fen tse-li). Similar regulations existed for military officials. Further regulations are contained, along with disciplinary regulations, in early editions of the *Collected Institutes* and in the *Statutory Amendments* (Ta-Ch'ing hui-tien tse-li or shih-li of the Ch'ien-lung, Chia-ch'ing, and Kuang-hsu eras).

2. *TCHT:CC*, 8/4b; *TCHT:KH*, 11/4b.

3. *LPTL, LPCFTL*, 1/1a–2a or *Hsin-tsuan LPCFTL* 1/1a–2a. See also chapter 1, pp. 19–20.

4. *TCHT:Khsi*, 12/9b–10a; *TCHTSL:CC* 75/1a–b; *Hsin-tsuan LPCFTL*, 15/18a. This offense also came under the purview of the Board of Punishment.

5. *Hsin-tsuan LPCFTL*, 15/7a.

6. *Ibid.*, 15/15a–b. The gentry involved in such offenses were to be dismissed from any office or brevet rank which they may have held, or if *sheng-yuan* or *chien-sheng* degraded (i.e., to commonality).

7. *TCHTSL:CC*, 70/21b–22a. Provincial treasurers and judges were allowed 40, intendants and prefects 30, first-class and second-class prefects also 20, and assistant department and district magistrates and below 10. Wives or women attendants accompanying male attendants were not to exceed these numbers. Apparently local officials did not always feel bound by these limits, for in 1760 regulations were passed requiring superior officials to check into this matter. *Ibid.*, 22a.

8. *Hsin-tsuan LPCFTL*, 15/35a–36a. E.g., as of 1736 district magistrates were required to report to their superiors, within three months of arriving at their post, the names, age, native district, and specific position of all personal servants in their employment. *TCHTSL:CC* 70/22a.

9. Ch'ü, *Local Government*, pp. 96 and 113.

10. *Hsin-tsuan LPCFTL*, 15/32b–33a.

11. This is based on a comparison of the *LPTL* of 1843 with the *Hsin-tsuan LPCFTL* and the *Liu-pu CFTL*. These are dated 1827 and 1887 respectively. They were issued in Chekiang.

12. The origin and evolution of the *ch'u-fen tse-li* is a subject awaiting further research. The distinction of administrative from penal law as such is early, as the studies by Hulsewe and Balazs show. Prior to the Ch'ing, the distinction had to do principally with punishment, rather than with the nature of the offense. Offenses, whether of an administrative or criminal nature, were both called *tsui*, and the administrative offenses were contained in the successive penal codes. On the other hand, officials were very early able to receive special treatment, under such provisions as the *pa i* (eight deliberations—for privileged groups) or *kuan-tang* (matching office, i.e., commuting punishment in terms of loss of service).

The Ch'ing continued to refer to administrative offenses as *tsui* and continued to stand by the administrative offenses and penalties already stipulated in the penal code. Under their rule, determination of civil administrative offenses (in most cases) and imposition of administrative penalties (in all cases) came under the management of the Board of Officials. They also added so many supplemental statutory regulations that it became administratively desirable to group the administrative offenses and penalties separately.

Hence the *ch'u-fen tse-li*. In addition to certain administrative rewards, they include all penal and statutory offenses affecting conduct of administration committed by office, rank, or degree-holders. They include only penalties based on administrative commutation. The penalties not eligible for commutation remained under the jurisdiction of the Board of Punishment and are not included in the *ch'u-fen tse-li*.

It would be interesting to know when and how jurisdiction over administrative offenses was separated from that over penal offenses, when and how the concept of *ch'u-fen* emerged, and when and how administrative offenses were distinguished into those of a public and private nature? Presumably the concept of *ch'u-fen* postdates the principle of *kuan-tang*, which Balazs traced back to the Ch'en dynasty (557–89). The present research led by chance to the mention of the term *ch'u-fen* in a T'ang imperial order of 750. See *Tang hui-yao*, 69/1217. The Columbia University Library contains separate publications of the *ch'u-fen tse-li* dating as early as the Yung-cheng reign, which may throw light on the matter. Examination of the *TCHTTL* and *SL* has so far failed to produce results. The Harvard Library *ch'u-fen tse-li* date only from the Tao-kuang reign, by which time the distinction is ingrained in the regulations.

13. Many examples of these are given by Ch'ü in *Local Government*, *passim*, especially chs. 7 and 8.

14. This list does not of course include all the reviews and examinations associated with the examination and appointment systems.

15. The levels of competence were as follows: ability (*ts'ai*) was assessed as long, normal, and short (*ch'ang, p'ing, tuan*); integrity (*shou*) as clear, normal, or turbid (*ch'ing, p'ing, cho*); quality of government (*cheng*) as diligent, normal, or negligent (*ch'in, p'ing, tai*); age (*nien*) as young, medium, or old (*ch'ing, chung, lao*). See *TCHTSL*, ch. 80.

16. *Ibid.* The Yung-cheng edicts are repeated in ch. 81 under the heading "Impeachment of Provincial Officials" (*wai-kuan ts'an-ho*). It is incorrect to regard the changes in administrative enactment as "technical and procedural, and therefore not of major importance" as does one recent authority. The issues on which they are based were of central importance. The edicts and statutes make it clear that the emperors, and many of their officials, knew this.

17. See above, chapter 8, pp. 108–9 and note 5.

18. *Ming shih*, 825.0–1.

19. *K'ao-ch'eng* regulations are in *TCHT:Khsi*, ch. 25 or in *TCHT:YC*, ch. 33, which provides a brief resume of the *k'ao-ch'eng* fiscal administration. The following are examples of rewards and punishments under the system:

a) rewards as established in 1665:

COLLECTED AND DELIVERED WITHIN ONE YEAR	REWARD: RECORDING IN MERIT
50,000 taels or less	one
50,000–100,000 taels	two
100,000 taels or over	three

no rewards for local officials who did not at the same time complete the collections of grain and miscellaneous taxes. *TCHT:YC*, 33/7b, 8b.

b) punishments as of 1726:

DEFICIENCY IN COLLECTION	PENALTY
one-tenth	fined 6 months' formal salary
two-tenths	fined 1 years' formal salary
three-tenths	demoted one rank in salary
four-tenths	demoted two ranks in salary
five-tenths	demoted one rank in office
six-tenths	demoted two ranks in office
all promotions stopped until tax deficit made good	

seven-tenths	demoted one (later three) ranks in office
eight-tenths	demoted two (later four) ranks in office
	all transferred
nine-tenths	dismissed

The penalties given in Ch'ü, *Local Government*, which are more severe, are from later sources. Ch'ü gives examples of the increased late eighteenth- and early nineteenth-century rewards, *ibid.*, p. 288, note 35.

20. *TCHT:Khsi*, 99/1a, *TCHT:YC*, 138/1a.

21. *TCHT:Khsi*, 99/5b–6a.

22. *Ibid.*, 6a–13b. For example, the reward paid to a commoner for apprehending robbers was 20 taels per robber at the start of the Shun-chih reign. In 1672 it was reduced to 10 taels for one robber, 20 for two. *Ibid.*, 13b.

23. Some of the early regulations for the registration of male adults for fiscal assessment (*pien-shen*) involve the *li-chia* system. A regulation of 1648 required registration to be investigated and equalized according to the *li* and the *chia*. After the freezing of the *ting* quota in 1713 (see chapter 14), a regulation of 1716 allowed that if a family could not replace a registered male who had reached the age of retirement (sixty *sui*), he could be replaced from the same clan, or *failing that* the same *chia* or land registration unit (*t'u*). But these regulations are concerned with registration of *ting*, not with the *li-chia* as such. The regulation of 1716 shows how little importance the central government attached to the *li-chia* system by that date. See *TCHT:YC*, 30/24a, 27b–28a.

24. According to one early Ch'ing official, the tax rates of Su-chou and Sung-chiang prefectures had begun rising during the Sung and Yuan dynasties. In 1317 the Su-chou summer levy of silk stood at 22,400 catties (*chin*); the autumn grain levy was 882,100 bushels (*shih*) in Su-chou and over 600,000 bushels in Sung-chiang. By the end of the Yuan, said this writer, the taxes were very unregulated and burdensome. *Wu-hsien chih*, 44/13b–14a.

But the real trouble for Su-chou and Sung-chiang began when these areas came under the control of Chang Shih-ch'eng, a rival of Chu Yuan-chang's (later Ming T'ai-tsu) for the imperial succession. It took Chu a long time to overrun them, and in his anger he not only confiscated a great deal of land belonging to "big clans" and "rich people" but also fixed the tax rates according to the existing private rent rates. *Ibid.*, 44/2b, 13b–14a. See also *Tzu-chih hsin-shu*, 1/36a. In Wu-hsien itself, official (confiscated) land was more than a third greater in registered area than commoner land. *Wu-hsien chih*, 45/1a.

Under Emperor Ming T'ai-tsu's aegis, the Su-chou autumn grain levy accordingly rose to 2.75 million bushels, higher than that of any individual province. The Sung-chiang autumn grain levy rose to 1.11 million bushels. See *TMHT*, 24/4b–10a. Ming T'ai-tsu's young and peaceable grandson issued an edict, following his succession, saying that the heavy tax rates in Kiangsu and Chekiang were only intended to punish obstinate people on one particular occasion. They must be reduced (to as little as one-third the existing rates). However, the usurping Emperor Ch'eng-tsu simply raised them again. See *Ming shih*, 824.3–4.

Thus in both sixteenth-century state tax lists, the Su-chou autumn grain levy stood at 2.04 million bushels and in the later list was still only exceeded by two provincial totals —those of Chekiang and Kiangsi. See *TMHT*, chs. 24 and 25. In the early Ch'ing, the

Su-chou and Sung-chiang tax rates were still the highest in the country. The flight of the poor from these prefectures was noted as early as 1426. See *Ming shih*, 824.3–4.

25. Memorial of Governor Han Shih-ch'i in *Wu-hsien chih*, 44/7b–8a. This applied only to payment in "commuted kind," i.e., money.

26. Memorials of Han Shih-ch'i, Mu T'ien-yen, Shao Chih-te, *ibid.*, ch. 44 and *Tzu-chih hsin-shu*, ch. 1.

27. In 1724, for example, four of the existing districts in Su-chou prefecture were divided into two (Wu-hsien was left untouched). *T'ung-k'ao*, 7301.2.

28. For those of Wu-hsien, see its annals, 45/19b–31a.

29. *T'ung-tien*, 2655–6.

30. See memorials of Yao Wen-jan, President of the Board of Punishments between 1666–68, and Li Chih-fang (1622–94) who served as Grand Secretary from 1687 to 1688. In Lu Yueh, *Ch'ieh-wen-ch'ai wen-ch'ao*, 23/14b ff and 18b ff.

Wang Yu-p'u, in his commentary to article 15 of the K'ang-hsi sacred edict (Unite the *pao-chia* in order to suppress robbery and banditry), said that one of the reasons why people did not report on bandits was their fear of the dishonesty of local officials: "The local officials are not really honest toward the people but think only of their own reputations. What they most dread is that robbers and bandits will affect their *k'ao-ch'eng* (record)." Wang continued with the familiar charge that when an owner of stolen property reported the theft, the magistrate, instead of going after the thief, first cross-examined and confused the owner. Even though he might arrest the thief and recover the stolen property, he would worry the owner to death. Therefore those who were robbed did not dare submit information, for fear of incurring the resentment of both the officials and the thieves. See F. W. Baller, *The Sacred Edict*, pp. 157–58. Several similar remarks are noted by Hsiao in his study of the *pao-chia* in *Rural China*.

31. *T'ung-tien*, 2657.2.

32. *TCHTSL:CC*, 68/1a–b (on *ti-hsiao* or commutation).

33. *TCHTSL*, chs. 80 and 81.

34. *TCHTSL:CC*, 67/14a–15a (under *k'ai-fu*, restoration to office).

35. *HCCSWP*, 16/1a ff. Ku's biography is in *Kuo-ch'ao ch'i-hsien lei-cheng*, 110/5a ff. Prior to becoming a censor he had served in the Hanlin Academy. Ku also attacked the administrative practice of buying commodities for official use at prices fixed by officials and not at the current market prices (*kuan-chia*); and he denounced the ways and means by which office underlings profiteered out of civil litigation.

36. The emperor's response is given in Ku's biography, 110/5b–6a.

37. Wang Hui-tsu scored a success on these lines shortly after arriving at his first administrative post (as magistrate of Ning-yuan in southern Hunan). See *Hsiao-shan hsien-chih kao*, 18/5a, and *Hsueh-chih i-shuo* B, No 73, cited in E. Balazs, *Political Theory and Administrative Reality in Traditional China* (London, SOAS, 1965), p. 62.

38. See *HCCSWP*, 16/5b–6b; *Yin-hsien chih*, 25/34b–35a; *Kuo-ch'ao ch'i-hsien lei-cheng*, 242/49a ff.

Chou Hao provides a good example of the struggle to become a local official. Born in 1754, he became a *chü jen* in 1779 at the relatively early age of twenty-five. After sixteen empty years he was selected in 1795 under the *ta-t'iao* system as a district magistrate and sent out to Chekiang. His first district magistracy seems to have come in 1797. In the next fourteen years he served in several different district posts in Chekiang. He was transferred (*tiao*) to Yin-hsien (an "important" post) in 1803 and served there from 1803 to 1809 and again from 1810 to 1811. During his service as a magistrate, he was noted for a variety of achievements, including settling of law suits, suppression of piracy, dike reconstruction, and famine relief. In fact, after his success at Yin he was specially transferred to P'ing-yang to aid in famine relief.

In 1811 he was promoted to first-class assistant prefect of Chia-hsing, in charge of coastal defenses. He stayed in that post for some ten years, during which he served briefly as acting prefect. He was promoted to prefect of Chang-chou in Fukien in 1821 and died in office two years later at the age of sixty-nine.

It was as a magistrate that Chou made his mark. He was highly respected at Yin, and the editors of its gazetteer devoted nearly four sides (two pages) to an account of his service there. As an assistant prefect he appears to have been conscientious at his duties, but found the time to take a practical interest in agricultural production. It is said that he once told some commoners in Chia-hsing: "My family are all farmers by calling. There is nothing we don't know about plowing and reaping. You can't fool me on that!" See *Chia-hsing fu-chih* 18/25b. As a prefect he appears to have made little impact. Unlike the gazetteers of jurisdictions in which he had previously served, that of Chang-chou contains no record of his service. The publication of his critique in the *HCCSWP* brought his career to the attention of the discriminating compiler of the *KCCHLC*, who described his family and his record at some length.

39. Wang himself suffered from the disciplinary system. He began his career in the office handling the Four Treasuries compilation, was evaluated as meritorious, and transferred to a magistracy in Shansi. He rose steadily through intermediate posts (including that of Prefect of Su-chou) to treasurer of Chekiang, where he endeavored to bring the system of customary fees under control. In 1796 he was demoted two grades and transferred, but in consideration of his past service appointed provincial judge of Kiangsi. The next year he became treasurer and later governor of Fukien, serving in that post for four years. Subsequently he held several high metropolitan posts. After returning to the provinces as governor-general of Fukien-Chekiang, he was eventually involved in a scandal and dismissed the service. He died a year later.

In the memorial quoted here Wang also recommended the employment of talented men in important posts, no matter whether they were qualified by length of service or free of impeachment on public offenses (the Chia-ch'ing emperor's edict approving and promulgating the latter suggestion is dated 1813. See note 3 above for sources). *HCCSWP* 16/4a–5b. Biographical accounts are in *Ch'ing shih*, 4476–77 and several other leading biographical sources.

13: Surveillance of rural life

1. Edicts on this subject are in *TCHT:YC*, 138/33a ff and in *TCHTSL*, ch. 158; also in *T'ung-k'ao* below as cited.

2. *TCHT:YC*, 138/33a–35a; *T'ung-k'ao*, 5051.3, 5055.1–2.

3. *T'ung-k'ao*, 5051.3; Huang Liu-hung, *Fu-hui ch'üan-shu*, 23/1a.

4. Order of 1727, *TCHT:YC*, 138/36a.

5. Most of these were covered in separate orders of 1757. See *TCHTSL*, ch. 158. For earlier orders, see the following: Bannermen, orders of 1686 and 1697, *TCHT:YC*, 138/33a; Aborigines, edict of 1726, *ibid.*, 138/33b–34a; Shed people, order of 1725, *ibid.*, 30/30b ff, and order of 1739, *TCHTSL*, ch. 158 (for later orders, see Hsiao, *Rural China*, p. 575, n. 24); Boatmen and fishermen, orders of 1729, 1747, and also orders of 1760 and 1765, *TCHTSL*, ch. 158; Farmers in Mongolia, order of 1743, *ibid.*; Clans, order of 1726, *T'ung-k'ao*, 5055.2; Gentry, order of 1727, *TCHT:YC*, 138/35a–b; *T'ung-k'ao*, 5073.1. Taiwan: order of 1733, *TCHTSL*, ch. 158.

6. Cited by Chou Liang-kung (1612–72) in *Tzu-chih hsin-shu*, 13/15a–17a. Opinions

such as these and the following are extracted from sources which cite them only to refute them.

Chou served as a magistrate in the last years of the Ming dynasty. For his stormy career, see *Eminent Chinese*, pp. 173–74.

7. Huang, *Fu-hui ch'üan-shu*, 21/1a.

8. Huang, in *HCCSWP*, 74/5a (but originally from the above source).

9. Cf. Huang Chung-chien in *HCCSWP*, 74/2b–3a. The account in the twentieth-century *T'ung-kuan hsien-chih*, ch. 18, section 2, also begins in this vein. The *pao-chia* system was then still in operation.

10. Chou Liang-kung in *Tzu-chih hsin-shu*, 13/15a–17a.

11. Lit. "before it budded." T'ao Yuan-ch'un, in *HCCSWP*, 74/3b. T'ao served as magistrate of Ch'ang-hua district (Kwangtung) from 1694 to c.1698. He died in office from overwork. *Ch'ing shih*, 5098.6.

12. Chou Liang-kung, *Tzu-chih hsin-shu*, 13/15a–17a. See also a proclamation by Lü Yuan-liang, a *t'ing* administrator: "Whereas the first duty of your official is to bring peace to the people . . ." He served in Chiang-ning prefecture in the early K'ang-hsi period. *Tzu-chih hsin-shu*, 13/21a–22a; *Chiang-ning fu-chih*, 16/24a, later edition, 21/3a. Lü goes on to tell the people that they cannot have peace if they do not cooperate in exposing criminals. He berates them for their foolishness in tolerating gambling, drunkenness, fugitives, etc., and orders the watch-groups henceforth to investigate, restrain, and secretly report any criminal activities. Any who accept bribes or conceal such matters will be punished. Secret reports, it may be noted, were recommended by those who feared that otherwise they would not get any reports. (The practice is also advised for this reason by Huang Chung-chien, and in the early nineteenth century by Wang Chih-i. It is rejected by the Chia-ch'ing emperor. See Edict of 1814, *Ch'ing hsü t'ung-k'ao*, 7759.2.) The whole tone of the proclamation is defensive and reproachful.

13. See Shen T'ung in *Pao-chia shu*, 3/7b ff. Also cited as editorial footnote in *Jih-chih lu*, 3/73–74. For the *Chou li* source see *Chou li*, 34/2. Shen obtained the lowly ninth rank but retired to look after his elderly parents and did not return to office. He died in 1752. See *Eminent Chinese*, pp. 647–48.

14. Lu Shih-i, in *Pao-chia shu*, 3/1b.

15. E.g., Wang Fu-chih, Chu Tse-yun. Members of the School of Han learning, such as Hu Wei and Yen Jo-chü, were beginning in the late seventeenth century to dismantle parts of basic classical texts as forgeries or later additions.

16. *Pao-chia shu*, 2/1a ff. The inclusion of the more recondite evildoers cited here was the work of the Ch'ien-lung emperor. See his edict of 1747 in *TCHTSL*, ch. 158. Earlier orders speak only of robbers, bandits, fugitives, and thieves, especially the first two.

17. Yang Ching-jen, *Ch'ou-chi pien*, 27/15a, which also contains all of Yeh's text (7b–14b).

18. *Pao-chia shu*, 2/12a.

19. E.g., edict of 1727, *TCHT:YC*, 138/36a; statement from Board of Revenue in 1757 on the division of duties between watch-group heads and village constables, *T'ung-k'ao*, 5062.1; edict of 1818 in response to a memorial of Governor-General Wang Chih-i on this problem, *Ch'ing hsü t'ung-k'ao*, 7759.2; edict of 1815, *ibid.*, 7760.1–2; Tseng Kuo-fan, *Tsou-kao*, 2/30a–b as cited by Hsiao in *Rural China*.

20. Huang Liu-hung alludes to the part played by a *ti-fang* in investigating a homicide. *Fu-hui ch'uan-shu*, 14/22b–25a.

21. *HCCSWP*, 74/8a–9b.

22. *T'ung-kuan hsien-chih*, 26/9b–10a.

23. Huang Liu-hung, *Fu-hui ch'üan-shu*, 21/1b, 4a.

24. E.g., edict of 1757, *TCHTSL*, ch. 158; Huang Liu-hung in *Fu-hui ch'üan-shu*, 21/4a–b or *HCCSWP*, 74/4a; Shen T'ung, in *Pao-chia shu*, 3/7b; Huang Chung-chien, in *HCCSWP*, 74/2b–3a.

The concept of rotational leadership, established by the *li-chia* system, continued to exercise influence over the *pao-chia* system in the seventeenth and eighteenth centuries. This may have been where surviving elements of the *li-chia* organization were used as a base on which to set up *pao-chia* forms. Huang Liu-hung speaks of *chia* of the *pao-chia* as forming eleven families, with the *chia* leader either coming from the eleventh family or from the ten families in turn. This eleven-family form differs from the standard *pao-chia* forms, and is a relic of the 110 family system of the *li-chia*. In Huang's time the *li-chia* administration was generally in an advanced state of decay, but its forms still survived widely. The *pao-chia*, although now backed by Ch'ing edicts, was still far from being an empire-wide institution, and its immediate form was a matter for local decision.

In these circumstances Huang found it necessary to argue against rotational leadership, because it would bring stupid, weak, or indigent people into a job requiring time and determination. As he pointed out, the *chia* head was established for the purpose of finding out if there were robbers, fugitives, or wicked persons among the ten families, not just to prepare a head count. In 1757 the Board of Revenue advised against rotational leadership on similar grounds. *T'ung-k'ao*, 5062.1.

25. This problem, well known to those engaged in security activities in populous near-subsistence countries, was pointed out by, among others, the Chia-ch'ing emperor, in an edict of 1814, *Ch'ing hsü t'ung-k'ao*, 7759.2; Huang Chung-chien, Yeh P'ei-sun, *Pao-chia shu*, 2/5b–6a; and Chang Hui-yen, *HCCSWP*, 74/5a–6b (for his biography see *Eminent Chinese*, pp. 42–43).

26. Ho, *Population*, p. 37.

27. *T'ung-k'ao*, 5033.1–2; *TCHTSL*, ch. 157.

28. *Ch'ing hsü t'ung-k'ao*, 7757.2.

29. *Ibid.*, 7757–58; edicts in *TCHTSL*, ch. 158.

30. *Ibid.*, ch. 158.

31. *TCHTSL*, ch. 397; *TCHT:YC*, 77/1a. The edict ruled out the use of "local big-shots," servants, and retainers, "wicked" clerks and "verminous" runners in *hsiang-yueh* offices. In other words, it did not want the offices, or the system, to be taken over by people with any local pull and used to further their own influence.

The use of the six maxims for the *hsiang-yueh* predates the Ch'ing. In 1599 a magistrate of T'ien-t'ai district (in Chekiang) set up a *hsiang-yueh* system. He chose spacious monastaries and temples for meeting places, and selected elderly men as heads. Twice a month they were to lead the masses in explaining the six maxims. They were also to encourage good, warn against evil, and foster genuine government. *T'ien-t'ai hsien-chih*, 3/5b–6a. There was, in fact, a lack of uniformity in late Ming *hsieng-yueh* systems. As with the Single Whip reforms or the *pao-chia* systems of that period, they were not masterminded by the central authority.

32. *TCHTSL*, ch. 397.

33. A translation of the maxims is given in, Hsiao, *Rural China*, pp. 187–88. The form of each is "do such and such [a duty] so as to effect such and such [a desirable end]." Compare this with the unequivocal form of such mandates as the six maxims or the ten commandments, which merely say "do [or do not do] such and such."

34. In 1686. *TCHT:YC*, 77/1b; *TCHTSL*, ch. 397.

35. In 1712. *Ibid.*

36. *Ibid.*, which give the whole text of the Maxims and Amplification.

The following Western-language translations may be consulted on this subject:

William Milne, *The Sacred Edict*. Translates the maxims, the amplification by the Yung-cheng emperor, and the commentary by Wang Yu-p'u. A pioneer translation with room for improvement.

A. Theophile Piry, *Le Saint Edict*. An annotated French translation of the maxims and amplification, with accompanying text. Considerably more reliable than the former, with extensive notes as an aid to study.

F. W. Baller, *The Sacred Edict*. Translates the maxims and the commentary by Wang Yu-p'u (but not the amplification), with accompanying text. Workmanlike, but sententious and uncritical. Includes text of amplication as appendix.

37. Wang Yu-p'u did not help matters by including a number of disparaging remarks on local officials and gentry in his popularized commentary.

38. *Tuan-ch'ang hsien-chih*, 12/33b–34b. The magistrate drew the idea of elder (*chang*) from the Ch'in and Han title of magistrates of smaller districts.

39. *Hu-k'ou hsien-chih*, 7/21a–22b.

40. This is its title in the *TCHTSL* and in some later gazetteers.

41. In 1729. *TCHTSL*, ch. 397.

42. In 1737. *TCHTSL*, ch. 398. An official had noted as early as 1655 that each district office only had one copy of the laws and that the ordinary people could not get to hear them, therefore lawbreakers were many. He requested that the provincial authorities be told to take the laws relevant to the people and order the local authorities to expound them during the spring and fall slack season. They should also order the educational officials constantly to expound and practice them with their licentiates. *T'ung-k'ao*, 6600.2. The K'ang-hsi emperor undoubtedly had this idea in mind in formulating his eighth maxim, "Expound the laws so as to warn the stupid and obstinate." T'ien Wen-ching, in an article on the conduct of the public lectures in the *Ch'in-pan chou-hsien shih-i*, noted that the magistrate was also to take the printed articles of the penal code and expound and display them, so that the people would know them and "tremble with respect." *Ibid.*, 8b. The principle of expounding the laws had its precedent in the *Chou li*, as the Yung-cheng emperor pointed out in his amplification.

43. *Ch'in-pan chou-hsien shih-i*, 8a–b; *Yung-hsin hsien-chih*, 5/85b–86a.

44. This conclusion is based on a sampling of some thirty district gazetteers. Other institutions for improving the people's morals, such as the rural wine-drinking ceremony, continue to receive mention, which makes the omission of the *hsiang-* or *chiang-yueh* the more conspicuous.

14: IMPACT OF FISCAL POLICIES

1. *TCHT:Khsi*, 20/7b.

2. Edwin G. Beal, *The Origin of Likin*, p. 3.

3. In that year the land tax produced 21.576 million taels of silver for the central government. The adult male *ting* tax produced 3.009 million taels, plus 12,570 bushels of rice. *TCHT:Khsi*, 20/7b, 23/7b. It is impossible to give a precise estimate of the cash value of this rice, as it would depend on its place of origin, the condition of the harvest, and the current cash-silver exchange rates (market and official), but it would be on the order of less than 12,000 taels.

4. This represents an increase of 18 percent. See *TCHT:YC*, 30/1b, 8a. In view of

local resistance to any increase in existing fiscal units, its achievement should not be underestimated. See Ho, *Population*, p. 33.

The regulations on registration of *ting* (*pien-shen*) are in *TCHT:Khsi*, 23/1b ff, and in *THCT:YC*, 30/24a ff. The increase or decrease in registered *ting* was taken into account in the *k'ao-ch'eng* assessment of local officials. Order of 1660, *TCHT:Khsi*, 23/17b.

5. See *TCHT:YC*, 54/12b, 17a, 18b–19b.

6. *Ibid.*, 54/21b–22a. The fixed salary rates are given in, among other places, *TSCC*, ching-chi, ch'üan-heng 78, k'ao 8/3a.

7. Ch'en Teng-yuan, *Chung-kuo t'ien-fu shih*, p. 222, citing the K'ang-hsi *Shih-lu*.

8. Ku Yen-wu, *T'ing-lin wen-chi*, ch'ien-liang B; also in *HCCSWP*, 29/3a–4a.

9. Ch'en Teng-yuan, *Chung-kuo t'ien-fu shih*, p. 213.

10. *TSCC*, ching-chi, hsiang-hsing, 133 hui-k'ao/17a.

11. Ch'en, *Chung-kuo t'ien-fu shih*, p. 213.

12. *TCHT:YC*, 54/23a.

13. *Ch'ing shih*, 4077.6–7; Ch'ü, *Local Government*, p. 219, n. 73, citing Wang Ch'ing-yun, *Shih-ch'ü yü-chi*, 3/46b–47a.

14. Since 1656 the *ting* assessment was conducted every five years. The totals obtained in 1661, 1685 and 1724 were as follows:

	NO. OF *ting*	SILVER ASSESSMENT (TAELS)	GRAIN ASSESSMENT *shih*
1661	21,068,609	3,008,900	12,570
1685	23,417,448	3,136,932	12,715
1724	24,854,918	3,291,229	⎧12,794 ⎩26,150 beans

SOURCE. *TCHT:YC*, 30/1b–17a.

15. *Ibid.*, 30/27a.

16. Edict of 1712. *T'ung-k'ao*, 5025.3.

17. *TCHT:YC*, 30/27a. This was what he proposed in the edict of 1712 above. His ministers agreed to it. The proposal was then promulgated in a "gracious proclamation" (*en-chao*) in 1713. For forms of imperial utterance, see Fairbank and Teng, *Ch'ing administration*, pp. 95–96.

18. *TCHT:YC*, 30/27b–28a.

19. Cited in Ho, *Population*, p. 211. On Kung (1792–1841), see *Eminent Chinese*, pp. 431–34.

20. In 1661 Shansi paid up 614,964 taels in *ting* levy. Kiangnan (Kiangsu and Anhwei) came next with 403,000 taels, and Chihli next with 352,000 taels. Some provinces paid well under 100,000 taels. In 1685 Shansi paid 561,543 taels, to Chihli's 387,000 taels, and Kiangsu's 258,000 taels; and in 1724, 573,268 taels, to Chihli's 378,000 taels, and Kiangsu's 249,000 taels. Much or most of Kiangsu's original *ting* levy was by then incorporated in the land tax. The significance of the Shansi figures is that they are the largest unincorporated *ting* sums. This has bearing on the incidence and degree of fulfillment of the levy. While the income from the Shansi *ting* zigzagged, the actual number of registered male adults went up steadily: 1,527,632 in 1661; 1,649,666 in 1685; and 1,768,657 in 1724. Evidently 1685 was a bad year for male adults and tax collectors in Shansi. Figures from *TCHT:YC*, ch. 30.

21. These are the reasons given in 1745 for not amalgamating the land and labor taxes in certain districts in Shansi (at a time when all the rest of the country except Kweichow

had completed the amalgamation). See *T'ung-k'ao*, 5029. 1. Shansi's fiscal backwardness is discussed by Wang Ch'ing-yun in *Shih-ch'ü yü-chi*, 3/28–36b. See also Ho, *Population*, pp. 31–32 and Ch'ü, *Local Government*, p. 286, n. 23. The amalgamation was not completed in Shansi until 1837. After the Yung-cheng period, fiscal conditions in Shansi do not provide a safe indication of conditions in other areas.

22. From biography of Kao Ch'eng-ling, provincial treasurer of Shansi, in *Ta-Ch'ing Chi-fu hsien-che chuan*, 30/29b–31b.

Shansi's *ting* rates rose as high as 4 taels per male adult, and Shensi's as high as 7 taels. In Shun-ti'ien (Chihli), they went up to 2.6 taels; in Kiangsu to 0.2 taels; in Hunan to 0.8 taels; in Kwangtung to 1.3 taels. *TCHT: YC*, ch. 30.

23. Shansi is particularly vulnerable to drought. For its most disastrous drought, see Ho, *Population*, pp. 231–32.

24. *Ch'ing shih*, 4077.6–4078.4. No-min made his proposal for the retention of the *huo-hao* in 1724.

25. *Ibid.*, and biographical source in note 22 above.

26. The quote, a useful handle for fiscal proposals, comes from the Tribute of Yü. Legge, p. 141.

27. *Ta-Ch'ing Chi-fu hsien-che chuan*, 30/29b–31b. Kao's figures for the tax quotas were 2.3 million taels in land tax, and 650,000 taels in *ting* tax. These compare with the *Hui-tien* figures for 1724 of 2,284,125 taels land tax (plus 45,770 bushels of grain) and 573,268 taels in *ting* tax. Kao's higher figure for *ting* is probably based on the quota for "equal service" (*chün-yao*) and artisans (*kung-chiang*), given in the Shansi gazetteer together as 651,124 taels. *Shansi t'ung-chih*, T'ung-chih edition, 58/7b. Kao was emboldened to press for amalgamation, since this had been approved for Chihli in 1723.

28. Ch'en, *Chung-kuo t'ien-fu shih*, p. 213.

29. From the *Doctrine of the Mean*, 20/14; Legge, p. 410.

30. From *Sung shih*, chih-kuan chih; cited by Morohashi, 44144.180.

31. From Wang Ch'iung (d. 1532), *Shuang-chi ts'a-chi*, reproduced in *TSCC*, ching-chi, ch'üan-heng, ch. 79, lu-chih pu, i-wen/1b.

32. *Ibid.*, 7b.

33. *T'ung-k'ao*, 5231.3–5232.2.

34. The rates are in *TCHTSL:CC*, 139/9a–15a, under the title "wastage surcharge" (*sui-cheng hao-hsien*). It is misleading of Hsiao to describe the surcharge as "tacitly legalized" (*Rural China*, p. 85). It was recommended, opposed, determined, promulgated, and apportioned, according to standard decision-making procedures. It was meant to be temporary, but that is not the same thing as "tacit."

35. On this, see Ch'ü, *Local Government*, p. 218, n. 63, citing the distribution of *huo-hao* income by the Honan provincial administration.

36. This is discussed, primarily as it affected the lower Yangtze region, by Ch'üan Han-sheng, "Mei-chou pai-yin yü shih-pa shih-chi Chung-kuo wu-chia ko-ming ti kuan-hsi," from the *Bulletin of the Institute of History and Philology* (May 1957), pp. 517–50.

37. Ch'en, *Chung-kuo t'ien-fu shih*, pp. 214–15, citing the biography of Shih-se in the *Ch'ing-shih lieh-chuan*, 15/28b–29a. The emperor, afraid that the practice would spread to other provinces, ordered Shih-se (then governor of Szechuan) to get rid of it permanently!

38. *T'ung-k'ao*, 5233.1; Wu Chao-hsin, *Chung-kuo shui-chih shih*, II, 39.

39. One of Wang Chih-i's complaints was that the disciplinary regulations for exceeding the time limits in collecting taxes were too severe. The normal deadline in the

eighteenth century was one year. In 1788 the Board of Revenue had approved a deadline of three months on the collection of grain from southern regions for military provisions, failing which magistrates should incur actual demotion and dismissal (i.e., not suspended until the arrival of a supplementary deadline). This regulation appears to have produced the grain; but it forced magistrates in Fukien to send in false reports or raid the granaries to fulfill the quota. Wang was writing about thirty years later. *HCCSWP*, 16/4a–5b.

40. Ch'en, *Chung-kuo t'ien-fu shih*, p. 215.

41. See Ch'ü, *Local Government*, pp. 29–30.

42. Ch'en, *Chung-kuo t'ien-fu shih*, pp. 211–12; Ch'ü, *Local Government*, p. 135, and also pp. 141–42 on customary practices in the collection of grain tribute.

43. These malpractices are detailed at length in Hsiao, *Rural China*, ch. 4.

44. *HCCSWP*, 16/6a.

15: Social conflict: the problem of litigation

1. This conclusion is manifest in the massively documented study by Hsiao, *Rural China*, which should be read as an illustration of this conflict and its dimensions.

2. See *Analects*, 20/1–2. The Ch'ing theory of penal administration is surveyed by Alabaster in *Notes and Commentaries on Chinese Criminal Law*. He noted in its favor that: 1) punishments for serious offenses were fixed—they could not be determined at the whim of local or provincial judges; 2) mitigation was not left up to local judges but was weighed by the Board of Punishments; 3) punishments were matched with crimes and applied consistently (This is truer of theory than of practice. Nevertheless, compared with the substantial latitude in treatment of offenders found in different regions or even under different individual judges in present-day America, administration of serious offenses was remarkably consistent throughout the Chinese empire); 4) capital punishments were frequently commuted; 5) various provisions such as privilege, circumstances, acts of grace (amnesties), acted as further mitigating factors; 6) accessories to capital offenses were in most cases not liable to the death penalty; only one life was demanded for each life lost. If an accessory died in prison, the principal's sentence was commuted.

Alabaster viewed the defects of the penal law as: 1) the use of torture; 2) the sentence of lingering death (However, in many cases the criminal was ordered to be killed with the first blow. The purpose of cutting up the body was to prevent the survival of the spirit); 3) the punishment of the cangue (a large wooden halter); 4) the concept of the legal responsibility of seniors for crimes committed by their subordinates; 5) social reluctance to interfere in crimes. From Introduction, p. xlix and lxiii to end, and 1/11–13.

Alabaster also noted the differentiation of penalties according to the social status and seniority of offenders and victims. This has caused offense to some Western commentators, but it was consistent with prevailing cultural values. It compares with the burning of "witches" or the execution of minors for stealing, still practiced in eighteenth-century Europe. Minors were accorded privileged treatment under the Ch'ing penal law.

As Alabaster pointed out, the aim of the penal laws and statutes was to relate punishments accurately to the specific circumstances of each case. The laws defined crimes; the statutes, which were alterable, adapted them to circumstances. The Ch'ing rulers intended that the laws and statutes be neither too tolerant nor too severe. The K'ang-hsi emperor, in an edict of 1679, noted that statutes had been added to make the people fear the law and avoid causing trouble, but he was deeply concerned that the new regulations "might be too severe." See *T'ung-k'ao*, 6608.1. The Yung-cheng emperor, drawing on themes from the *Shu ching*, *Chou li*, and *Hsun-tzu*, said that the laws were established so that people might know them and thereby avoid crime, end disputes, transform customs, and eliminate the need for laws. He said that he himself paid the greatest attention to law for the sake of these ends. *Mu-ling shu chi-yao*, 7/1b–2a; *Sacred Edict and Amplification*, Article 8.

3. Signs displaying these two laws and their attendant penalties were hung over the gateway of district administrative offices. Liu Heng, *Tu-lü hsin-te*, introduction by Wu Chia-pin. The Yung-cheng emperor somewhat optimistically told the people that if they knew these two laws they would do away with the habit of bringing suits. *Sacred Edict and Amplification*, Article 8.

4. These and other definitions are from Morohashi, 35266.

5. See Wilhelm, *I Ching*, II, 51–56. Text from Harvard-Yenching index.

6. *Analects*, 12/13; repeated in *Great Learning*, 4; *Chou li*, under ta-ssu-k'ou.

7. From *TSCC*, ching-chi, hsiang-hsing 133, sung-chieh, hui-k'ao/20b–21a. For "probity," the text reads "clearing (business) in a scrupulous manner." T. R. Jernigan, *China in Law and Commerce*, p. 19, cites, without source, a statement which he attributes to the K'ang-hsi emperor, condemning suits on principle and ordering courts to treat plaintiffs "without pity" so that they should be "disgusted with the law." The passage is repeated in Van der Sprenkel, *Legal Institutions in Manchu China*, p. 77. It is hard to believe that such a rigid attitude could have been taken by this emperor. The reader can see that the K'ang-hsi emperor was sensitive to administrative problems, flexible rather than rigid, generally opposed to severity, and conscious of the educational function to be played by law. Possibly these sentiments belong to the nineteenth century, when there is more of a rigidity in imperial statements. Certainly the passage, as translated, does not jibe with early Ch'ing policy on litigation.

8. *Sacred Edict and Amplification*, articles 3, 8, 12.

9. Wang Hui-tsu, *Ping-t'a meng-hen lu*, A, under 1766 (25b–27a).

10. *Ibid.*, 27a–b.

11. *Ibid.*, under 1760.

12. *Ibid.*, under 1758.

13. The difficulty was compounded by the fact that legal secretaries could not be present in court during formal hearings. The court was public, the secretaries private. As a secretary, Wang Hui-tsu came as close to circumventing this barrier as possible by standing where he could hear the proceedings. In his writings Wang himself distinguished the legal responsibilities of secretary and magistrate, saying that a secretary could advise according to reason and law (*li* and *fa*) whereas a magistrate had to take account of feelings and circumstances (*ch'ing* and *shih*). *Hsueh-chih*, A, 1. But Wang gained his distinction as a secretary because he did not limit his advice to *li* and *fa*; he also questioned secretarial opinions based solely on these factors. See *Ping-t'a meng-hen lu*, A, case of Hsu T'ien-jo and Mrs. Chiang, nee Yü, under 1761; *Tso-chih yao-yen*, No. 21, p. 8 (a secretary plays down a charge of adultery against a husband and unwittingly exposes the wife to a charge of bigamy). In *ibid.*, No. 35, p. 15, Wang advises secretaries to take account of circumstances in formulating judicial decisions.

14. *Hsin-tsuan LPCFTL*, 47/15a–16a. In his edict ordering these penalties, the Chia-ch'ing emperor noted that magistrates were still observing the deadlines for reporting large cases and not daring to delay; but in suits under their own jurisdiction (on this distinction, see Ch'ü, *Local Government*, p. 117) they were doing as they pleased, delaying and putting off petitioners, allowing underlings to "deceive and extort," and causing "entanglement without end."

15. Morohashi, 35266.3, citing the *Kuei-hsin tsa-shih* by Chou Mi (1232–after 1308).

16. *TCHTSL*, ch. 112, under 1725 (repeated by the Ch'ien-lung emperor in 1736).

17. *T'ung-k'ao*, 6619.1. Wang Yu-p'u, in his commentary on the duties of scholars, proclaimed that those who fomented litigation, although licentiates in name, were base riffraff, and a disgrace to the schools! Baller, *The Sacred Edict*, p. 66 (article 6).

18. Wang Hui-tsu, *Hsueh-chih*, A, No. 44, p. 14.

19. *Ibid.*, Nos. 41 and 49, pp. 12–13, 16.

20. Mu-han, *Ming-hsing kuan-chien lu*, 27b–29b.

21. Liu Heng, *Yung-li, yung-yen*, 58a–b and *Kuo-ch'ao hsien-cheng shih-lueh* (No. 7 in Ch'ing Biographical Collections) 54/8a–9b.

22. See Wang Hui-tsu, *Hsueh-chih*, A, Nos. 48 and 60, pp. 15–16, 19.

23. Mu-han, *Ming-hsing kuan-chien lu*, 30a–b; Wang Hui-tsu, *Hsueh-chih*, A, No. 58, p. 18: *Tso-chih yao-yen*, No. 20, p. 8.

24. Mu-han, *Ming-hsing kuan-chien lu*, 30a.

25. *TCHTSL:CC*, 90/3a ff; *TCHTSL*, ch. 112, under 1812.

16: GOVERNMENT BY MEN: THE STRUGGLE TO UPHOLD POLITICAL HUMANISM

1. *Hsun-tzu chi-chieh*, ch. 12, "The way of the *chün*," p. 1. For the views of Shang Yang, see *Shang chün shu*, ch. 2–5 and 7–8. In his translation of this work Duyvendak, like Watson, sometimes translates *ssu* (private) as "selfish." Shang Yang was in fact trying to give "private" the perjorative connotation of "selfish." Unless the reader knows this, he will think that the charge is moral when it is in fact political. Shang Yang was a past master in the art of ideological warfare.

2. *Doctrine of the Mean*, 20/2,4; see Legge, p. 405.

3. *T'ung-k'ao*, 5232.1. The emperor also introduced a new auditing system. After it had improved the management of the Board of Revenue, it was ended. See Ho, *Population*, p. 211.

4. *Analects*, 13/2.

5. *HCCSWP*, 18/15b ff. The rejoinder, by Kung Ching-han (1747–1802) is in *Pao-chia shu*, 3/3a ff. On Kung, see *Eminent Chinese*, p. 446. His ideas deserve further study.

6. *Shu ching*, ch. 3, Counsels of Yü, 2 (Legge, pp. 58–59). See *Sacred Edict and Amplification*, Article 8.

7. Mu-han, *Ming-hsing kuan-chien lu*, introduction, la.

8. Yuan Shou-ting, *T'u-min lu*, 4/14a–b.

9. Liu Pao-nan, *Lun-yü cheng-i*, pp. 28–29, commenting on *Analects*, 2/3.

10. *HCCSWP*, 16/4a; *hsin-tsuan LPCFTL*, 1/1b.

11. Wang Hui-tsu, *Ping-t'a meng-hen lu*, A, under 1752; *Tso-chih yao-yen*, No. 1, p. 1. The father of the novelist Shen Fu served throughout his career as a secretary. Shen's portrait of him, although intended to be sympathetic, is of a lonely and defensive man. He liked to think of his family as a "scholar household." See "Six Chapters of a Floating Life," in Lin Yutang, *The Wisdom of China and India*, pp. 964–1050. Another translation of this work is by Shirley M. Black. See also the following opinion in Wu Ching-tzu, *The Scholars*, p. 233: "Even teaching and secretarial work are not proper careers. If, however, you are brilliant enough to pass the examinations, you immediately reflect credit upon your whole family."

12. *Hsiao-shan hsien-chih kao*, 18/5a.

13. See examples in Chang, *Income*, Appx 3, pp. 243 and 247 (Chu Ch'i and Wang Ching-k'uan. Wang compiled in his leisure a collection of model sayings by legal specialists entitled *Hsing-ming-chia ko-yen. Yunnan t'ung-chih* 187/7b).

The very title of secretary of law, *hsing-ming*, is itself "legalist" in derivation. See Creel, "The Meaning of *Hsing-ming*," in *What Is Taoism?* ch. 5.

14. Wang Hui-tsu, *Tso-chih yao-yen*, No. 25, p. 11.

15. *Mencius*, 2A3.1.

16. The last six words are paraphrased. From *HCCSWP*, 11/2b–3a. Among the officials Jen listed were Chu-ko Liang, Han Ch'i (Sung), and Yü Chien (Ming). Chu-ko Liang is especially noted for having compared himself with Kuan Chung.

Jen Ch'i-yun (1670–1744) was a model of perseverance. He obtained his provincial degree at the age of fifty-three and his metropolitan degree ten years later. He served only in metropolitan administration, rising through the Censorate to vice-director of the imperial clan court. He was a close student of Mencius and Chu Hsi. *Ch'ing-shih lieh-chuan*, 68/32b ff. Several biographies of him exist in leading Ch'ing biographical collections.

17. Although widely current, the use of "Legalism" or "Legalists" to represent *fa* and *fa-chia* is unsatisfactory for a number of reasons. As a reader has pointed out, *fa* constituted only one aspect of the school of thought which Han Feitzu represented. *Shih* "authority" and *shu* "tact" or "technique" were equally important. Second, *fa* itself applied not only to laws but to all regulations, enactments, and policies of a coercive or systemic nature. The "Legalists" were less interested in "law" (as that term is commonly understood) than in systematic control of political resources. This continued to be a major objective of imperial policy, despite the repudiation of "Legalist" writings and philosophers as such.

For a discussion of the administrative methods of early Legalists and their association with the teachings of Shen Pu-hai, see Creel, "The *Fa-chia*: 'Legalists' or 'Administrators'?" in *What Is Taoism?* ch. 6.

18. Hsu Tung, *Mu-ling shu*, 1/51b, editorial note.

BIBLIOGRAPHY

Note: the following bibliography lists sources which have been cited more than once, and others which have been of use in supplying information or analysis relevant to this study. It does not include sources such as gazetteers utilized for the date of an official's degree or term of service. All the works cited in this study have been consulted at the Harvard University libraries except those marked "Columbia," which are unavailable at Harvard.

For further bibliographic notes, see the following: Western-language literature on the examination system (chapter 2, note 1); the Ch'ing official appointment system (chapter 3, note 2); handbooks commonly consulted by Ch'ing local administrators (chapter 3, notes 56–60); the *Hsiao ching* (chapter 5, notes 11–12); General Sources for the study of Chinese local administration before the Ch'ing (chapter 7, note 11); Translations of the Sacred Edict (chapter 13, note 36).

CHINESE AND JAPANESE SOURCES

Chao I. *Nien-erh shih cha-chi.* Peking, 1963 ed.

Ch'en Ch'i-t'ien. *Han Fei-tzu chiao-shih.* Shanghai, 1940.

Ch'en Teng-yuan. *Chung-kuo t'ien-fu shih.* Shanghai, Commercial Press, 1936.

Chin-shan hsien-chih. Eds. of 1751 and 1878.

Ch'in-pan chou-hsien shih-i. See under T'ien Wen-ching.

Ch'ing hsü t'ung-k'ao. Ch'ing-ch'ao hsü wen-hsien t'ung-k'ao. Shanghai, Commercial Press, 1935.

Ch'ing shih. Taipei, 1961.

Ch'ing shih lieh-chuan. Chung-hua Book Company, 1928. (Ch'ing biographies, No. 2.)

Chou li. Ssu-pu pei-yao ed.

Ch'ü Tui-chih. *Wang Hui-tsu chuan-shu.* Shanghai, Commercial Press, 1935.

Ch'üan Han-sheng. "Mei-chou pai-yin yü shih-pa shih-chi Chung-kuo wu-chia ko-ming ti kuan-hsi," *Li-shih yü-yen yen-chiu-so chi-k'an* (Bulletin of the Institute of History and Philology), XXXVIII (May 1957), 517–50.

Ch'üan Tseng-yu, "Ch'ing-tai mu-liao chih-tu lun," *Ssu-hsiang yü Shih-tai,* 31 (Feb. 1944), 29–35.

CKHCF. Orita Yorozu. *Ch'ing-kuo hsing-cheng fa.* Chinese ed, tr. by Ch'en Yü-nien. Shanghai, 1906.

CSCS. *Chin-shen ch'üan-shu* (see also MHCCCS, *Man-han chueh-chih ch'üan-shu*).

Fang Chao-ying and Tu Lien-che. *Tseng-chiao Ch'ing-ch'ao chin-shih t'i-ming pei-lu.* Cambridge, Harvard Yenching Index Series, 1941.

Fang Ta-chih. *P'ing-p'ing yen*. 1887 (Columbia).

Hai Jui. *Hai Jui chi*. Peking, Chung-hua Book Company, 1962.

Han Feitzu. See under Ch'en Ch'i-t'ien.

HCCSWP. Ho Ch'ang-ling, ed. *Huang (Ch'ing)-ch'ao ching-shih wen-pien*. 1896 ed.

Hsiao-shan hsien-chih kao. 1935.

Hsin-t'ien hsien-chih. 1812.

Hsin-tsuan LPCFTL. *Hsin-tsuan li-pu ch'u-fen tse-li*. 1827.

Hsü Dau-lin (Tao-lin). "Ch'ing-tai k'ao-shih yü jen-kuan chih-tu," in Chang Ch'i-yun, ed., *Chung-kuo cheng-chih ssu-hsiang yü chih-tu shih lun-chi*. Taipei, 1955.

—— *Chung-kuo fa-chih shih lun-lüeh*. Hong Kong, Cheng-chung Book Company, 1953.

Hsü Nai-p'u, comp. *Huan-hai chih-nan wu-chung*, preface 1859.

Hsü Pei chuan chi. Miao Ch'üan-sun, comp. 1893. (Ch'ing Biographies, No. 5.)

Hsü Ta-ling. *Ch'ing-tai chüan-na chih-tu*. Peking, Yenching University, 1950.

Hsü Tung, comp. *Mu-ling shu*. 1838.

—— *Pao-chia shu*. 1848.

Hsuntzu. *Hsün-tzu chi-chieh*. Wang Hsien-chien, ed. Shanghai, Commercial Press, 1929.

Hu-k'ou hsien-chih. 1818.

Huang Liu-hung. *Fu-hui ch'üan-shu*. 1893 ed.

Hung Yeh (William Hung), Nieh Ch'ung-ch'i, et al. Harvard Yenching Indices to *Lun-yü*, *Meng-tzu* and other classics.

HWHTK. *Hsü-wen-hsien t'ung-k'ao*. Shanghai, Commercial Press, 1935.

KCTL. *K'o-ch'ang t'iao-li*. 1790.

Ku Chieh-kang. *Shang-shu t'ung-chien*. Harvard Yenching Index Series, 1936.

Ku Yen-wu. *Jih-chih lu*. Shanghai, Commercial Press, 1933.

—— *T'ing-lin wen-chi*. Ssu-pu pei-yao ed.

Ku Yen-wu wen. T'ang Ching-kao, ed. Shanghai, Commercial Press, 1928.

Kuo-ch'ao ch'i-hsien lei-cheng. Li Huan, comp. (Ch'ing Biographies, No. 3.)

Kuo ch'ao hsien-cheng shih-lüeh. Li Yuan-tu, comp. (Ch'ing Biographies, No. 7.)

Li chi. Ssu-pu pei-yao ed.

Li-yang hsien-chih. 1811.

Liang Chang-chü, *Ch'eng-wei lu*. 1884.

Liu Chün-jen. *Chung-kuo ti-ming ta tzu-tien*. 1930.

Liu Heng. *Tu-lü hsin-te*, Ts'ung-shu chi-ch'eng ed. 1939.

—— *Yung-li yung-yen*. 1827 (Columbia).

Liu Pao-nan. *Lun-yü cheng-i*. 1933 ed.

LPCFTL. *Liu-pu ch'u-fen tse-li*. 1887. (See also *Li-pu tse-li*, 1843 and *hsin-tsuan li-pu ch'u-fen tse-li*, 1827.)

LPCHTL. *Li-pu ch'üan-hsüan tse-li*. 1886(?).

LPTL. *Li-pu tse-li*. 1843.

Lu Yueh, comp. *Ch'ieh-wen chai wen-ch'ao*, preface 1775.

Lü K'un. *Shih-cheng lu*. 1868 ed.

Ma Feng-ch'en. *Ch'ing-tai hsing-cheng chih-tu yen-chiu ts'an-k'ao shu-mu*. Peking University, 1935.

Mei Liang-fu. *Li-tai jen-wu nien-li pei-chuan tsung-piao*. Shanghai, 1959 ed.

MHCCCS. *Man-han chüeh-chih ch'üan-shu* (see also CSCS, *Chin-shen ch'üan-shu*).

Ming hui-yao. Peking, 1956 ed.

Ming shih. Taipei, 1962 ed.

MLSCY. *Mu-ling shu chi-yao*. Ting Jih-ch'ang rev. and ed., 1868.

Morohashi Tetsuji. *Dai Kan-Wa Jiten*. Tokyo, 1955–60.

Mu-han. *Ming-hsing kuan-chien lu*, preface 1845.

Ning-yuan hsien-chih. 1811, 1876.

Shang-hai hsien-chih. 1588.

Shang Yang. *Shang-chün shu chieh-chi ting-pen*. Chu Shih-ch'e, ed. Peking, 1956.

Shen Clan. *Hsiao-shan Ch'ang-hsiang Shen-shih tsung-p'u*. 1893.

Shen Pang. *Wan-shu tsa-chi*. Peking, 1961.

Ta-Ch'ing Chi-fu hsien-che chuan. Hsü Shih-ch'ang, comp. (Ch'ing Biographies, No. 10.)

T'ien-t'ai hsien-chih. 1683.

T'an Clan, Tam Yeu-wa (T'an Yao-hua), et al. *T'an-shih chih*. Hong Kong, 1957.

Tao-chou chih. 1820, 1877.

TCHT. *Ta-Ch'ing hui-tien*. Cited by edition as follows: Khsi (K'ang-hsi), 1690; *YC* (Yung-cheng), 1732; *CL* (Ch'ien-lung), 1764; *CC* (Chia-ch'ing), 1818; *KH* (Kuang-hsü), 1899.

TCHTSL. *Ta-Ch'ing hui-tien shih-li*. Kuang-hsü ed., 1899 (see also following entry).

TCHTSL:CC. *Ta-Ch'ing hui-tien shih-li*. Chia-ch'ing ed., 1818.

TCLL. *Ta-Ch'ing lü-li hui-chi pien-lan*, 1903.

T'ien Wen-ching and Li Wei. *Ch'in-pan chou-hsien shih-i*, in Hsü Nai-p'u, *Huan-hai chih-nan wu-chung*, preface 1859.

TMHT. *Ta-Ming hui-tien*. Taipei, 1963 ed.

TSCC. *Ku-chin T'u-shu chi-ch'eng*. Chung-hua Book Company ed., 1934.

Tu Lien-che and Fang Chao-ying. *San-shih-san chung Ch'ing-tai Chuan-chi tsung-ho yin-te*. Cambridge, Harvard Yenching Index Series, 1932.

Tuan-ch'ang hsien-chih.

T'ung-k'ao. *Ch'ing-ch'ao wen-hsien t'ung-k'ao*. Shanghai, Commercial Press, 1935.

T'ung-kuan hsien-chih. 1944.

T'ung-tien. *Ch'ing-ch'ao t'ung-tien*. Shanghai, Commercial Press, 1935.

Tzu-chih hsin-shu. Li Yü, comp., preface 1667.

Wang Feng-sheng. *Hsüeh-chih t'i-hsing lu*, in *Yüeh-chih ts'ung-cheng lu*, preface 1824.

Wang Hui-tsu. *Hsüeh-chih i-shuo*. Ts'ung-shu chi-ch'eng ed., 1939.

—— *Ping-t'a meng-hen lu*, in *Wang Lung-chuang hsien-sheng i-shu*. 1882–86.

—— *Tso-chih yao-yen*. Ts'ung-shu chi-ch'eng ed., 1937.

Wang Yang-ming. *Yang-ming ch'üan-shu*. 1925 ed.

Wu Chao-hsin. *Chung-kuo shui-chih shih*. Shanghai, Commercial Press, 1937.

Wu Ch'eng-lo. *Chung-kuo tu-liang heng-shih*. Shanghai, 1957.

Wu-hsien chih. 1933.

Wu-kung hsien-chih. 1662.

Yen Keng-wang. "Chung-kuo ti-fang hsing-cheng chih-tu," in Chang Ch'i-yun, ed., *Chung-kuo cheng-chih ssu-hsiang yü chih-tu shih lun-chi*. Taipei, 1955.

Yen Mao-kung, ed. *Ch'ing-tai cheng-hsien lei-pien*. 1932.

Yuan Shou-ting. *T'u-min lu*. 1839.

Yung-hsin hsien-chih. 1746.

WESTERN LANGUAGE SOURCES

Alabaster, Sir Chaloner. *Notes and Commentaries on Chinese Criminal Law*. . . . Ernest Alabaster, ed. London, 1899.

Balazs, E. *Le Traité Juridique du Souei-chou*. Leiden, Brill, 1954.

Baller, F. W. *The Sacred Edict*. Shanghai, China Inland Mission, 1921.

Bauer, Peter T. and Basil S. Yamey, *The Economics of Under-developed Countries*. Chicago, University of Chicago Press, 1957.

Beal, Edwin G. *The Origin of Likin*. Cambridge, Harvard University Press, 1958.

Biot, Edouard, trans. *Le Tcheou-li ou Rites des Tcheou*. 2 vols. Paris, 1851.

Brunnert, H. S. and V. V. Hagelstrom. *Present Day Political Organization of China*. Shanghai, Kelly and Walsh, 1912.

CAT. See under Sun, E-tu Zen.

Chan, Wing-tsit. *A Source Book in Chinese Philosophy*. Princeton, Princeton University Press, 1963.

—— "The Evolution of the Confucian Concept *Jen*," *Philosophy East and West*, Vol. IV, No. 4 (Jan. 1955), pp. 295–319.

Chang, Carson. *Wang Yang-ming*. New York, St. John's University Press, 1962.

Chang, Chung-li. *The Chinese Gentry: Studies on their Role in Nineteenth-century Chinese Society*. Seattle, University of Washington Press, 1955.

—— *The Income of the Chinese Gentry*. Seattle, University of Washington Press, 1962.

Chang Fu-jui. *Les Fonctionnaires des Song:* index des titres. Paris, Mouton, 1962.

Ch'ü Tung-tsu. *Law and Society in Traditional China*. Paris, Mouton, 1961.

—— *Local Government in China under the Ch'ing*. Cambridge, Harvard University Press, 1962.

Creel, H. G. "The Beginnings of Bureaucracy in China: The Origin of the Hsien," *JAS*, Vol. XXIII, No. 2 (Feb. 1964), pp. 155–84.

—— *What Is Taoism? And Other Studies in Chinese Cultural History*. Chicago, University of Chicago Press, 1970.

de Bary, Wm. Theodore et al. *Sources of Chinese Tradition*. New York, Columbia University Press, 1960.

Dobson, W. A. C. H. *Mencius*. Toronto, University of Toronto Press, 1963.

Dubs, H. H., trans. *The Works of Hsüntze*. London, Probsthain, 1928.

Duyvendak, J. J. L. *The Book of Lord Shang*. London, Probsthain, 1928.

Elmquist, Paul Oscar. *Rural Controls in Early Modern China*. Ph.D. thesis, Cambridge, Harvard University, 1963.

Eminent Chinese. Arthur W. Hummel, Chao-ying Fang, et al. *Eminent Chinese of the Ch'ing Period*. Washington, Library of Congress, 1944.

Fei, Hsiao-t'ung. *Peasant Life in China*. London, Routledge, 1939.

Fei, Hsiao-t'ung and Chang Chih-i. *Earthbound China*. London, Routledge, 1948.

Gulik, R. H. Van. *Dee Goong An: Three Murder Cases Solved by Judge Dee—An Ancient Chinese Detective Story*. Tokyo, 1949.

Ho, Ping-ti. *Studies on the Population of China*. Cambridge, Harvard University Press, 1959.

—— *The Ladder of Success in Imperial China: Aspects of Social Mobility 1368–1911*. New York, Columbia University Press, 1962.

Hsiao, Kung-ch'üan. *Rural China: Imperial Control in the Nineteenth Century*. Seattle, University of Washington Press, 1960.

Hsu, Cho-yun. *Ancient China in Transition: An Analysis of Social Mobility, 722–222 B.C.* Stanford, Stanford University Press, 1965.

Huang Pei. *A Study of the Yung-cheng Period.* . . . Ph.D. thesis, Bloomington, Indiana University, 1963.

Huang, Yen-kai. *A Dictionary of Chinese Idiomatic Phrases*. Hong Kong, Eton Press, 1964.

Hucker, Charles O. *The Censorial System of Ming China*. Stanford, Stanford University Press, 1966.

Hulsewe, A. F. P. *Remnants of Han Law*, Vol. I. Leiden, Sinica Leidensia, Vol. IX, 1955.

Karlgren, Bernhard. "Grammata Serica Recensa," Stockholm, *BMFEA*, XXIX (1957), 1–332.

—— *The Book of Documents*, Stockholm, 1950, Reprint from *BMFEA*, Vol. XXII.

—— *The Book of Odes*, Stockholm, Museum of Far Eastern Antiquities, 1950.

Kracke, E. A. *Civil Service in Early Sung China, 960–1067*, Cambridge, Harvard University Press, 1953.

Legge, James. *The Chinese Classics*. 2d ed. Oxford, Clarendon Press, 1893–95. 1. *Confucian Analects, The Great Learning* and *The Doctrine of the Mean*. 2. *The Works of Mencius*. 3. *The Shoo King; or, The Book of Historical Documents*. 5. *The Ch'un Ts'ew with the Tso Chuen*.

—— *The Texts of Confucianism*, in *Sacred Books of the East*. F. Max Müller, ed. Oxford, 1879–1885. Vol. II. *The Yi King*. Vols. III–IV. *The Li Ki*.

Li Chow Chung-cheng. *L'Examen Provinciale en Chine (Hsiang Che) sous la Dynastie des Ts'ing*. Paris, 1935.

Liang, Fang-chung, "Local Tax Collectors in the Ming Dynasty," in E-tu Zen Sun and John de Francis, *Chinese Social History*, Washington D.C., ACLS, 1956, pp. 249–69

—— *The Single Whip Method of Taxation in China*. Cambridge, Harvard University Press, 1956.

Liu, Hui-chen Wang. *The Traditional Chinese Clan Rules*. Association for Asian Studies, Monograph VII, 1959.

Myint, Hla. *The Economics of the Developing Countries*. New York, Praeger, 1965.

Shen Fu. *Six Chapters from a Floating Life*, in Lin Yutang, *The Wisdom of China and India*. New York, Random House, 1942, pp. 964–1050. See also Shirley M. Black, trans. *Chapters from a Floating Life*. London, Oxford University Press, 1960.

Skinner, G. William. "Marketing and Social Structure in Rural China," Part I, *JAS*, Vol. XXIV, No. 1 (Nov. 1964), pp. 3–43; Part II, *JAS*, Vol. XXIV, No. 2 (Feb. 1965), pp. 195–228.

Sprenkel, Sybille van der. *Legal Institutions in Manchu China*. London, Athlone Press, 1962.

Sun, E-tu Zen. *Ch'ing Administrative Terms*. Cambridge, Harvard University Press, 1961.

Swart, K. W. *Sale of Offices in the Seventeenth Century*. The Hague, Nijhoff, 1949.

Waley, Arthur. *The Analects of Confucius*. London, Allen, 1938.

Wang Gung-wu. *The Structure of Power in North China during the Five Dynasties*. Kuala Lumpur, University of Malaya Press, 1963.

Watson, Burton, trans. *Han Fei Tzu: Basic Writings*. New York, Columbia University Press, 1964.

Wilhelm, Richard, trans. *The I ching or Book of Changes*. Rendered into English by Cary F. Baynes. New York, Pantheon, 1950.

Wu Ching-tzu. *The Scholars*. Yang Hsien-yi and Gladys Yang, trans. Peking, Foreign Languages Press, 1957.

Yang, Lien-sheng. *Les Aspects Economiques des Travaux Publics dans la Chine Imperiale*. Paris, College de France, 1964.

Zi, Etienne. *Pratique des Examens litteraires en Chine*. Varieties Sinologiques, 5, Shanghai, 1894.

Glossary

Terms

ai	愛	chi-shih	記室
ch'a-hsuan	插選	chia	甲
ch'ai-wei	差委	chia-i-chi	加一級
chang shu-chi	掌書記	chiang-yueh	講約
ch'ang	長	chien-hsuan	揀選
ch'ang-sui	長隨	chien-sheng	監生
chen-pieh	甄別	ch'ien	錢
cheng	政	chih	知
cheng-hsuan	政選	chih-hsien	知縣
cheng-pi	徵比	chih-shan	至善
ch'eng-ting	成丁	chin	斤
chi-hsuan	急選	chin-shih	進士
chi-lu	記錄	ch'in	勤
chi-pan	即班	ch'in	親

ch'in-min	親民	fu-chien	監附貢
ch'ing	情	fu-kung	貢副
ch'ing	頃	fu-mu	母父
ch'ing	青	fu-pang	榜副
cho	濁	hao-hsien	羨耗
chou	州	hao-min	民豪
ch'u	除	hao-yu	右豪
ch'u-fen tse-li	處分則例	hsiang	鄉
ch'u-shen	出身	hsiang-ts'un	鄉村
chung	中	hsiang-yueh	鄉約
chung	忠	hsiao	孝
chung-teng	重戥	hsien	縣
chü-jen	舉人	hsien-chang	縣長
chün	郡	hsien-cheng	縣正
chüntzu	君子	hsien-ling	縣令
chün-hsien	郡縣	hsin	新
chün-yao	均徭	hsin-min	新民
en-kung	恩貢	hsing	性
fa	法	hsing-ming	刑名
feng-kung	奉公	hsiu-ts'ai	秀才
fu	府	hsü	序

hu	斛	li-chia	里甲
huan	環	li-lao	里老
huo-hao	火耗	liang	良
i	義	liang	兩
i-hsü	議敘	liang-chang	糧長
jen	仁	liang-chih	良知
jen	仕	lin-kung	廩貢
k'ai-fu	開復	liu	留
k'ao-ch'eng	考成	mou	畝
k'ao-man	考滿	mu	幕
ko-hsin	格心	mu-chih	幕職
ko-wu	格物	mu-ling	牧令
k'o-hu	客戶	mu-shu	幕書
kuan	貫	nien	年
kuan-chia	官價	pa-fa	八法
kuan-tang	官當	pa-i	八議
kung	公	pa-kung	拔貢
kung-chiang	工匠	pai-mi	白米
kung-sheng	貢生	pao-chia	保甲
kung tzu kung,	公自公	pao-p'i shih-ts'ao	剝皮實草
min tzu min	民自民	pieh	別

pien-shen	編審	ta-chi	大記
p'ing	平	ta-hsuan	大選
p'ing-yü	平餘	ta-hu	大戶
pu	補	ta-t'iao	大挑
shan	善	tai	怠
shen-shih	紳士	tai-shu	代書
sheng	升	t'ai-shou	太守
sheng-yuan	生員	tan	石/担
shih	士	ti	弟
shih	石	ti	帝
shih ta-fu	士大夫	ti-fang	地方
shih-yung	試用	ti-hsiao	抵銷
shou	守	ti-hsuan	抵選
shou-ling	守令	ti-pao	地保
shu	恕	ti-ting	地丁
shu	署	t'i	題
shu-chi	書記	tiao	調
sui	歲	ting	丁
sui-kung	歲貢	t'ing	廳
sung	訟	tou	斗
sung-shih	訟師	ts'ai	才

ts'ai-fu	財賦	t'ung-p'an	通判
tso-hsuan	坐選	tzu-hsing	子姓
tsui	罪	wai-kuan ts'an-ho	外官參劾
tsun	尊	wang	王
tu	都	yin-chien	引見
t'u	圖	yin-sheng	廕生
tuan	短	yu-kung	優貢
t'ung-li	同利	yü	獄

NAMES AND/OR TITLES

Chang Ch'i-yun	張起鈞	Ch'eng-tsu	成祖
Chang Tsai	張載	Chia-ch'ing	嘉慶
Ch'ang-chou	長洲	Chia-hsing	嘉興
Chao I	趙翼	Ch'ien-lung	乾隆
Ch'en Ch'i-t'ien	陳啟天	Chin-shan	金山
Ch'en Hung-mou	陳宏謀	Ch'ing-ch'ao t'ung-tien	清朝通典
Ch'en Teng-yuan	陳登原		
Cheng tzu t'ung	正字通	Ch'ing-ch'ao wen-hsien t'ung-k'ao	清朝文獻通考
Ch'eng Han-chang	程含章	Ch'ing shih	清史
Ch'eng Hao	程顥	Ch'ing shih lieh-chuan	清史列傳
Ch'eng I	程頤		

Chou Hao	周鎬	Hsin-t'ien	新田
Chou li	周禮	Hsü Kuang-ch'i	徐光啟
Chou Tun-i	周敦頤	Hsü Kuang-chin	徐廣縉
Chu Hsi	朱熹	Hsü Nai-p'u	許乃晉
Chu Shih	朱軾	Hsü Tao-lin	徐道鄰
Chu Shih-ch'e	朱師轍	Hsü pei chuan chi	續碑傳集
Chu Tse-yun	朱澤澐	Hsü Ta-ling	許大齡
Chu Yun	朱筠	Hsü Tung	徐棟
Ch'ü Tui-chih	瞿兌之	Hsü wen-hsien	續文獻
Ch'üan Han-sheng	全漢昇	t'ung-k'ao	通考
Fang Chao-ying	房兆楹	Hsun-tzu	荀子
Fang Ta-chih	方大湜	Hu-k'ou	湖口
Feng Meng-lung	馮夢龍	Huang Liu-hung	黃六鴻
Fu-chou	福州	Hui-shih t'ung-nien	會試同年
Hai Jui	海瑞	ch'ih-lu	齒錄
Han Fei-tzu	韓非子	Hung Liang-chi	洪亮吉
Ho Ch'ang-ling	賀長齡	Hung Yeh	洪業
Hsi yuan-lu	洗寃錄	Jen Ch'i-yun	任啟運
Hsiao ching	孝經	Juan Yuan	阮元
Hsiao-shan	蕭山	Kao Ch'eng-ling	高成齡
Hsieh Chin-luan	謝金鑾	K'o-ch'ang t'iao-li	科場條例

Ku Chieh-kang	顧頡剛	Lin Tse-hsü	林則徐
Ku-chin t'u-shu chi-ch'eng	古今圖書集成	Liu Chün-jen	劉鈞仁
		Liu Heng	劉衡
Ku Yen-wu	顧炎武	Liu Pao-nan	劉寶楠
Ku Yun-sheng	賈允升	Liu-pu ch'u-fen tse-li	六部處分則例
Kung Tzu-chen	龔自珍		
Kuo-ch'ao ch'i-hsien lei-cheng	國朝耆獻類徵	Lu Yueh	陸燿
		Lü Chih-t'ien	呂芝田
Kuo-ch'ao hsien-cheng shih-lueh	國朝先正事略	Lü K'un	呂坤
		Ma Feng-ch'en	馬奉琛
Lan Ting-yuan	藍鼎元	Mei Liang-fu	姜亮夫
Li chi	禮記	Man-Han chüeh-chih ch'üan-shu	滿漢爵秩全書
Li Kung	李塨		
Li-pu ch'üan-hsuan tse-li	吏部銓選則例	Ming hui-yao	明會要
		Ming shih	明史
Li-pu ch'u-fen tse-li	吏部處分則例	Morohashi Tetsuji	諸橋轍次
		Mu-han	穆翰
Li-pu tse-li	吏部則例	Mu-ling shu	牧令書
Li-yang	溧陽	(chi-yao)	輯要
Li Yü	李漁	Ning-yuan	寧遠
Liang Chang-chü	梁章鉅	No-min	諾敏

Pao Shih-ch'en	包世臣	Ta-Ch'ing lü-li	大清律例
Pi Yuan	畢沅	Ta-Ming hui-tien	大明會典
P'ing-hu	平湖	T'ai-tsu	太祖
P'ing-lo	平樂	T'an	譚
San-yuan	三原	Tao-chou	道州
Shang-hai	上海	T'ao Chu	陶澍
Shang Yang	商鞅	T'ien-t'ai	天台
Shen	沈	T'ien Wen-ching	田文鏡
Shen Chin-ssu	沈近思	Ting Jih-ch'ang	丁日昌
Shen Pang	沈榜	Tsung Chi-ch'en	宗稷辰
Shen-tsung	神宗	Tu Lien-che	杜連喆
Shen T'ung	沈彤	T'u-shu chi-ch'eng	圖書集成
Sheng-yü kuang-hsun	聖諭廣訓	Tuan-ch'ang	端昌
		Tung Kuei-fu	董桂敷
Shih ching	詩經	T'ung-kuan	同官
Shih-nan	施南	Tzu-chih hsin-shu	資治新書
Shu ching	書經	Wang Chih-i	汪志伊
Ta-Ch'ing chi-fu hsien-che chuan	大清畿輔先哲傳	Wang Feng-sheng	王鳳生
		Wang Hui-tsu	汪輝祖
Ta-Ch'ing hui-tien (shih-li)	大清會典事例	Wang Yang-ming	王陽明
		Wu Chao-hsin	吳兆莘

Wu Ch'eng-lo	吳承洛	Yin-hsien	鄞縣
Wu-hsien	吳縣	Yuan Shou-ting	袁守定
Yeh Ming-ch'en	葉名琛	Yuan Wen-kuan	袁文觀
Yeh P'ei-sun	葉佩蓀	Yung-cheng	雍正
Yen Keng-wang	嚴耕望	Yung-hsin	永新
Yen Mao-kung	嚴懋功	Yü Ch'eng-lung	于成龍
Yin-chi-shan	尹繼善	Yü-chih ta-kao	御製大誥

The calligraphy in the Glossary has kindly been prepared by Mrs. Loretta Pan.

INDEX

acting appointments (*shu*): and establishment of authority, 21; officials holding, 30–31, 62–64; under provincial control, 47

advancement in grade (*chia i chi*), 179

Alabaster, Sir Chaloner, 304*n*.2

altruism (*shu*): in *Analects*, 91; in Neo-Confucian thought, 94

Analects, The, 78, 93, 94, 96, 228; on the people, 79; on role of *chüntzu*, 79, 92

appointment to office, 45–55; candidates by purchase, 30, 37, 40; metropolitan graduates, 32–37; provincial graduates, 37; first-class senior licentiates, 37, 40; to office of magistrate, 46–49; to higher offices, 68–72; senior licentiates, 265*n*.43

assistant magistrate (*ch'eng*): number and salary during Ch'ing, 15–16; staff, 16, 296*n*.7; promotion, 46, 263*n*.2; and great selection system, 53; purchase of office, 54; during T'ang and Sung, 108, 284*n*.12; under Ming T'ai-tsu, 115, 116; during Ming, 133–35; function, 259*n*.5

assistant officials: reduction of, during Ch'ing, 15, 45, 69, 75, 140–41, 227; in aftermath of T'ang, 107; during Sung, 108; under Ming T'ai-tsu, 115; during Ming, 132–35; functions, 259*n*.5; staff, 294*n*.7

audiences (*yin-chien*), 173, 179–80, 196

avoidance, 20–22, 49, 227

awe (*tsun*), 86, 134

bandits: arrest of, under *li-lao* system, 113; rehabilitation of, 148, 256; and *pao-chia*, 148–49, 185, 189; in early Ch'ing regulations, 175–76; official fear of, 297*n*.30

bannermen: officeholding among, 26–30, 45; behavior of unemployed, 178; in *pao-chia*, 186, 298*n*.5

Board of Officials (*li-pu*): management of Disciplinary Regulations, 18, 20, 175, 180, 294*n*.12; and appointment to office, 46–53, 202; publication of Disciplinary Regulations, 172

Board of Punishment (*hsing-pu*), 220, 304*n*.2

Board of Revenue (*hu-pu*), 284*n*.11, 306*n*.3; and purchase system, 54, 262*n*.23; receives copies of *li-chia* and *ting* registers, 111, 198; reviews tax collection, 174–75; and *pao-chia* system, 192, 299*n*.19, 300*n*.24; tightens tax collection deadlines, 304*n*.39

Board of Rites (*li-pu*), 116

Board of War (*ping-pu*), 175; and Disciplinary Regulations, 260*n*.17

Book of Changes (*I ching*), 78, 100; on way of the *chüntzu*, 91; on Heaven as originator, 100; on *sung*, 214

Studies of the East Asian Institute

The Ladder of Success in Imperial China, by Ping-ti Ho. New York, Columbia University Press, 1962.

The Chinese Inflation, 1937–1949, by Shun-hsin Chou. New York, Columbia University Press, 1963.

Reformer in Modern China: Chang Chien, 1853–1926, by Samuel Chu. New York, Columbia University Press, 1965.

Research in Japanese Sources: A Guide, by Herschel Webb with the assistance of Marleigh Ryan. New York, Columbia University Press, 1965.

Society and Education in Japan, by Herbert Passin. New York, Bureau of Publications, Teachers College, Columbia University, 1965.

Agricultural Production and Economic Development in Japan, 1873–1922, by James I. Nakamura. Princeton, Princeton University Press, 1966.

Japan's First Modern Novel: Ukigumo of Futabatei Shimei, by Marleigh Ryan. New York, Columbia University Press, 1967.

The Korean Communist Movement, 1918–1948, by Dae-Sook Suh. Princeton, Princeton University Press, 1967.

The First Vietnam Crisis, by Melvin Gurtov. New York, Columbia University Press, 1967.

Cadres, Bureaucracy, and Political Power in Communist China, by A. Doak Barnett. New York, Columbia University Press, 1967.

The Japanese Imperial Institution in the Tokugawa Period, by Herschel Webb. New York, Columbia University Press, 1968.

Higher Education and Business Recruitment in Japan, by Koya Azumi. New York, Teachers College Press, Columbia University, 1969.

The Communists and Chinese Peasant Rebellions: A Study in the Rewriting of Chinese History, by James P. Harrison, Jr. New York, Atheneum, 1969.

How the Conservatives Rule Japan, by Nathaniel B. Thayer. Princeton, Princeton University Press, 1969.

Aspects of Chinese Education, edited by C. T. Hu. New York, Teachers College Press, Columbia University, 1969.

Documents of Korean Communism, 1918–1948, by Dae-Sook Suh. Princeton, Princeton University Press, 1970.

Japanese Education: A Bibliography of Materials in the English Language, by Herbert Passin. New York, Teachers College Press, Columbia University, 1970.

Economic Development and the Labor Market in Japan, by Koji Taira. New York, Columbia University Press, 1970.

The Japanese Oligarchy and the Russo-Japanese War, by Shumpei Okamoto. New York, Columbia University Press, 1970.

Imperial Restoration in Medieval Japan, by H. Paul Varley. New York, Columbia University Press, 1971.

Japan's Postwar Defense Policy, 1947–1968, by Martin E. Weinstein. New York, Columbia University Press, 1971.

Election Campaigning Japanese Style, by Gerald L. Curtis. New York, Columbia University Press, 1971.

China and Russia: The "Great Game," by O. Edmund Clubb. New York, Columbia University Press, 1971.

Money and Monetary Policy in Communist China, by Katharine Huang Hsiao. New York, Columbia University Press, 1971.

The District Magistrate in Late Imperial China, by John R. Watt. New York, Columbia University Press, 1972.

Law and Policy in China's Foreign Relations: A Study of Attitudes and Practice, by James C. Hsiung. New York, Columbia University Press, 1972.

Japan's Foreign Policy, 1868–1941: A Research Guide, edited by James William Morley. New York, Columbia University Press, forthcoming.

DATE			